INVENTING THE OPERA HOUSE

In this book, Eugene J. Johnson traces the invention of the opera house, a building type of worldwide importance. Italy laid the foundation for theater buildings in the West, in architectural spaces invented for the commedia dell'arte in the sixteenth century, and theaters built to present the new art form of opera in the seventeenth. Rulers lavished enormous funds on these structures. Often they were among the most expensive artistic undertakings of a given prince. They were part of an upsurge of theatrical invention in the performing arts. At the same time, the productions that took place within the opera house could threaten the social order, to the point where rulers would raze them. Johnson reconstructs the history of the opera house by bringing together evidence from a variety of disciplines, including music, art, theater, and politics. Writing in an engaging manner, he sets the history of the opera house within its broader early modern social context.

Eugene J. Johnson is Amos Lawrence Professor of Art, Emeritus, at Williams College.

INVENTING THE OPERA HOUSE

THEATER ARCHITECTURE IN RENAISSANCE AND BAROQUE ITALY

EUGENE J. JOHNSON

Williams College

Photographs by Ralph Lieberman

CAMBRIDGE
UNIVERSITY PRESS

University Printing House, Cambridge CB2 8BS, United Kingdom

One Liberty Plaza, 20th Floor, New York, NY 10006, USA

477 Williamstown Road, Port Melbourne, VIC 3207, Australia

314–321, 3rd Floor, Plot 3, Splendor Forum, Jasola District Centre, New Delhi – 110025, India

79 Anson Road, #06–04/06, Singapore 079906

Cambridge University Press is part of the University of Cambridge.

It furthers the University's mission by disseminating knowledge in the pursuit of education, learning, and research at the highest international levels of excellence.

www.cambridge.org
Information on this title: www.cambridge.org/9781108421744
DOI: 10.1017/9781108377669

© Eugene J. Johnson 2018

This publication is in copyright. Subject to statutory exception and to the provisions of relevant collective licensing agreements, no reproduction of any part may take place without the written permission of Cambridge University Press.

First published 2018

Printed in the United States of America by Sheridan Books, Inc.

A catalogue record for this publication is available from the British Library.

Library of Congress Cataloging-in-Publication Data
NAMES: Johnson, Eugene J., 1937- author.
TITLE: Inventing the opera house : theater architecture in Renaissance and baroque Italy / Eugene J. Johnson, Williams College.
DESCRIPTION: New York : Cambridge University Press, 2017. | Includes bibliographical references.
IDENTIFIERS: LCCN 2017034813 | ISBN 9781108421744 (hardback)
SUBJECTS: LCSH: Theater architecture–Italy–History. | Architecture, Renaissance–Italy. | Architecture, Baroque–Italy.
CLASSIFICATION: LCC NA6840.I7 J64 2017 | DDC 725/.8220945–dc23
LC record available at https://lccn.loc.gov/2017034813

ISBN 978-1-108-42174-4 Hardback

Cambridge University Press has no responsibility for the persistence or accuracy of URLs for external or third-party internet websites referred to in this publication and does not guarantee that any content on such websites is, or will remain, accurate or appropriate.

for Leslie
con tanto amore
and
in memory of
Celeste Love Thornton

CONTENTS

List of Figures   *page* ix

Acknowledgments   xvii

INTRODUCTION   1

1 FERRARA AND MANTUA, 1486–1519   7

2 ROME, 1480s–1520   21

3 EARLY THEATERS IN VENICE AND THE VENETO   47

4 SIXTEENTH-CENTURY FLORENCE, WITH EXCURSIONS TO VENICE, LYON, AND SIENA   70

5 EARLY PERMANENT THEATERS AND THE COMMEDIA DELL'ARTE   105

6 THEATERS IN THE ANCIENT MANNER AND ANDREA PALLADIO   122

7 DRAMA-TOURNEY THEATERS   152

8 FERRARA, PARMA, PESARO, AND THEATERS OF GIOVANNI BATTISTA ALEOTTI   173

9 SEVENTEENTH-CENTURY THEATERS IN VENICE, THE INVENTION OF THE OPERA HOUSE   205

10 SEVENTEENTH-CENTURY THEATERS FOR COMEDY AND OPERA   227

11 TEATRO DI TORDINONA IN ROME, QUEEN
   CHRISTINA OF SWEDEN, AND CARLO FONTANA   254

   AFTERWORD   277

Appendix   280
Notes   283
Bibliography   307
Index   323

FIGURES

1	Giuseppe Piermarini, Teatro alla Scala, Milan, 1776–78, plan of ground floor	page 3
2	Giuseppe Piermarini, Teatro alla Scala, Milan, 1776–78, longitudinal section	4
3	Giuseppe Piermarini, Teatro alla Scala, Milan, 1776–78, cross section	5
4	Reconstruction of courtyard of Palazzo Ducale, Ferrara, for performance of 1486	9
5	Reconstruction of the temporary theater in Palazzo Ducale, Ferrara, 1493	11
6	Andrea Mantegna, Camera Picta (Camera degli Sposi), Palazzo Ducale, Mantua, dated 1474	14
7	Andrea Mantegna, *Triumphs of Caesar*, Vase Bearers	15
8	Reconstruction of theater in Palazzo della Ragione, Ferrara, 1502	18
9	Palazzo di San Sebastiano, Mantua, garden façade	20
10	Michelangelo Buonarotti, *Bacchus*, marble	22
11	Palazzo della Cancelleria, Rome, courtyard	23
12	Baldassare Peruzzi, Villa Farnesina, Rome, 1511, garden façade	24
13	Baldassare Peruzzi, Villa Farnesina, Rome, schematic plan of ground floor	25
14	Anonymous, Villa Farnesina garden façade, drawing, first half of sixteenth century	26
15	Villa Farnesina, schematic reconstructions of possible seating arrangements, according to the description of Egidio Gallo, 1511	27
16	Stage with actors from the edition of Plautus, Venice, 1518	28
17	Sebastiano Serlio, Colosseum, Rome, exterior, Book III	29
18	Sebastiano Serlio, Theater of Marcellus, Rome, Book III	30
19	San Marco, Rome, façade	31
20	Marten van Heemskerk, view of Vatican from east with Benediction Loggia, drawing	32
21	Palazzo Ducale, Urbino, Sala del Trono, view of interior	33
22	Palazzo Ducale, Urbino, partial plan of piano nobile; north is directly to the right; west is at the top	34

x FIGURES

23	Theater on the Capitoline Hill, 1513, plan at right, Codex Coner	41
24	Reconstruction of the Theater on the Capitoline Hill of 1513, after Arnaldo Bruschi	42
25	Marten van Heemskerk, view of St. Peter's, Rome, under construction with Bramante's temporary structure of 1513 to protect the high altar, Roman Sketchbook II, drawing	43
26	Antonio da Sangallo the Younger, Raphael's project for Villa Madama, Rome, plan, begun c. 1516	45
27	Jacopo de' Barbari, map of Venice, 1500, detail showing pedimented portico of Palazzo dei Camerlenghi at foot of Rialto Bridge as it still stood in 1508	49
28	Venice, Piazza San Marco and Piazzetta, plan	52
29	Jacope de' Barbari, Piazza San Marco, detail of map of Venice, 1500	53
30	Venice, Procuratie Vecchie, rebuilt sixteenth century on the model of the original twelfth-century buildings shown in Fig. 29	54
31	Gentile Bellini, detail of *The Procession of Corpus Domini in Piazza San Marco*, 1496	55
32	Matteo Pagan, detail from *Procession of the Doge on Palm Sunday*, engraving, 1556–59	56
33	Giacomo Franco, *Execution of Bulls in the Piazzetta on Fat Thursday*, from *Habiti d'Huomeni et Donne Venetiane*, 1610	57
34	Venice, view of Piazzetta from Bacino	58
35	Sebastiano Serlio, stage set based on view of Piazzetta from Bacino	60
36	Sebastiano Serlio, frontispiece of Book III	61
37	Sebastiano Serlio, theater at Pola, from Book III	62
38	Sebastiano Serlio, plan of the theater at Vicenza, 1537, from Book II	63
39	Sebastiano Serlio, longitudinal section of the theater at Vicenza, from Book II	64
40	Sebastiano Serlio, comic set, Book II	65
41	Sebastiano Serlio, tragic set, Book II	66
42	Sebastiano Serlio, satiric set, Book II	67
43	Giovanni Maria Falconetto, Loggia Cornaro, Padua	68
44	Cricoli, Villa Trissino, façade	69
45	Michelozzo di Bartolomeo, Palazzo Medici, Florence, façade, 1444	71
46	Medici Palace, Florence, second courtyard	72
47	Palazzo Gonella–Venier, Venice (the wide, pedimented facade at right, behind the bridge), demolished.	74
48	Giorgio Vasari, *Adria, spirit of the Adriatic Sea*, drawing, ink and wash	75
49	Lyon, theater of 1548, reconstruction of plan and four walls	77

FIGURES

50	Lyon, theater of 1548, reconstructions of north (top) and south walls	80
51	Leon Battista Alberti, Sant'Andrea, Mantua, nave, designed 1470	81
52	Sebastiano Serlio, elevation of Donato Bramante, exterior wall of upper level, Cortile del Belvedere Vatican Palace, Rome, Book IV	81
53	Sebastiano Serlio, Verona, Porta dei Leoni, Book III	82
54	Lyon, theater of 1548, reconstruction of plan	83
55	Lyon, theater of 1548, reconstruction of stage	84
56	Baldassare Lanci, set for *La Vedova*, 1569, drawing	85
57	Sebastiano Serlio, Ancy-le-Franc, chateau, courtyard, 1540s	86
58	Salone dei Cinquecento, Palazzo Vecchio, Florence, plan with reconstruction of theater of 1565	87
59	Siena, Palazzo Pubblico, rear façade	88
60	Bartolomeo Neroni (Il Riccio), proscenium and stage set of Teatro degli Intronati, Siena, 1560	89
61	Federico Zuccaro, *Landscape with hunters and view of Florence*, sketch for first curtain of Theater of 1565	90
62	Giorgio Vasari, Palazzo degli Uffizi, Florence, piazza looking north toward Piazza Signoria	95
63	Palazzo degli Uffizi, piazza looking south toward the Arno	96
64	Giovanni da Bologna, statue of Cosimo I, Palazzo degli Uffizi, Florence	97
65	Giorgio Vasari, Palazzo degli Uffizi, east wing, section of northern end	99
66	Palazzo degli Uffizi, axonometric drawings of north end of east wing, cut away to show reconstructed interior of Vasari's theater. The position of the royal dais is not clear, and so it does not appear in this reconstruction (Satkowski, Fig. 12)	100
67	Palazzo degli Uffizi, staircase landing outside entrance to Uffizi theater with bust of Francesco I by Giovanni da Bologna.	101
68	Jacques Callot, theater of the Uffizi, interior, 1617, etching	104
69	Gabriele Bertazzolo, map of Mantua, 1628, detail showing the complex of Palazzo Ducale in center foreground	108
70	Donato Bramante, San Biagio, Rome, plan, Codex Coner	110
71	Bologna, Palazzo del Podestà, exterior	114
72	Teatro Baldracca, Florence, plan in 1717	116
73	Giacomo Barozzi da Vignola, project for Palazzo Farnese, Piacenza, cross section of courtyard with elevation of theater	123
74	Giacinto Vignola, copy of project by his father, Giacomo Vignola, for Palazzo Farnese, Piacenza, plan showing two levels	124
75	Jakob Binck, tournament in the Belvedere Courtyard	125
76	Andrea Palladio, plan of a Roman theater, from Barbaro Vitruvius, 1567	126

FIGURES

77	Andrea Palladio, section through a Roman theater from Barbaro Vitruvius, 1567	127
78	Andrea Palladio, elevation of *scenae frons* of a Roman theater from Barbaro Vitruvius, 1567	128
79	Basilica, Vicenza, interior of *salone*	129
80	Alessandro Maganza (attrib.), *Amor Cost.*, *1562*, fresco, Vicenza, Teatro Olimpico, 1590s	130
81	Alessandro Maganza (attrib.), *Sofonisba, 1562*, fresco, Vicenza, Teatro Olimpico, 1590s	131
82	Andrea Palladio, theater of 1562, Vicenza, schematic digital reconstruction	133
83	Andrea Palladio, theater of 1562, Vicenza, schematic digital reconstruction	133
84	Andrea Palladio, Teatro Olimpico, 1580–85, view of interior from level of peristyle	136
85	Andrea Palladio, Teatro Olimpico, Vicenza, 1580–85, plan	137
86	Andrea Palladio, Teatro Olimpico, view of cavea from stage	137
87	Andrea Palladio, Teatro Olimpico, interior from stage	138
88	Teatro Olimpico, "Pianta del Teatro," detail of Fig. 97	138
89	Andrea Palladio, Teatro Olimpico, stairs leading from peristyle level to balustrade level	139
90	Andrea Palladio, Teatro Olimpico, balustrade level	140
91	Teatro Olimpico, exterior, southeast façade on Stradella del Teatro Olimpico	141
92	Andrea Palladio, Teatro Olimpico, longitudinal section	142
93	Andrea Palladio, Teatro Olimpico, "Gradi con le Loggie," detail of Fig. 97	143
94	Palladio, Teatro Olimpico, view of stage left side of interior	144
95	G. Ruffoni, Teatro Olimpico, Vicenza, view of cavea and orchestra in 1650 The ceiling, with birds flying, may not be original	145
96	Palladio, Teatro Olimpico, view of stage	146
97	Iseppo Scolari (after Ottavio Bruti Revese) proscenium and stage of Teatro Olimpico, 1620, engraving	147
98	Teatro Olimpico, exterior of building with a rusticated portal added to theater (by Scamozzi?) in sixteenth century	148
99	Teatro Olimpico, Vincenzo Scamozzi, detail of scenery, 1584–85, viewed through Royal Door	149
100	Teatro Olimpico, central street of set with equestrian statue at end, detail of Fig. 97	150
101	Teatro Olimpico, stage from balustrade level	151
102	Sabbioneta, plan of the city	154
103	Vincenzo Scamozzi, Odeon, Sabbioneta, exterior from northwest, 1588–90	155
104	Odeon, Sabbioneta, exterior from southwest	156

FIGURES

105	Antonio Lafrery, elevation of Donato Bramante, Palazzo Caprini, later House of Raphael, Rome, first decade of sixteenth century, engraving (demolished)	157
106	Vincenzo Scamozzi, Odeon, longitudinal section and plan	158
107	Odeon, Sabbioneta, digital reconstruction of interior, looking west	158
108	Scamozzi, Odeon, view of interior from stage	159
109	Scamozzi, Odeon, peristyle with statues of Olympian gods	160
110	Odeon, Sabbioneta, fresco of trimphal arch over door in west wall	161
111	Odeon, Sabbioneta, fresco of triumphal arch on east wall	161
112	Scamozzi, Odeon, view of center of peristyle and wall with Roman emperors	162
113	Scamozzi, Odeon, view of stage from ducal throne	163
114	Giovan Battista Coriolano, view of the theater in Bologna of 1628, etching	165
115	Detail of Fig. 114, showing spectators in compartments near the proscenium	166
116	Detail of Fig. 114, showing curved seating to stage right of the entrance to the theater	167
117	Giovan Battista Coriolano, view of stage of theater in Bologna of 1628	168
118	*Ermiona*, Act II, Scene V, proscenium	169
119	Giacinto Lodi, miniature of the interior of the Sala Grande, Palazzo del Podestà, Bologna	171
120	Giovanni Battista Aleotti, map of Ferrara, 1605, detail showing location of Teatro degli Intrepidi at letter A	174
121	Giovanni Battista Aleotti (attrib.), plan of Teatro degli Intrepidi, Ferrara, c. 1605	175
122	Teatro degli Intrepidi, Ferrara, digital reconstruction	176
123	Oliviero Gatti, engraving of Giovanni Battista Aleotti's proscenium and tragic set, Teatro degli Intrepidi, Ferrara, 1618	178
124	Giovanni Battista Aleotti, Teatro Farnese, Parma, 1617–18, interior from stage	180
125	P. Mazza, plan of Palazzo della Pilotta, Parma, nineteenth century	182
126	L. A. Feneulle, Palazzo della Pilotta, Parma, longitudinal section through staircase and Teatro Farnese, c. 1780	184
127	Palazzo della Pilotta, Parma, exterior. The theater is in the wing in the center of the photo	186
128	Palazzo della Pilotta, Parma, ground floor vaults and entrance to staircase	186
129	Palazzo della Pilotta, Parma, single ramp staircase leading up from ground level	187
130	Palazzo della Pilotta, Parma, view from second landing down single ramp stair	188

131	Palazzo della Pilotta, Parma, view from second landing up toward door of theater	188
132	Palazzo della Pilotta, Parma, dome over staircase	189
133	Palazzo della Pilotta, Parma, monumental entrance to theater	190
134	Giovanni Battista Aleotti, Teatro Farnese, Parma, stage	191
135	Giovanni Battista Aleotti, Teatro Farnese, Parma, north side wall	191
136	Andrea Palladio, Basilica, Vicenza, exterior, designed 1546	192
137	Tourney in the Piazza Maggiore, Vicenza, 1680	193
138	Teatro Farnese, anonymous nineteenth century painted view of interior, showing ceiling painting demolished in nineteenth-century	193
139	L. A. Feneulle, Teatro Farnese, Parma, plan of theater and staircase, c. 1780	194
140	Teatro Farnese, plan showing a corridor above seats and a forestage	195
141	Teatro Farnese, plan showing existing windows and seats turned to face stage	196
142	Giovanni Battista Aleotti, Teatro Farnese, Parma, vaulted corridor above stepped seats	196
143	Giovanni Battista Aleotti, project for the Teatro Farnese with four levels of seating, a royal box, and deep proscenium	197
144	Giovanni Battista Aleotti, Teatro Farnese, detail of seats, triumphal arch, and proscenium	198
145	Giovanni Battista Aleotti (attrib.), sketches for Pesaro theater of 1621	199
146	Giovanni Battista Aleotti, detail of Fig. 144	199
147	Digital reconstruction of Pesaro theater of 1621	200
148	Francesco Guitti, letter of February 18, 1628 to Enzo Bentivoglio	202
149	Teatro degli Obizzi, Ferrara, view of interior, engraving, 1660	204
150	Giacomo Torelli, set for prologue of *Bellerofonte*, with view of Venice just risen from the sea	215
151	Giacomo Torelli, proscenium and set for prologue of *Venere Gelosa*	216
152	Tommaso Bezzi, plan and section of Teatro SS. Giovanni e Paolo, Venice, 1691–95	218
153	Teatro SS. Giovanni e Paolo, Venice, digital reconstruction of longitudinal section	220
154	Interior of Teatro S. Giovanni Grisostomo, Venice, etching, 1709	223
155	After Nicodemus Tessin, sketch plan of nine central boxes of Teatro S. Giovanni Grisostomo	224
156	Teatro Formagliari, Bologna, 1641, plan in 1802	229
157	Francesco Galli Bibiena, Teatro Filarmonico, Verona, longitudinal section, drawing, 1716	230

FIGURES

158	Paris, Salle des Machines, plan	235
159	Bartolommeo Feris, "Francesco d'Este, Duke of Modena, inspects his theater," etching, 1659	236
160	Detail of Fig. 159	237
161	Silvio degli Atti, Teatro della Pergola, Florence, view from the stage, etching, 1658, pl. I	239
162	Silvio degli Atti, Teatro della Pergola, Florence, view of proscenium, etching, 1658, pl. I	240
163	Teatro della Pergola, Florence, plan, early 1690s	241
164	Teatro degli Intronati, Siena, longitudinal section	244
165	Teatro degli Intronati, Siena, plan, early 1690s	245
166	Luigi Vanvitelli, project for tower added to Palazzo della Ragione, Fano, drawing	247
167	Fernando Galli Bibiena, view of proscenium and interior of Teatro della Fortuna, Fano, engraving, c. 1719	248
168	Teatro della Fortuna, Fano, longitudinal section after Gabriel Pierre Martin Dumont, 1777	249
169	Cross section after Gabriel Pierre Martin Dumont of Teatro della Fortuna, Fano, inserted into cross section of Palazzo della Ragione, Fano, by Arcangelo Innocenzi	250
170	Giacomo Torelli, *Cortile Regio*, set for *Il trionfo della continenza considerato in Scipione Africanus*, pen and watercolor, 1677	251
171	Giacomo Torelli, *Galleria*, drawing, set for *Il trionfo della continenza considerato in Scipione Africanus*, pen and watercolor, 1677	252
172	Antonio Tempesta, detail of map of Rome, 1598, with Palazzo Riario at lower right	255
173	Anonymous, Project for a theater for Queen Christina of Sweden in Via Lungara, Rome, alongside Palazzo Riario	256
174	Anonymous, Project for a theater for Queen Christina of Sweden in Via Lungara, Rome, across from Palazzo Riario	257
175	Giovanni Battista Nolli, detail of the Piccola Pianta di Roma, 1748. The location of the Teatro Tordinona is marked by the oval	259
176	Plan of houses on ground level of site of former Tor di Nona prison	260
177	Plan of first Teatro Tordinona inserted into abandoned Tordinona prison	261
178	Views of the exterior of Teatro Tordinona c. 1670–71 (upper) and c. 1695 (lower), drawing, c. 1695	262
179	Anonymous, project for Teatro Tordinona, c. 1671–72	265
180	Anonymous, project for Teatro Tordinona, variant of Fig. 179	266
181	Carl Fredrik Adelcrantz, "Design of a theater to be built for Queen Christina of Sweden, invention of Cav. Carlo Fontana," copy after a drawing of Carlo Fontana	267

182	Two variations of the box for Queen Christina shown in Fig. 181	268
183	Carlo Fontana, "Plan of the Amphitheater as it is at present with the temple that is proposed to be built" (from Fontana)	269
184	Superimposed plans of first Teatro Tordinona (smaller) and second	270
185	Carlo Fontana, Project for second Teatro Tordinona, 1695	271
186	Carlo Fontana, "Established profile of the Teatro di Tor di Nona," signed	272
187	Carlo Fontana, "Profile in perspective of the said theater"	273
188	Digital reconstruction of Teatro Tordinona as shown in Figs. 186 and 187, Soane 6 and 8	274
189	Digital reconstruction of auditorium of Teatro Tordinona based on Figs. 186 and 187, Soane 6 and 8	275
190	Carlo Fontana, "Plan of Teatro di Tor di Nona . . . by order of Ill. str.mo Palavicino gov. of Rome," signed	276
191	Zaha Hadid, Guangzhou Opera House, 2003–11, interior from stage	278

ACKNOWLEDGMENTS

When I first started to look into this subject in the late 1970s, I was on sabbatical in Rome. Many hours of reading in the Biblioteca Hertziana convinced me that too much basic research in too many places needed to be done to produce a reasonable work in a lifetime. When I hesitantly returned to the problem twenty years later, I found a host of splendid new studies by Italian scholars that ranged up and down the peninsula. I offer my profound thanks for all of their efforts. In particular I would like to single out Elena Povoledo and Lodovico Zorzi, whose work stands as the foundations of the impressive structure of studies of the history of Italian theater architecture now erected by Italian scholars. Gratitude to many of them is expressed at appropriate points in the text. Their work, taken together, made this book possible. The illustrations for the book are largely drawn from Italian archives, libraries, and museums. Almost without exception, the employees of those institutions have been marvelously helpful.

My interest in opera, which sparked the desire to investigate the architecture of the opera house, was kindled by my grandmother, Celeste Love Thornton, who listened to broadcasts from the Met almost every Saturday afternoon of the opera season. I often listened with her. My interest greatly intensified when I met and then married Leslie Nicholson, who was studying opera singing in Florence when a mutual friend, Marcia Hall, introduced us. We celebrated our fiftieth wedding anniversary in 2015. Leslie has read more versions of the manuscript than either of us can count. The happy results of her advice can be found on almost every page. As Otello says to Desdemona (albeit in a far, far less happy context), "Ancor un bacio." And to my sons, Eugene and Nick Johnson, a big hug for all sorts of technical advice and support.

The splendid new photographs that grace these pages were taken by my old friend and colleague, Ralph Lieberman. In gratitude to Ralph, I once paraphrased a famous papal remark: "God has seen fit to give us Ralph Lieberman. Let us enjoy him." Three Williams undergraduates, Grace McEniry, Benjamin Hoyle, and Troy Sipprelle, have contributed crucial drawings. Additional photos were taken by two other Williams alumni, Henry Schmidt and Ranana Dine. Assistance with Italian came from another student, Sara Vitale. I thank them all heartily. Colleagues and scholars who have lent a needed hand at one point or another include Stephen Astley, Bruce Boucher, Molly Bourne (more times than I can count), Zirka Filipczak, Catherine Girard, Beth Glixon, Werner Gundersheimer, Mari Yoko Hara, Johanna Heinrichs, Meredith Hoppin, Michael J. Lewis, Elizabeth McGowan, Charles Paquette, Sara Piccolo, Linda Reynolds, Leon Satkowski, Martin Soderstrom, Stefanie Solum, Amanda Wilcox, and Livio Giulio Volpi Ghirardini. To them I offer unending gratitude. Two anonymous readers for the Cambridge University Press made numerous helpful suggestions. I would like particularly to thank the acquisitions editor at CUP, Beatrice Rehl, for her support and advice and my copy editor, Susan Thornton, for her painstakingly careful work.

A fellowship from the Gladys Kriebel Delmas Foundation enabled me to spend time in the Venetian archives to pursue the history of Venetian theaters as it appears in the minutes of the Council of Ten, and a Visiting Scholar's position at the American Academy in Rome provided the chance to do the research to write Chapter 11.

Very generous financial support has been provided by the office of the Dean of Faculty of Williams College. I am particularly grateful to Megan Konieczny, Assistant Dean of the Faculty, for her help.

INTRODUCTION

This is an architectural success story. A new type of building, the opera house, or *teatro all'italiano*, arose out of complex theatrical developments in Italy between the fifteenth and seventeenth centuries. Quickly the type spread throughout Europe and then its colonies, so that for four hundred years and more it influenced the design of theaters around the world. Few new building types of modern times have been more successful.

The book explores the architecture of the Italian theater from temporary court theaters erected by Italian princes in the late fifteenth century through the theaters for commedia dell'arte of the sixteenth to the public opera houses of the seventeenth. The book is selective; too many theaters were constructed or projected during these centuries to discuss in one volume. Despite the large numbers built, only three still stand. For most we have verbal descriptions; for a few there are drawings. This book is often an exercise in imagining lost structures, aided, where possible, by digital reconstructions.

Architecture is an art in the service of specific functions. Opera demanded its own architecture. As a public art form, opera began in the seventeenth century in Venice, growing out of theatrical and musical developments of the previous hundred and fifty years, each of which required its own architectural setting. The first stirrings of modern theater in the late fifteenth century were antiquarian revivals of the comedies of the Roman playwrights Plautus and Terence, which had not been performed since antiquity because of opposition from the church. Works by contemporary authors quickly joined their ancient counterparts. Musical interludes between acts, called *intermedi*, with singing, dancing, and elaborate sets and stage machinery, became so popular as part of court spectacles that they sometimes overwhelmed the plays they punctuated. As the sixteenth century approached its middle years, commedia dell'arte, a homegrown commercial art form, came to be performed widely. At the same time, theaters built at court by rulers housed elaborate "medieval" tourneys, presented either as single spectacles or as insertions between the acts of plays. At the very end of the cinquecento the new musical form of opera was introduced in Florence by a group of learned gentlemen who believed that by including sung dialogue in performances they were reviving the way Greek plays had been performed. Opera swiftly became a court spectacle for invited audiences to participate in dynastic celebrations. Often in the seventeenth century lavish musical performances, with singers and musicians and elaborate costumes and sets, would be presented simultaneously with tourneys featuring beplumed knights in fabulously rich armor jousting on horseback. One such, produced in Padua in 1636, led to the first public performance of an opera for a paying audience in Venice the next year. That took place in an existing theater built for commedia dell'arte, but within a year or two the first purpose-designed commercial opera theater rose in the same city. After that, the *teatro all'italiano* proliferated.

    By the second half of the eighteenth century the form reached full maturity. The finest example, Giuseppe Piermarini's Teatro alla Scala, rose in the center of Milan between 1776 and 1778[1] (Figs. 1–3). There the auditorium is surrounded by six levels of seating, with the bottom four containing private boxes and the upper two galleries for the less well-off. The boxes are a crucial feature of this new type of theater. During a performance the box holders, on view to the rest of the audience, are as much a part of the spectacle as what happens on stage. As Antonio Pinelli noted, the rulers "no more are the only ones to be simultaneously spectators and objects of attention; the cornice of the box frames like a miniature proscenium, the representation of the bourgeois rite of seeing and being seen, the spectacle within the spectacle which, with time tends ... almost to prevail over the central action."[2] The boxes (*palchi* in Italian) are arranged in a horseshoe shape to face a stage almost equal in depth to the auditorium, that depth necessary to house elaborate scenic effects (Fig. 1). In section, the auditorium is revealed to have a low vaulted ceiling. Between the auditorium and the stage lies the orchestra pit. The proscenium arch divides the auditorium from the stage area, which rises to the same height as the auditorium to provide fly-space for the scenery (Fig. 2). Opening night of the annual opera season in Milan pits the spectacle of fashion on one side of the proscenium against the spectacle of a new production on stage.

    Because the vast literature on these theaters is mostly the work of Italian scholars, the story told here is difficult of access for those who do not read their

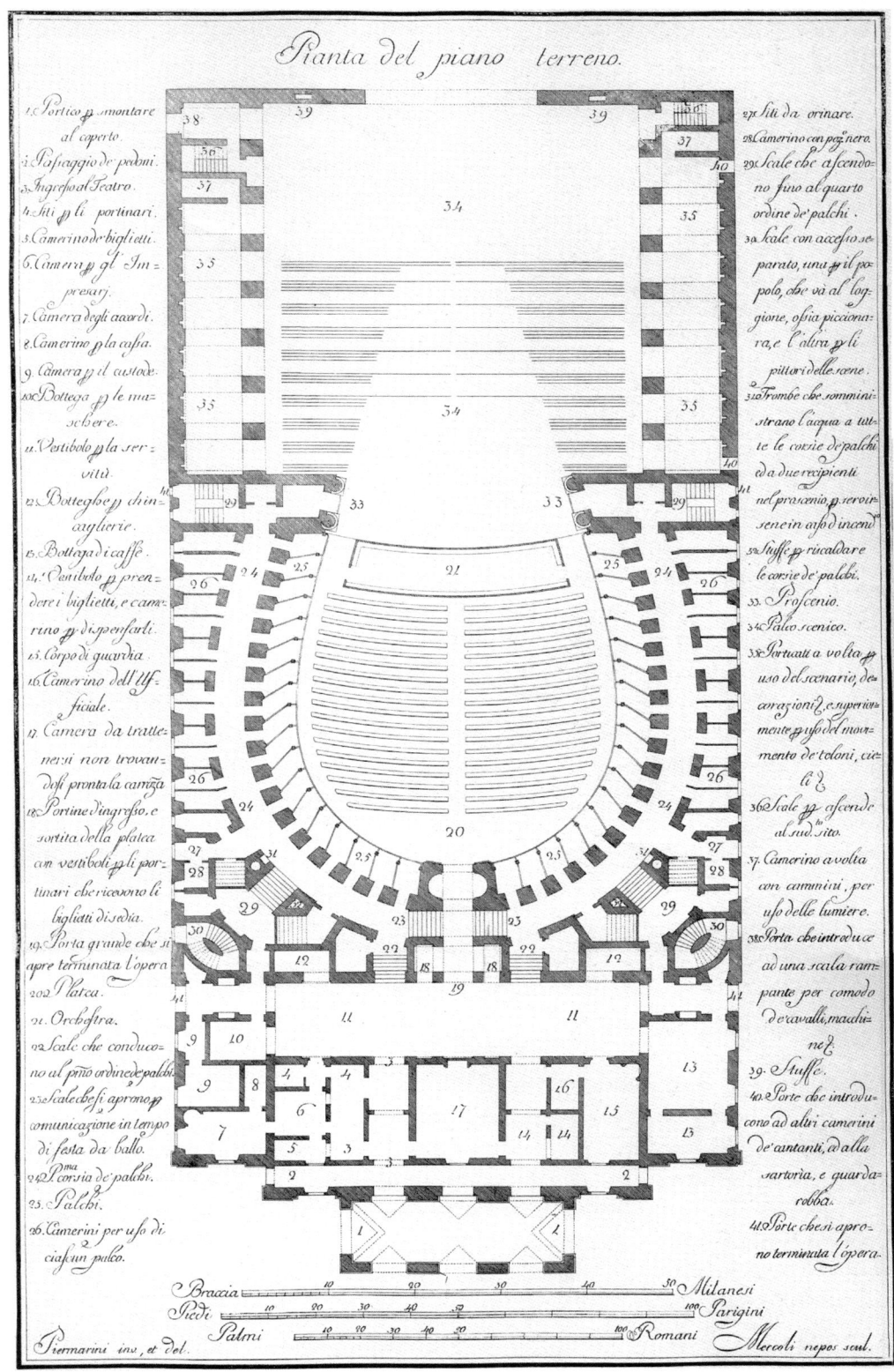

FIG. 1 Giuseppe Piermarini, Teatro alla Scala, Milan, 1776–78, plan of ground floor (from Piermarini. Art in the public domain)

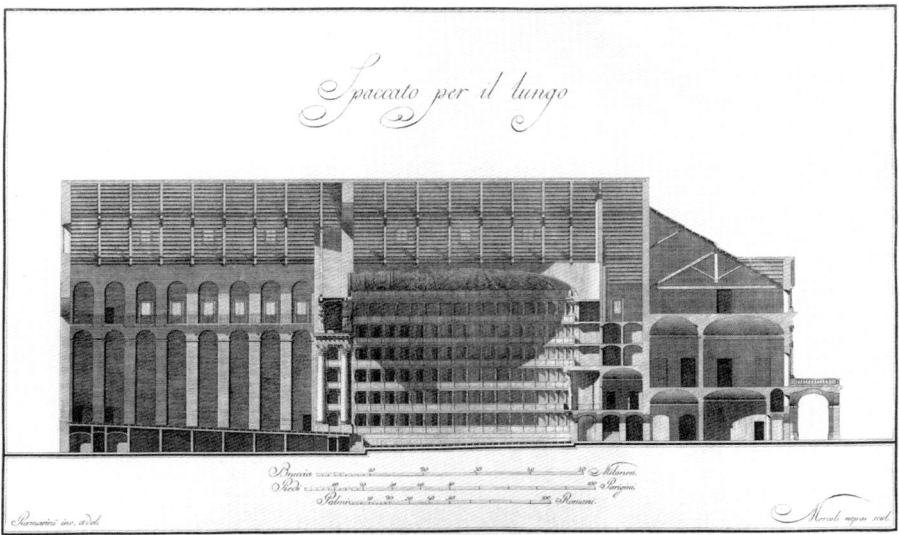

FIG. 2 Giuseppe Piermarini, Teatro alla Scala, Milan, 1776–78, longitudinal section (from Piermarini. Art in the public domain)

language. One purpose of this book is to bring the story to the attention of a wider audience. Another purpose is to draw together buildings often discussed separately, or in groups defined by geography (the theaters of Venice, say), so that the origins of this remarkable new building type can be understood in something of its complexity and inventiveness. In studies of Italian Renaissance and Baroque architecture, theaters have generally received less attention than churches, palaces, or villas. The dearth of surviving monuments is surely one reason for this neglect, but a failure to take seriously the importance attached to theatrical spectacles at the time may well be another. A vast amount of talent and money were invested in these activities. Italian theaters were built for many reasons in many forms: by single rulers, by groups of educated patrons, or by entrepreneurs out to make a profit. The motivation could be political, intellectual, financial, antiquarian, or a combination of factors. The money lavished by rulers on theatrical projects makes clear the political benefits they hoped to achieve from them.

For reasons of space, the book focuses on what was actually constructed or designed for a specific site. Relatively little time is devoted to architectural writings of the period about theaters, either ancient or modern.[3] A summary knowledge, however, of what the period knew of ancient theaters is essential, because in the beginning theater designers had only what the ancients had built or written for inspiration. For knowledge of theaters of the past, architects and patrons turned to the texts of the Roman architect Vitruvius and of the Renaissance architect Leon Battista Alberti, whose writings are discussed in the Appendix.

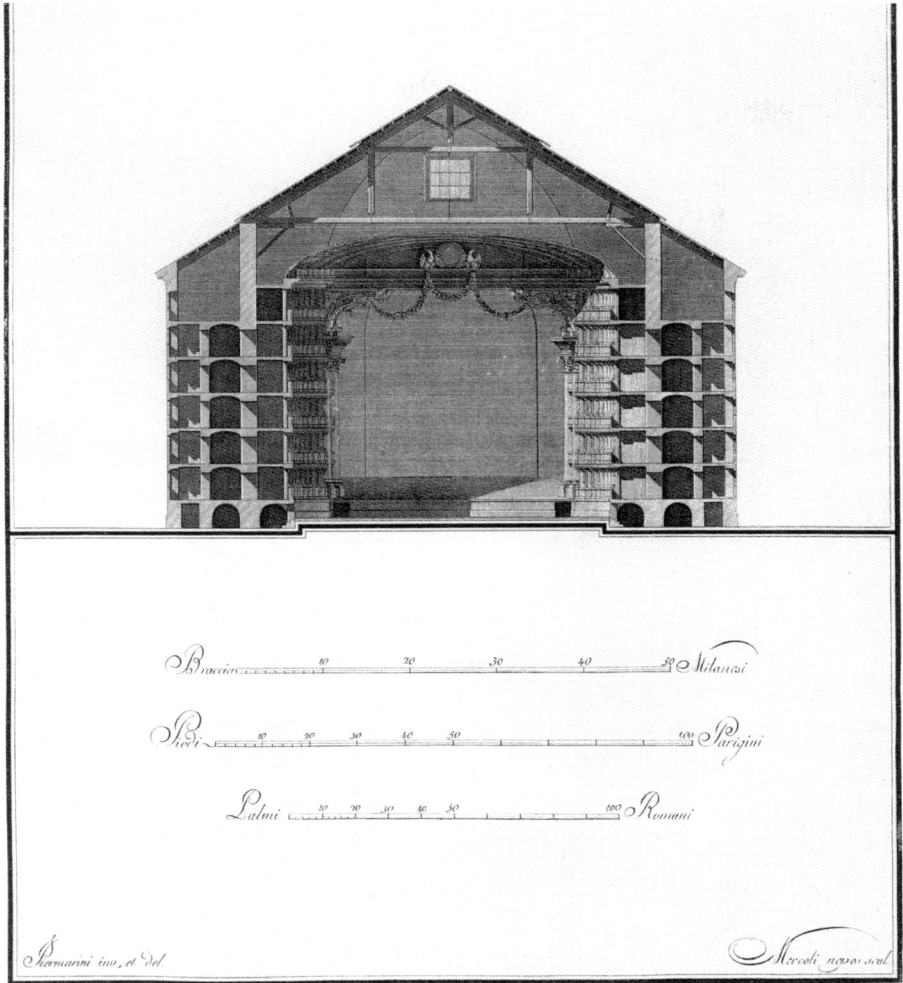

FIG. 3 Giuseppe Piermarini, Teatro alla Scala, Milan, 1776–78, cross section (from Piermarini. Art in the public domain)

The theaters noted here almost never had exterior architecture of interest. Theaters that embellish urban settings with noble architecture arrive mainly in the eighteenth century. What mattered in earlier efforts was the interior: how the audience was accommodated and what that audience saw when it arrived for the performance. What the audience saw on stage – that is, scene design – is a subject of study on its own.[4]

The organization of this book is geographical and chronological, although one might also say political and social and chronological, since differences in location mean differences in governmental and social forms. Theaters developed at secular courts have their own trajectory, while those under the purview of the papacy another. The societies of states with oligarchic rather than dynastic rule created theaters that suited their different needs. All of these developments took place on a narrow peninsula with a more or less common language in which word of what was new in, say, Florence was quickly transmitted to Venice or Rome or Mantua, where that novelty could be fused with theatrical traditions developed locally. Or ignored. Rivalry was intense. Troupes of players, particularly from the mid-sixteenth century on, roamed the countryside, bringing word of theaters in which they had played. An essential means of transmitting architectural ideas in these moments were the traveling performers themselves, even if they have left us no visual records. With the development of opera in the seventeenth century, the troupes came to include singers, musicians, scene designers, and anyone else who might be needed as the group set up shop in one center after another. In this vital moment of theatrical creativity, architecture played an essential role.

1

FERRARA AND MANTUA, 1486–1519

For the carnival season of 1486 Ercole I d'Este, Duke of Ferrara, ordered a performance of the *Menaechmi*, a comedy by the Roman playwright Plautus, in the courtyard of his palace. That he did so is of capital importance. For the first securely dated time since antiquity an ancient comedy, albeit in an Italian translation, was performed for a large group of people in a semipublic space. (In Rome Cardinal Raffaele Riario may have presented publicly a Roman comedy slightly earlier, but the date is not sure. See Chapter 2.) Like other renaissance princes, Ercole was educated in classical literature, read Latin well enough to quarrel with a learned translator, and had a taste for the verbal and visual arts of the Roman past. He enjoyed at his court the presence of an eminent humanist polymath with an abiding interest in ancient theater, Pellegrino Prisciani, whose advice must have been crucial for the choice of the play, a choice that is not hard to understand. The *Menaechmi*, about identical twins who find each other after being separated at an early age, is amusing and a bit bawdy, just the thing to delight a carnival crowd. By entertaining his citizenry, Ercole was acting like a Roman emperor, precisely the kind of ancient behavior an ambitious renaissance prince emulated. He may even have believed that the comedies he presented were a means to educate his subjects in the proper conduct of their lives. Ercole was so proud of the plays he produced that he eventually took them on the road. In 1493 he brought three productions to Pavia to entertain the court of the Duke of Milan, Ludovico Sforza, whose niece, Anna Sforza, was the first wife of

Ercole's heir, Alfonso I.[1] The fame of his enthusiasm for the theater was such among his contemporaries that the architect Cesare Cesariano, in his commentaries on Vitruvius, wrote: "In such things in our times Ercole d'Este, Duke of Ferrara, delighted."[2] Ercole was the only contemporary figure Cesare included among a long list of ancient patrons of plays.

Theater at court was never separate from politics. For a specific historical reason, Ercole had more than entertainment in mind; his lavishing of always-scarce resources on a handsomely mounted theatrical event was designed to lead to the payback of a more secure polity. In 1486 he needed just such a dividend. Between 1482 and 1484 Ferrara fought a disastrous war against Venice and Pope Sixtus IV. Ercole lost territory, including the city of Rovigo, to invading Venetian forces. His besieged capital of Ferrara had been on the verge of starvation when the wily Sixtus abruptly changed sides and allowed relief to reach the city. The Peace of Bagnolo of September 8, 1484 ended the war on bad terms for Ercole, who had to cede to Venice the territory its armies had taken.

During the carnival of 1485, Ercole had done little to take his subjects' minds off their recent defeat. He actually passed a good part of carnival in Venice, at Venetian expense.[3] His subjects grew restive at his inattention to the affairs of their state. His production of a play by Plautus during the carnival of 1486 was an attempt to signal the return of his domain to normality, and to focus his citizens on something new by presenting a wholly unheralded form of entertainment.[4] In this, he seems to have taken the advice of Pellegrino Prisciani, who began a treatise on theaters, *Spectacula*, with these words to the duke, to whom the treatise is dedicated: "First those ancient and most wise Greeks, and then the Italians, instituted spectacles in their cities, not only to entertain and please the people, but also for the not small utility of their republics. In truth, few other events in cities are more apt to that sweet and natural desire of man [to be part of a society] than these spectacles."[5]

A huge crowd packed the *cortile nuovo* of the Ducal Palace, stuffing itself between the wooden risers where the ducal party and important guests sat against the north side of the open, almost-square space, and the stage, raised against the south wall[6] (Fig. 4). The production had two foci, the ruler and the play – the state and the entertainment it provided. No great distances separated the duke, the audience, and the performance. In the princely party were Ercole's fourteen-year-old daughter, Isabella d'Este, as well as her fiancé, Francesco II Gonzaga, the young Marquess of Mantua whom she married in 1489. Francesco and Isabella would make their own contributions to renaissance theatrical history. Women who were members of the court or the upper class watched from the risers, from under the porticos of the courtyard, and from the windows of the palace. Males of similar status occupied separate parts of the risers or had to stand. Women who were not members of the court or

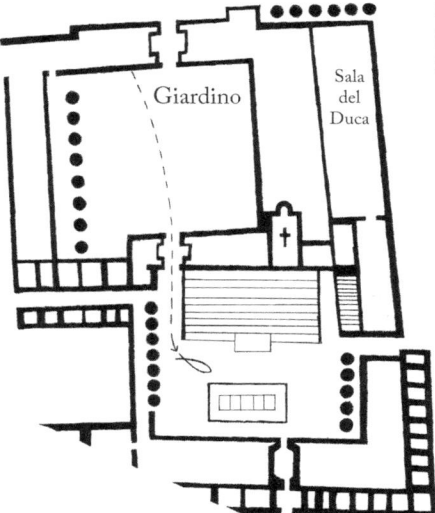

FIG. 4 Reconstruction of courtyard of Palazzo Ducale, Ferrara, for performance of 1486, after Povoledo, 1974 (Drawing: Troy Sipprelle)

upper classes seem to have been excluded, since no places appear to have been provided for them. It is not clear who else may have been admitted to the courtyard, but since the populace wore masks at carnival, it would have been difficult to restrict the audience to the aristocratic or rich.[7] On the other hand, if Ercole had wanted everyone in the city to see the play, he could have staged it in the piazza just outside the palace.

The stage, made of wood like the risers, showed a cityscape, including five separate houses with battlements, each with a window and a door that the actors used for entrances and exits. A contemporary described the painted houses as worthy of any gentleman and also noticed the presence on stage of an inn.[8] Early in the performance a large boat (a special effect not required by the script), manned by ten oarsmen, made its way through the audience to the stage. The boat brought one of the Menaechmus twins, heroes of the comedy, from Syracuse to the Greek city of Epidamnos, where his lost brother, for whom he is searching, turned out to live.

No building was constructed for this event, only temporary seating and a stage with scenery. Although the play was Roman, nothing about the architectural setting emulated the theaters built by the ancients, save for the fact that the performance space was outdoors and the audience sat on steps. The set continued the use of individual houses that had characterized medieval religious plays presented in public squares. For the duke, the advantage of having the performance outdoors was obvious. He need build no large new space to accommodate a once-a-year event, and he need not allow the throng inside his palace. Outdoor settings have the obvious drawback of vulnerability to bad weather. Carnival takes place in the dead of winter, when the climate in northern Italy is far from toasty. For the following year, the seats and stage in the courtyard were rearranged, with the stage to the east and the risers to the west,[9] so that the women of the court could watch in greater comfort from windows of the palace. The comedy was rained out, and so in 1489 Ercole moved the theatrical events of carnival indoors, thus surely reducing the size and diversity of the audience. Inside comedies at carnival remained for the rest of his reign, during which he sponsored at least fourteen different plays by Plautus and Terence, plus a new play, *Cefalo*, by Niccolò da Correggio.[10]

In 1489 Ercole celebrated the marriage of Isabella to Francesco Gonzaga with a series of performances of comedies to entertain guests come to Ferrara for the joining of the dynasties. The marriage was one of the more important of the late fifteenth century, not least for its impact on the history of the theater. Isabella, as Marchioness of Mantua, became a great patron of the arts, particularly of painters. Her husband had been raised to be a knowledgable patron of architecture, an attribute required of a reigning prince. Isabella sought such training for herself. In 1491 she wrote to Francesco that she was being instructed in architecture by Pellegrino Prisciani, who introduced her to Vitruvius: "I have begun to learn architecture, so that when your lordship speaks to me of your buildings, I will understand it better."[11] Husband and wife were both avid devotees of the theater. She was present at a remarkable number of important theatrical events, not just in Mantua and Ferrara, but even in Rome. The competition between the courts of Ferrara and Mantua, now joined by marriage, produced major theatrical moments.

We do not know how the theater, inserted into the great hall of the palace in Ferrara, was organized for the marriage of Isabella and Francesco, but we do have descriptions of a perhaps-similar arrangement two years later, for the celebration of the wedding of Alfonso I d'Este and Anna Sforza, an event that brought richer, more powerful Milan into the theatrical competition among courts.[12] Plautus' *Menaechmi* was again performed, together with two plays by Terence, *Andria* and *Amphitryon*. The set, this time with four houses, was placed across one short wall of the great hall of the d'Este palace, while tiers of benches were arranged in a U-shape in front of the stage (Fig. 5). The risers took up only about half of the space of the long narrow room, leaving the other half open for dancing prior to the performances, so that guests could stretch their legs before being confined to their seats.[13]

If Isabella could not be in Ferrara for carnival, she had someone on the spot to report theatrical events. Such was the case for the carnival of 1499, when an actor, Iano (Giovanni) Pencaro, wrote letters between February 9 and 13 that described in great detail the costumes and *intermedi* for three plays, *Trinummus* and *Poenulus* of Plautus, and *Eunuchus* of Terence, produced by the duke. In his first letter, Pencaro gave an account of the way the theater of that year was arranged.

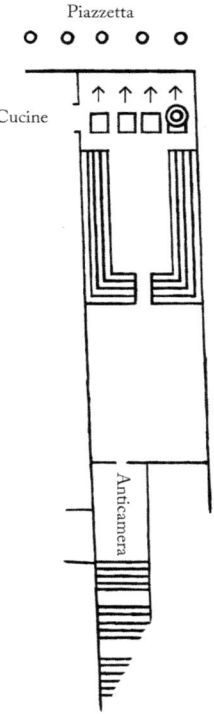

FIG. 5 Reconstruction of the temporary theater in Palazzo Ducale, Ferrara, accordring to the description of the theater at the time of the marriage of Alfonso I d'Este and Anna Sforza, 1493, after Povoledo, 1974 (Drawing: Troy Sipprelle)

And to paint for your ladyship how it is, you need to exercise your imagination a bit, and recall the *sala grande* of the court as it was for other comedies. The stage for the actors is, as usual, along the wall with windows. On the other side is the tribunal (risers), the first step of which is not raised as usual one foot above the floor, but four feet. Above that rise nine steps. The tribunal, set against the long wall, attached by brackets as you know, is much larger than usual. The brackets used to project four feet from the wall, now they are eight feet. The tribunal rises almost to the ceiling, with its railing and columns, all covered with cloth and greenery with the ducal arms and devices, beautiful to see. All the seats are covered with red, white and green cloth [the d'Este colors]. The rest of the room is treated in the usual way. At the credenza end is a tribunal, and a similar one on the other side."[14]

Pencaro, then, described a rectangular room with a stage set under the windows along one long wall and faced by three separate sets of risers for the audience: one against the other long wall and two, the other "tribunals" where the ruler and most important guests probably sat, placed perhaps at right angles to the stage. Atop the risers of the "tribunals," which began four feet off the floor, columns rose almost to the height of the ceiling. If the risers against a long wall were set eight feet in front of that wall, as Pencaro says, then there was a walkway between the columns and the wall of the room. The arrangement of steps for seating set well above the floor and rising to support a row of columns above them surely derives from Vitruvius's description of Roman theaters, which he says had colonnades above the seating that were open on the side toward the stage and closed by solid walls at the back. These colonnades, according to Vitruvius, served acoustical purposes. The local student of ancient theaters, Pellegrino Prisciani in his *Spectacula*, repeats Vitruvius's call for such colonnades.[15] It has often been suggested that Prisciani may have had some influence on the architecture of the theaters at the d'Este court; in this case that influence seems evident. The year 1499 may mark the earliest moment in which an imitation of a Vitruvian theater was constructed in a princely Italian palace. How many people the room held is a question Pencaro raised but avoided answering. He told Isabella that some had estimated the crowd at six, seven, eight, or even nine thousand, without endorsing any number. The estimates were surely exaggerated, but that the room was crowded Pencaro made clear: "The people were so tightly packed that one could scarsely put one's hand to one's nose without having one's arm above one's neighbor's shoulder."[16]

In Ferrara, they developed a preference for illumination by torches rather than natural light. In a subsequent letter of February 10, Pencaro noted that when a play was performed during daylight hours, curtains were drawn over the windows to make the hall dark, and torches lit to illuminate the scene.[17] This may be the earliest evidence we have for a room deliberately darkened to simulate nighttime. One may well ask why the stage was placed under the windows rather than opposite them, so that light would come in over the shoulders of the audience to illuminated the stage. The apparent answer to that question is that the risers for the audience rose so high that they would have blocked the windows. The draped windows may also have been opened for ventilation. Imagine all those people and the smoke from all those burning torches.

In early February of 1501 Isabella was in Ferrara for a series of plays performed during carnival. The guest of honor was the Queen of Hungary, Beatrice of Aragon, who was returning to her native Naples after her childless marriage to Vladislaus II had been annulled by the pope. Beatrice was the younger sister of Isabella's deceased mother, Eleanora of Aragon. Both were daughters of the King of Naples. Isabella reported on the plays in letters to her husband, and in one she relates that she, her aunt the queen, her father, and a few others were seated atop a small tribune in the middle of the room, so that they were architecturally separated from the rest of the audience and very much in the audience's view. Although this practice may have been going on in Ferrara for a decade or so, Isabella's letter is the first mention we have of such a structure, the forerunner of the royal boxes that appear in later theaters.

She noted that some in the audience had been displeased by the crudeness of some of the language in the plays.[18]

THE MANTUAN THEATER OF 1501

Later in the same month in Mantua, Isabella and Francesco created a temporary theater that was architecturally far more ambitious than anything her father had built in Ferrara. Quite possibly, the theater was designed by Andrea Mantegna, court painter to the Gonzaga. We know quite a lot about this theater, because Ercole d'Este's ambassador in Mantua, Sigismondo Cantelmo, sent him on February 23 a long account of its appearance, to keep the duke up-to-date on what the rival court was doing.[19] The ambassador assured Ercole that the theater merited comparison with any temporary theater, ancient or modern. Doubtless the duke was both impressed and jealous.

The theater, according to the ambassador, was rectangular, in a ratio of about three to four. The audience was accommodated, somewhat unusually, on risers placed against one long and one short wall. One set of steps was reserved for women, and the other for "Germans, trumpeters and musicians." Presumably some important German-speaking visitors were in town. The other two sides of the room had "scenes given to actors." The performance apparently took place, unusually, along two sides of the room. According to the ambassador's letter, a series of now-lost paintings of the *Triumphs of Petrarch* by Andrea Mantegna was hung on the front of the stage. These *Triumphs* frequently were transported around the Gonzaga realm to decorate temporary theaters that Francesco ordered constructed in his palaces or villas. If the princely party sat apart on a platform, or tribune, raised in the center of the floor, like the one in Ferrara, the ambassador's account makes no mention of it. Nor does the ambassador tell us where the male guests were placed, but custom probably dictated their being seated on benches on the floor. In the letter there is no sense of how the audience entered the theater space to take their seats. Elena Povoledo believes that passageways behind the stepped seats were necessary, but if there were such passages, the Ferrarese ambassador did not so note.[20]

According to Cantelmo, the long sides of the room had "eight architraves with corresponding columns well proportioned to the width and height of said arches," and the short sides had six. (Thus Cantelmo's statement that the proportions of the room were 3 to 4). Probably the ambassador was describing separate architectural elements consisting of a round arch framed by two columns or pilasters supporting an architrave. Such an arrangement would have recalled the exterior of the Colosseum in Rome, the greatest theatrical monument to come down from antiquity and thus a particularly appropriate source for the architecture of a theater. In the previous decade Mantegna had

FIG. 6 Andrea Mantegna, Camera Picta (Camera degli Sposi), Palazzo Ducale, Mantua, dated 1474 (By concession of the Ministry of Cultural Resources and Tourism)

spent two years in Rome painting a chapel in the Vatican Palace, and so he certainly knew the Colosseum. These architectural elements were richly embellished, the bases and capitals sumptuously colored and ornamented with leaves, while the arches were decorated with reliefs of flowers. Similar decorations are found on the painted pilasters in Mantegna's frescoes in the Camera Picta (Camera degli Sposi) in the Ducal Palace in Mantua, dated 1474 (Fig. 6). Inside the arches hung curtains of gold or green cloth. To the ambassador, the architecture recalled "an enduring building of antiquity, full of delight," just what the architect and the Gonaga rulers wanted him to think.

On one long side of the theater hung six of the *Triumphs of Caesar*, a series of nine paintings by Mantegna (Fig. 7). Mantegna's *Triumphs* each measure 9 feet, 1 ½ inches (2.78 m) in width, or 6 Mantuan *braccia*.[21] Their deployment would have required a large room.[22] The choice of rooms of appropriate size in Mantua in 1501 was limited perhaps to two. The theater may have been erected in the principal hall of the twelfth-century Palazzo della Ragione, the dimensions of which, 56.4 × 17.2 m, were sufficiently large, but it is difficult to reconcile Cantelmo's proportions of 3 × 4 with those measurements, unless the theater occupied only part of the space.[23] Another possible site is the Sala di Pisanello in the Gonzaga Palace, which measures 17 × 9 m.[24] Again, the theater would have occupied only part of the room. The ambassador does not specify where the *Triumphs of Caesar* were placed in relation to the audience.

FIG. 7 Andrea Mantegna, *Triumphs of Caesar*, Vase Bearers (Hampton Court Palace) (Royal Collection Trust / © Her Majesty Queen Elizabeth II 2017)

Presumably they were behind the stage and across the room from the audience, so that they would have been visible during the entire performance, as would the *Triumphs of Petrarch*, attached to the front of the stage platform. Above the columns and architraves – probably directly over the centers of the columns – stood "tall statues of silver, gilt and many metallic colors, part fragments, part whole." The *faux* fragments deliberately increased the sense of the antiquity of the theater. This antiquarian, archaeological character was entirely congruent with antiquarian and archaeological details frequently found in Mantegna's paintings.

There are many problems in understanding Cantelmo's letter, and so no graphic reconstruction is attempted here. Were the Mantegna *Triumphs of Caesar* actually framed by the architecture? Maybe so, but probably not. Cantelmo gives the width of the arches as approximately 4 braccia, whereas we know that the paintings are half again as wide. He also tells us that the arches were filled with gold or green curtains, used as the performance required. Presumably the curtains hung from rods, like the painted curtains in the Camera Picta (Fig. 6). Curtains that concealed actors before they came on stage or after they exited were standard in early performances of ancient plays, and so it makes sense to imagine that the arches acted as a backdrop to the action, at stage level. In this case, then, the paintings would have hung above the entablatures that surmounted the arches. Because the actors would have needed space to move around behind the curtains, the pictures may have been hung behind the set on the upper wall of the room, or they may have been attached to a temporary wall that rose above the arches.

Over the whole room hung a turquoise cloth "starred with those signs which that very evening were appearing in our hemisphere." The stars were made of tin, as were figures set among the stars that represented the signs of the zodiac.[25] Although the theater was constructed in an interior space, it was tricked out to seem to be outside, particularly as in an ancient theater described by Alberti, who wrote that it was covered by a starry cloth (see Appendix). The stage walls resembled the exterior walls of a famous Roman building, the Colosseum, and the ceiling depicted the sky that hung over Mantua that very night. The interest in making modern indoor theaters appear to be outdoor spaces like those of ancient theaters may well have begun in this very room. Certainly, it is the earliest example of such an indoor/outdoor inversion in a modern theatrical space of which we have specific knowledge.

The most curious part of the ambassador's letter is his description of four tall columns set across one of the corners of the room, presumably that corner connecting the walls given to the actors. The columns may have served as a screen in front of a grotto that appeared "very natural," or they may have enclosed the grotto in some fashion.[26] The columns bore representations of the four winds. Above the columns and the grotto was a "sky, brilliant with lights that resembled shining stars." There one saw a rotating wheel of zodiacal signs, with the sun and the moon in their respective houses. Inside that wheel was the wheel of Fortune, with the motto *I rule, I have ruled, I will rule*, and a gilded statue of the fickle goddess, holding a scepter with a dolphin. This display of the unending movement of time – the zodiac and the rotation of sun and moon in an allegorical starlit heaven – contrasted with the representation over the hall of the actual sky over Mantua on the day of the performance. Under that temporary sky filled with tin stars hung, as we will see, the arms of temporal powers. Over those powers, as the decorations made clear, ruled Fortune, as uncontrollable and eternal as time itself.

The decorations of the theater were designed to celebrate both the Holy Roman Emperor, Maximillian I, and Francesco Gonzaga. The Romanness of the stage architecture reinforced the imperial Roman subject matter of

Mantegna's *Triumphs of Caesar* (Fig. 7). The whole room was an homage to the emperor, the contemporary Caesar, whose arms were displayed with particular prominence. The military subject matter of the paintings also celebrated the military prowess of Francesco Gonzaga, who had led Italian forces at the Battle of Fornovo, 1495, against an invading French army. The battle had a complex outcome, however. The supposedly defeated French actually achieved their goal of breaking through the Italian lines into Lombardy, but the Italians humiliated the French by seizing all their baggage. Gonzaga claimed, because of this "victory," to be a new Caesar in terms of his skill in battle. If Mantegna's paintings above the stage were a constant reminder of imperial and military glory, the stage became, at the end of each performance of the four plays presented on it, the site where Francesco became the star of the show.[27] Each night he appeared in one of two "inventions," specially commissioned from the playwright Niccolò da Correggio. One of these featured Francesco himself conversing with personifications of Italy and Mantua.[28]

Coats of arms that signaled the Gonzagas' position in the world were displayed on all four sides of the room. On a lower level, under the arches, were devices of the marquis and marchioness, and the arms of Isabella's father and of Albrecht, Duke of Bavaria, the brother of Francesco's mother, Margaret Wittelsbach. The present and previous marchionesses were thus honored by the inclusion of the arms of the heads of their houses, while the alliances by marriage that the Gonzaga had contracted with Bavaria and Ferrara were signaled. Higher up, on the shorter walls, were the arms of the King of France and the Signoria of Venice, more potent powers with whom Gonzaga at that moment had contracts for military service and with whom he needed to keep cordial relations. Venice, the expansionist neighbor to the east, had particularly to be kept happy (in 1509 Francesco ended up a captive of Venice for a year). On the longer walls were the arms of the pope and the Holy Roman Emperor, liege lords, respectively, of Ferrara and Mantua. Surely the emperor's arms were on the same wall as the *Triumphs of Caesar*. The emperor was also honored in the lighting fixtures of the room: a set of three-branched sconces decorated with gilded shields displaying the doubled-headed eagle of the Hapsburgs. All these armorial decorations expressed the hierarchy of power in the Gonzagas' world. The arms of the marquis and marchioness and of their Bavarian and Ferrarese relatives, all vassals of greater powers, were embedded in the architecture *all'antica*. Above that architecture rose the arms of the independent powers on whose good will Gonzaga fortunes depended. The sophistication and learning exhibited by the architecture and by Mantegna's *Triumphs*, however, were the Mantuans' alone to claim. The theater both honored the emperor and challenged him on a level at which the Gonzaga could compete — the patronage of art and learning.

FERRARA AND MANTUA AFTER 1501

Even after receiving such a detailed account of a theater constructed in Mantua, Ercole d'Este did not try to rival it in sophistication when, in the following year, his son Alfonso I married for a second time, the new bride being Lucrezia Borgia, daughter of the pope, Alexander VI, and, unlike her father, no stranger to holy matrimony. Isabella attended her brother's wedding and reported in lengthy letters to Francesco the details of the festivities. The temporary theater was now constructed in the main room of the Palazzo della Ragione, adjoining the Ducal Palace.[29] The room was of considerable dimension, in a rough proportion of 3 to 1; Isabella writes 146 by 46 feet, presumably using the Ferrarese foot, since the Mantuan unit of measure was the *braccia*.[30] Against one long wall rose thirteen rows of risers, divided into three sections by two walls. Women sat in the central section, male guests to either side. The men's risers were reserved for out-of-town guests. Should any spaces in the men's sections be left vacant, they could be occupied by Ferrarese gentlemen.

According to another eyewitness account, the seats were arranged in a circular shape. Elena Povoledo has reconstructed this arrangement as having a central section parallel to the a long wall of the room, with the two side sections curving toward the stage[31] (Fig. 8). Such an arrangement suggests an attempt to replicate the semicircular or semielliptical seating of ancient theaters, perhaps for the first time since antiquity. On the other hand, it is possible that the pair of smaller risers described by Pencaro in 1499 also were curved in plan. Pencaro doesn't say. The only decorations of the room were green, white, and red cloths (d'Este colors again) covering the seats and the ceiling. (No classicizing architecture to conjure ancient Rome or Vitruvius here. Not even the row of columns from 1499.) The stage opposite the benches consisted of a wall the height of a man, crenellated to resemble a city wall, above which rose six houses for the actors – "not fancier than usual," Isabella noted dryly.[32] The ceiling also boasted five coats of arms, the papal in the middle, flanked by those of the King of France and the ducal arms of the

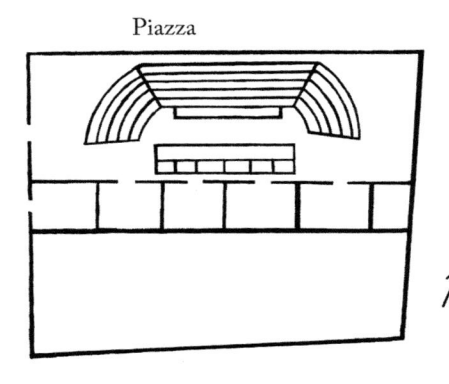

FIG. 8 Reconstruction of theater in Palazzo della Ragione, Ferrara, 1502, after Povoledo, 1974 (Drawing: Troy Sipprelle)

d'Este. Farther to the side were intertwined arms of d'Este and Borgia and the old arms of her family. Isabella concludes on a condescending note: "I saw nothing else worthy of note. The beams of the ceiling are still of wood, undecorated. I don't know if they will cover them further."[33]

Ercole had decided to spend his money on fabulous costumes for the five plays that were presented.[34] As he had done previously in 1499, he ordered an independent parade of the costumes "so that it would be known that all the costumes had been made new, and that those for one comedy would not have to serve for another." There were 110 costumes for the plays, and even more for the *intermedi*, the lively musical and dance performances that took place between the acts of the plays. About *intermedi* more later.

Ercole was the first Renaissance prince to start to construct a purpose-built theater, and so he may be the first ruler since antiquity so to do. Sadly, he did not live to see a performance in a completed building. In 1503, he began to erect the Sala dalle Comedie, a new structure attached to the southwest corner of the Ducal Palace, on land previously occupied by houses that the duke ordered razed.[35] The space was large, measuring 62 (or 63) × 122 Ferrarese feet.[36] The walls, originally planned to reach a height of 10 m, were increased to a height of 42 Ferrarese feet (17 m) at the duke's orders, so that they loomed over surrounding buildings. Twenty-five buttresses stabilized the exterior walls. (Were they merely structural, or did they have an elegant architectural character?) There is no sense in the documents of the location of entrances to the *sala*; nor do we have any sense of its fenestration. A payment of 1504 for seventy large steps (*schaloni*) suggests that the seating on the interior was being built as the structure neared completion. Ercole died on January 25, 1505, before the hall was finished, and his son, Alfonso I, abandoned the project and ordered some of its timbers recut and used elsewhere. This first permanent theater turned out to be all too impermanent. In Ferrara, permanent theaters often did not last.

Ferrara had another theatrical novelty up its sleeve: the painted set in one-point perspective. For the carnival of 1508 a new play by Ludovico Ariosto, *Cassaria*, was presented in the Sala Grande of the Ducal Palace. Isabelle d'Este was not present, but she received an account of the performance by letter. Bernardino Prosperi, her correspondent, wrote: "What has been best of all in these celebrations and performances was the scenery, made by a M. Peregrino a painter who works for his lordship, a perspective construction of a land with houses, churches, bell towers and gardens, which one never got one's fill of looking at."[37] The set by Pellegrino da San Daniele[38] has not survived, although there have been attempts to find a reflection of it in a drawing in ruinous condition in Ferrara.

In Mantua in the last years of his life Francesco Gonzaga, sick with syphilis, lived in the relatively small Palazzo di San Sebastiano, which he had

FIG. 9 Palazzo di San Sebastiano, Mantua, garden façade (Photo: Comune di Mantova)

constructed between 1506 and 1512 across town from the huge family palace.[39] In the long, narrow *salone* on the *piano nobile* he installed his beloved *Triumphs of Caesar*. Directly below the *salone* at ground level the new palace had a large (c. 26 × 7 m) open loggia that faced an extensive garden (Fig. 9). Completed in 1506, the loggia was the site of performances of classical comedies.[40] During carnival season in the winter, the open arcades of the loggia were sealed off by temporary canvas enclosures.[41] The stage erected inside the loggia for the carnival of 1513 he ordered kept in place until his wife, Isabella, returned from Milan, so that the performance of the *Andria* could be repeated for her.[42] Francesco was a devotee of Plautus, copies of whose plays he assiduously sought, even from as far away as the French royal library at Blois. He kept himself well informed of theatrical events in Italy, corresponding, for instance, with Cardinal Raffaele Riario in Rome. He may have thought of his loggia at the Palazzo di San Sebastiano as his own version of the permanent structure for theatrical performances, the first of modern times, that his father-in-law, Ercole d'Este, had set out to build just before Francesco began his modest palace for his declining years.

2

ROME, 1480s–1520

As early as the middle of the fifteenth century there may have been a plan to build a new theater in Rome. Leon Battista Alberti may have designed a theater for Pope Nicholas V. In his biography of Nicholas, the humanist Gianozzo Manetti describes a vast, parklike space that Nicholas hoped to lay out east of the Vatican Palace. In this garden would have risen three buildings: in the center a theater, on one side a chapel, and on the other a multifunctional auditorium for speeches, conclaves, coronations, and papal benedictions, with an attached treasury. Manetti says the theater will be constructed with marble columns and vaults, a notion that accords strikingly with Alberti's stress in his treatise, *de re aedificatoria*, on the use of columns and vaults in the design of theaters.[1] Alberti wrote his treatise on architecture largely or wholly during the pontificate of Nicholas, to whom he dedicated the work, and he appears to have been Nicholas's architectural adviser. While this evidence is entirely secondhand, it allows one to hypothesize, with due caution, a lost Albertian design for a theater with vaults and marble columns, possibly resembling the ancient theaters he contemporaneously described in his treatise.[2] What Manetti's text allows us to know is that around the middle of the fifteenth century, there was already a desire to resurrect the architecture of ancient Roman theaters. That a pope considered building a theater on Vatican land is a stunning fact, given the checkered later history of the building of theaters in Rome (see Chapter 11).

PATRONAGE OF CARDINAL RAFFAELE RIARIO

If north Italian courts were in the vanguard of modern theatrical performances, one Roman cardinal, Raffaele Riario, was equally early, or perhaps earlier, as a patron of theater. Riario, a nephew of Pope Sixtus IV, is notorious in art history as the man who apparently commissioned and then rejected Michelangelo's first major piece of sculpture, *Bacchus*, 1496–97 (Fig. 10). That Riario was interested in acquiring a statue of Bacchus accords with his interest in plays, since that god was the ancient patron of theater.

We know about the cardinal's theatrical activities in large part from the preface to the first printed edition of Vitruvius's treatise, *de architectura*, written by Sulpizio da Veroli, a humanist scholar who dedicated the volume to Riario. Apparently the book was published in Rome in 1487–88, and so Riario's theatrical activities took place before this hazy publication date.[3] A letter of 1486 states that performances of Plautus' *Epidicus* and Seneca's *Hyppolitus* were staged on consecutive days on the Capitoline Hill and then in Campo de' Fiori near the cardinal's house.[4] In his preface to Vitruvius Sulpizio claimed for himself the honor of having trained the young men of Rome to perform tragedies, but he gave the cardinal credit for having erected the stages on which the tragedies were performed, as well as the backdrops. He exhorted the cardinal to give Rome a permanent theater building, but the cardinal never did.[5]

FIG. 10 Michelangelo Buonarotti, *Bacchus*, marble (Museo del Bargello, Florence) (Photo: Ralph Lieberman)

FIG. 11 Palazzo della Cancelleria, Rome, courtyard (Photo: Stefanie Solum)

Although pagan dramas were regarded with suspicion in certain church circles, their performance in the papal city was justified by the claim that they trained young men to speak Latin clearly and forcefully, a skill necessary for success as an orator. Ancient dramas were revived in Rome under the tutelage of Pomponio Leto, the assumed name of a humanist educator who trained the sons of the best families in Rome in Greek and Latin. His students performed the plays produced by Riario. Because one student so skillfully portrayed the role of Phaedra in *Hyppolitus*, that player, Tomaso Inghirami, became known as "Fedra" for the rest of his life.

According to Sulpizio, these performances of ancient Roman comedies and tragedies, "which Rome had not seen for many centuries," had taken place all over the city: in the middle of the Forum, then in the Mausoleum of Hadrian (Castel Sant'Angelo) with Pope Innocent VIII present, then in the cardinal's house, then in the middle of the Circus, where the whole population was admitted. The cardinal was the first to have commissioned painted scenery, Sulpizio claimed, but his description of the scenery is too vague to allow scholars to agree on what precisely he meant. He failed to tell us what provisions the cardinal made to accommodate his sometimes large audiences. Did everyone simply stand? Or bring their own seats? Or were there risers? Did any women attend? If so, where did they sit? Did the pope have a special dais at the performance he attended? In short, the only architectural information Sulpizio specifically provided is the five-foot height of the stage.

This ambitious program of performances, some deliberately staged in great monuments of Roman imperial times, stressed continuity between present and

FIG. 12 Baldassare Peruzzi, Villa Farnesina, Rome, 1511, garden façade (Photo: Stefanie Solum)

past. In the Forum, we are told, the five-foot-high stage was beautifully decorated, and we can assume that the stages erected elsewhere would have been of a similar size and decor. Probably one stage was disassembled and re-erected in other sites.[6] One suspects that only the play given before the pope, in an ancient building that had become a papal fortress, had a carefully selected audience. The effect on the population of Rome must have been remarkable; truly no such entertainments had been offered in the city since imperial times.[7]

Probably in 1489, Cardinal Riario began to build the largest palace in Rome after the Vatican, the vast Cancelleria[8] in whose courtyard a goodly audience could have been accommodated, with spectators lining the two stories of arcades that surround the open space as well as sitting on temporary seating in the middle of the courtyard (Fig. 11). In 1492 Riario celebrated the capture of Granada from its Muslim rulers by Ferdinand and Isabella of Spain with several performances in Rome. One was a dramatic piece by Carolus Verardus (Carlo Verardi), *Historia Baetica*, that told the story of the siege of Granada. Verardus says that the production appeared in the magnificent house of the cardinal, perhaps in the courtyard of the Cancelleria, even if the palace was still under construction.[9] That the columns of its arcades are said to have come from the nearby ancient theater of Pompey suggests a happy coincidence of ancient and modern functions. Michelangelo's *Bacchus* may have been intended to preside over this space. As one walks around *Bacchus*, the figure changes, as Ralph Lieberman pointed out, from a man standing in a graceful

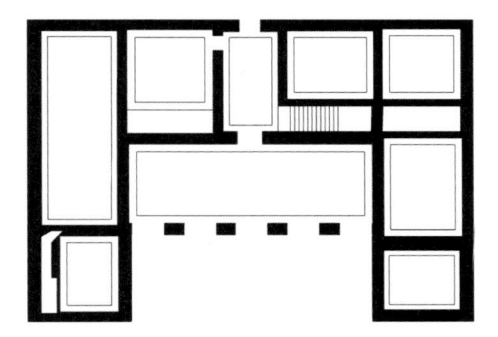

FIG. 13 Baldassare Peruzzi, Villa Farnesina, Rome, schematic plan of ground floor (Drawing: Benjamin Hoyle)

contrapposto pose (Fig. 10) to one who is staggering under the influence of the wine in his raised drinking cup.[10] Michelangelo's "theatrical" revelation of character in this stationary statue suggests that the young genius was trying to give his patron something wholly appropriate to the patron's interests in theater, even if that patron turned out not to want it.

VILLA FARNESINA

Subsequent theatrical developments in Rome often were connected to Riario's family. In 1503 Riario's cousin, Giuliano della Rovere, became Pope Julius II. Julius always needed money, much of which was supplied by his banker and close associate, Agostino Chigi from Siena. Chigi, having achieved almost monopolistic control of the production of alum, crucial for dyeing cloth and thus for the very important European cloth trade, amassed a fortune that came to include, at the time of his death in 1520, some 900,000 ducats in specie and objects safeguarded in his house.[11] In 1505 Chigi bought property on the Vatican side of the Tiber, along a street, the Via Lungara, newly laid out by Julius II through mostly open land. On this property he created a suburban residence cum office, surrounded by elaborate gardens. The elegant house (Fig. 12), designed by an untried young Sienese artist, Baldassare Peruzzi, may have been begun on April 22, 1506,[12] an auspicious day for Chigi and Rome. By 1509 it was largely completed,[13] but still not quite finished in 1511.[14] Here Chigi lived, conducted business, and put on extravagant entertainments that frequently included theatrical performances. The building is now known as the Villa Farnesina, after the papal family, the Farnese, who acquired the property later in the sixteenth century.

U-shaped in plan (Fig. 13), the house opens to the garden through a five-bay loggia flanked by projecting wings (Fig. 12). This façade was the principal entrance to the house. The round-arched openings of the loggia are framed by pilasters that support an entablature, an arrangement that recalls the exterior of the Colosseum and the ancient Theater of Marcellus, which could be seen

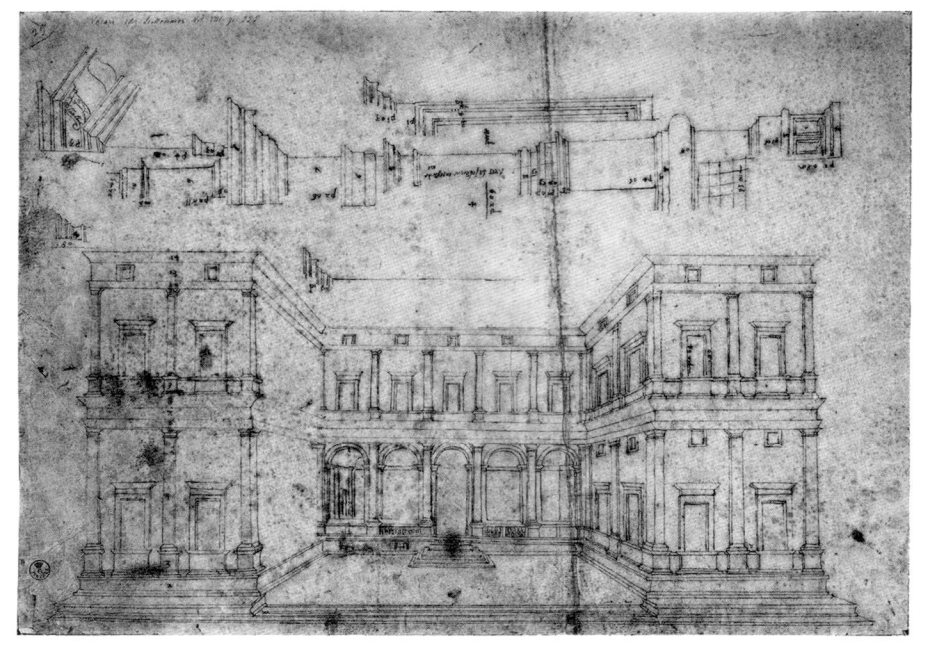

FIG. 14 Anonymous, Villa Farnesina garden façade, drawing, first half of sixteenth century (Florence, Gabinetto dei Disegni e Stampe degli Uffizi, UA 365)

from the top floor of the villa.[15] As the house appears in early drawings,[16] it once rose higher above ground level than it does today (Fig. 14). A flight of steps led down from the central bay of the loggia to a platform enclosed by the projecting wings. From this platform a low, broad flight of steps descended to the level of the garden. In this part of the villa the theatrical performances took place.

We have no specific description of the staging of a comedy or a tragedy at the villa, but we do have a written seating plan from the celebratory poem about the villa published by Egidio Gallo in 1511. Gallo places "knights" on two rows of seven steps, with other seating reserved for "princes" and dukes, with popes presiding over it all.[17] "Knights" probably indicate men of substance; "princes" could be cardinals, the princes of the church; and "dukes" visiting rulers or their representatives. In such a Roman, all-male environment, only men would be present, unless the consort of a ruler were a special guest. I would propose two possible reconstructions of the seating plan described by Gallo (Fig. 15). One would place a bank of seven steps against each side wall of the court, with seating for the princes, dukes, and popes in a separate section set in the garden and facing the loggia. Such an arrangement accords very well with the seating created only two years later, in 1513, for the theater on the Capitoline Hill. Seven steps could easily fit into the space between

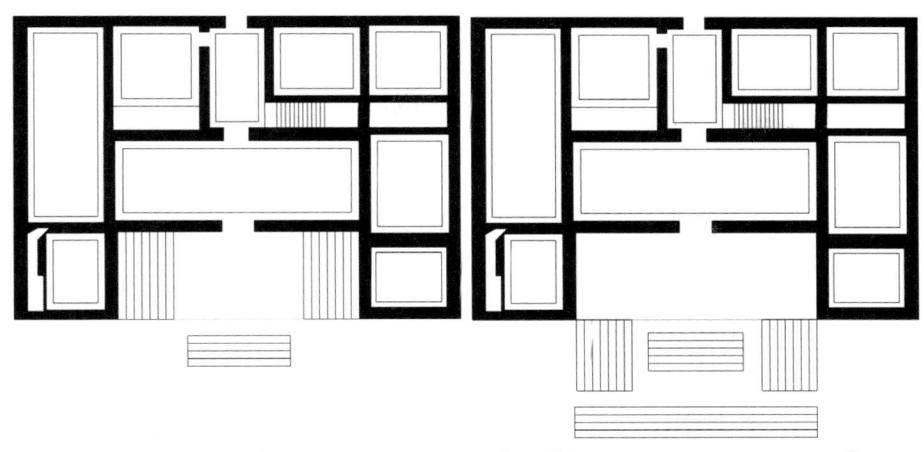

FIG. 15 Villa Farnesina, schematic reconstructions of possible seating arrangements, according to the description of Egidio Gallo, 1511 (Drawings: Benjamin Hoyle)

the floor of the courtyard platform and the sills of the windows in the villa's wings. Seating on fourteen steps stacked vertically would have covered part of the windows and occupied too much of the surface of the platform. The steps would have had a limited width, however, and thus a limited capacity. To answer that objection, one might suggest a second possible reconstruction that would have the entire audience facing the loggia, with two separate sets of seven steps flanking seating in the center for the most important spectators, and additional seating behind those worthies.

The loggia offered an ideal backdrop for the action; similar arrangements of arched orders were frequently used as backdrops for theatrical performances, such as we see in an illustrated edition of Plautus published in Venice in 1518 (Fig. 16). For intimate recitations of poetry or performances of music, the guests possibly sat under the loggia and watched the performers either against the backdrop of the garden or at one end of the loggia. Such flexibility seems desirable. In the same years Francesco Gonzaga in Mantua used the loggia of his Palazzo San Sebastiano (Fig. 9) for theatrical performances even during carnival, when the weather is north Italy is cold.[18] At such times, all of his guests and performers would have been inside the loggia, with the openings temporarily filled in to keep the weather out.[19]

Julius II felt free to use the villa, only half a mile from the Vatican, even when Chigi was out of town. In July of 1511, while Chigi was on a mission to Venice, the pope twice brought his hostage, Federico II Gonzaga, the young heir to Mantua and son of Francesco and Isabella, to the villa to be entertained.[20] During both visits they dined and enjoyed a performance.[21] In July 1512 Chigi entertained Federico at a dinner preceded by a pastoral performed

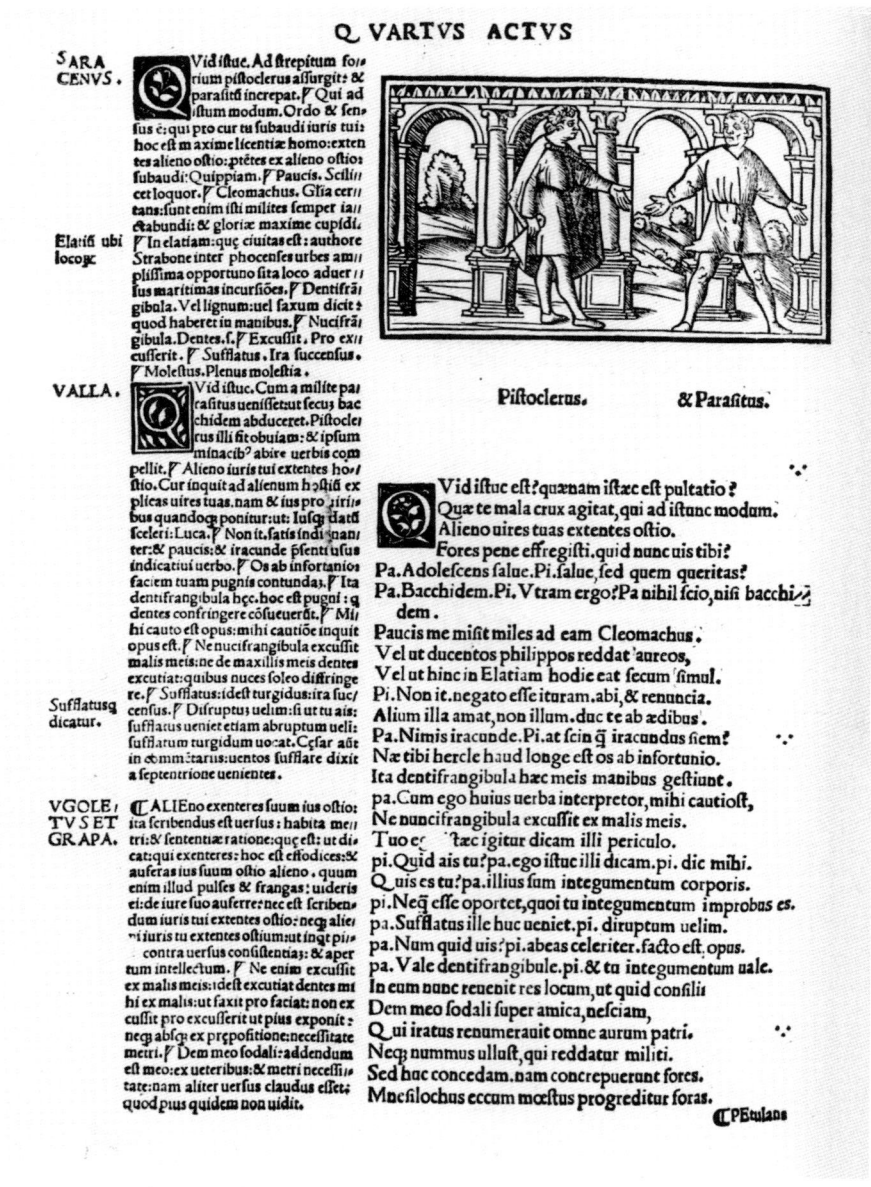

FIG. 16 Stage with actors from the edition of Plautus, Venice, 1518 (Venice, Museo Civico Correr)

by a group of boys and girls from Siena.[22] One imagines that their untrained voices required their performing inside the loggia.

The choice of an architectural form derived from the Colosseum (Fig. 17) and the Theater of Marcellus (Fig. 18) for the five bays of the loggia can hardly have been accidental, since the villa was meant to serve as a theatrical space.

FIG. 17 Sebastiano Serlio, Colosseum, Rome, exterior, Book III (Chapin Library of Rare Books, Williams College)

We have already encountered its use in the Mantuan theater of 1501 (see Chapter 1). In fifteenth-century Rome the Colosseum motif, reproducing either the half columns of the Roman building or substituting pilasters, had been adopted in important buildings: the façade of the church of S. Marco incorporated into the Palazzo Venezia (Fig. 19), the incomplete Benediction Loggia erected in front of St. Peter's (Fig. 20), both from the 1460s; and the

FIG. 18 Sebastiano Serlio, Theater of Marcellus, Rome, Book III (Chapin Library of Rare Books, Williams College)

façade of the Belvedere of Innocent VIII in the Vatican of the 1480s. In all these cases, arches enclosed in a trabeated order framed either the act of viewing, or of being viewed, or both. The Belvedere loggia looked out on a splendid view of the Roman campagna. The loggias of S. Marco and St. Peter's had a more complex function. They were benediction loggias, from which the pope (the Venetian Paul II at S. Marco) could view and bless a crowd assembled in front of the churches.[23] At the same time the building presented the pope, framed by an arch and engaged columns, to the viewing public. Thus the designs of these loggias fit Ovid's definition of a theater as a place to see and be seen.[24] The benediction loggias also acted as entrances to the churches, just as the loggia of Chigi's villa served as the entrance to his house.

FIG. 19 San Marco, Rome, façade (Photo: Stefanie Solum)

URBINO, 1513

The influence of Rome extended into the papal states, that part of central Italy under the direct political control of the popes. An elaborate performance of *La calandra*, a contemporary play written by Bernardo Dovizi da Bibbiena,[25] took place at the court of Urbino in 1513 during carnival season,[26] at the behest of the twenty-two-year-old Francesco Maria I della Rovere, Duke of Urbino, nephew of Julius II and cousin of Cardinal Riario. In the winter of 1510 he had married Eleonora Gonzaga, daughter of Francesco and Isabella d'Este;[27] the wedding had been celebrated by a number of performances of plays in Rome.[28] The author, not present in Urbino, was in Rome, employed in the papal court. Because the papal nephew had been confirmed in the papal fief of the Duchy of Urbino by the pope himself, who was in the process of making Francesco Maria duke of neighboring Pesaro and hoping to make him lord of Siena, we should see this Urbinate performance as ultimately a Roman event.[29]

A long report of the play is contained in a letter of February 6, 1513 written by that famous authority on Renaissance manners Baldassare Castiglione, author of *The Courtier*.[30] Castiglione, a nobleman from the Gonzaga territories of Mantua who played an important role in Italian diplomacy and court life in the early sixteenth century, directed the play. An anonymous contemporary report, now in the Vatican Library, both corroborates and disagrees

FIG. 20 Marten van Heemskerk, view of Vatican from east with Benediction Loggia, drawing (Vienna, Albertina, 2.17.2) (Photo: Art Resources, NY)

with Castiglione's.[31] Preparations took at least four months, according to Castiglione, and so planning must have begun at the end of the previous summer. That moment accords with the political situation in Italy during the summer of 1512. In that year, Francesco Maria had reconciled with his uncle, Julius II, after previously siding with the French against Julius. Although the French won the bloody battle of Ravenna that year, they lost their hold in Italy. At the Congress of Mantua, hosted by Isabella d'Este in August of 1512, the Italian powers, the Spanish king, and the Holy Roman Emperor agreed on a new disposition of Italian states. Milan went back to a Sforza (Isabella's nephew), and Florence was returned to the Medici through the intervention of a Spanish army. Francesco Maria abandoned his French connection and returned to his uncle's good graces. Peace was restored (if briefly) on the Italian peninsula. The carnival of 1513 in Urbino celebrated that return of peace.[32]

The temporary theater and its set were surely designed by the court architect, Girolamo Genga.[33] On one side of the vast Sala del Trono[34] of the ducal palace (Fig. 21 and 22) was the stage, raised on a platform edged by crenellations and flanked by two towers,[35] so that the front of the platform looked like a "most natural" city wall. Musicians were placed on the tops of the towers: shawms, horns, and trombones on one, trumpets on the other. On stage behind the crenellations edging the platform was an open space for the actors that represented an area inside the city between the walls and the nearest houses. To this point, both texts are clear and agree. Other parts of the descriptions, however, present difficulties of interpretation.

The Sala del Trono is a large, vaulted room (c. 34 × 14 m) with three tall windows that go down to the floor set deeply into the long north wall, and two fireplaces flanked by two large doors on the south (Fig. 22). The short wall

FIG. 21 Palazzo Ducale, Urbino, Sala del Trono, view of interior (Photo: Scala/Art Resources, NY)

to the east is next to the grand staircase that leads up to the hall from the ground floor, while the western short wall is contiguous with two rooms in the private apartments of the duke and duchess. Doors that open into these rooms are located in the northwest corner.

In the vault of the room are twenty-one rosettes arranged in three parallel rows of seven. Both descriptions agree that enormous balls of greenery were suspended from these rosettes; the foliage may have dampened the bothersome resonances that masonry vaults can create. Iron wires threaded through the balls of greenery hung down from the rosettes to hold suspended candelabra that lit the room brightly. According to both sources, there were thirteen candelabra, each in the shape of a letter that spelled out the words DELICIAE POPULI (the A and E of Deliciae were combined into one letter). Inexplicably, Castiglione says that there were thirteen candelabra because there were thirteen rosettes. The Vatican manuscript tells us that the first I of DELICIAE hung above an eight-sided temple that was part of the scenery, and Castiglione says that the temple was in the center of the stage.[36]

The audience, according to Castiglione, was seated on risers placed only on one side of the room. Above them hung a set of Flemish tapestries, no longer known, that told the story of the Trojan War. Above the tapestries was a large entablature with a blue frieze on which appeared, in large white letters, the words: BELLA FORIS, LUDOSQUE DOMI EXERCEBAT ET IPSE / CAESAR: MAGNI ETENIUM EST UTRAQUE CURA ANIMI.[37] The

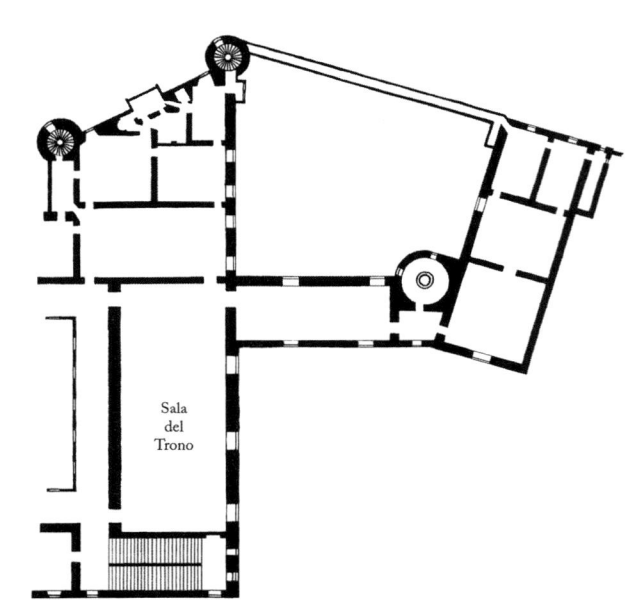

FIG. 22 Palazzo Ducale, Urbino, partial plan of piano nobile; north is directly to the right; west is at the top (Drawing: Troy Sipprelle)

Sala del Trono

inscription, probably composed by Castiglione, may be translated as "Even Caesar himself used to conduct wars abroad and games at home, for a great spirit has concerns of both kinds."[38] Although the entablature continued around the room, it bore the inscription only on the wall above the seats.[39]

Where the stage was placed in the room is a crucial question that the contemporary observers fail to answer. Their reports have been analyzed by Elena Povoledo[40] and Franco Ruffini,[41] with different outcomes. Povoledo does not specify where the stage may have been placed, but she seems to think that it was on one of the long walls. Ruffini argues that it was erected against the short wall at the western end of the space, so that the performers could have used the adjoining rooms in the princely apartments as backstage areas. Backstage spaces were surely necessary, and so it makes sense that the stage would have been built next to these doors.

Most plausible is to place the stage against the long window wall and the risers against the opposite wall with the fireplaces – probably between them. Castiglione makes clear that there was only one set of seats. Had the seats been against the window wall, there would have been a problem placing the continuous inscription above them, as well as the tapestries. In theaters constructed in Ferrara, the stage often had been placed against a long wall with windows,[42] and in the Mantuan theater of 1501 the wider part of the stage was against a long wall. Covering the windows with scenery would have eliminated daylight, so that the candelabra could provide controlled lighting, again as we have seen in Ferrara. The tower at the west end of the stage would have covered the two doors into the adjoining ducal rooms, so that performers might come and go unseen. The stage was sufficiently elevated above the floor of the room so that performers could pass under it to make entrances or exits through the other tower or through trap doors. Conceivably, the deep recesses in front of the windows could have been used, with the help of a few steps or short ladders, for the actors to make entrances and exits toward the center of the stage. The play requires the presence of two houses; the two deep windows located toward the center of the long wall, if hidden behind the set, could have provided concealed access to those houses.[43]

If our reconstruction is acceptable, then the seven letters of the word DELICIAE would have hung from the seven rosettes above the stage, in view of the audience, to announce the pleasures the spectators were to experience. POPULI, appropriately, would have hung above the heads of the audience, perhaps with no letter hanging from the central rosette to maintain symmetry. In that case, an astute observer might have inserted the central I of DELICIAE into the void in the middle of POPULI to make a punning reference to the pope himself: POP I ULI. Such play with the significance of single letters was not unknown at the time.[44] In the shorter prologue for the Urbino performance, its author (Castiglione or Bernardo Dovizi) stresses the delights ("diletti") the play was to provide the audience.[45] The prologue makes clear that conceptually the performance consisted of two parts: the play, spoken in Italian; and the audience, delighted by what they saw and heard. Spectators in this arrangement would have been able conveniently to enter and exit the hall through both doors leading from the corridor that connected to the grand staircase. Trumpets played them in and out of the room.

Wrote Castiglione: "The room came to be like a moat in the earth, crossed by two walls, like dams (*sostegni d'acqua*)." Although this is not an easy statement to interpret with certainty, it suggests that a parapet parallel to the wall across the front of the stage rose in front of the risers for the audience. These two walls acted like dams not only to enclose the intervening, moatlike space, but also to define both parts of the performance, the play and the spectators (Deliciae and Populi). The wall in front of the audience would also have conformed to the descriptions of ancient theaters by Vitruvius and Alberti. Genga, the presumed designer, turned the Sala del Trono into a remarkably unified spatial experience, in which the whole room was given over to the illusion that the audience was seated on one side of the moat of a city, whence they watched actions that took place in the city itself. Conceptually, the hall became part of the continuous outdoor space of the moat encircling the city,[46] with the balls of foliage, as the author of the Vatican MS noted, appearing to be clouds in the sky.[47] The city of Rome, in which the play unfolded, was presented illusionistically in a one-point-perspective design that employed two- and three-dimensional devices. Transporting the audience to Rome underlined the Roman context of the entire event.

The set, according to Castiglione's description, was dazzlingly complex: "The scene was imaginary, with streets, palaces, churches, real streets, and everything in relief, but aided by wonderful painting and well understood perspective." In other words, some of the scenery was in three dimensions, some in two. Buildings, according to Castiglione, included an eight-sided temple and a triumphal arch carrying an equestrian figure and flanked by altars bearing vases that flamed throughout the performance. The faux buildings were decorated with sculptural reliefs, and in certain places there were "jewels of glass that appeared most real." The earlier version of this idea of an illusionistic city as a set, in Ferrara in 1508, had hardly taken the concept so far. Moreover, the appearance of a temple and a triumphal arch represents a major step beyond the medieval holdovers of crenellated houses with a door and a window that we encountered in Ferrara in 1486 and later.[48] According to a contemporary observer, Sebastiano Serlio, Genga on another occasion designed a landscape set of surpassing richness and variety for the Duke of Urbino, with vegetation made of silk and water courses filled with an endless number of woodland animals, all interspersed with coral and mother of pearl.[49]

Particularly impressive were the *intermedi*, conceived by Castiglione and presented as musical entertainments between the acts. Urbino in 1513 was not the place such entertainments first appeared; that honor apparently goes to Ferrara in the previous century. But this is a good place to introduce the *intermedi*, because those at Urbino were fully mature, beautifully produced, and carefully described by two relatively trustworthy reporters, Castiglione and the anonymous author of the Vatican manuscript. *Intermedi* had nothing to do with the plot of the play whose acts they punctuated. Instead, they were independent elements that usually featured music and dance, as well as elaborate costumes and stage devices. *Intermedi* often presented learned fantasies whose interlocked themes produced a message dictated by whoever paid for the performance. In time, *intermedi* came to overwhelm the plays they were originally designed to punctuate, and their extravagant musical numbers paved the way for musical theater.

At Urbino the first *intermedio* featured the ancient hero Jason, who entered armed and dancing. He was met by two fire-breathing bulls, whom he yoked and used to plow the ground, in which he sowed dragon's teeth. The sown teeth produced armed men who rose from below stage through trap doors: "first half their heads, then down to their necks, then to half their bodies, then to their thighs, finally standing on their feet, completely armed, with nude swords in hand."[50] These warriors danced a *moresca* and tried to kill Jason, who killed them. At the end of the carnage, Jason exited "with the golden fleece on his shoulder, dancing excellently."

The next three *intermedi* featured triumphal carts bearing ancient gods. First appeared Venus, in a cart drawn by doves. Around her cart danced amorini, and then nine young men came on stage to dance. Neptune, in a cart pulled by two half-horses with the fins and scales of fish, dominated the next *intermedio*. His cart was followed by eight dancing sea monsters. After the next act Juno appeared in a cart set on a cloud and pulled by two peacocks. Although Castiglione does not tell us whether the cart was actually airborne, he was certainly stunned by the peacocks: "so beautiful and so natural that I did not know how it was possible." Dancers costumed as eagles, ostriches, sea birds, and parrots accompanied Juno. From these descriptions we learn that the stage floor was far enough above the floor of the hall to allow the warriors to move under it and emerge from trap doors, and we also learn that there had to be a large enough entrance from at least one side of the stage to accommodate the triumphal carts of the gods, plus a backstage area to store them. If the carts were not made fully in the round, to save money, they would have entered from one side of the stage and exited the other. In that case, the two towers at either end of the stage would have had to be large enough to contain all of them at one time.

"When the comedy was over, there was suddenly borne on stage an Amorino (did he actually fly?) . . . who declared in a few verses the significance of the intervals." The battle between "earthly brothers" in the first *intermedio* signified that "wars are between those who are near to each other and should make peace." The three gods, representing love, the sea, and the air, then came to throw out war and discord and to unite the world in concord. All of that would hardly have been self-evident to the audience, who must have felt relief when the Amorino gave them to understand what they had been looking at. The political point of the *intermedi* became clear. Italy had just undergone a difficult period of war, in which most of Europe, joined in the League of Cambrai, had ganged up on Venice. Julius II had sponsored the league to oppose the expansionist ambitions of the Venetian state. Once Venice had been humbled, Julius switched sides to counter growing French influence and brought about a cessation of the hostilities. Peace was now "on-message" from the Vatican, as the papal nephew's carnival entertainment made the audience understand.[51] The performance concluded when four concealed voices, accompanied by concealed violas, "sang a song with a beautiful musical air, almost a speech in honor of Love." On stage, love replaced war, whose constant presence in history was signaled by the story of the Trojan War told in the tapestries hung opposite the stage.

The inscription on the wall over the audience summed up, in a most flattering way, the manner in which the performance celebrated the role of Julius II both as a war-making and peace-making pope, the great spirit who conducted both battles abroad and games at home, as the Latin inscription put it. The last word of the first line, "ipse" (himself), and the first word of the second, "Caesar," placed a particular emphasis on that ancient leader whose name Julius II had adopted.[52] The first Pope Julius[53] was not the man Julius sought to invoke by taking his name, but rather Julius Caesar. The two words, "ipse Caesar," would have appeared right in the center of the inscription, and thus right in the center of the wall above the audience.[54] Few in an audience well versed in Latin would have missed the allusion, tinged for some with sadness, for Julius was mortally ill in Rome. Thus did theater and politics continue to join together in Renaissance Italy.

ROME OF LEO X

Julius II died two weeks after the performance of *La calandra*. His successor, elected the next month, was Cardinal Giovanni de' Medici, who chose the name Leo X. He took the Duchy of Urbino away from Francesco Maria I della Rovere and gave it to his nephew, Lorenzo de' Medici, in an effort to establish a large Medici state in central Italy.[55] Leo was a friend, however, to Benardo Dovizi da Bibbiena, whom in the fall of 1513 he named a cardinal, thereafter known as Cardinal Bibbiena.

Isabella d'Este went to Rome in 1514 to look after her state's welfare, to see the sights, and to solidify her contacts at the papal court. There Leo X honored her with a splendidly staged performance of Cardinal Bibbiena's *La calandra*, directed by the author and given in the Vatican itself, since the honoree was a ruling marchioness and ally. It was unusual for comedies to be given lavish productions in the Vatican. Alexander VI Borgia enjoyed comedies and had them performed frequently for his amusement, even into the wee hours, but he spent little or nothing on the staging.[56] For example, he ordered a performance of the *Menaechmi*, that consistent favorite, in 1502 to celebrate the marriage of his daughter Lucrezia to Alfonso I d'Este, Isabella's brother. But he chose a room too small to accommodate scenery. Not so for the production Pope Leo X offered Isabella in 1514, for which the architect of the Farnesina, Baldassare Peruzzi, designed impressive sets that gave Isabella a chance to see the work of the man who became the most advanced scene designer of the time in the very first year of his stage activity.[57]

Leo X Medici, a son of the famous Lorenzo the Magnificent, took his father's patronage of art to even more elevated heights, now that he had Rome and the universal church as the platforms from which to launch his ambitious artistic program. "Since God has given us the papacy, let us enjoy it," he is reported to have said. Gaining the papacy gave the Medici family, who had wielded unofficial political power throughout much of the fifteenth century in Florence by mean of wealth and guile, a legitimacy they had not previously possessed. Leo sought to enhance his family's status by honoring its male members, the presumptive heirs to the family's possessions that had been seized by the commune of Florence when it unceremoniously pitched the Medici out of town in 1494, two years after Lorenzo died. Leo declared his brother Giuliano and his nephew Lorenzo citizens of Rome, and in September 1513, he inducted them into Roman citizenship in an elaborate spectacle carried out in a large temporary theater erected for the occasion on the Capitoline Hill, the first purpose-built theater since antiquity that we know to have been the site of an actual performance.[58] A correspondent of Isabella d'Este, who sent her a lengthy description now unfortunately lost, said, in a remarkable understatement, that it was "so beautiful and extraordinary that Rome had not seen a similar celebration in many years."[59] The choice of the Capitoline Hill was no accident. It had been the symbolic heart of the whole Roman Empire, and since the Middle Ages the hill had served as the seat of the Roman civic government, which operated under the auspices of the pope, who was both the secular and religious ruler of the city.

Since the return of the popes to Rome from Avignon in the early fifteenth century, various of them had sought to revivify the Capitoline Hill. At midcentury Nicholas V, the first of these popes with a comprehensive plan to return Rome to its former architectural glory, constructed a new building on the hill, the Palazzo dei Conservatori, in the new Renaissance architectural style. In the 1480s Sixtus IV began to assemble the first outdoor public collection of sculpture, placing on the hill large Roman statues that had been unearthed in the city. During Sixtus's pontificate Plautus' *Epidicus* was given on the hill in 1486. In 1511 the Conservatori, governors of Rome, had honored young Federico Gonzaga with a performance of the *Menaechmi* in their palace.[60] The Capitoline Hill was the focus of papal efforts to revive civic life in Rome, and Leo surely chose the site for that reason. It would have been inappropriate, even for Leo, to hold the secular ceremony of citizenship in the Vatican. He was also trying to curry favor with the citizens of Rome, whose ability to govern themselves had been seriously infringed by Julius II.

The reasons for constructing this theater being political, Leo saw to it that its architecture and decoration stressed his intended message of celebrating an alliance between Florence and Rome, supposedly stretching back to antiquity, that brought the weight of Roman history down on the side of his family. Accordingly, the architecture of the theater was classical. Several written descriptions of the structure have come down to us, as well as a contemporary plan, and from these it is possible to reconstruct with some certainty what it looked like. The entrance wall, as much as 30 m wide, was divided into five arches flanked by six free-standing columns with gilded bases and capitals. The central arch framed the entrance, while the other arches contained paintings that celebrated the friendship between ancient Romans and Etruscans, ancestors of the modern-day Tuscans of Florence. Above the arches was an attic story with symbols of Florence – a lion and ball – and Rome – the she-wolf – as well as representations of the Arno and Tiber, the rivers of the two cities. It would have been hard to miss the point. It would also have been clear that the free-standing columns framing the arches, as well as the attic story, were elements taken directly from Roman triumphal arches, so that the entrance to the theater, which confronted spectators as they climbed up the slope of the hill from the center of the city, declared a Medician triumph.[61] The other exterior walls were undecorated.

Those outside walls, roughly 18 m high and probably made of wood, enclosed an interior space that measured approximately 20 × 25 m.[62] In height and width, the theater would have been roughly the same size as the entrance court of the Farnesina. A contemporary plan in the Codex Coner (Fig. 23) gives us a rather clear picture of the layout, since its details largely accord with the surviving written descriptions, even though the drawing shows a larger version of the design than actually built.[63] Against three walls rose banks of steps for seating, five rows according to the plan, seven (the same number we encountered at the Farnesina) according to the verbal descriptions. The U-shaped organization of the seats, divided in the middle by the path of the entrance, was like the arrangement in the palace in Ferrara for the wedding of 1491. The risers were raised up on a podium (cf. Vitruvius), the level of which was the same as the floor of the stage. All the interior walls were articulated by evenly spaced square columns. The back wall of the stage was pierced by five doors that mirrored the five arches of the façade. The doors were of a size that one would find in a private house (presumably a large one, however). Through the stage doors, covered by gold cloths, the actors entered and exited. In the side walls of the stage were two similar doors for the entrance and exit of triumphal carts. The plan, strangely, shows the only means of access to the risers from ground level to have been the doors at the sides of the stage. The other openings in the side walls probably admitted light and air, not people, since they would have been elevated considerably above ground. The whole interior was covered by a blue, white, and green striped awning. An altar stood center stage for the celebration of mass that opened the ceremonies. It was replaced by a lectern for the speakers, which was then removed for the banquet, the procession of triumphal carts, and the performance of the comedy. The most important people sat on the stage, so that they were part of the spectacle, rather than spectators.

Ralph Lieberman has made the plausible suggestion that the architecture of the theater was largely prefabricated.[64] According to the contemporary accounts, it was erected in only a few days, but the paintings that decorated it were the product of work that stretched over a longer span. In other words, the paintings were brought completed onto the hill and set into a quickly assembled framework. We are told that those who were not invited to sit inside cut holes in the paintings in order to look in at the action. That probably

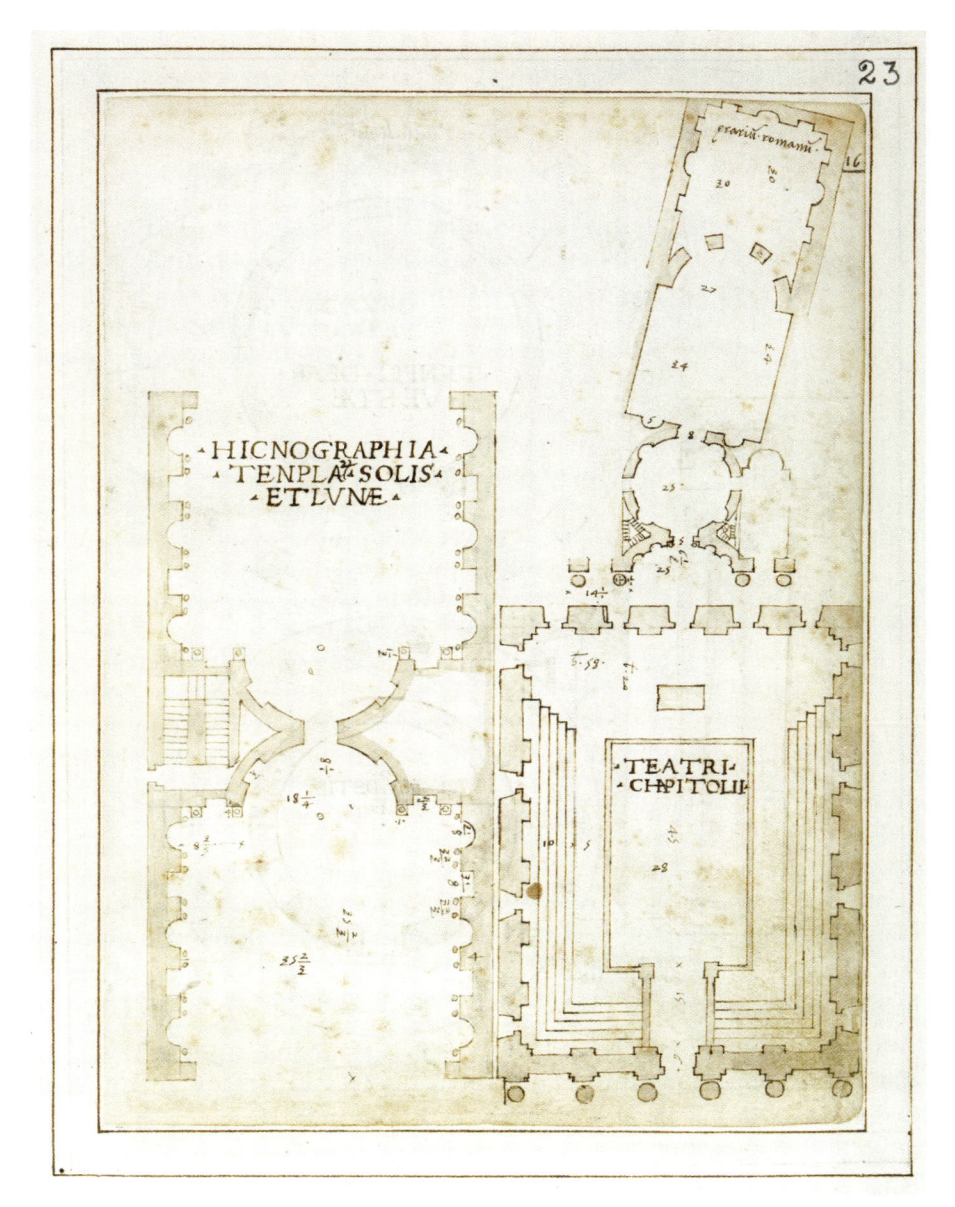

FIG. 23 Theater on the Capitoline Hill, 1513, plan at right, Codex Coner (© Sir John Soane's Museum, London, 115, 23)

means that there was no backing behind the paintings, or between paintings that were hung back to back on the outside and inside of the entrance wall.

According to contemporary accounts, a Florentine, Pietro Rosselli, built the theater, but it is not likely that he designed it. Arnaldo Bruschi has convincingly attributed the theater to Giuliano da Sangallo, a Florentine architect

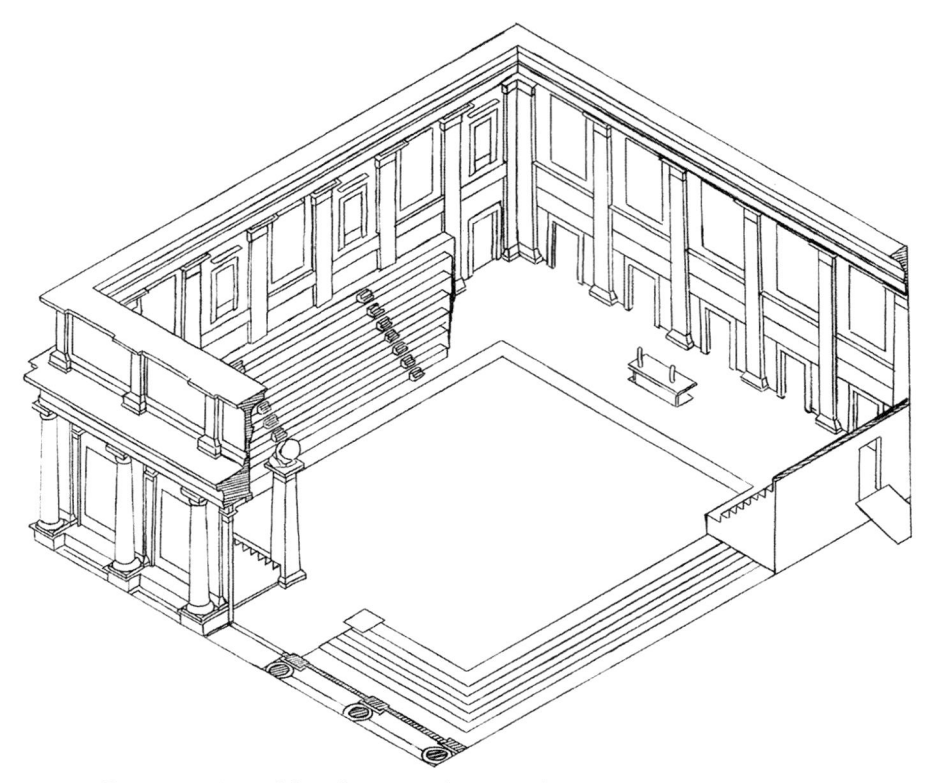

FIG. 24 Reconstruction of the Theater on the Capitoline Hill of 1513, after Arnaldo Bruschi (Drawing: Troy Sipprelle)

who had worked for Lorenzo the Magnificent and had hurried down to Rome from Florence after the election of Leo X.[65] Bruschi published a most helpful reconstruction of the theater (Fig. 24). The design of its façade is remarkably like the façade that Donato Bramante had designed in the spring of 1513 for a temporary structure to protect the altar and apse of the church of Old St. Peter's while the new St. Peter's was under construction (Fig. 25). We know Bramante's building from sixteenth-century drawings; it disappeared once the enormous new church had been completed. That Giuliano and Bramante knew each other's designs is likely, and it is hard to say which may have come first. Both expressed triumph, one Christian, one secular.

Above the doors at the rear of the stage were five paintings, the central of which showed the founding of Florence by Romans. On the opposite wall – the inside of the entrance wall – to the left of the entrance was a painting that showed a theater full of people "with those who recite comedies on the stage, called actors, who appear with their acts, gestures and words to delight and give pleasure to the people looking on." Connected to this painting was a Latin inscription, LUDI SCENICI AB HETRUSCUS ADCOEPTIO, that

FIG. 25 Marten van Heemskerk, view of St. Peter's, Rome, under construction with Bramante's temporary structure of 1513 to protect the high altar, Roman Sketchbook II, drawing (Berlin, Kupferstichkabinett, Staatliche Museum) (Photo: Volker-H. Schneider/Art Resource, NY)

gave a perhaps-inflated importance to the contribution of the Etruscans to the history of the theater in ancient Rome.

Modern Romans turned out in huge numbers to see the theater. One chronicler says that old folks who had not left their houses for a long time roused themselves to come out, "and only God knows if they will leave their houses again." Matrons and virgins, seldom permitted even to venture forth to church, were allowed to visit the theater. Only a small, elite group gained admission to the theater to witness the ceremonies, banquet, procession, and play, however. The contemporary chronicler Paolo Palliolo tells us that men stationed at the doors "did not allow every manual laborer and vile plebeian to enter, but only those whose aspect was deigned worthy of such a spectacle."[66] Those who had been repulsed peeked through cracks in the structure, or the windows, or holes they cut in the structure or its decorations. Not even all those possibly considered "worthy" were able to enter. Some noblemen and clergy watched from windows of the nearby Palazzo dei Conservatori, and certain Roman aristocrats even built balconies on the façade of the Palazzo dei Conservatori so that they could see and hear the speeches and performances in the theater. (It's not clear how they managed to see around the striped awning that covered the interior.)

What a show it was. A procession with musicians brought Giuliano to the theater from the papal palace (Lorenzo was not present). Mass was said at an altar set up on stage. Speeches were given. A lavish banquet was provided on stage, with such rare dishes as a roasted wolf, recovered in its own skin and appearing to nurse human twins. The audience watched their betters eat. Triumphal carts wheeled across the stage to pay homage to Giuliano. When the performance of Plautus' *Poenulus* in Latin, deliberately unintelligible to "manual laborers and vile plebeians," ended the festivities in the afternoon of the second day, the stage was so crowded by the seated honoree and important guests there was barely room for the actors. The comedy was repeated in the Vatican on September 18, with fifteen cardinals; the ambassadors of Milan, Florence, and France; and hundreds of guests present.[67]

If we think of this theater as like the Mantuan theater of 1501, but inverted and erected outside, we will not be far wrong. The arches flanked by columns of the entrance wall recalled, just as did the arches and columns on the walls of the Mantuan theater, the Colosseum and the Theater of Marcellus – just as the loggia of the north façade of the Farnesina had recalled the same structures.[68] Thus the architecture deliberately referred to ancient theatrical structures whose forms had already been revived in contemporary theater architecture. But the theater did not follow the semicircular plan of Roman theaters. Instead, the shape of the rectangular palace halls and palace courtyards that housed contemporary theaters was continued here. It was not a lack of knowledge of the shape of ancient theaters that led Leo to have the Capitoline Hill theater constructed as if it were part of a contemporary palace complex. Rather, he seems deliberately to have wanted to recall such temporary theaters in palaces, presumaably to stress his own role, and that of his family, as legitimate (or ideally legitimate) contemporary sovereigns. This was the type of temporary theater that a sovereign built.

The first theater in the ancient, semicircular manner of modern times, at least as far as we know, Raphael designed for the Villa Madama in Rome, another Medici project (Fig. 26). Begun around 1516, the building was never finished, and so we know Raphael's design only from drawings.[69] The long axis of the villa, running roughly north/south, was laid out against the slope of Monte Mario. At the approximate center of this layout was a circular courtyard through which an east/west cross-axis was to pass. On the uphill, or western, end of this cross-axis Raphael placed his theater, taking advantage of slope of the hill down to the east toward the bed of the Tiber. The steps of the theater would have served as the entrance to the villa from a road that ran alongside it higher up the hill. The *scenae frons* of the theater would have been its eastern wall, contiguous with the western wall of the circular courtyard. Raphael's

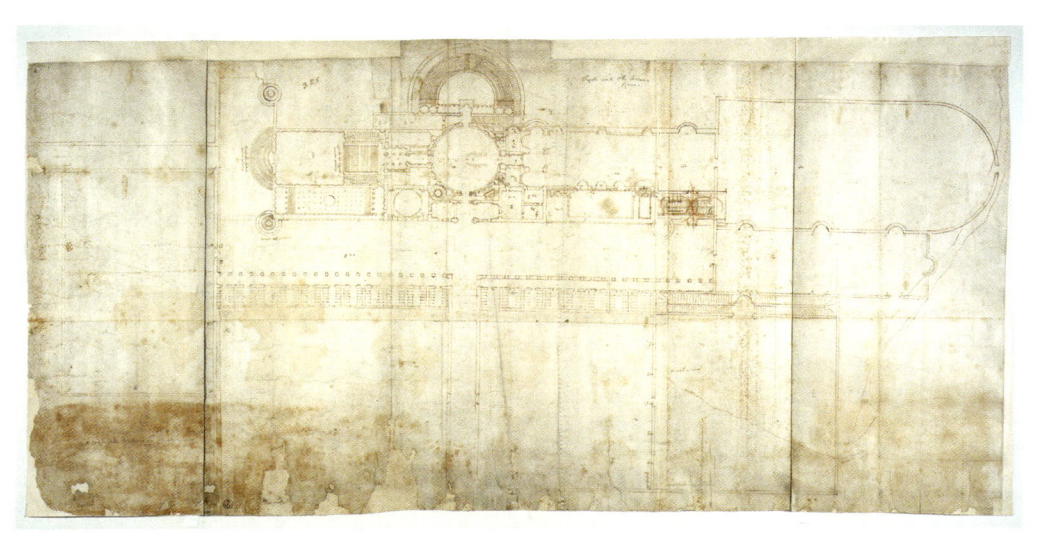

FIG. 26 Antonio da Sangallo the Younger, Raphael's project for Villa Madama, Rome, plan, begun c. 1516 (Florence, Gabinetto dei Disegni e Stampi degli Uffizi, UA 314)

interest in ancient buildings is well documented in a letter he wrote to Leo X urging their preservation, and so the archaeological correctness of his design comes as no surprise here. The archaeological rightness of the architecture goes along with the deliberately Roman character of the plays written to entertain Leo and his court.[70]

In Rome in 1519 Leo took another important step in the development of the theater as an architectural experience. A performance of Ariosto's *I suppositi* was given on March 6 in the residence of the papal nephew, Cardinal Innocenzo Cibo, under the patronage of the Medici pope.[71] According to the Ferrarese ambassador to Rome, the pope stationed himself at the entrance to one of the cardinal's antechambers, so that he could allow in only those he wanted to attend the performace. Then, when all were assembled in the antechamber, he stood at the entrance to the room in which the theater had been constructed "and without confusion with his blessing he let enter whom he pleased" His Holiness as ticket taker and usher, as it were. No earlier account of making so much of the actual admission of the audience to a theater seems to have come down to us. Leo may have been the first to recognize the possibilities inherent in a before-play space, a space that will come to be immensely important in later theaters – one thinks of the great staircase hall at the Paris Opéra.

The theater constructed for this occasion consisted of rows of risers for seating placed against the wall opposite the stage. According to the Ferrarese ambassador, as many as 2,000 men were present, but that is surely an exaggeration. The pope sat at the bottom of the steps, on a platform raised five risers above the floor. To either side of him cardinals and ambassadors sat in a row "according to their station." Here too we find a moment of some importance, in which a ruler uses the arrangement of seating in the theater to reinforce the hierarchy of positions at his court. To view the stage, the audience had to look across the raised figure of the pope, who had seated to either side of him, in an order that he had approved, the most powerful members of his court. Around him, Leo's name blazed in lights. The candelabra that lit the theater were in the shape of letters that spelled out LEO PONS. MAXIMUS, with each letter carrying five torches, in a continuation of the idea of lights shaped like letters from Urbino. The stage scenery was by none other than Raphael. Unfortunately, no sure representation of this scenery has come down to us. The Ferrarese ambassador noted that the set contained perspective openings, which probably represented the streets of a town, while the ambassador from Venice wrote that the sets were magnificent and represented Ferrara precisely as it was.[72] Although the French in the audience were scandalized by bawdy remarks that came from the stage, Leo laughed loudly.

The theater of 1519 continued, then, the general type of the court theater, now some thirty years old. The seating did not take up the U-shaped plan of the theater on the Capitoline Hill, probably because Leo wanted all the audience literally looking at the play over his shoulders. Leo was the focus of the event, his name literally up in lights.

3

EARLY THEATERS IN VENICE AND THE VENETO

The theatrical situation in Venice was as unique as its geography, government, and society. Aqueous Venice was ruled not by a hereditary prince, or by a tyrannical warlord, or by the pope, but by a group of rich families who decided at the end of the thirteenth century to exclude newcomers to their ennobled numbers. The laws of the city were created by an assembly, the Maggior Consiglio, in which sat all the male members of these families who had reached the age of eighteen. From this unmanageably large group were appointed smaller ruling bodies that actually ran the city and its empire on a day-to-day basis. There was an elected leader, the doge, who lived in the great Ducal Palace, but that palace was in many ways a communal palace, used by the entire aristocracy, rather than the residence of a ruling prince. The doge, whose powers were severely restricted in order to prevent his taking over the state, rarely sponsored theatrical performances.

The aristocrats, who loved the theater, banded together in groups to produce plays, particularly during the carnival season, when Venice gave itself over to the public pursuit of pleasure. Carnival began just after Christmas and ended on the Tuesday before the first day of Lent, which usually occurred in February. Plays were given either in the palaces of great families or in rooms, called *stanze* in Venetian documents, fitted out as theatrical spaces. We have no description of these *stanze*, and so we have no idea how they were disposed architecturally. Venetian palaces have a standard arrangement of rooms that conforms to a well-developed building type. Each floor of a palace has a long, narrow central room, flanked to either side by suites of smaller rooms. Often the central room is lit by windows set in both of the short end walls. If a performance were held inside a palace, it would have been in a room of this type, which could accommodate a fairly large number of people. Venetian palaces generally did not have large interior courtyards that could be devoted to theatrical performances. Given the Venetian climate – cold and rainy, or even snowy, in winter – holding the performances indoors made sense.

The best information we have on theatrical performances in Venice in the first decades of the sixteenth century comes from a remarkable diarist, Marin Sanudo, an aristocrat who somehow managed to write down everything of importance that happened in Venice every day of his adult life. These diaries were published in fifty-four volumes at the end of the nineteenth and the beginning of the twentieth centuries,[1] and so what Sanudo had to say is available to anyone with the patience to decipher his sometimes-cryptic writing in Venetian, a language often different from modern Italian.

During the carnival of 1508 (1507 according to the Venetian calendar, in which the new year arrived on March 1), as Sanudo informs us, a man named Francesco Cherea presented the *Menaechmi* of Plautus in a *stanza* at San Cassiano in Biri. "It was most beautiful," Sanudo writes.[2] Cherea was the stage name of a gentleman from Lucca, Francesco de' Nobili. He took the name Cherea from a character in Plautus' *Eunuchus*, a role he must have played with success.[3] He began to organize theatrical performances from which, it seems, he derived profit. Later in the same carnival season a rustic comedy – Sanudo uses the words "comedia vilanescha" – was put on in the same *stanza*.[4] Both ancient and modern comedies, then, were offered for the pleasure of Venetians, who paid to attend the performances. The *stanza* is identified by the church nearest to it, San Cassiano. Naming theatrical spaces after nearby churches became a Venetian tradition, so that theaters in the city came to bear the names of saints, even though what took place in them was rarely holy.

The night before the rustic comedy was put on, another comedy by Plautus was performed before a large crowd, perhaps in a different location. What is remarkable about this performance is that two of the leading citizens of the city took important roles: "Anzolo Trevisan, *capo* of the Council of Ten, and Zaccaria Dolfin, a counselor to the doge, accepted the execution of the parts and performed them."[5] The Council of Ten was the single most powerful ruling body in the Venetian republic; every month two of its members became its heads, or *capi*, by rotation. The office of counselor to the doge was also of great importance. If the play were put on today by similar folk in Washington, DC, the leading roles might be taken by the secretary of defense and the president's chief of staff. Sanudo's account reveals a situation that continued in

Venice for some time. There were private performances by members of the nobility, presumably for their own kind, and then there were more public performances sponsored by an impresario for profit.

Francesco Cherea was an ambitious man.[6] At the end of 1508 he tried to gain the use of a most prominent public building, the Palazzo dei Camerlenghi, for the performance of his comedies during the coming carnival.[7] He proposed to the *capi* of the Council of Ten and to another governing body that controlled the building that he should rent its loggia, or columned portico, at Rialto for this purpose. We know something of the appearance of this portico from the map of Venice published in 1500 by Jacopo de' Barbari (Fig. 27). With tall columns supporting a pediment, it faced a relatively large open space at the west end of the then- wooden Rialto Bridge. Presumably the columns would have served as the backdrop for the productions, while the audience would have gathered in the open space before the portico. Rialto was the most important commercial area in Venice, the business center of a city whose business was commerce. Rialto at that time boasted the only bridge that crossed the Grand Canal to connect the two halves of the city. One might say that Cherea tried to rent the equivalent of Times Square. Venetians were leery of turning over any important part of their city to one person, even for a brief time, and so the request was denied.

FIG. 27 Jacopo de' Barbari, map of Venice, 1500, detail showing pedimented portico of Palazzo dei Camerlenghi at foot of Rialto Bridge as it still stood in 1508 (Venice, Museo Civico Correr)

Cherea's proposal struck fear into the hearts of the Venetian ruling class. On December 29, 1508 the Council of Ten issued an extraordinary decree, banning theatrical events at any time and at any place in the city, unless the council gave permission for the performance. According to the decree, the performance of comedies had been introduced into the city only recently.[8] The council predicated its decree on its self-assumed role of protecting the morals of the youth of Venice, now in danger of being corrupted by the "many shameful, lascivious and indecent words and actions" that characterized this novel form of entertainment. The membership of the council changed annually at the end of September. No one could serve two successive terms, and so Anzolo Dolfin, the *capo* who had taken a role in a comedy the preceding winter, was no longer a member. But both men who had acted in that comedy were councillors to the doge in December 1508, and so they were still able to cast votes in the Ten, which actually consisted of seventeen members: the members of the Ten, plus the doge and his six councillors. How they voted is not recorded.[9] The penalties imposed for not observing the new law were severe. They could include a year in jail, banishment from Venice and its territories for five years, a large fine, or two years of banishment from the Maggior Consiglio for a nobleman who permitted such a performance in or near his house. Although this law was frequently ignored during subsequent years of the century,[10] it produced a catastrophic effect on two new theaters of considerable architectural importance in the 1580s.

From time to time the law put a damper on the activities of a series of organizations of young Venetian nobles, known as the Compagnie della Calza.[11] Each of these companies, which dated back to the early fifteenth century, lasted only briefly, during the years their members came into manhood. The members, from wealthy patrician families, pooled resources to produce entertainments in which the young men took the principal parts. The name Compagnie della Calza refers to the costumes the young men adopted. Each group chose a particular combination of colors for the tights they all wore. One group might, for instance, have red tights on their right legs and yellow and blue on the left. We know such brightly colored garments from many fifteenth century Italian paintings. (Translating *calza* into English as "tights," so that a group would be called a Company of Tights, is problematic; even more ambiguous would be Hose Company. We will stick to the Italian phrase.)

In some years as many as four separate companies operated at once, with the permission of the Council of Ten. During the carnival of 1520 (1519 m.v., modo veneziano, that is, the Venetian manner of starting the new year on March 1) Sanudo tells us that one group, the Ortolani, arranged a dinner followed by dancing outside in Campo San Polo.[12] Four days later another group, the Immortali, sponsored the performance of a comedy by the Paduan playwright Ruzzante at the Foscari palace on the Grand Canal,[13] while on the same day at the Loredan palace near San Marcuola a third company, the Trionphanti, put on Terence's *Adelphi*, with the members of the company taking all the roles. The next day the Trionphanti presented the *Aulularia*.[14] Three days later a fourth company, the Zardinieri, presented a contemporary play in dialect by Ruzzante in the house of one of the procurators of St. Mark, Domenico Trevisan.[15] Not every year was so busy, and there were years in which the Council of Ten absolutely forbade the presentation of any theatrical performance by any group, no matter how aristocratic.

The plays were usually part of elaborate celebrations that included dances and banquets that lasted into the wee hours. Husbands and wives attended together. The stages for the plays might be a makeshift arrangement inside the palace, but sometimes they could be part of elaborate constructions outside the palace. At Ca' Foscari the Immortali constructed a floating bridge across the Grand Canal, as well as a large, partially covered platform in front of the palace. Spectators also stood in the palace windows. Once the performance was over, bridge and platform were dismantled.[16]

Not all of the celebrations organized by these groups took place at carnival, and not all of the structures built to hold these celebrations were designed to be fixed in one place. In July of 1530 a company called the Floridi built a floating theater supported on two boats. Its platform was decorated with two figures of marine monsters, one an old man and the other a (presumably more attractive) woman. Over the whole was a canopy decorated with beautiful tapestries. Eighty-seven young women came aboard to dance, while the stage was rowed by many boats up the Grand Canal to the Rialto Bridge and then back to Piazza San Marco.[17]

The next day, in the rain, the women once again danced on the moving stage as it was towed up the Grand Canal. They stopped in front of Ca' Foscari to watch a man dive from the highest balcony into the water, a stunt he repeated twice. Then a boat race was held on the Grand Canal, after which the theater was towed to the island of the Giudecca, to which a temporary bridge had been built over a line of boats. The foreign ambassadors joined the party, and they dined aboard the theater with the women who had been dancing. Sanudo found the food poor and improperly served. After dinner, there was more dancing on the floating stage, then a procession of servants dressed up as various animals on the fondamenta, or quay, of the Giudecca. With the animals came representations of "the world in the form of a sphere, a city in the shape of Venice, and the Inferno."[18]

All of this goes to show the imaginative ways the Venetians used their city as a huge stage set, against which images of the world, the city, and the lower

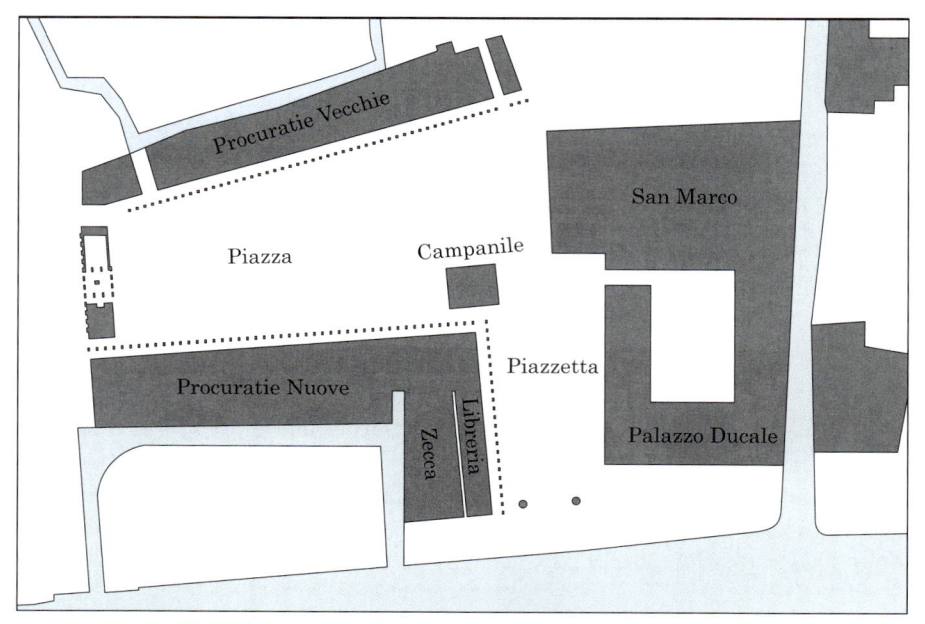

FIG. 28 Venice, Piazza San Marco and Piazzetta, plan (Drawing: Benjamin Hoyle)

depths could be presented – to say nothing of beautiful young women from the best families dancing on the waters. Venetians built sets within the great set of the city, using its architecture and water as both backdrops and stages. At the same time the city became an auditorium to accommodate spectators. The relationship between stage and audience was as fluid as the city's site. A floating construction might even be called a "Teatro del Mondo" (Theater of the World), adding still yet another dimension to the theatrical nature of the city and its environment.

One part of Venice was the most "theatrical": Piazza San Marco and its smaller appendage, the Piazzetta (Fig. 28). Here, in its heart, the city produced its most important public festivals and theatrical events. By Sanudo's time the piazza already had been employed for such purposes for several centuries. A letter from the poet Petrarch of August 10, 1364 describes the celebrations of a Venetian military victory in Crete. On consecutive days a race and a joust were held in the piazza. The doge and the leading men of the city watched the spectacle from seats, protected by awnings, placed above the façade of the church of San Marco (Fig. 29). Petrarch sat next to the doge, and so his description is firsthand. The crowd down below was so great that "as the saying goes, a grain of millet couldn't have fallen to earth. The great square, the church itself, the towers, roofs, porches, windows were not so much filled as jammed with spectators." Against the front of the building that formed the north side of the square – to Petrarch's right as he looked down from his

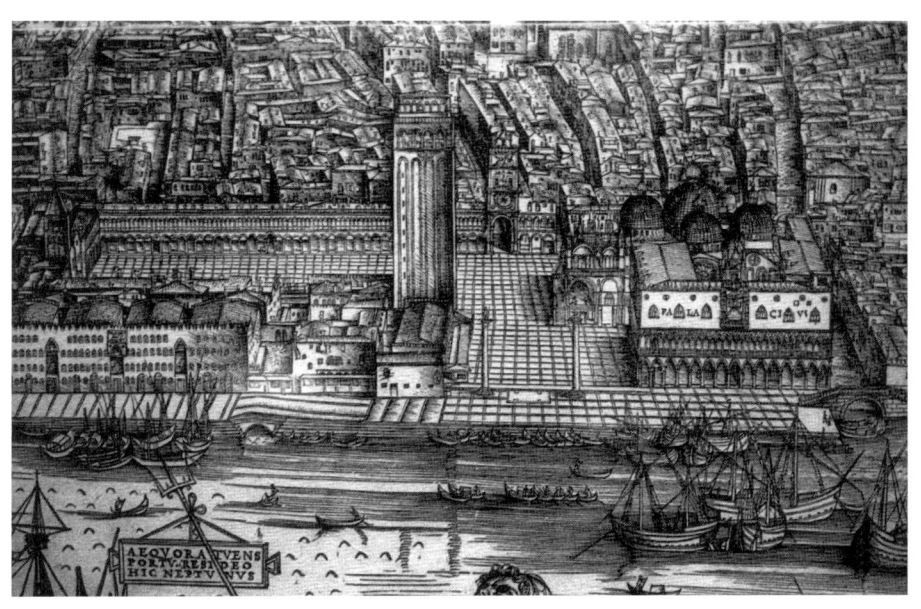

FIG. 29 Jacope de' Barbari, Piazza San Marco, detail of map of Venice, 1500 (Venice, Museo Civico Correr)

perch – a grandstand had been erected to hold four hundred "young women of the flower of the nobility, very beautifully and splendidly dressed." Not only did they adorn the public square, but they also provided a "brilliant reception for invited guests." Venice never lost the opportunity to put spectacle to diplomatic use. Among those at the festival were "certain high noblemen from Britain, kinsmen of the king, who had journeyed here by sea to celebrate our victory."[19] You can be sure that back home they had never seen anything quite like the show Venice put on.

From the twelfth century, and perhaps even earlier, spectators jammed the windows of the buildings surrounding the piazza on festive days. The grandstand for the young women that Petrarch describes stood against the Procuratie Vecchie, a long arcaded structure built in the twelfth century. (The present structure dates from the sixteenth century, but it follows the model of its predecessor closely) (Fig. 30). According to the thirteenth century chronicler Martino da Canal, women ascended to the windows in the Procuratie to watch a tourney held in 1254 in Piazza San Marco to celebrate the accession of Doge Renier Zeno.[20] As Gentile Bellini presents the building at the left edge of his famous painting of 1496, *The Procession of Corpus Domini in Piazza San Marco*, each window is occupied by one or two women watching the action in the square (Fig. 31). A similar situation is shown in the engraving by Matteo Pagan, *Procession of the Doge on Palm Sunday*, 1556–59 (Fig. 32). Venetian paintings of the fifteenth and sixteenth centuries demonstrate that windows

FIG. 30 Venice, Procuratie Vecchie, rebuilt sixteenth century on the model of the original twelfth-century buildings shown in Fig. 29 (Photo: Ralph Lieberman)

all over the city were used this way. The eyewitness character of these pictures, pointed out by Patricia Fortini Brown, assures us that such depictions of details of Venetian life are unlikely to be largely fictitious.[21]

Building temporary grandstands in the piazza was also common. Around 1610 Giacomo Franco, in his engraving of the execution of bulls in the Piazzetta on Fat Thursday (*giovedì grasso*) from his *Habiti d'Huomeni et Donne Venetiane* (1610), shows temporary seats for spectators erected in front of the doge's palace and the Libreria di San Marco (Fig. 33). A third set of stands appears in the lower left corner, to suggest that the north end of the Piazzetta was enclosed by seats as well. To the south, toward the water, there are no seats; spectators stand on the pavement. Franco's engraving demonstrates that the Piazzetta could be fitted out as a theatrical space with seating on three sides, and that the openings in both flanking buildings were used as places from which important spectators could see and be seen. Temporary grandstands for spectators had been erected in the Piazzetta much earlier, of course. For example, for a tourney in honor of the condottiere Bartolomeo Colleoni in 1458 rows of seats were arranged opposite the Palazzo Ducale.[22]

FIG. 31 Gentile Bellini, detail of *The Procession of Corpus Domini in Piazza San Marco*, 1496 (Venice, Galleria dell'Accademia) (Photo: Ralph Lieberman)

The Piazza (Fig. 29), the Piazzetta, and the Ducal Palace that flanked the Piazzetta (Fig. 34) were used over and over again as sites to entertain important visitors. When a visit from the young marquess of Mantua, Federico II Gonzaga, impended in 1519, the Immortali, the Compagnia della Calza that had produced plays at carnival that year, took it upon themselves to entertain him. He was made an honorary member of the group, which planned to build two structures in the Piazza on which to mount an entertainment. One would

FIG. 32 Matteo Pagan, detail from *Procession of the Doge on Palm Sunday*, engraving, 1556–59 (Venice, Museo Civico Correr)

be a grandstand for the visitor, the doge, and the ladies; the other would be a stage for a performance and for dancing that would follow.[23] There were murmurs around town that this would not be permitted, because such a construction to entertain a visitor had never been erected in the Piazza before. In Venice precedent reigned supreme. Novelty of any kind in the conduct of public life was viewed with deep suspicion.

On May 25 Gonzaga had an audience with the doge, after which the Immortali asked the doge for permission to build their temporary structures in the Piazza. The doge said, according to Sanudo, "We are well content, and we give you our room," by which he meant the very large outdoor room outside his palace. Sanudo was shocked: "The celebration will be in Piazza San Marco at night: a new and unheard of thing."[24] The doge retired to his chambers for a few days, and some of the old men in the government began to raise questions about his decision. The doge's counselors reaffirmed it, however, and construction of the grandstand and stage began. At just this moment, word arrived that a great Turkish war fleet was about to set sail, an ominous development for the Venetians, who were engaged in constant strife with the Ottomans over control of the eastern Mediterranean. People began to say that at such a perilous time an unprecedented nighttime celebration in Piazza San Marco would be inappropriate. The Immortali decided to dismantle the structures and move them to the Giudecca,[25] where on May 29,

FIG. 33 Giacomo Franco, *Execution of Bulls in the Piazzetta on Fat Thursday*, from *Habiti d'Huomeni et Donne Venetiane*, 1610 (Venice, Museo Civico Correr)

FIG. 34 Venice, view of Piazzetta from Bacino (Photo: Ralph Lieberman)

1519 the celebration in honor of the marquess finally took place. There were a regatta, dancing, dinner, rockets over the canal, and, finally, the performance – a tale of Hercules going to the underworld to take Proserpina away.[26] The marquess must have been pleased to have a story about Hercules staged in his honor. Ercole d'Este was his grandfather.

Building public grandstands was not without risk. Sometimes they fell down. During that same festive carnival of 1519, when four companies were producing plays and dances, a grandstand erected in Campo Santa Maria Formosa for a bull chase collapsed on people standing under it. Seven people were killed and many others badly hurt. "It was a very horrible thing to see," wrote Sanudo, "brains on the ground, heads without bodies."[27]

The most outrageous public spectacle of the year in Venice took place on Fat Thursday, the day that marked the beginning of the last six frenetic days of carnival. Several pigs and at least one bull (Fig. 33) were taken into the Ducal

Palace and condemned by a judge, with the doge, his counselors, and the foreign ambassadors in attendance. The pigs were turned loose in the Piazzetta, where, to the great enjoyment of the crowd, they were chased, captured, and beheaded, and so was the bull, or sometimes the bulls. The meat was distributed to the populace.[28]

Andrea Gritti, doge from 1523 to 1538, found this scene embarrassingly indecorous, and so he tried to improve it by joining it to a lavish theatrical performance subsidized by the state. He hired Francesco Cherea, the man who had wanted to rent the loggia at Rialto some years earlier, to produce the first of these spectacles for the carnival of 1526 (m.v.). Cherea erected a large grandstand in the middle of the piazza for the doge, the important men of the government, and the ambassadors, and then he surrounded the Piazza with other grandstands for which admission was charged. The grandstand seats were filled with masqueraders and women, and the Piazza itself was crowded with spectators who watched for free. At one end of the Piazza was a stage surrounded by curtains. Five pigs were chased and killed, and then a bull suffered the same fate. It rained a bit. The curtains on the stage fell to reveal an old world to one side and a new world to the other, with four giants occupying the corners of the stage. From a grotto dancers and singers emerged, the singers offering a song about renewing the old world. Sanudo provides a numbingly detailed account of what followed, which included a fire-breathing serpent and a boy dressed as an angel who recited verses about the old world. Finally, the old world caught fire, the new world remained, and the whole thing was over. "It was an extremely poor performance (*brutissima festa*)," wrote Sanudo, "and everyone said awful things about Cherea."[29]

Here Andrea Gritti, a man of no mean ambition for himself and his city, had hired Cherea to develop in "the doge's room" the equivalent of what princes in neighboring states had been doing for some time, both inside and outside their palaces. The whole Piazza was turned into an auditorium, with the principal political actors on a raised platform in the middle, the audience arranged around them on grandstands, with a stage at one end of the space. This being Venice, however, money entered the picture. The grandstands were not provided freely by the doge. If you wanted a seat, you had to pay for it, just as you had to pay for seats in the *stanze* where comedies were performed. Such performances continued for the rest of Sanudo's life in the Piazza on Fat Thursday; one is struck by how boring they must have been. Excruciatingly high-minded and crushingly allegorical, they celebrated the virtues of Venice in stylized tourneys.

After Sanudo's death in 1536, copious records like his of theatrical performances in the city diminish abruptly.

FIG. 35 Sebastiano Serlio, stage set based on view of Piazzetta from Bacino (Florence, Gabinetto dei Disegni e Stampe degi Uffizi, UA 5282) (Photo: Alinari/Art Resources, NY)

SEBASTIANO SERLIO IN VENICE

Sebastiano Serlio, who moved to Venice from Rome, saw the Serenissima as a stage set (Fig. 35).[30] Serlio was the only writer of an architectural treatise during the sixteenth century to include in his published work illustrations of a theater he had actually designed.[31] Serlio's books on architecture hold a special place in the history of architectural publications.[32] He was the first to publish a book illustrated with actual buildings, mostly ancient, or with buildings of his own design. Born in Bologna, Serlio worked professionally in Pesaro between 1511 and 1515; there he knew theatrical spectacles created by Gerolamo Genga in nearby Urbino, whose duke was also lord of Pesaro.[33] He moved on to Rome, where he was trained by Baldassare Peruzzi and where he came to possess drawings that Peruzzi had made of ancient Roman buildings. Serlio must have been keenly aware of Peruzzi's theatrical endeavors. It is not clear that Serlio could read Latin, but by 1521 Vitruvius had been translated into Italian in the sumptuous volume published in Como by Cesare Cesariano. That Serlio knew Vitruvius well cannot be doubted.

In 1527, after the Sack of Rome by troops of the Holy Roman Emperor Charles V, Serlio moved to Venice, where he designed very little but where he

FIG. 36 Sebastiano Serlio, frontispiece of Book III (Chapin Library of Rare Books, Williams College)

began to publish his books on architecture. As if deliberately to confuse bibliophiles, Serlio did not bring out these books in the numerical order he gave them. Book IV, devoted to the ancient orders of architecture, appeared first in 1537, followed three years later by Book III, which recorded the appearance of ancient Roman buildings and a few contemporary structures, notably Bramante's Tempietto and his design for the church of St. Peter's in Rome. In 1540 Serlio moved to France to become architect to Francis I. In Paris Books I and II appeared simultaneously in 1545, the former dealing with geometry and the latter with perspective. Serlio explained this curious sequence of publication as a marketing ploy: the material in the first two books would be difficult for some readers. He enticed his public with the more immediately appealing Books IV and III, to soften them up to buy I and II.

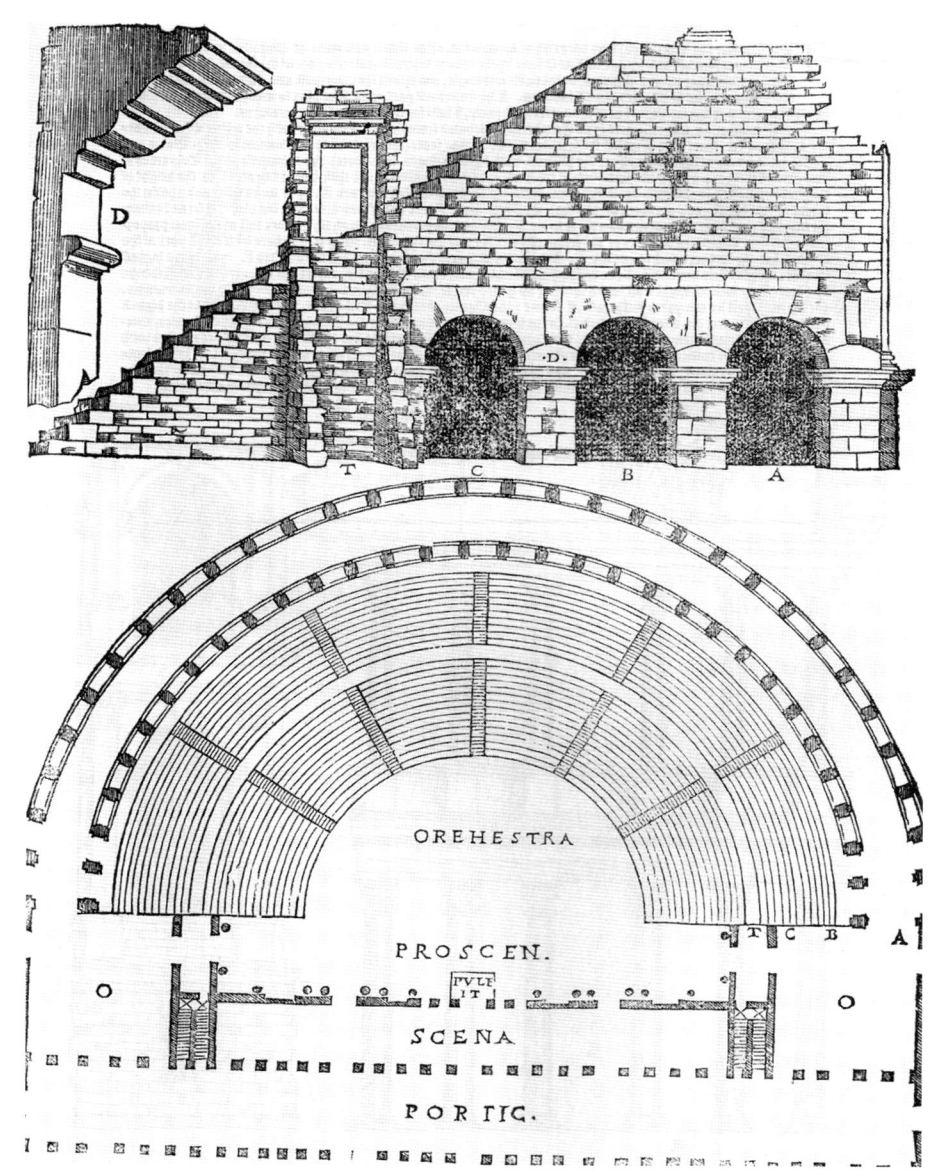

FIG. 37 Sebastiano Serlio, theater at Pola, from Book III (Chapin Library of Rare Books, Williams College)

Book III opens with a particularly magnificent frontispiece in which rusticated arches, set amid fallen architectural members, bear the motto ROMA QUANTA FUIT IPSA RUINA DOCET ("What Rome was the ruins themselves demonstrate")[34] (Fig. 36). In this book he illustrated and described three ancient theaters, which were given pride of second place immediately

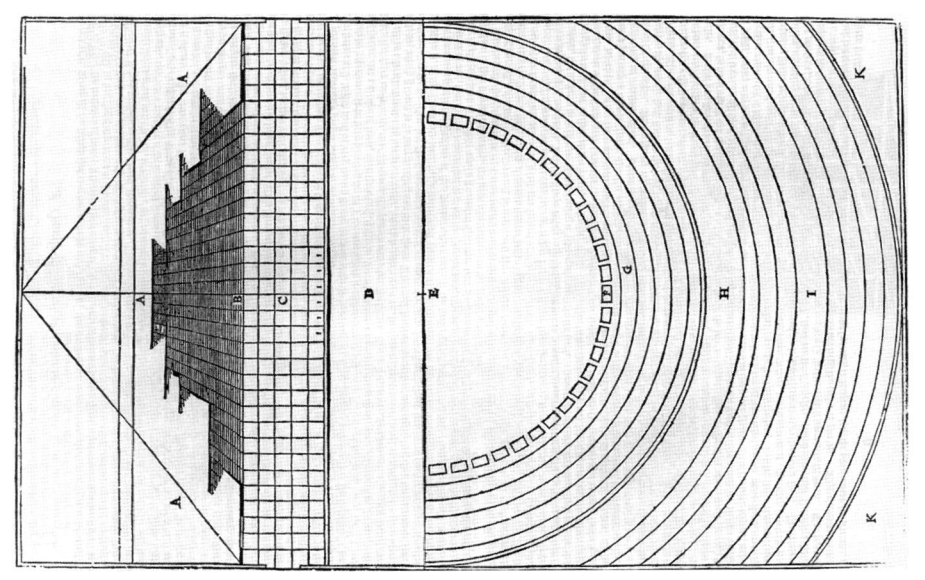

FIG. 38 Sebastiano Serlio, plan of the theater at Vicenza, 1537, from Book II (Chapin Library of Rare Books, Williams College)

following ancient and modern religious structures. These, the first drawings of ancient theaters to appear in print, are of the Theater of Marcellus in Rome (Fig. 18), the theater at Pola on the Dalmatian coast (Fig. 37), and that at Ferento north of Rome.[35] All share a common plan: seats arranged in a semicircle that face a rectangular stage across the flat edge of the half-circle of the orchestra. Rows of columns decorate the stages of the first two, and those theaters also are enclosed by round-arched porticoes articulated by engaged columns or pilasters. For many in the sixteenth century, Serlio's woodcut illustrations would have provided the first opportunity to imagine the appearance of ancient theaters.

Of equal or perhaps greater importance for the history of theater architecture is the theater that Serlio illustrates in Book II, based on a theater that he himself constructed in Vicenza in 1539 in the courtyard of a palace belonging to the da Porto family.[36] This is the earliest published representation we have of a theater actually built in the Renaissance. Serlio offers us a plan (Fig. 38) and a longitudinal section (Fig. 39), stating that they represent the theater in Vicenza more or less as he built it, although the plan is adapted to fit the publication. He devotes more than half the length of the courtyard to seating, arranging the seats in steps supported by the wooden framework shown in the section. At ground level, or the level of the orchestra, the seats form a half-circle, but as the steps for the audience rise, their arcs are cut off by the walls of the space into which they are fitted. Serlio here attempts to put a Roman

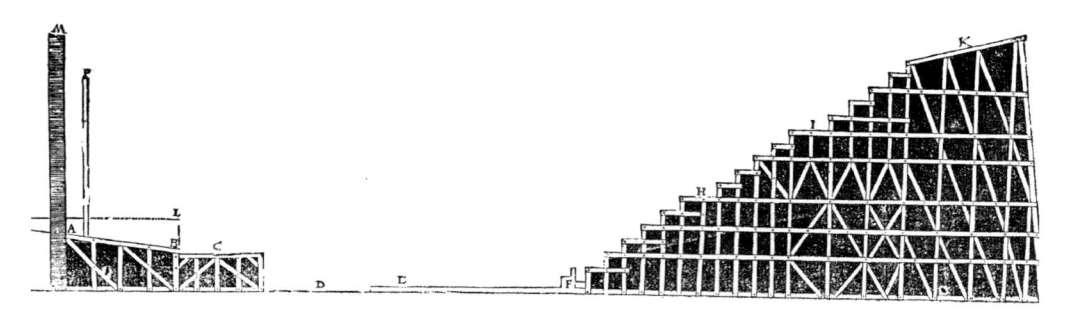

FIG. 39 Sebastiano Serlio, longitudinal section of the theater at Vicenza, from Book II (Chapin Library of Rare Books, Williams College)

theater inside a modern interior. As he notes, most theaters of his day were constructed in large halls rather than outdoors; those rectangular halls were almost never large enough to accommodate the full half-circles of the seating of a Roman theater.

On the floor of the orchestra are seats for the most important noblemen, following Vitruvius's statement that senators had their seats arranged in a semicircle on the edge of the orchestra (F on the plan). He separates the audience by sex and class. The most important noblewomen sit on the lowest step just behind the most important men (G). On the next several rows sit lesser noblewomen, who then are separated by a walkway (H) from noble men seated above them. A second walkway (I) separates the nobles from lesser nobles at the top of curved steps. Circulation among these parts of the theater is provided by steps set at the center of the semicircular rows. At the top of the seating are two small, triangular areas (K) for common folk, standing on a slanted floor that allowed them to see over the heads of men in front of them.

According to the section (Fig. 39), the orchestra (E) on which the great nobles sat was raised a step above the proscenium floor (D), which lies at ground level. This long, narrow rectangle led to the stage (C), a rectangle of exactly the same dimensions. Serlio says that in Vicenza his stage was 12 feet deep and 60 feet wide. If he used the Vicentine foot, which Palladio gives as 35 cm in his *Quattro Libri*, then his stage would have been 4.2 m deep and 21 m wide. Whatever the actual dimensions, Serlio states that the stage was large enough to accommodate the *intermedi*, which featured carriages (pulled by real horses?) and elephants (composed of costumes with men inside?) and thundering Moorish dancers. The stage, he says, was "perhaps, or rather without doubt, the largest built in our times." Because the published plan has no scale, we cannot easily assign dimensions to it. He tells us, however, that the palace courtyard in which the theater was erected had a width of 80 feet, or a sizable 28 m, if Serlio was using the Vicentine foot.

FIG. 40 Sebastiano Serlio, comic set, Book II (Chapin Library of Rare Books, Williams College)

A second part of the stage (A–B in the section) angles upward behind the first area (C) to meet the rear wall of the hall (M). In front of that rear wall Serlio places the back wall of the stage (P), leaving a passageway so that actors could move unseen from one side of the stage to the other. On the slanted floor of this second part of the stage rose perspectival sets that gave the illusion of extending much farther into space than they actually did. The height of the vanishing point of the perspective is located at (L), roughly the eye level of noblewomen sitting on the second step above the orchestra, or more or less at the eye level of actors on stage. Here we have the earliest representation that has come down to us of the relationship between the viewers in the audience and the vanishing point of a perspectival set. As is well known, one-point perspective works best if the eye of the viewer is at the same level as that of the vanishing point. In a theater in which a one-point perspective set is presented to an audience that is seated at many different levels, the perspective works best for only a very few. The problem of unifying the audience with the illusion of

FIG. 41 Sebastiano Serlio, tragic set, Book II (Chapin Library of Rare Books, Williams College)

the set, never fully solved, is abundantly clear in Serlio's section. In his theater, Roman seating and Renaissance perspectival illusion awkwardly come together. The very best point in the theater for viewing the set actually would have been on the stairs in the center of the audience, a place where no one sat.

The principal subject of Serlio's Book II is perspective, or how to draw things so that they appear on the page as they appear in nature to the eye. He brings Book II to a close with woodcuts of three stage sets designed according to the principles of one-point perspective.[37] His sets he called his own contribution to the art of drawing in perspective. Following Vitruvius, he designs settings for comedy, tragedy, and satyr plays. The first two show urban scenes, the comic (Fig. 40), marked by the houses of ordinary people, shops, and a bordello; the tragic (Fig. 41) with the houses of great men. For the satyric plays (Fig. 42), there is a landscape with trees, rough paths, and rustic cottages of a type common in the Veneto. We should probably imagine a set similar to one of these erected on his Vicentine stage. All three show steps leading up from the orchestra to the stage, but such steps do not appear in his plan of the theater. Sometimes, such steps were painted on the front of the stage to create the illusion that the audience could easily walk up onto the stage, or actors

FIG. 42 Sebastiano Serlio, satiric set, Book II (Chapin Library of Rare Books, Williams College)

could easily descend to the orchestra. At the time of Serlio's production in Vicenza, actors often sat in the front row and used such steps to make entrances. Steps connecting the stage and the orchestra could have come in handy to add variety to the movements of the actors, or to allow the wild "Moorish" dancers of the *intermedi* to have greater space for their antics. Here, if the male performers sat in the front row, they would have been sitting next to the most important noblemen. One doubts that such impropriety would have been allowed.

LOGGIA CORNARO, PADUA, AND VILLA TRISSINO, CRICOLI

Alvise Cornaro, a rich Paduan polymath, was a citizen of the Venetian state, but he was not a member of the aristocratic families of Venice proper who ruled Padua and its territories. Theater was one of his many interests. In Padua he built two structures, the Loggia Cornaro, dated by an inscription 1524

FIG. 43 Giovanni Maria Falconetto, Loggia Cornaro, Padua (Photo: Padovacultura)

(Fig. 43), and the somewhat later Odeon Cornaro, in the courtyard of his palace for the performance, respectively, of plays and music.[38] At his country estate near Este he is reported to have built a stone theater in the ancient manner, of which no trace remains. He also proposed bulding a theater in the ancient manner on an enlarged sandbar in the Venetian lagoon (see Chapter 6).

The Loggia Cornaro is of considerable importance. Placed across one of the short sides of the courtyard, the loggia is a five-bay structure based in part on the Theater of Marcellus in Rome (Fig. 18). The six piers of the loggia support five round arches. Engaged to the piers are Doric half-columns that carry a Doric entablature, above which rises a later addition, a second story articulated by Ionic pilasters set above the half-columns below. Instantly the loggia of the Farnesina in Rome (Fig. 12) comes to mind: a similarly articulated, two-story structure used for theatrical purposes. Cornaro surely knew this building, as did his architect, Giovanni Maria Falconetto, who had spent time in Rome.

That this particular disposition of architectural forms was understood at the time to signify a building of theatrical purpose is demonstrated by the illustrations in an edition of 1518 of the comedies of Plautus, published in Venice and likely known to Cornaro and Falconetto (Fig. 16). The same forms, used in the same way, occur a decade later, also in Venetian territory, in the façade of the Villa Trissino at Cricoli, outside Vicenza (Fig. 44). In the 1530s the medieval

FIG. 44 Cricoli, Villa Trissino, façade (Photo: Hans A. Rosbach)

villa was modified by Gian Giorgio Trissino, who inserted the two-story classical south façade between two existing towers. A well-traveled noble humanist, educator, and playwright, Trissino had been in Rome at the time of Leo X and surely visited the Farnesina. He was the patron of Andrea Palladio, but it is far more likely that Trissino designed his villa than Palladio, who came into Trissino's orbit while the villa was under construction. At his villa Trissino had plays performed, presumably in front of this façade, in emulation of what occured at the Farnesina and in front of the Loggia Cornaro in Cornaro's palace.

4

SIXTEENTH-CENTURY FLORENCE, WITH EXCURSIONS TO VENICE, LYON, AND SIENA

No city in Italy in the mid and late sixteenth century had a more vigorous development of court theater than Florence under the Medici dukes.[1] Particularly to celebrate dynastic weddings, but also to honor important visitors, the Medici produced a series of spectacular theatrical events.

FLORENCE, 1539, THEATER FOR MEDICI WEDDING

The male line of the primary branch of the Medici family ended in 1537 with the assassination of Alessandro de' Medici, first Duke of Florence, by his cousin Lorenzino. Within days a member of the secondary branch of the family, Cosimo, ascended to power at the age of 18. Although his hold on power at first was tenuous, Cosimo eventually brought about political stability and concentrated the control of the state in his hands. In 1539 Cosimo, at the behest of Charles V, married Eleanora of Toledo, daughter of the Spanish viceroy of Naples. Eleanora brought with her money, an important alliance and a relationship to the Spanish royal family. The Medici had been bankers; they needed blue-blooded connections to bolster their legitimacy. Although the marriage was one of political convenience, and even political necessity, it turned out to be a happy one. Eleanora and Cosimo had eight children.

For their wedding a lavish entertainment was prepared in the second courtyard of Michelozzo's imposing fifteenth-century Medici palace[2] (Figs. 45 and 46). The courtyard was fitted out in ways that are reminiscent of the

FIG. 45 Michelozzo di Bartolomeo, Palazzo Medici, Florence, façade, 1444 (photo: Ralph Lieberman)

theater constructed on the Capitoline Hill in Rome in 1513, when earlier men of the Medici family had been inducted into Roman citizenship. The courtyard was given a temporary ceiling of blue cloth – a false sky under the real one – beneath which Medici arms were suspended. At the short south end of the couryard, in front of a crimson satin cloth with gold fringe, stood the table for the newlyweds and guests of honor. Six painting were hung on each of the long side walls. On the east side were scenes from the history of the Medici family, focused on its greatest men: Cosimo il Vecchio, Lorenzo the Magnificent, and Popes Leo X and Clement VII, plus a scene that featured Cosimo's father, Giovanni delle Bande Nere, a man who had made his way in the world as a rather successful *condottiere*. On the west walls hung six parallel scenes from the life of the new duke, ending in a representation of the official marriage of Eleanora and Cosimo that had already taken place in Naples. History painting was featured here, but unlike the Triumphs of Caesar

FIG. 46 Medici Palace, Florence, second courtyard (Visual Resources, Williams College)

in Mantua in 1501, or the scenes from Etruscan and Roman history in the Roman theater of 1513, the history was recent, even up-to-the-minute. Cosimo had accomplished relatively little in his 20 years, but he was made to seem a great hero.

On July 9, 1539 Antonio Landi's comedy *Il Commodo* was presented on the stage, set at the north end of the courtyard and fitted out with an elaborate representation of the coastal city of Pisa, through which Eleanora had passed on her triumphal entry into Florentine territory. The five acts of the play were framed by intermedi by Giovanni Battista Strozzi the Elder, in charge of the production. The play was preceded by a banquet in the first courtyard of the Medici palace, from which the guests proceded into the neighboring courtyard, illuminated by torches held by *amorini* suspended from the ceiling – love lighting the way for the happy couple. On stage Pisa was recognizable becase of the presence of the Leaning Tower and the dome of the baptistery, but the rest of the city was made up of 'bizarre' houses and 'capricious' palaces – in other words, buildings invented for the occasion. In front of the stage was a trench fitted out as the river Arno, and on the audience side of the trench were painted steps that appeared to lead down from the stage to the audience. The designer of the sets was Bastiano da Sangallo, sometimes known by his nickname of Aristotele.

Bastiano da Sangallo was an important figure in the emerging art of scene design. Unfortunately, no visual record of his set of Pisa has come down to us. To make visually clear the unity of time in the play, Sangallo create a sun that moved across the stage. He attached a lantern with torches inside it to an arc that curved up behind the houses of the set. In front of the lantern was a glass globe filled with water and surrounded by an aureole symbolizing the rays of the sun. As the time in the play progressed from morning until night, the 'sun' rose to center stage and then descended and disappeared. From the *faux* Arno in front of the stage aquatic creatures emerged during one of the *intermedi*. During other *intermedi* bits of scenery, such as a grotto for Silenus, were wheeled onto the stage in front of Pisa, apparently visible at all times. There seems to have been no curtain to conceal the fixed set between the acts, a situation that perhaps duplicated the one in Urbino of 1513. We do not know how the audience was accomodated.

VENICE 1542

Only two years later, in 1541, the thirty-year-old artist Giorgio Vasari was invited to Venice by his fellow native of Arezzo, the writer Pietro Aretino, to design a theater and set for the production of Aretino's play, *La Talanta*, at carnival during the following winter.[3] Vasari had been Bastiano da Sangallo's assistant at the Medici wedding festivities. Patron of the Venetian production was a recently constituted *Compagnia della Calza*, the Sempiterni. As the site for their theater the Sempiterni had contracted for the use of a large palace still under construction. Antonio Foscari has identified this building as the Palazzo Gonella, later Valier, which rose on the west side of the Cannaregio Canal near the church of San Giobbe and the Ponte dei Tre Archi[4] (Fig. 47). The building burned in the late eighteenth century, but views of it made earlier in that century survive. It was a two-story structure with a broad façade on the canal. Across the center of the piano nobile stretched an unusually wide balcony in front of a fourteen-arch arcade that marked the presence of the main room(s) of the palace behind them. The theater Vasari designed stood behind this arcade, probably with its length at right angles to the canal. The church-like, pedimented frontispiece that rose above the eight central bays reflects the width of the central room, covered by the shed roof that runs at considerable length behind the pediment (Fig. 49). Neither the plan nor the architect of the palace are known.

In the shell of this unfinished building – only the walls and roof had been constructed – Vasari created an elaborate and elegant room to hold the audience. We have a good idea of what it looked like because Vasari sent a long description to a Florentine patron. Later in his life Vasari included a description of the theater in the edition of 1568 of his *Vite* (*Lives of Artists*).[5]

FIG. 47 Palazzo Gonella-Venier, Venice (the wide, pedimented facade at right, behind the bridge), demolished. (Etching from Domenico Lovisa, *Il Gran Teatro di Venezia*, Venice, Museo Civico Correr)

The two accounts do not entirely agree, and scholars have not found it easy to reconcile conflicting details.[6] A couple of drawings for the theater from Vasari's hand have also come down to us. On the basis of the descriptions and the drawings Jürgen Schulz reconstructed the appearance of the long side walls and the ceiling.[7] In the description in the *Vite* Vasari gives the length of the room as 70 braccia. The Florentine braccia measured something over half a meter, and so the room was a good 35 meters long, or well over 100 feet.[8] The width is given as 16 braccia, or something over 8 meters, making the room long and narrow, just as one would expect such a hall in a Venetian palace to be. Vasari says that the huge crowd and all the lights made the room hot and stuffy.

    The room was entered through a door that resembled a triumphal arch. This is not a detail to be ignored, because it may well be the earliest evidence we have for an entrance of some architectural pretension designed specifically for a theater space. By bringing the audience through a triumphal arch, Vasari was preparing them for the triumphant representations of Venice and its empire that lined the walls. Against the long sides of the room Vasari arranged two rows of benches for women. Above the benches, each wall was decorated with four large painting, *en grisaille*, that showed allegorical representations either of the overseas possessions of Venice, or the rivers of Venetian territory on the mainland, or of Venice itself. One painting combined representations of the Tiber and the Arno. Flanking these eight paintings, four per wall, were

10 herms on each wall that framed niches holding allegorical figures of Virtues, such as Justice or Prudence, that represented the virtues of the Venetian state.

Herms were understood in the sixteenth century to represent territorial boundaries.[9] In Roman literature they were associated with the god of boundaries, Terminus. When Terminus, through auguries, refused to have his shrine on the Capitoline Hill moved to make way for a new temple of Jupiter, the augurs took that to mean that the boundaries of Rome would be eternal. In the sixteenth century, Venice consistently promoted itself as a new Rome, and so the herms that framed the allegorical depictions of Venetian territories underscored this notion. In the frieze that ran above the paintings and the herms – indeed, directly over the heads of the herms – were representations of the lion of St. Mark (the lion with his feet in the water, as Vasari put it), a principal heraldic device of Venice. Venice herself was personified by Adria, the spirit of the Adriatic Sea, who was shown as a beautiful nude woman with one foot in the water and the other on the rock on which she sat, to signify Venice's power on sea and land. This scene is preserved in Vasari's sketch now in the Rijksmuseum, Amsterdam[10] (Fig. 48).

Over this celebration of Venetian empire and glory stretched a coffered and carved wooden ceiling filled with paintings representing time. Four large

FIG. 48 Giorgio Vasari, *Adria, Spirit of the Adriatic Sea*, drawing, ink and wash (Amsterdam, Rijksmuseum)

canvases, in oil, depicted Dawn, Day, Night and, depending on whether you believe Vasari's letter or his words in the *Vite*, either Evening or Time. These four large pictures were surrounded by 24 smaller pictures that represented the hours, each marked to make clear which hour each figure represented. One day, then, symbolically floated above the heads of the audience. That day could be understood as representing the cyclical repetition of time, or else the actual day of the performance. Or both. The room, in turn, could be understood to embody both the space of one day and the space controlled by Venice. The notion of the single day was reinforced by a very large glass globe, produced by the skilled artisans of the glassworks on Murano, filled with liquid and lit from behind. The globe, an allegorical sun like the one Bastiano da Sangallo had designed for Cosimo de' Medici's wedding, moved slowly from one side of the stage to the other during the course of the performance to indicate that the play took place during one day. Thus was the Aristotelian unity of time maintained, while the unity of place was given by the fixed set depicting Rome. If this all sounds suspiciously like the Mantuan theater of 1501 in its political content and representation of time, that surely is no coincidence, although it is unlikely that Vasari knew anything about the theater in Mantua. Rather, both presented the same themes of politics and time that were ubiquitous in sixteenth century theatrical spaces.

    The configuration of the stage in this theater is less easy to reconstruct, because Vasari did not describe it precisely. It probably occupied one end of the 70 braccia length of the room, so that the decorated walls and ceiling would actually have been shorter than 70 braccia.[11] The scenery involved several traditional houses through which characters in the play entered and exited. The houses probably were arranged along two sides of the stage according to the rules of one point perspective, so that they appeared to get smaller as they stood farther upstage. The backdrop boasted a painted depiction of famous Roman monuments. A character in the play describes what was depicted on this backdrop: buildings from all over the city joined together in a symbolic collage of Rome. The description sounds not unlike what appears in various Peruzzi drawings of stage sets representing the eternal city, so that what the Venetian audience saw may not have been too different from what Roman audiences at performances designed by Peruzzi saw. Vasari probably used a raked stage, but there is no hard evidence to that effect. The arrangement of the auditorium itself conformed to a type already established for court theaters. The decoration of the walls, however, would appear to have been quite innovative, although tied in some ways to the decorations of the second courtyard of the Medici palace for the wedding of Cosimo and Eleonora, on which Vasari had worked as Bastiano da Sangallo's assistant.

LYON 1548

Florence was a financial power. Colonies of its merchants and bankers were established in major commercial centers of Europe, such as Lyon, the largest metropolis in France after Paris and a center of European trade. In September 1548 the recently crowned Henry II of France and his queen, the Florentine Catherine de' Medici,[12] made a triumphal entry into Lyon that was the occasion

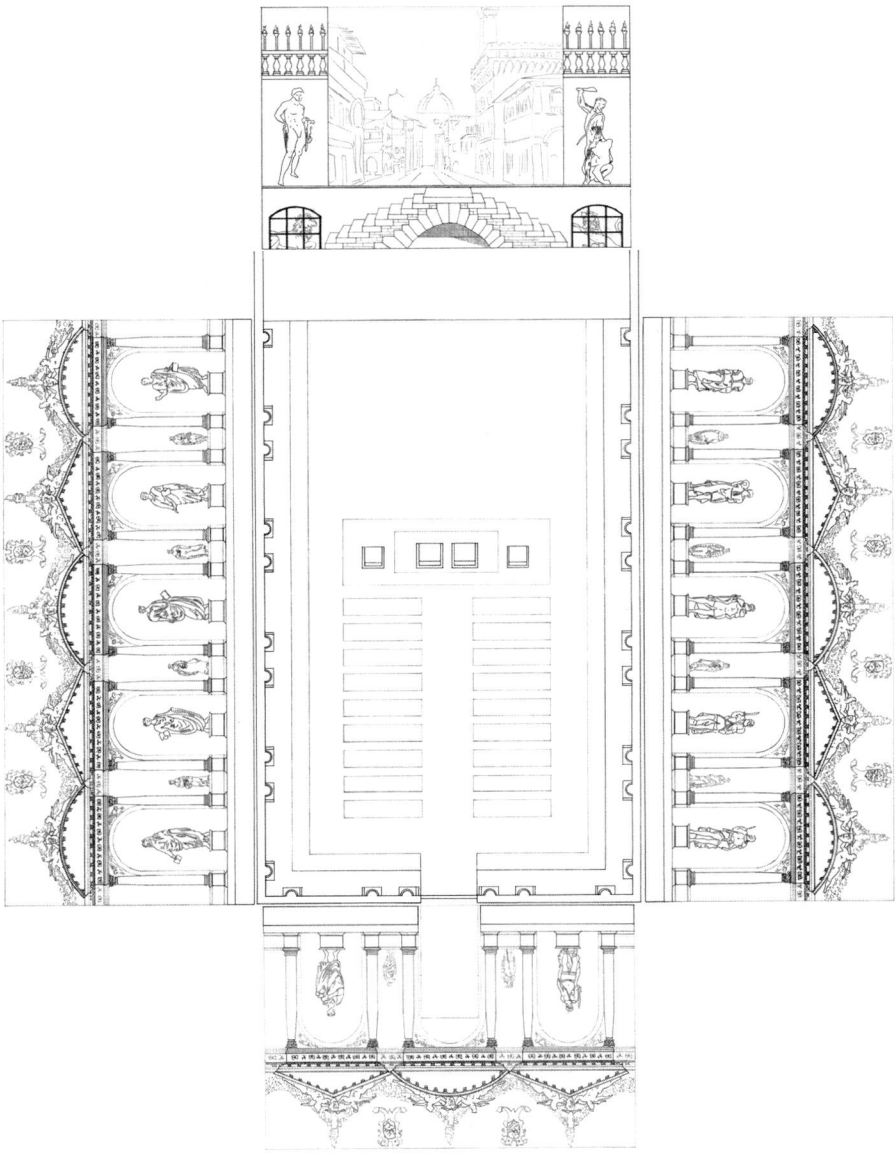

FIG. 49 Lyon, theater of 1548, reconstruction of plan and four walls (Drawing by Grace McEniry)

for the first performance of a modern Italian comedy in France, presented in a temporary theater constructed according to the latest Italian ideas of theater architecture.[13] Among the moving forces behind this theatrical event were the Florentine merchants in Lyon and the city's archbishop, Ippolito d'Este, Cardinal of Ferrara and grandson of Ercole I d'Este. In Lyon, at the confluence of the Rhone and the Saône, various Italian traditions of theater came together.

The play was Cardinal Bibbiena's *La Calandra*, first performed in Urbino in 1513 and then in Rome in 1514 under the first Medici pope, Leo X. The actors were a troupe imported from Florence,[14] and the artists who created the architecture of the theater, the decorations of that room, and the set on the stage all seem to have been Italian – indeed Florentine – with one major exception.

The entry of the royal couple into Lyon was described in a book published by a French humanist, Maurice Scève. Shortly thereafter an Italian translation of Scève's work was issued by a Florentine with the initials F.M. The Italian version contains a much more detailed description of the modifications Ippolito made to his archibishop's palace for the festivities. Indeed, F.M.'s description is so detailed in terms of measurements that he seems to have had access to the architectural drawings, or to the architect himself. The following account is largely based on F.M.'s.

Ippolito, as Cardinal Protector of France, held a position in the French court that required him to honor the king and queen extravagantly. Although the burghers of Lyon organized the elaborate entry processions that the king and queen followed on succeding days, Ippolito controlled what happened in and around his palace, in which the royal couple lodged. In front of the palace he erected, as the final temporary monument the royal processions passed, a tall triumphal column surmounted by a figure of victory to honor Henry. He built a noble classical door through which the royal couple passed into his Gothic palace. Inside, he completely remodelled the two rooms devoted to playgoing, so that no sense of the original late medieval style of the interiors remained. The entrance hall, entered through a door in its south wall, was painted to look as if it had rusticated lower walls, and heavy rustication was painted around the windows in the west wall. The Gothic ceiling was concealed by a cloth painted to look like sky, so that the room became a fictitious outdoor court. Opposite the three windows, in the east wall, a noble new doorway led into the theater space. The door was surmounted by a pediment over which putti held up a crescent moon, a device of Henry's, inscribed with the royal motto. Flanking the door were larger than life-size, gilded, terra-cotta statues of a man and a woman, he holding a shield with the arms of Lyon, she holding the single red lily of Florence. Both figures pointed to a shield over the center of the door bearing the fleur-de-lis of the French monarchy. An inscription in Latin, placed near the female statue, begged the lilies of France not to despise the little lily of Florence. This door announced, in a way, the message that would be developed in the space of the theater itself. One cannot help but see this doorway as a parallel to the triumphal arch through which Vasari made his Venetian audience pass into his theatrical space. In both cases, the entrance portals made the theater space more important.

Opposite the door, against the west wall, were two gilded reclining statues that honored Henry through their identical inscriptions HENRICO INVICTISSIMO D.D.[15] The heavily rusticated walls, like those of a fortress, alluded to Henry's putative military prowess, which he had had little occasion to demonstrate. The spectator's experience of entering the entrance hall, making a 90-degree turn to the right, passing through the elaborate new door and entering the theater made the theater the climax of a carefully calculated architectural promenade. Such cleverly wrought sequences of contrasting architectural spaces had been developed in Italy in the preceding decades by such masters as Michelangelo in the Laurentian Library in Florence or Jacopo Sansovino in the Libreria di San Marco in Venice.

If the entrance hall largely celebrated Henry, the theater was devoted in good part to Catherine. The French were not happy to have a queen descended from a family of bankers. A principal object of the theater was to raise her status in the minds of her subjects.

The medieval Salle Saint-Jean[16] was given a modern classical architectural system far more monumental than that employed by Vasari in Venice. F.M.'s extraordinarliy detailed description has permitted a reconstruction of the theater[17] (Fig. 49). The entrance door, in one of the short walls of the rectangular space, was opposite the stage. The three visible walls of the theater were articulated by Corinthian columns with gilded capitals that rose from a dado set above the two risers for spectators that lined the long and entrance walls in the shape of an elongated U. The columns, which carried an entablature, were arranged in pairs, except for single columns that flanked the corners of the room. Ten columns on each of the long walls alternated with five arches, while the columns of the entrance wall flanked three arches, with the entrance door cut into the central bay (Fig. 50). Springing from pilasters set against the columns, the arches framed gilded terra cotta statues. To the right as one entered were men in armor who represented Italian military leaders, some belonging to the Medici family, while to the left were writers in togas, including the Tuscans Dante, Petrarch and Boccacio.[18] On the wall surfaces between the paired columns smaller, painted, allegorical female figures personified cities or towns of Tuscany.[19] Just as Venetian territories had been represented in Vasari's theater, Florentine possessions were present here. The room in Lyon, then, was devoted to a celebration largely of Tuscany, of which Catherine's cousin, Cosimo, now bore the title of duke. Florence itself was depicted in the backdrop of the set. The emphasis on Florentine

FIG. 50 Lyon, theater of 1548, reconstructions of north (top) and south walls (Drawings by Grace McEniry)

accomplishments was not lost on the local commentator, Maurice Scève, who wrote:

> ... the large figures were twelve in number, six togate in the ancient manner and crowned with laurel, representing six Florentine poets: the six others armed in the ancient manner for the six ancestors of the house of Medici, who were the first restorers of Greek and Latin letters, architecture, sculpture, painting, and all the other good arts by them revived and introduced into Christian Europe, which the rudeness of the Goths had devastated for a long time.[20]

The room's system of piers, articulated by paired columns or pilasters, alternating with round arches went back to the nave of the Florentine architect Leon Battista Alberti's Sant' Andrea in Mantua, designed in 1470 (Fig. 51). Alberti had derived this system from Roman triumphal arches, the classical guise he gave his façade of Sant'Andrea. It had been taken up by Donato Bramante in the walls of the upper level of the Cortile del Belvedere in the Vatican under Julius II[21] (Fig. 52). From there it appears to have spread to France as a form appropriate to royal palaces. Francis I used it in

FIG. 51 Leon Battista Alberti, Sant'Andrea, Mantua, nave, designed 1470 (Photo: Ralph Lieberman)

FIG. 52 Sebastiano Serlio, elevation of Donato Bramante, exterior wall of upper level, Cortile del Belvedere, Vatican Palace, Rome, Book IV (Chapin Library of Rare Books, Williams College)

his rebuilding, for instance, of the royal chateaux at Blois and Saint-Germain-en-Laye, where his son who became Henry II was born. With a cloth ceiling painted to resemble the sky (a nod to Alberti's description of ancient theaters), the theater space at Lyon was meant to be understood as an outdoor courtyard like the one used in the Medici wedding of 1539. Ippolito d'Este and the Florentine merchants of Lyon were indeed bringing the latest Italian architectural and theatrical ideas to France, and in so doing, they were honoring the Florentine-born French queen as well as the king's political ambitions.

Appropriately, the architecture was not as solemn as a church interior. There were playful touches, starting with the mannered rhythms of the wall articulation. Pediments rose over the arches, presumably spanning the distance between the columns that flanked the arches, to frame the statues from above (Fig. 51). The columns adjacent to the arches were visually double-functioning elements that could be paired either with the column standing on the other side of a painted allegory or on the other side of an arch framing a statue.

There seems to have been a deliberately punning reference to a specific Roman monument, The Porta dei Leoni in Verona, recently illustrated in Sebastiano Serlio's Third Book, published in 1540[22] (Fig. 53). Serlio remarks on the unusual nature of this arch, actually a city gate, which at ground level

FIG. 53 Sebastiano Serlio, Verona, Porta dei Leoni, Book III (Chapin Library of Rare Books, Williams College)

SIXTEENTH-CENTURY FLORENCE

has two openings, rather than the normal one or three. The arches, which spring from pilasters, are framed by Corinthian/Composite columns that carry an entablarture bearing a pediment over each arch. The relationship to the walls of the theater in Lyon seems hardly accidental: an ancient arch associated with lions multiplied more than a dozen or more times to celebrate the triumphal entry of Henry and Catherine into the city of Lyon, whose lions were actually depicted in paintings that decorated the stage.

To the cloth ceiling, painted to look like the sky, were affixed stars and planets made of mirrors decorated with tinsel. All of this was lit by amusing sconces and chandeliers. Dragons hung by their tails down the columns, spreading their multi-colored wings and sticking out their fiery tongues to support torches. A second, higher row of lights was part of a frieze with protruding dragon heads that simultaneously bit the tails of interlaced snakes and supported torches. Across the ceiling flew twenty putti, each with a bow and arrows in one hand and a torch in the other. Dragons were an heraldic device of Ippolito d'Este. One might see them here as a not-so-secret signature. Torch-bearing *amorini* had flown overhead for the Medici wedding of 1539. In both cases, the putti must have represented love bringing the marriage partners together.[23] In Lyon they served to belie the actual situation of the royal couple. Conjugal bliss was something Henry and Catherine never enjoyed, given his attachment to Diane de Poitiers.

Seating in the room was carefully thought out (Fig. 54). The rows of risers were made comfortable by covering them with oriental rugs. On the floor of

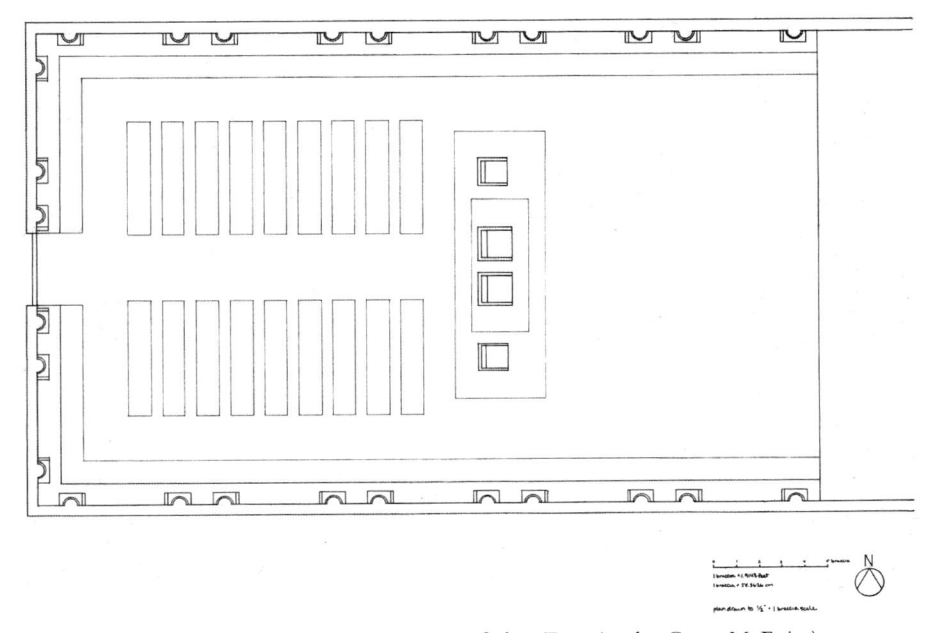

FIG. 54 Lyon, theater of 1548, reconstruction of plan (Drawing by Grace McEniry)

FIG. 55 Lyon, theater of 1548, reconstruction of stage (drawing by Grace McEniry)

the room, the first 16 braccia were given over to two sets of benches, separated by aisles from the risers and divided by the central aisle. At the end of that aisle was the royal dais, the first for which a clear description in known. It rose in two levels only a modest half braccia above the floor, so as not to compromise the sight lines of the audience. The dais was 12 braccia wide and 4 braccia deep, with an upper level for the chairs of the king and queen that measured 6 × 2 braccia. The couple was one of two foci of the room, just as Leo X had been. On the lower step other members of the royal family occupied chairs, while ladies of the court arranged themselves on oriental carpets (did they actually sit on the floor for four hours?) laid on the 5 braccia of floor between the dais and the stage. The U-shaped arrangement of the risers and the separate platform for the rulers both go back to fifteenth century Ferrara, but a similar layout of benches is not, as far as I know, mentioned in earlier documents.

The second focus of the room was the raised stage, which almost everyone saw over the heads of the royal couple (Fig. 55). The front of the stage was painted with illusionistic stairs, like those of the stage of the Medici wedding of 1539, that appeared to give the audience access to the stage. Hidden behind the front of the stage were actual steps used by actors at the end of the performance, when they left the stage to enter the audience to lavish praise on Henry and offer a gift to Catherine.

What framed the stage is difficult to reconstruct from F.M.'s description. To stage left and right there were some loggia-like arrangements, topped by gilded

FIG. 56 Baldassare Lanci, set for *La Vedova*, 1569, drawing (Florence, Gabinetto dei Disegni e Stampe degli Uffizi, 404 P) (Photo: Scala/Art Resources, NY)

balustrades; each loggia included a painted colossus of Samson or Hercules. At the bottom of these structures were trompe-l'oeil windows behind which one descried lions, as in Lyon, or the marzocco of Florence. Somewhere on the stage were the houses necessary for the entrances and exits of the actors. At the back of the stage hung a perspective drop painted by a Florentie pupil of Andrea del Sarto, Nannoccio della Costa San Giorgio, that depicted Florence, whose major monuments – the dome and belltower of the cathedral and the tower of Palazzo Vecchio – could be recognized, at least by those in the audience who knew the city.[24] We have based our reconstruction on Baldassare Lanci's scene design of the center of Florence for the production of *La Vedova* in Florence in 1569 (Fig. 56). The set in Lyon resembled Serlio's Comic and Tragic sets, published in his Book II in Paris in 1545 (Figs. 41 and 42).

Indeed, it now seems clear that Serlio must have designed the architecture of the theater, even if neither F.M. nor Scève mentioned his name (Serlio was from Bologna, not Florence). The walls of the Lyon theater, as we have reconstructed them from F.M.'s description, bear a striking resemblance to those of the courtyard of the Chateau of Ancy-le-Franc, Serlio's surviving

FIG. 57 Sebastiano Serlio, Ancy-le-Franc, chateau, courtyard, 1540s (Photo: Christophe Finot)

masterpiece that was being brought to completion at the time of the Lyon entry[25] (Fig. 57). Serlio was artistically and even physically close to Ippolito d'Este. He had recently designed Ippolito's house at Fontainbleau, the now demolished Hôtel de Ferrare, or Grande Ferrare (1544–46); in 1548 he and his family were actually living on the upper floor of the Grande Ferrare, directly over the cardinal's nose, as it were.[26] The date announced for the king's intended entry into Lyon gave the city little time to prepare. Ippolito surely turned immediately to his house architect to come up with a theater design fit for a royal couple. Luckily he had at hand perhaps the best qualified man in Europe to do so.

The king himself, according to Maurice Scève, requested the performance of an Italian play as part of the festivities surrounding his entrance into Lyon – clearly to raise the status of his queen. The decor of the theater, stressing the leading role of Florence in recent cultural history and the role of the Medici as the current ruling family of the city, made Catherine out to descend from a family worthy of an alliance with the royal family of France. Maurice Scève, as we saw, recognized this message. If it is true that Henry chose the play, then his was the intelligence behind this landmark event in the history of French theater. The queen probably participated in the preparations by summoning the troupe of players from Florence, as a later Florentine source suggested.[27] The Florentine colony in Lyon also must have helped with securing the services of the artists and artisans who came from their home town.[28] Ippolito d'Este went deeply into debt to finance his part of the festvities, spending perhaps 10,000 ducats, a huge amount.[29] In later life Ippolito continued his extravagant patronage of architecture by constructing the magnificent gardens of the Villa d'Este at Tivoli outside Rome.

The performance of the play, a novelty in a French royal entrance into a city, was a huge success. It was given again on the night after the first performance, ostensibly for the citizens of Lyon for whom there was no room in the theater the first time around. The royal couple enjoyed the first performance so much, however, that they showed up unexpectedly for the second, accompanied by members of the court. The burghers of Lyon had to retire, and so the play was given a third time the following week for the local folk. We are told that the actors went back to Florence well paid.

FLORENCE, THE MEDICI WEDDING OF 1565

In Florence in 1565 Vasari fitted out the enormous Salone dei Cinquecento in Palazzo Vecchio (Fig. 58) for a performance of *La Cofanaria* by Francesco d'Ambra to celebrate the marriage of the heir to the duchy, Francesco, to Giovanna d'Austria, sister of the Holy Roman Emperor, Maximillian II.[30] This was a signal event in Medici history. Francesco's mother, Eleanora of Toledo, was not a princess, but rather the daughter of the Spanish viceroy of Naples who was the second son of a Spanish grandee, the Duke of Alba. Cosimo, unable to command a royal consort for himself, could provide one for his heir. Four years later, in 1569, Pope Pius IV elevated Cosimo to the title of Grand Duke of Tuscany.

The choice of the Salone dei Cinquecento as the site for the performance was in itself important. In 1540, the year after his marriage to Eleanora, Cosimo

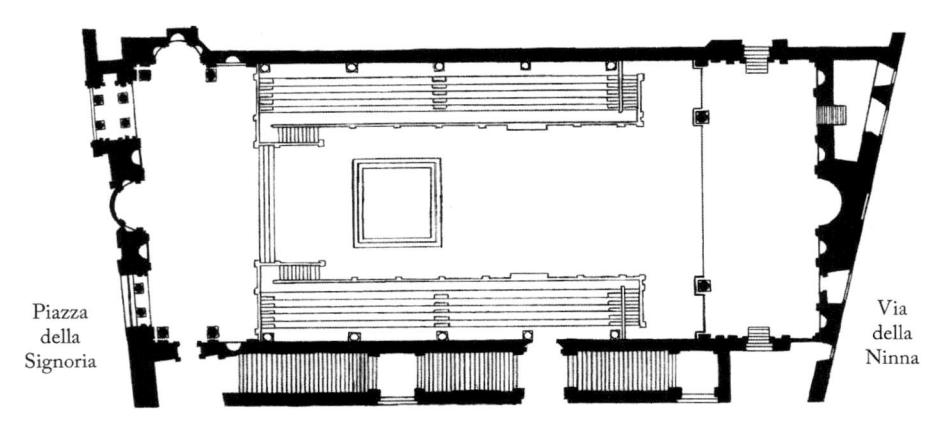

FIG. 58 Salone dei Cinquecento, Palazzo Vecchio, Florence, plan with reconstruction of theater of 1565 (Drawing: Troy Sipprelle)

abandoned the fifteenth-century family palace where he had been married (Fig. 46) and moved into Palazzo Vecchio, physically taking possession, for his own use, of the most important symbol of Florentine government. At the end of the fifteenth century, after the Medici had been exiled from the city by the monk Savonarola, a huge new hall had been added to the civic palace to house the deliberations of the most important citizens. To give Florentine government by oligarchy a proper setting, Savonarola chose to copy the great Sala del Maggior Consiglio in Palazzo Ducale in Venice, where the Venetian patriciate made decisions of state. The walls of the new space were to have been decorated by Leonardo da Vinci and Michelangelo with scenes of famous battles from Florentine history. Converting the hall built for a government by many into one dedicated to the dynastic triumphs of an autocrat vividly represented the new political order in Florence. When Cosimo was first named duke in 1537, he was saddled with the remnants of the old oligarchical government. By the time he married his son to a Hapsburg, he had utterly marginalized these trappings of the old polity.

Turning a hall that had been used as the meeting site for an old representative government into a room for entertainment was no novelty in 1565 for Cosimo. In 1555, after a long and bloody siege, Cosimo had conquered Siena and made it part of his duchy. In celebration of his first official visit in 1560 to that city, he ordered the Sala del Consiglio Generale in the Palazzo Pubblico (Fig. 59), where the major governing body of Siena had met since 1342,

FIG. 59 Siena, Palazzo Pubblico, rear façade. Wing to right contains on upper floors former Sala del Consiglio Generale converted to Teatro degli Intronati (Photo: Ranana Dine)

FIG. 60 Bartolomeo Neroni (Il Riccio), proscenium and stage set of Teatro degli Intronati, Siena, 1560 (London, Victoria and Albert Museum. Art in the public domain)

converted into a theater. Nothing could have made his displacement of the old order clearer. Cosimo may have been emulating the policy of the papal legates who had ruled Bologna from the time of Julius II. As early as 1547 they had allowed the aristocrats of the city to organize entertainments in the great hall of the Palazzo del Podestà, where the previous oligarchical government of Bologna had met.[31] In Siena a stage and seating were constructed in the old hall, on designs of the Sienese architect and painter Bartolomeo Neroni, known as Il Riccio. We have no idea how Riccio arranged the seating, but a view of the stage with his perspectival scenery showing a cityscape is preserved[32] (Fig. 60). The urban scene may reflect the encounter that Riccio had with Baldassare Peruzzi in the mid-1530's.[33] Riccio's proscenium consisted of two robust Doric piers supporting an entablature with hevy brackets that support a projecting cornice that seems to cast shadows. Two statues, probably painted, decorated the face of each pier, with Poetry and Comedy occupying the upper niches and the Romans Augustus and Scipio Africanus the lower.[34] This arrangement foreshadows the well-known proscenium designed by Giovan Battista Aleotti for the Teatro degli Intrepidi in Ferrara in the first decade of the next century (see Chapter 8). Aleotti's design produced numerous progeny, of which Riccio's proscenium may be understood as the grandparent. The design continues the Serlian motif of stairs in front of the stage, with low

FIG. 61 Federico Zuccaro, *Landscape with Hunters and View of Florence*, Sketch for first curtain of Theater of 1565 (Florence, Gabinetto dei Disegni e Stampe degli Uffizi, 11074) (Photo: Alfredo Dagli Orti/Art Resurces, NY)

windows to either side. Designed only twelve years after the proscenium in Lyon, this one may be the earliest of which an actual representation is known.

To return to Cosimo's Florence: the Sala dei Cinquecento occupies an irregular site, so that its plan is trapezoidal (Fig. 58). Vasari made the interior seem to be a regular rectangle by cutting off the short ends with parallel elements. At the north end, opposite the stage, he inserted a large Serliana to give light. He arranged seats along the side walls, atop a terrace raised about eight feet above the floor and protected by a balustrade, to accommodate some 360 women.[35] The wooden seats, intended to be reused, could be dismantled or set up in eight hours. The walls above the seats were hung with tapestries, and above the tapestries were frescoes of the most important cities under Cosimo's rule. Note the repetition of territorial possessions from Lyon and from Vasari's theater in Venice. In the middle of the hall rose a dais, raised on three steps, on which sat the duke and duchess, the newlyweds and foreign ambassadors, all the center of attention and on axis with the Serliana in the north wall. This arrangment bears a striking resemblance to the seating arrangement in Lyon in 1548, which certainly would have been known in Florence through F.M.'s published description. The men of the audience occupied benches placed around the dais. Vasari understood the relation of the parts of the audience to each other: "Thus the gentlewomen from their height saw the stage and all the men and gentlemen, and in like manner the men and gentlemen saw the stage and the gentlewomen. One could desire neither more beautiful nor more sumptuous nor more proud a sight." Ovid himself might hardly have put it better. Enrica Benini has stressed the importance of the lavish and colorful costumes of the audience, bathed in colored light, for the overall effect.[36] Silver statues of female figures held large crystal globes, illuminated from behind, that were filled with water of different colors, a technique Vasari had learned from his master.[37] There were enough globes to represent the many hours that the whole spectacle required.[38] Time and territory once again were signalled.

Vasari raised the height of the ceiling considerably, thus making the proportions of the Saalone even more imposing. From the ceiling he suspended lights in the form of crowns. Like the heraldic devices in the Gonzaga theater of 1501, these crowns displayed the place of the Medici in the political firmament. Three crowns were shaped like the papal tiara to signal the three Medici popes, Leo X, Clement VII and the current Pius IV, an extraordinary number for one family. Three more represented Holy Roman Emperors: Charles V, Ferdinand I, father of the bride, and Maximillian II, her brother. There was a royal crown to represent Catherine de' Medici, now queen mother of France, and a crown that represented the newlyweds. These last two were suspended in the middle of the hall and surrounded by four ducal coronets. The lights in the chandeliers were made brighter by passing through water suspended in refracting glass. The hall glowed with the dynastic achievements of the Medici.

The raised stage was placed on the short side of the room to the south, at the same level as the terrace of the women's seats. The stage was framed by two Corinthian columns, which formed what was once thought to be the very first proscenium arch in history, but that honor now seems to go to the theater in Lyon.[39] Between the columns hung a curtain painted by Federico Zuccaro that showed a ducal hunt taking place in a landscape with the city of Florence in the background (Fig. 61). This early proscenium arch, then, literally acted as a picture frame. Zuccaro's sketch for this curtain, preserved in the Uffizi, gives us the appearance of one of the earliest such curtains. When the curtain disappeared, another picture was revealed – a set that represented an actual quarter of Florence. The purpose of the curtain was to conceal the stage scenery from prying eyes during the days before the performance, so that the appearance of the scenery would be a *coup de théâtre*.

Unfortunately we have no drawing of this set, but we do have a contemporary description: "The scene represented Florence in that part we call Santa Trinità, in which appeared the bridge [the Ponte Santa Trinità] as it was before it was destroyed in the flood of 1557, with the street of via Maggio as far as San Felice in Piazza. And likewise the palaces and houses that surround that place, as well as the addition of a triumphal arch in the middle, with the Arno and Danube rivers." Via Maggio was one of the major urban developments of the reign of Cosimo I, and so the set represented modern Florence prospering under Medici rule.[40] As Ludovico Zorzi pointed out, the focus on Via Maggio recalls a passage from the Tuscan writer Benedetto Varchi: "Of all the regions of Italy Tuscany is the most beautiful, of all the cities of Tucany Florence is the most beautiful, of the four quarters of Florence Santo Spirito is the most beautiful, and of all the streets of the quarter of Santo Spirito via Maggio is the most beautiful."[41] The triumphal arch depicted the symbolic confluence the Arno and the Danube through the Medici-Hapsburg union.

The intermedi that framed the acts of the play included adventurous stage effects, perhaps the most ingenious of which occurred at the very beginning of the performance. A cloud descended from the ceiling, bearing Venus seated in a gilded chariot pulled by two swans. The goddess was accompanied by the three Graces and the four Seasons. As they descended, the rest of the Olympian deities were revealed seated in their Olympian fastness. At the end of the scene the cloud bore Venus and her seven companions back into the sky. To accomplish this feat, the goddess and her retinue must have been carried on a platform that was raised and lowered by ropes on pulleys.

Other *intermedi* involved elaborate effects that rose up from beneath the stage or opened up in the stage floor. In the third *intermedio* little hills grew out of the stage, and in the fourth holes opened from which emerged Discord, Anger, Cruelty, Rape and Revenge, each accompanied by two Furies. All of these effects were apparently worked out by Vasari's assistant on this production, the young Bernarado Buontalenti, whose formidable talents came to play an even more important role two decades later. The quick appearance and disappearance of many performers at once was made possible by Vasari's provision of considerable backstage space, a major innovation of this theater.[42] Vasari gave them the possibility of moving around unseen behind the set before making their entrances. In earlier instances, there had been little room backstage. Sometimes actors sat in the front row of the audience and entered the stage by steps that connected that platform to the floor on which the audience sat. Vestigial steps were painted on the front of the stage of 1565, as they had been on the stage in Lyon of 1548 (Fig. 55) and Siena of 1560 (Fig. 60).

Over the architrave that spanned the distance between the columns of the proscenium rose the Medici coat of arms, borne by putti, while flying nude figures held torches that lit the stage. Again we find torch-bearing amorini to bring the happy pair together. The whole apparatus – stage, hall, audience – was a celebration of Medici power, with the rulers at the center of the show. The flexible room did not serve only as a theater, however. After the play, the audience withdrew and then returned to find a banquet hall. After eating, the guests again withdrew and returned to find the room converted to dancing, which lasted til dawn.

THE PALAZZO DEGLI UFFIZI AS A THEATER

The Medici continued to use views of their city and its cultural heritage as the sets for theatrical performances that served dynastic purposes. In 1569, to honor the visit of the Archduke Karl of Austria, brother of Francesco's bride, the Medici produced Giambattista Cini's play *La Vedova*, with the set by Baldassare

Lanci that showed the political heart of Florence (Fig. 56). The audience looked at a representation of Palazzo Vecchio, the medieval town hall that the Medici now occupied as their residence and that now symbolized their rule. In the distance rose Filippo Brunelleschi's dome of Florence Cathedral, moved for the occasion a bit to the east of its actual position so that this staggering achievement of Florentine architecture would be visible on stage. In front of Palazzo Vecchio appeared the three sixteenth-century statues that grace the Piazza Signoria, including Michelangelo's *David*. To stage right one made out the arcade of the Loggia dei Lanzi, while to stage left appeared the northernmost bays of the east wing of Palazzo degli Uffizi, then under construction. Lanci's set represented past and present architectural achievements of Florence and the symbols of Medici control.[43] According to a contemporary observer, Ignazio Danti, Lanci used *periaktoi*, rotating vertical triangular prisms with different scenes painted on each side, to make possible quick set changes.[44] The scene of Palazzo Vecchio gave way to the Ponte Santa Trinità, another site in Florence, and that in turn to the nearby village of Arcetri. In this production, the unity of place established by the single city set earlier in the century was abandoned for a far more fluid movement of the action from one site to another, and for a far more elaborate celebration of Florentine territory.

By inference Lanci's set placed the audience in the new, open, public space in the center of the Uffizi, suggesting thereby that the piazza of the Uffizi could be understood as a theatrical space in which an audience looks at Piazza Signoria and its monuments as if they were represented in a stage set (Fig. 62). Vasari, the favored architect of Cosimo I, began construction of the Uffizi in 1560 to house the bureaucracy of Cosimo's newly created autocratic state. The open space of the Uffizi is notoriously difficult to interpret.[45] To begin with, it is not clear if it is a street or a courtyard or a piazza or all three (piazzale, the name currently given to it, is surely anachronistic). Each of these urban typologies has its own peculiar qualities. Vasari, its architect, called the space a street, and that makes sense in terms of its long, narrow shape and in terms of the way it replaces a new street that Vasari had laid out on the site in 1546 to connect Piazza Signoria with the Arno. The dramatic perspective view down the Uffizi to Palazzo Vecchio has something of the quality of a view down a long, straight street. On the other hand, the building that surrounds and creates the space does so by means of porticos placed on three sides, a characteristic of many Italian piazze and courtyards (Fig. 63). The space seems at once too wide for a street and too narrow for a piazza or courtyard. My own sense, shared by a number of scholars who have written about the space, is that it is deliberately ambiguous in its nature, capable of meaning different things at different times. Such ambiguity is hardly unknown in the art of mid-sixteenth century Italy.[46]

We do know that on some occasions the Piazza degli Uffizi was used for public events that were "theatrical" in nature: it was illuminated in honor of

FIG. 62 Giorgio Vasari, Palazzo degli Uffizi, Florence, piazza looking north toward Piazza Signoria (Photo: Ralph Lieberman)

important guests; the funeral cortege of Cosimo I in part formed in the porticos before moving from Piazza Signoria to the Medici parish church of San Lorenzo; and it was used for solemn entrances into the city.[47] As such, it functioned something like the Piazzetta in Venice, also an adjunct to the largest and most important public space of that city.[48] Like the Piazzetta, the Uffizi connects the major public space to water (Fig. 33). Cosimo seems to have intended the permanent presence of an audience in this space, in attendance at the permanent "show" of Medici power and Florentine cultural prowess in Piazza Signoria and the cathedral dome. At the end of the open space toward the Arno a statue of Cosimo by Giovanni da Bologna stands under an arch on the piano nobile to face Piazza Signoria (Fig. 64). Cosimo almost seems as if he were in a royal box looking down the rectangular space of a court theater at Lanci's set for *La Vedova*. Originally, the figure of Cosimo was to have been carved by Vincenzo Danti as a seated figure, a more likely pose for a theater-goer.[49] In the twenty niches of the piers at ground level Cosimo intended to place statues of famous Florentine men.[50] Cycles of famous men were fairly common in the Renaissance, and Vasari himself had written that the ancients had placed statues of virtuous men in public places to urge desire for virtue and glory on the part of citizens.[51] A set of *uomini famosi* installed in a public space like that of the Uffizi, however, is rare, if not indeed unique in the sixteenth century. These statues

FIG. 63 Palazzo degli Uffizi, piazza looking south toward the Arno (Photo: Ralph Lieberman)

vividly recall those installed in the theater in Lyon of 1548, which also represented famous Tuscans (Fig. 50). The Uffizi statues, only finally carved and set up in the nineteenth century (Fig. 63), would have formed a permanent audience stationed on the ground below the seated ruler, just as the gentlemen of the audience in the Salone dei Cinquecento were arranged on the orchestra floor below Cosimo, his family and his guests. It is certainly tempting to see this arrangement as a permanent allegory of the theater of a royal court. Previous writers, struggling to define the exterior space of the Uffizi, appear not to have considered the way that space relates to the rectangular shape for temporary theaters set up in the palaces of rulers that by 1560 had become standard. One of the many ways the Uffizi can be interpreted, then, is as a permanent theater of the Grand Duchy of Tuscany.

One can also look at the open space of the Uffizi from the opposite direction, from the north end, from Piazza Signoria (Fig. 63). Standing there, one is "on stage," observed by the duke and, if one is Florentine, by one's ancestors. If viewers realize this fact, they can come to understand that they are part of the ceaseless drama of Florentine life. Alison Fleming has rightly argued that the space of the Uffizi should be understood as a theater of urban life,[52] even though she did not recognize the connection to the architecture of theaters. Like others who have studied the space, she points out the fact that

FIG. 64 Giovanni da Bologna, statue of Cosimo I, Palazzo degli Uffizi, Florence (Photo: Ralph Lieberman)

a viewer can look at it in two ways. It is precisely this duality of points of view that links the Uffizi space to the Piazzetta in Venice, which Vasari knew well. The Piazzetta is also an urban theatrical space.[53] Sebastiano Serlio had used a view of it from the south, or the water's edge, as the basis for a scene design[54] (Fig. 35), and indeed the view through the Piazzetta north to the Torre dell'Orologio has often been compared to Renaissance one-point perspective scene designs. If, however, one looks from the north, with one's back to the clock tower, one looks past the flanking porticos of the Ducal Palace and the Libreria di San Marco, which converge on the two columns that act like a proscenium arch framing the waters of the Bacino as if they were a set imitating the sea, a commonplace in contemporary scene design (Fig. 33).

When Vasari was in Venice in 1542, Jacopo Sansovino's Libreria di San Marco, begun 1537, was under construction, and Vasari sought out its architect, a fellow Tuscan. Although the Libreria was not very far along,[55] Vasari would surely have learned how the Piazzetta was used for theatrical "performances," not the least of which were the public executions that took place with some frequency between the columns (Fig. 33). And he may have learned from Sansovino how the windows in the piano nobile of the Libreria were eventually to be used almost like theater boxes (a later invention, as we will see) for the procurators of Saint Mark, the Venetian patricians who were building the Libreria, to view events in the Piazzetta (see Chapter 5). Risers were often set up in the Piazzetta to accommodate spectators, in a manner similar to the way risers were arranged along the side walls of temporary theaters in palaces. The experience of the Piazzetta seems to have been important for Vasari when he designed the Uffizi. Perhaps even his two columns that form the Serliana at the southern end of its open space and frame the view of the Arno may recall the columns of the Piazzetta. The two columns of Venice must have been in his mind when he designed the proscenium arch for the Salone del Cinquecento in 1565, five years after he began construction of the Uffizi.

It is no accident that the sets for the plays of 1565 and 1569 both focused on parts of Florence that were being transformed under Cosimo. Andrea Mariotti has pointed out the uniqueness of the contribution of Cosimo and Vasari to the history of city planning: "[Their] transformation of an urban structure from polar to linear represents an absolute novelty on an international level, because it is the first time that piazze, streets and bridges were tied together to create a true urban continuum."[56] Via Maggio and the Uffizi were two of the most important parts of that new understanding of urban space.

THE MEDICI THEATER IN THE PALAZZO DEGLI UFFIZI

Vasari's Uffizi served many purposes, one being to house a large, new, purpose-built, permanent court theater to replace his makeshift conversion of the Salone dei Cinquecento.[57] In the Salone Vasari, one recalls, had introduced an important novelty, backstage space that gave actors the possibility of moving around unseen behind the set before making their entrances. But even with this convenient new space, the stage of the Salone was not deep enough to house the increasingly lavish court spectacles the Medici wished to put on. Lanci's *periaktoi* took the shallow stage of the Salone about as far as it could go (Fig. 56). Vasari's new theater space in the Uffizi, 55.10 × 20.30 × 14 m tall,[58] was divided into two parts, with a stage roughly half as deep as the length of the long, rectangular auditorium, to which he gave a sloping floor to enhance the audience's ability to see the fabulous things that were to happen on stage. The slope of the floor, toward the south and the Arno, was made possible by decreasing the heights of the vaults of the ground floor rooms of the Uffizi beneath the theater, a sign that the theater was planned from the outset[59] (Fig. 65).

The theater apparently was not completed until it was used for the celebration of the wedding in 1586 of Cosimo I's daughter, Virginia (borne by his second wife, Camilla Martelli), to Cesare d'Este, who in 1597 became Duke of Modena.[60] For the marriage Bernardo Buontalenti, Vasari's assistant for the productions in the Salone dei Cinquecento, decorated the interior of Vasari's auditorium so that it seemed to be a garden, with trellises containing symbols

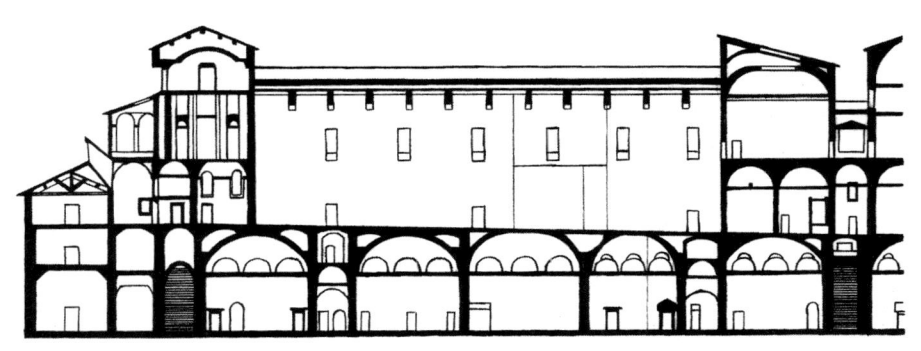

FIG. 65 Giorgio Vasari, Palazzo degli Uffizi, east wing, section of northern end. The theater is the long, two-story space with slanted floor above the ground floor vaults (Drawing: Troy Sipprellle)

of fecundity, fruits, rabbits and deer, overhead. Live birds were released after the audience entered. Here the auditorium space itself became a means to transport that audience to another place, long before the curtain went up and the set revealed a part of Florence in which they were not actually sitting. Women again sat on carpeted steps arranged against three walls of the auditorium (Fig. 66), and men again sat on benches surrounding the dais meant to show off the royal personages and important guests. So many were eager to see the play that separate performances for men and women were arranged, making the question of separate seating for the sexes moot. No drawings of this theater are known.

Cosimo's son, Francesco I, second grand duke and half-brother of the bride, took great pride in this theater. For the wedding he ordered a series of performances of the comedy *L'Amico Fido* by Count Giovanni Bardi to entertain not only important guests, but also the citizens of Florence. Remarkably, the performances extended into the season of Lent. Vasari had connected the theater to the city by an elegant staircase that rises from under the portico of the open space of the Uffizi up to the door of the theater. The position of the staircase makes clear that the theater was not just for members of the court.[61] The landing on which the entrance to the theater was located presented theater-goers with an architectural conundrum. Climbing the final steps to the landing, they faced an elegant triple portal. A bust of Francesco I by Giambologna rises above the central door (Fig. 67). One expects these three doors to lead to an important space, but they open into a dark, airless chamber. This portal, which Detlef Heikamp has dated to 1585, was doubtless designed by Buontalenti.[62] Francesco I stood at the top of the stairs, under his own bust and in front of this elaborate backdrop, to usher the audience toward the actual door of the theater, which opened to the grand duke's right. Vasari at Venice had given the act of entering the theater architectural importance, a notion that was continued in the theater at Lyon. Here in the Uffizi, under Francesco

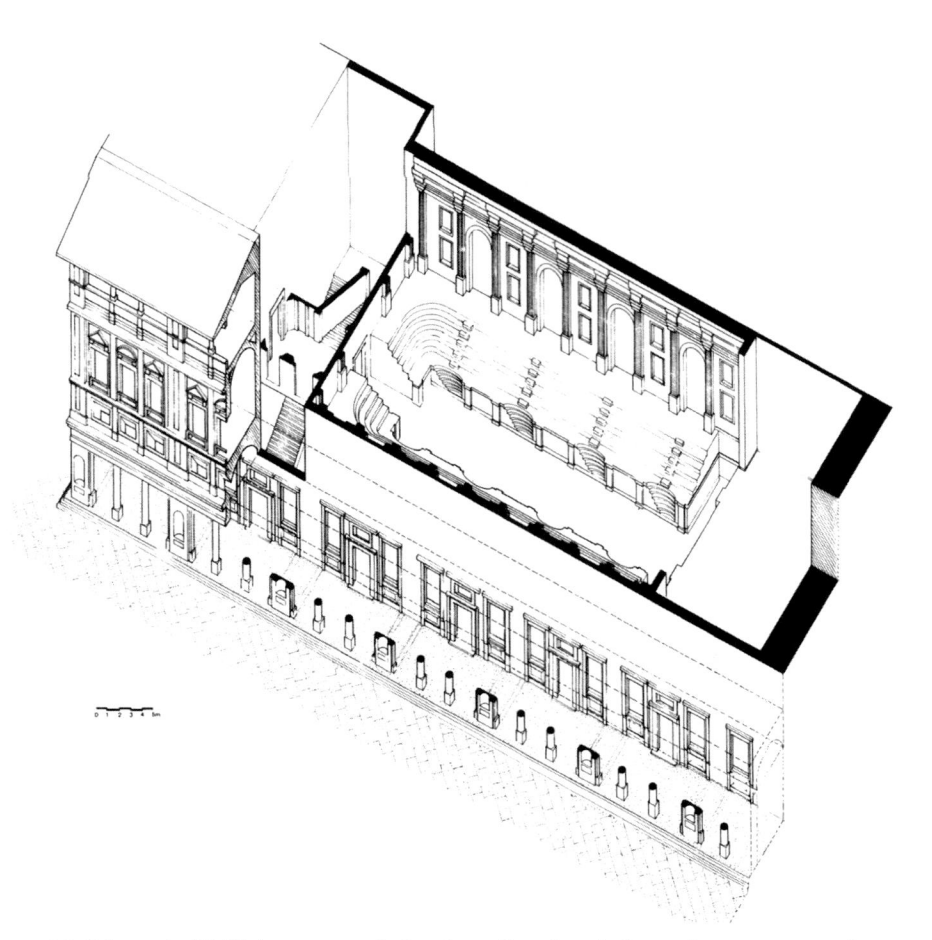

FIG. 66 Palazzo degli Uffizi, axonometric drawings of north end of east wing, cut away to show reconstructed interior of Vasari's theater. The position of the royal dais is not clear, and so it does not appear in this reconstruction. (Satkowski, fig. 12)

I, the architectural backdrop of the triple door framed the public graciousness of the prince, who met the visitor from his elevated position at the top of the stairs. But there was also an admonition in this arrangement. The gracious duke, ushering visitors into his theater, deflected them from the more elaborate door behind him that surely appeared to lead into the restricted world of his residence. Did Francesco know that his forebearer, Leo X, had similarly played doorman at his theater in Rome in 1519?

Buontalenti designed six separate sets, one for each intermedio, that hid the fixed set of Florence used during the play and made full use of the ample new stage. The scenes changed from the heavens, populated by all the gods, in the first *intermedio*, to a vast cavern in the second. A contemporary description gives us the flavor of this scene: "the earth opened [to reveal] a most fearsome cavern, filled with cruelest fire and dark flames" in which appeared the entire

FIG. 67 Palazzo degli Uffizi, staircase landing outside entrance to Uffizi theater with bust of Francesco I by Giovanni da Bologna. Entrance to theater was at left (Photo: Gabinetto Fotografico, Galleria degli Uffizi, Florence)

flaming city of Dix surrounded by the Stygian swamps and populated by devils and furies. In the third *intermedio* a desert landscape bloomed, in the fourth there was a marine scene with figures disporting themselves on the waves, and in the fifth a storm with lightning in a cloud-filled sky gave way to a rainbow.

FLORENCE, THE MEDICI WEDDING OF 1589

In 1589, for the wedding of Grand Duke Ferdinando de' Medici[63] to the granddaughter of Catherine de'Medici, the French princess Christine of Lorraine, the Medici put on what was probably the most sumptuous theatrical performance of the entire century. Buontalenti remodeled the Uffizi theater a second time, turning it into a monumental hall with a giant order of Corinthian pilasters framing nine round-arched bays along each side.[64] On the east there were four windows, while on the west there were openings into the gallery that ran along Vasari's courtyard/piazza outside. Seating for women continued to be on steps along the sides and across the wall opposite the stage. Saslow suggests that these seats may have been modular elements reused from the performance of 1586.[65] Again, men sat on benches on the floor, and a dais held the chairs of the ruling family and guests of note.[66] Lighting was provided by sixteen chandeliers, hanging from panels of the coffered ceiling, that bore the coats of arms of the bride and groom under a crown. A half-oval staircase connected the floor of the hall to the stage, the edge of which was marked by a balustrade that concealed footlights. The proscenium featured statues of the Arno and the Moselle, rivers of the homelands of the newly-weds. Buontalenti made an important improvement for the benefit of some of the musicians, now accomodated on a newly-installed platform over the door, from which they could actually see what was happening on stage.[67] Where the other musicians were placed behind the sets is not clear. The audience, of course, could enjoy being surrounded by music.

Three stage curtains teased the audience's sense of place. A red house curtain dropped to reveal a second curtain, painted to look like a continuation of the architecture of the rest of the room to create what a contemporary called a "perfect amphitheater." This curtain, in turn, dropped to reveal a depiction of the city of Rome. Then Rome fell to uncover a set of the city of Pisa, a Medici possession and the setting for the action of the play, *La Pellegrina*, written some years earlier by Girolamo Bargagli for Ferdinando, but never performed. For this wedding, however, the dusted-off play was not the thing. Instead, all the stops were pulled out for the *intermedi*, six musical interludes performed, first before the play began and, subsequently, after each of its five acts. The stage was made deeper by almost 3 m. to accomodate the much more elaborate stage machinery that Buontalenti designed for this dynastic extravaganza, thus depriving the auditorium of seating space.[68] Every *intermedio* had its own elaborate set, often with moving parts. Figures in lavish costumes designed by Buontalenti, whose drawings are preserved, floated down to the stage on clouds, or dove into what appeared to be ocean waves. There was another hellish grotto with flames. At the end the Olympian gods descended from the skies to bless the happy couple and augur a new golden age for Florence. The whole was designed for political purposes; the libretto of the *intermedi* was published so that it could carry the news of the alliance of France and Tuscany throughout the courts of Europe, as well as the notice that the Medici produced unrivalled spectacles.

In 1600, to celebrate another alliamce between Tuscany and France – the marriage of Maria de'Medici to Henry IV placed a second Medici queen on the French throne – Buontalenti again remodelled the theater in the Uffizi.[69] For the most important guests, Buontalenti converted the musicians' gallery over the door into a kind of royal box for the duke and duchess and the most important guests, thus liberating the floor of the theater for dancing during the *intermedi*. The seating for the audience seems to have been in some way turned into a half oval, so that at the end of the whole performance Buontalenti could cause a curtain to fall that depicted a half-oval theater that offered almost a mirror image of the actual theater (the order was Doric instead of the Corinthian of the pilasters of the auditorium) to the astonished audience

We see the interior of Buontalenti's theater in the Uffizi in an etching by Jacques Callot that records a performance on February 6, 1617 to celebrate the marriage of Cosimo II's sister, Caterina, to Ferdinando Gonzaga, Duke of Mantua (Fig. 68). The room has the basic articulation that it had in 1589. Giant pilasters along the side walls support the cross-beams of the coffered ceiling. Rows of steps to either side provide seating, and the half-oval steps at the front of the stage connect stage and floor. Giulo Parigi, the designer of the production, has added two curving ramps to embrace the steps and offer an easy path for dancers to leave the stage and perform on the open floor. Callot adopts the high view point which the rulers and important guests enjoyed from the converted musicians gallery over the door. He seems to suggest, however, that these great personages descend toward the auditorium floor on steps that did not exist. Below them Callot arranges a multitude of well-dressed figures, both male and female, who stand in a truncated oval that suggests a continuation of the oval form Buontalenti introduced in 1600. Since again there is no need for a royal dais, the empty floor is given over to dancing. According to Nagler,[70] the scene depicted by Callot occurred at the end of the first *intermedio*, when knights and ladies descended from the stage (the figures on stage are holding hands) to dance on the floor. The grand duke and grand duchess

FIG. 68 Jacques Callot, theater of the Uffizi, interior, 1617, etching (Gabinetto dei Disegni e Stampe degli Uffizi, Florence) (Photo: Scala/Art Resources, NY)

themselves joined in the dancing with the performers, becoming active participants rather than passive members of the audience. The participation of rulers in the spectacle, going back to Francesco Gonzaga in 1501 (and maybe earlier), here continues into the next century, where it will become an ever more important part of theatrical events at court.

5

EARLY PERMANENT THEATERS AND THE COMMEDIA DELL'ARTE

Ferrara was home to the first complete, permanent theater building erected and actually used since antiquity, as far as we know.[1] The story of this theater, built by Alfonso I d'Este, is a short, sad one. In existence as early as 1529, it was destroyed by fire on December 2, 1532, when the marriage celebration of Renée de France and Ercole II d'Este took place. The *Menaechmi* of Plautus, translated into French in honor of the bride, was to be given, but on the very night of the performance the theater burned. The poet and playwright Lodovico Ariosto, literary star of the Ferrarese court, apparently gave advice on the theater's form, about which we know very little except that it had a permanent set in the form of a generic city that could stand for any town in which a play might be set.[2] The prologue to a play presented in the theater tells us that "what you thought was Ferrara yesterday is Cremona today."[3]

MANTUA, COURT THEATER

The earliest permanent theater for which we have an actual description of its architectural form was built in Mantua by the court architect Giovanni Battista Bertani, an artist of considerable inventive powers. The building, approaching completion in 1549, may not have been entirely fitted out until 1551. Mantua under the successors of Francesco and Isabella continued to be a city with a rich theatrical life, even if the Gonzaga could never quite afford to satisfy their voracious appetite for art. The theater was commissioned from Bertani by Cardinal Ercole Gonzaga, regent during the minority of the heir to the duchy, Francesco Gonzaga, the grandson of Francesco and Isabella. In 1550 Francesco died at age seventeen, to be succeeded by his younger brother, Guglielmo, for whom the cardinal continued to act as regent.[4]

We have a description of this theater in a short passage from a poem written by one Raffaello Toscano to celebrate the city of Mantua. The poem was published in 1586, five years before the theater was destroyed by fire and replaced by another, whose architect is not known.[5]

Toscano devotes only sixteen lines to the theater, but from that brief notice quite a clear picture emerges:

> Rich is the scene: where the actors intent
> On beautiful works gather often,
> Whose proud and noble ornaments
> Show how much art Art has placed here.
> Of hewn beams and of wood painted
> Or carved in relief, and there quickly follows
> A city, which seems to be filled
> With as many arts and virtues as once had Athens.
>
> Against the great Stage which gracefully slopes
> Bertani the architect places a thousand steps,
> That half a circle make, and there one ascends
> With great ease up to the roof;
> Below is a field, where the fiery Mars
> Often lights the breasts of his followers:
> Temples, Towers, Palaces and Perspectives;
> And figures are there that appear live.[6]

The poet's opening blast, "Rich is the scene," sets the stage for enumerating the forms and materials of the scenery that came together to make a city comparable to ancient Athens: a high-flown claim, but one that tells us of the ambition to rival the ancients that stands behind the theater's design. The sloping stage, then, held a permanent set of a cityscape. Anything performed in Mantua in the court theater during the second half of the sixteeenth century appeared before an unchanging cityscape. Once again, "Ferrara yesterday, Cremona today." The last two lines of the next stanza indicate that all the arts were used for the scenery: the architecture of the stage buildings, the sculptural figures that appeared to be alive, and the perspectival paintings that created an illusion of depth behind the three-dimensional structures.

Opposite the gracefully sloping stage Bertani, according to the poem, raised "a thousand steps ... with which one ascends with great ease up to the roof." A thousand steps seem unlikely, but surely there was a tall range of steps opposite the stage that led to a level near the ceiling. The steps were arranged in a half-circle. That, of course, is a crucial point. Greek and Roman theaters had semicircular seating, and Bertani's theater deliberately imitated their form. Opposite the presumably classical architecture of the city on the stage stood an arrangement of steps that was genuinely classical in its form and function.

At the base of the steps was an open area that also served for performances. The poet's image of Mars, the god of war, inflaming the breasts of his followers in this space indicates that it was used for faux-medieval tourneys, a pastime that delighted sixteenth century court audiences. This is the first clear instance we have of an indoor theater designed for both plays and tourneys, a type that persisted in popularity well into the seventeenth century. Those later theaters invariably have an open space that intervenes between the end of the steps and the front of the stage. According to a description dated 1606 of the successor theater to Bertani's, his design had had such a space between seats and stage that was maintained in the newer structure.[7] The Mantuan theater may well have been the originator of this type of plan. As such, it should be celebrated for the invention of a new type of theater building, although it seems not to have been given the credit to which it is due. Theaters for tourneys have a distinct history well into the following century, a history explored in Chapters 7–9.

Chronologically, Bertani's theater stands between two far-better-known designs. It opened a bit more than a decade after Sebastiano Serlio's theater of 1539 in Vicenza (see Chapter 3) and more than three decades before Andrea Palladio's Teatro Olimpico, Vicenza, inaugurated in 1585 (see Chapter 6). Both of these theaters had curved seating and a stage set of a city. Probably a direct inspiration for Bertani's theater was the illustrated account of Serlio's Vicentine theater that he published in 1545 in his Book II (Fig. 38), but Bertani also leaned heavily on Vitruvius and Alberti.

In its permanence, the Mantuan theater was unlike most of its predecessors. Theater architecture was no longer for the moment, but at least for the foreseeable future. As a permanent theater, Bertani's had to be accessible to the public. Some scholars believe that instead of putting the theater inside one of the rooms of the extensive and ever-expanding Gonzaga palace, Bertani built a new shell to contain it outside the walls of the palace, on an important piazza of the city. If that were the case, then Bertani's was one of the earliest free-standing buildings erected to house a permanent theater. By the middle of the sixteenth century going to theatrical performances sponsored by ruling princes had become part of normal life in some court cities. It would make sense to put a new theater between the palace and the town in order to keep the crowds out of the princely residence.

Evidence that the theater was located inside the palace, however, is offered by Gabriele Bertazzolo's map of Mantua of 1628 (Fig. 69). That

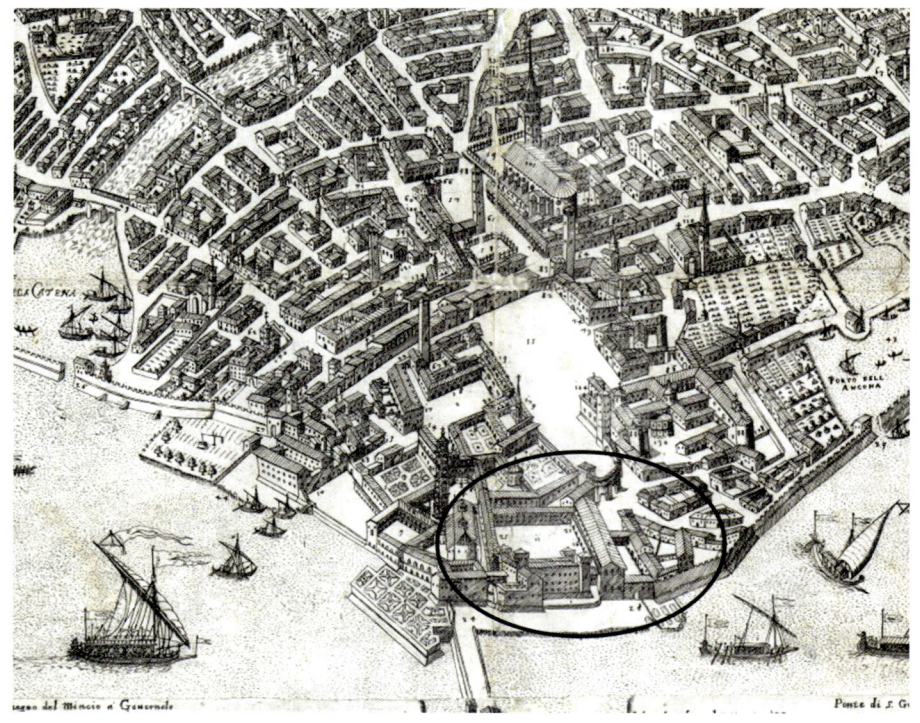

FIG. 69 Gabriele Bertazzolo, map of Mantua, 1628, detail showing the complex of Palazzo Ducale in center foreground. The theater is the rectangular building marked by the oval (Photo: Mantova: Settore Promozione Culturale e Turistica della Città)

map identfies the court theater by the number 4 in a rectangular wing of the palace located just inside the walls and very near the surrounding lake, between the medieval Castello S. Giorgio and the Porta San Giorgio, a main entrances to the city. This possibility seems the more likely, although by 1628 Bertani's theater of c.1550 had burned and been replaced by another. Also supporting the supposition that Bertani's theater was in the palace is the fact that in the 1580's Duke Guglielmo Gonzaga decreed that during carnival any citizen, except ecclesiastics, could enter the theater masked but could not go into adjacent parts of the ducal residence.[8] By this date it seems safe to assume that both men and women were welcome to join the audience, although they would have been seated separately. An easily accessible theater was another example of princely largesse – of that duty of a good prince to patronize the arts, embellish his realm and entertain his citizens. Since the Mantuan theater, in either location, was connected to the palace, the prince and his party could enter and leave with ease. If entrance to the theater was at ground level, then knights on horseback easily could have entered to joust.

ROME 1550

Most likely in 1550, and thus contemporary with Bertani's theater in Mantua, a commercial theater was fitted out in Rome, according to Giorgio Vasari, in Rome at the time. He tells us that Giovanni Andrea dell'Anguillara, "a truly rare man in every sort of poetry," put together a company of people of various talents and erected an "apparatus" for playing comedies before "gentlemen, lords and great personages."[9] In clerical Rome, no women allowed. The site for the theater was Palazzo SS. Apostoli, a large ecclesiastical residence next to the church of the same name. The theater, according to Vasari, was quite beautifully decorated by two members of the troupe, the painter Battista Franco and the sculptor Bartolomeo Ammanati. Each contributed works of his own specialty. Because Ammanati could not have been in Rome until after April 17, 1550, when he was married in the Marche,[10] the theater presumably dates from the spring or early summer of that year. By some time in May Vasari had arranged for Ammanati to receive the commission for carving two statues for the Del Monte chapel in S. Pietro in Montorio, the family chapel of Pope Julius III, elected the previous February. Julius III loved the theater, and so it is likely that his ascending the throne of Peter made it possible for a commercial theater to open in the city.

The seating area consisted of steps so ordered that they accomodated people of various rank; that is, architectural consideration was given to the classes of spectators who paid to see the performances, just as seating by class had occurred in Serlio's theater in Vicenza. Cardinals and other high prelates, who might not want to be seen in public at performance of a comedy, got special treatment. These worthies, unique to Roman society, were provided with "some rooms" where they could view the comedies through shutters without being seen themselves. Not only was the seating arranged to accomodate different classes, but also members of the highest class, princes of the church, were given the priviledge of being in a public place without anyone knowing they were present. In court theaters, rulers wanted to be the center of the show. In Rome, cardinals avoided being part of the show at all. When the newly elected pope, Julius III, enjoyed the performance of comedies, he did so in the Vatican palace.[11] The troupe spent so much money on the theater that they could not collect sufficient box office receipts to cover expenses. The space being too small, Giovanni Andrea dell'Anguillara moved the whole apparatus into an unused church, San Biagio in Strada Giulia, somehow fitting his scenery and seats and shuttered rooms and paintings and sculptures into the new space. The plan of the church is that of a cross, with three equal arms, and a fourth, longer arm that served as the nave (Fig. 70). Anguillara somehow must have forced the stage and seating into that shape. There, says Vasari, he presented many comedies "to the incredible satisfaction of the people and

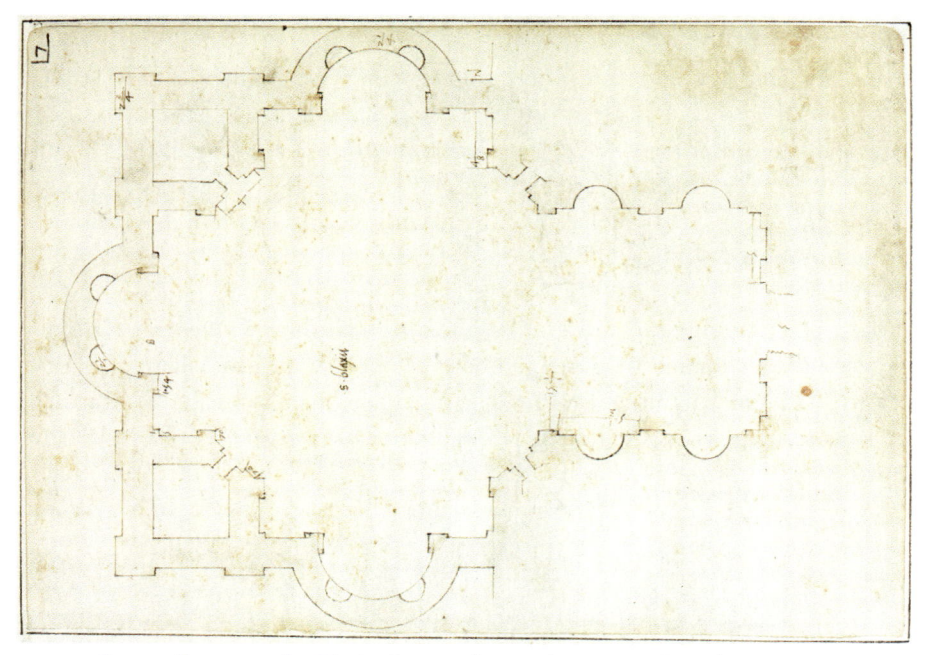

FIG. 70 Donato Bramante, San Biagio, Rome, plan, Codex Coner (©London, Sir John Soane's Museum, 115, 11)

courtiers of Rome." Vasari suggests that the new space could accommodate a more varied audience in terms of class, a fact that permitted casting a wider net for a paying audience. Vasari closes this passage by mistakenly telling us that it was in this theater that commedia dell'arte was invented. We know that not to be the case, but Vasari's mention of the 'Zanni,' – the characters of commedia dell'arte – means that such a troupe or troupes performed in Giovanni Andrea dell'Anguillara's theater. We have no idea how long this theater remained open. By June of 1551 Anguillara may already have left Rome.[12] At least for a while in Rome there was a permanent theater in which both amateurs and professionals performed comedies in a hall fitted out to accomodate the several classes that frequented it.

Commedia dell'Arte

A crucial development in the history of the theater in Italy, and indeed in Europe, during the sixteenth century was the rise of commedia dell'arte, a popular form of entertainment performed by troupes of "strolling players," to steal a phrase from Cole Porter. We know little of how, where or when these companies of professional actors, who made their living through performance, began. According to the Venetian Marin Sanudo, players from Rome appeared as early as 1528 in a private palace on the island of Murano.[13] During the carnival of 1533, again according to Sanudo, a troupe of actors from Rovigo performed in a palace of the noble Priuli family, also on Murano. The audience, which Sanudo said was large, paid to attend. Sanudo wrote that the performance was good and the *intermedi* featured music and numerous *buffoni*.[14] The carnival of 1533 was a particularly jolly one in Venice. "This land at present is at peace, and much given to Venus and Bacchus," Sanudo wrote.[15]

The earliest legal document we have for the creation of a commedia dell'arte troupe dates from 1545, a contract signed in Padua by a small group of men under the leadership of a certain Ser Maphio.[16] This group seems to have performed in Venice in 1546 and 1549; in the latter year they left Venice for Rome to play carnival there. They may well have appeared in the theater in the palace of SS. Apostoli or in the church of S. Biagio (Fig. 70). The dates are right and coincide with the establishment of permanent theaters in Mantua and Rome, surely intended to house regularly available troupes of professional actors.

These troupes varied wildly in quality. Some were composed of people on the very fringes of society who could seem an outright threat to public order. Other troupes became the favorites of kings and princes and enjoyed prosperity and fame. By the 1560's women were as important as men in the troupes; some female comics became internationally famous and fairly well off.[17] At the great Medici wedding of 1589, marked by one of the principal theatrical extravaganzas of the entire century, the commedia dell'arte star Francesca Andreani brought the house down with a mad scene partly performed in fractured French. Her appearance delighted (and honored) the French bride, Christine of Lorraine. Often a troupe would contain at least one husband and wife team.

In the early years of commedia dell'arte the players had to play wherever they could find space. Sometimes it would be a hall in a palace, sometimes it would be a rented hall in a less distinguished building; eventually there were theaters designed to accommodate their work. They used simples sets, which they carried with them, and their costumes also came along in the baggage. The sets consisted mostly of a painted backdrop, perhaps with a view of a town, and two houses, placed to either side of the stage, through which the performers made their exits and entrances. Players might appear in the windows of houses, as we know from the depiction of performances illustrated in the *Corsini scenarii* from the second half of the sixteenth century.[18] The audience was accomodated in a casual manner. Perhaps the hall would contain stools to rent. Perhaps not. Women could not be in the audience, unless separate seating was provided for them. In many (most?) cases, then, the audience was all male, at least until later in the sixteenth century.

The description of a modest theater in Venice that the English traveler Thomas Coryat experienced during his visit to that city in 1608 probably gives us a good idea of what many of these theaters from the previous century were like.[19] Coryat, hardly innocent of national pride, found the theater quite inelegant by English standards, nor was he impressed by the quality of the scenery and the costumes. Much of his description is devoted to the dress of the courtesans who sat on a balcony or two above the male members of the audience, who perched on rented stools on the ground floor. From the scraps of information Coryat supplies, it would seem that the theater consisted of a single rather shabby room or courtyard, with a stage at one end and a balcony or balconies for the courtesans. The men (some noble) and women, masked, exchanged words during the performance, even though it could not have been easy for the spectators to have recognized each other, given the effectiveness of the masks that Coryat described. What most amazed Coryat was the presence of women on stage, something for which the all-male casts of English plays had not prepared him. The women charmed him; amazed, he felt that they performed quite as well as the men. (!) He seems to have been unaware that this theater could hardly have been open more than a year, or that it must have been hastily cobbled together after the expulsion of the Jesuits from Venetian territory in 1607 as part of the settlement of a bitter feud between Venice and the papacy. Essentially no theaters had operated in Counter-Reformatory Venice between 1585 and 1607, but by May of that year at least one troupe of "Zanni" was operating in the city.[20]

By the middle of the sixteenth century, then, theatrical spaces began to be set up to accomodate the traveling players. They could be at princely behest, as in Mantua, or they could be constructed or outfitted by private citizens on the lookout for profit, as in Rome. Exemplary of the latter was the proposal by a Mantuan Jew, Leone de' Sommi (identified in documents as "Leone hebreo"), who in 1567 petitioned Duke Guglielmo Gonzaga for permission to set up a "stanza" for the presentation of comedies "by those who go about performing for a price." He requested a monopoly on such an enterprise for ten years. In return, he offered to give two sacks of wheat annually to the poor.[21] Leone was supported in his request by a ducal cousin, Francesco Gonzaga, Count of Novellara, who found the proposal useful both for the poor and the pleasure of the city. The count seems to have consulted with Leone about his plans, for he believed that Leone intended a commodious room where ladies and gentlemen could attend plays decently.[22] There is no record of the duke's reply to the request for permission.

Mantua was a city with an apparently unique relationship between the Jewish community and theater.[23] As early as 1525 Jewish groups were performing comedies in the city, and by the second half of the century they were regular performers in the court theater and suppliers of costumes and scenery.

The fame of Mantua's Jewish comedians was widespread; in 1605 Carlo Emanuele of Savoy knew enough about them to mention them in a letter to Vincenzo I, whose heir was to marry Carlo Emanuele's daughter.[24] Counter-reformatory antisemitism was resisted by the dukes of Mantua well into the following century. In the winter of 1598–99, Vincenzo, whose passion for the theater was close to unrivaled, was the first ruler, it would seem, to establish and sponsor his own troupe of players.

Comedy was a hot commodity in Mantua in the summer of 1567.[25] Two companies were playing there simultaneously, and the city was split in its allegiances to the two principal actresses, Flaminia and Vincenza.[26] Both theaters were filled. Even monks were going to the theater, as many as 25 at a time; the scandalized bishop was driven to prohibit his clergy from attending.[27] Comedy by this time was not something enjoyed only by the nobility and the rich. A report of the captain of the ducal guard notes a performance with a "good number of people of every type." This particular performance got a bit out of hand, when the audience demanded that some spectators, who were standing on the stage and blocking everyone else's view, get down. A young gentleman from Verona refused to move, until he was finally forced off, to the accompaniment of shouts and hisses. He said something untoward to the audience, then escaped before they could take revenge. At a later performance the audience recognized him, and he had to be spirited out of the theater and hidden in the house of the actors. At a still later performance he was forced to go on stage and apologize.[28] The presence in Mantua over a period of time of the young Veronese devotee makes clear that people came from miles around to stay in the city and enjoy the comedies. Comedies were good for the local economy.

The players earned their livings through the box office. The troupe of Flaminia performed in "the usual place," presumably Bertani's court theater designed almost twenty years earlier. Vincenza and her company worked in a private house fitted out to accomodate the plays.[29] At one point a performance was also given in the Palazzo della Ragione, or town hall. Leone de' Sommi, keenly aware of local interest in comedies, may actually have profited from the excitement. The house that Vincenza appeared in was located near the Jewish quarter, and Ferrucio Marotti believes it possible that Leone, who had a connection with Vincenza, may have opened his requested theater there after all.[30] Leone de' Sommi, successful director of comedies, wrote a series of four dialogues on the theater.[31] Mostly they concern advice on staging plays, a subject on which he was clearly experienced. The dialogues contain little of architectural interest, save for the points he made about lighting. It was important to use lights that did not smoke, he wrote, but since that was not generally possible, he advocated a ventilated stage. As he put it, without ventilation, by the end of the second act the stage was so filled with smoke that actors appeared no longer as men but as shadows.[32] He advised vents in the ceiling over the stage and holes in the floor below, so that the air, rising up, would carry the smoke away. Likewise, in the auditorium, he advocated vents in the ceiling above the places where he located a few torches. He used only a small number of lights in the auditorium, placed behind the audience, so that the playgoers could look from a dark house into a brightly lit stage. For comedies, he recommended uniformly bright lighting on stage, but in certain instances, if a tragic event took place, he would extinguish many of the stage lights to create a sense of horror in the audience.[33]

We have notices about comedies from other cities as well, such as Bologna. There, as early as 1547, the great hall on the *piano nobile* of the Palazzo del Podestà was given over to housing entertainments.[34] The palace had been built in the late thirteenth century as the seat of the administration of justice in the city (Fig. 71). Remodeled in the late fifteenth century, the structure continued to play its role as one of the city's principal governmental buildings until papal troops occupied Bologna in the name of Julius II. The old oligarchical government of the city was replaced by the rule of a single man, the papal legate. The Palazzo del Podestà, its great meeting hall lit by nine enormous windows, became an immense, unused relic of a past political situation. The legates, shrewdly, allowed the old aristocracy of the city to run its cultural affairs, and

FIG. 71 Bologna, Palazzo del Podestà, exterior. The nine windows in the façade light the great hall (Photo: Georges Jansoone)

so they took over the palace as the site for presumably politically-unthreatening entertainments. In 1598, for instance, the papal legate allowed a certain Giuseppe Guidetti to fit the room out with *palchi* for the performance of comedies, to sell fruit, and even to schedule ball games in the hall.[35] Such a conversion of a building of immense import to a civic polity into a place of entertainment was not unique to Bologna. Cosimo I later did the same in Siena and Florence, as we saw in the previous chapter.

FLORENCE, TEATRO DI BALDRACCA

In Florence, the Medici rulers wanted to keep comedies under their control, and so they constructed behind the Uffizi, in a seedy quarter called Baldracca, a theater where comedy troupes performed.[36] The theater was on the top floor of a multipurpose building with shops on the ground floor and store rooms on the first.[37] The building, and thus what went on in the theater, were controlled by the Dogana, the state customs office. There was one entrance for the paying public, and a separate corridor that connected the theater to the Palazzo degli Uffizi immediately to its west for the use of the Grand Duke and his guests. The duke and his party attended the comedies unseen, just as they could attend mass in the church of Santa Felicità in an enclosed, private space elevated above the main portal, thanks to Vasari's elevated corridor that connected the Uffizi with Palazzo Pitti and passed by the church after crossing the Arno. On the Uffizi side of the Baldracca there were rooms, or *stanzini*, screened from the view of the audience, that members of the court could enter directly. While ordinary citizens could enjoy the raucous fun of the comedies in public, the duke and his companions could enjoy the coarse jokes in private and thereby maintain the air of superiority on which their increasingly autocratic rule partly depended.

This theater was in operation probably as early as 1576, when we know the commedia dell'arte company of Pedrolino performed in Florence; the Gelosi followed the next year. It is mentioned in a rime, datable c. 1577, as "the new room [that] has been deflowered by the Zanni."[38] The name given to it normally in contemporary documents is *La stanzone delle Commedie*, the Big Room of the Comedies. This theater was not unique in being a separate venue for comedies directly connected to a princely palace. In Mantua Bertani's theater theater of c. 1550 was part of the Gonzaga palace. Such early theaters connected to palaces were the forerunners of the great opera houses that came to be constructed next to royal residences, such as the Teatro San Carlo in Naples, inaugurated in 1737.

A plan made of the Baldracca theater in 1717, after it had long been abandoned,[39] shows the rectangular space, 33 × 16 m, for performances, surrounded by corridors to the north, east, and west (Fig. 72). Beyond the

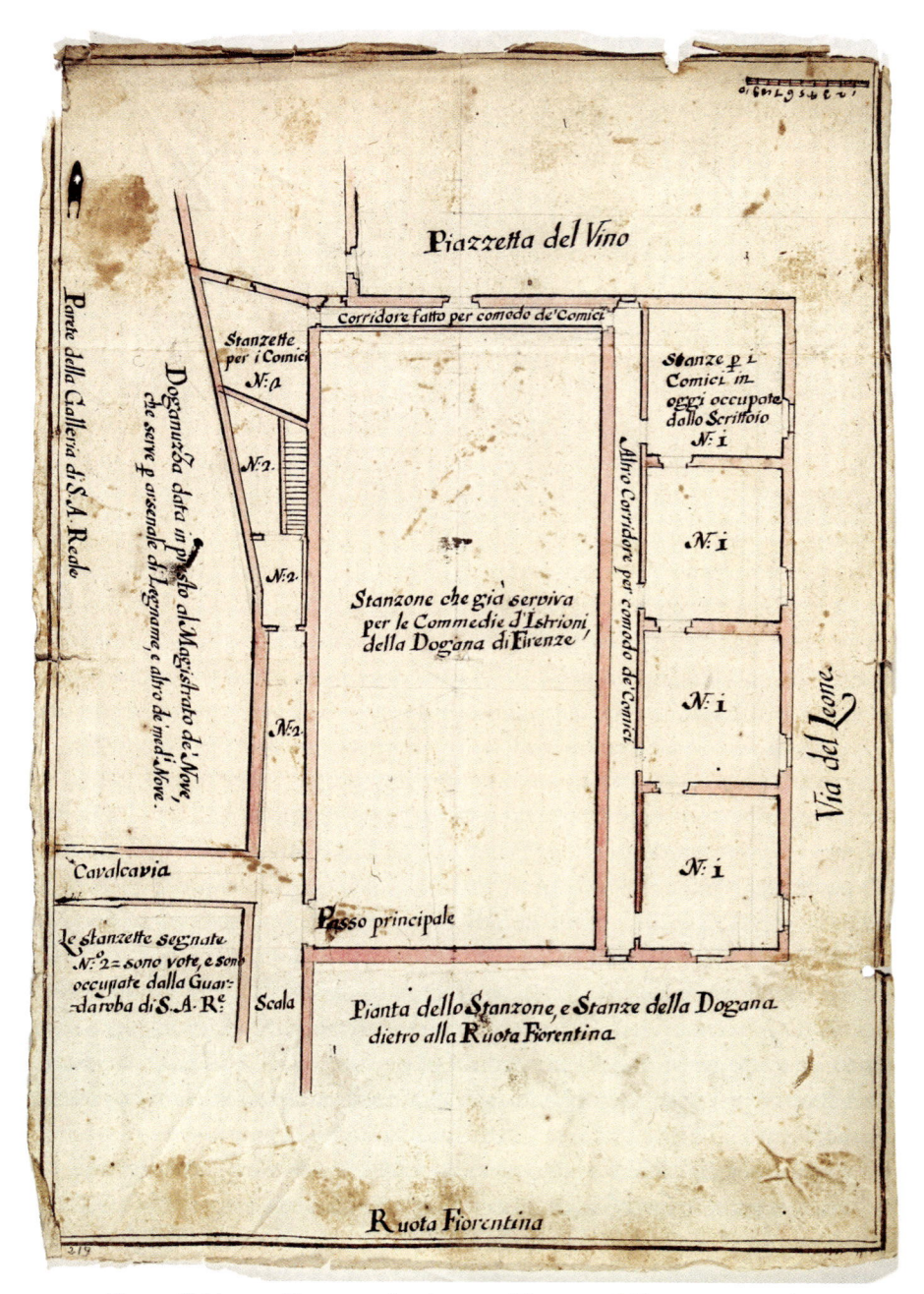

FIG. 72 Teatro Baldracca, Florence, plan in 1717 (Florence, Biblioteca Nazionale Centrale, Fondo non inventariato, f. III, insXI) (Photo: GAP, Florence)

eastern corridor are four squarish rooms for use of the performers, and there is a fifth room, of similar purpose but irregularly shaped, at the northwest corner. The corridors and rooms for the performers seem to have been thoughtfully planned to meet functional needs. Entering the building from the southwest is the "cavalcavia," the corridor that connected the theater to the Uffizi, and at the southwest corner of the theater itself is the public entrance. The *stanzone* is shown completely empty, and so one surmises that the stage and the *stanzini* (discussed later) that it once held had been removed before the plan was drawn.

A letter of December 25, 1618 from a court functionary, Cosimo Baroncelli, to Don Giovanni de' Medici, patron of the Confidenti, a commedia dell'arte troupe, makes clear that by that date the theater contained two or more levels of *stanzini* (little rooms),[40] which may or may not have been boxes. The letter is not easy to interpret, since we have no visual evidence with which to compare it. The pertinent parts of the letter for our purpose read:

> Cicognini had printed in praise of this lady [Lavinia, an actress] a poem, and at the end of the performance, he had some young men who were in the uppermost stanzini throw a large quantity of them down to the people who gathered them up to much applause.
>
> The Lord Cardinal had since last year the key to the stanzino of Your Excellency and he never returned it and having asked for it this year to accommodate the Lord Resident he made me send it back and he kept it three evenings and then ... he accommodated the Lord Resident [the ambassador of the Holy Roman Emperor] with a stanzino of those that are on the second level above that of the Most Serene Grand Duke. In the first days Monsignor Corcini who was here used the stanzino and then Sig. Tommaso Medici had it almost always, except in the last eight or ten days when Sig. Lione Nerli took it for his wife, with whom my wife has also sometimes gone to hear the comedies and with this circumstance I saw that many women who went to the stanzino of Sig. Antella passed by way of that of Your Excellency with complete freedom: that is, they used the same route and staircase of Your Excellency.[41]

From this letter we learn that there were numerous stanzini in the theater, some of which were under the permanent control, with a key, of individuals. There were a lower level of stanzini, including that of the Grand Duke; a second level above that; and perhaps one or more levels as well, from which young men showered the audience with a printed poem in praise of an actress. Annamaria Evangelista believes that this letter proves that there were boxes in the Baldracca by 1618,[42] which may have been the case, but there are also other ways of interpreting the document that complicate the picture. The Italian word for boxes, *palchi*, is not used in the letter, whereas *palchi* is used in the Venetian documents, discussed later, that concern the two theaters with boxes that opened in Venice in 1580. *Stanzini* may indicate small rooms that opened into the Baldracca but that were not *palchi*, at least not as we have come to know them in later history. The fact that many women could use the *stanzino* of Sig. Antella suggests that the *stanzini* were larger than the average Venetian box, which generally holds four, or perhaps six, people. The fact that those women used an access not readily available to the public to get to the Antella *stanzino* makes one think that at least some of the "little rooms" were accessible only by a select few, who did not enter the theater in the same way that the public came in. And the fact that Baroncelli felt compelled to tell Don Giovanni de' Medici that the women freely passed by his *stanzino* implies that they had to take a route different from the open corridors around boxes that existed in Venetian theaters. Circulation to and from the *stanzini*, in other words, was not easy. All of these suppositions that the letter raises are consistent with a view of the theater as open to a public who paid, but also open to the Medici and upper-crust Florentines through a separate entrance that led to rooms arranged on two or more levels that allowed a select few to enjoy the comedies without coming in contact with the ordinary folk in the theater, and possibly without being seen.[43] Furthermore, at least some of the *stanzini* were apparently under the direct control of members of the ruling family, who gave them to people they wanted to honor or please, whereas ticket sales to the public were supervised by the Dogana. On the other hand, by the third or fourth decade of the seventeenth century, if not earlier, there were *stanzini* that were rented by the Dogana to particularly high-class prostitutes, as Francesca Fantappiè has made clear.[44] The prostitutes had to pay a tax on their earnings. When business was bad, they requested a lowering of the tax, which went to a pious cause.[45] Boxes in Venice, as we will see, were built to make a profit for the impresarios who built the theaters. They were neither the tools of an autocratic state nor a means for raising charitable contributions.

VENICE, 1580–1585, THE MICHIEL AND TRON THEATERS

The most important permanent commedia dell'arte theaters for the subsequent history of theater architecture opened in Venice for the carnival of 1580. There were two, built not far from each other in the parish of San Cassiano by two noble families, the Michiel and the Tron, for profit. The two most famous commedia dell'arte troupes of the day played them, the Gelosi in the Michiel theater, the Confidenti in the Tron. Of both theaters we have no visual trace, but we can reconstruct something of their appearance from documents preserved in the records of the Council of Ten, the powerful body that after 1508 had to approve theatrical performances in Venice.[46]

Comedies were being performed by professional troupes in Venice in the 1560s (and earlier, according to Sanudo), but we do not know precisely where.[47] Venice was devastated by a plague in 1576; in that year all public gatherings were forbidden. As the city slowly got back on its feet, entertainment seems to have been crucial to its citizens' recovery of a sense of well-being. In the last years of the 1570s, the Ten approved theatrical events for carnival with invariably similar provisos: that the performances be decent and conclude at a reasonable hour of the night. Suddenly, in 1580, the language of approval changed radically. The Ten ordered that the places where comedies were to be performed be inspected by competent architects to make sure that they were safe. The new language signals a new architectural situation, and that situation was the invention of theaters with rows of superimposed boxes. We know from other documents that the boxes were surrounded by corridors and entered by doors. In the next few years decrees of the Ten insist that lights be lit in the corridors throughout the performances, and there are promises to the Ten from owners of the theaters and troupes of actors that the boxes would be kept open, so that nothing scandalous could occur in them.

The boxes solved the age-old problem of where to place men and women in theaters. A box, rented to a family for the season, could accommodate both sexes. No longer would wife and daughters have to sit in one part of a theater and husband and sons in another. We know this happened because of the comments of at least one prudish writer who strenuously condemned the patricians who took their daughters to comedies, where they heard the foulest language. The bawdiness of some of the plays was undeniable, and Venetians, who still have a penchant for earthy humor, enjoyed them tremendously. The boxes, with doors into corridors, also made it easy to leave one's seat in the middle of a performance. In previous theaters, audience members were generally trapped in their places for the duration of long entertainments. In an emergency, they had to disturb their neighbors.[48] From the very first year, there were complaints that the novel social situation these theaters created had encouraged bad behavior. The mixing of men and women in the boxes made assignations all too possible. Private spaces in a public building created a novel social architectural situation, to say the least. We have no direct first-person accounts, but Venetians seem quickly to have figured out how to use the boxes as if they were modern motel rooms. It is even likely that some of Venice's famous courtesans set up shop in the theaters.

The incentive for constructing the theaters was economic. Venetian nobles were always eager to make a ducat, and they saw a chance to profit from the great popularity that professional comedies at carnival had achieved, just as Leone de' Sommi had hoped to do in Mantua. The new type of theater with boxes grew out of the unusual structure of Venetian society, dominated not by a ruling prince but by an oligarchy of rich noble families. Those families could easily afford to assure themselves of relatively comfortable and private spaces at the theater by renting the boxes their fellow nobles had provided. The dense urban fabric of Venice, restricted to islands surrounded by water, also played a role. Stacking people up in tiers of boxes fetched a greater return from a small piece of real estate, just as skyscraper office buildings did in late-nineteenth-century America. We do not know exactly how, but the theater owners and the troupes of actors split the income from the rents and ticket sales. From what little evidence we have, the theaters seem to have started off as a great economic success. After the first year, Ettore Tron, owner of one of the theaters, claimed that he made a profit of 1,000 ducats, a handsome sum. We do not know how large the theaters were, or how many boxes each contained. They seem to have been constructed inside already-existing spaces, perhaps warehouses, and to have been made of wood. One can imagine a system of wooden beams supporting wooden floors, with thin partitions between the boxes. There is no indication that they made any visual impact on the surrounding city. Both theaters were next to canals, so that they could be reached by gondola. Many of the streets in Venice were not paved in the sixteenth century; noblewomen would not have wanted to slog through mud in their lavish dresses to get to a performance.

The scandalous behavior in the boxes and on stage created a strong reaction among the aging, pious patricians who ran the city. Their thinking about public morality was dominated by the Jesuits, a religious order created in the sixteenth century to strengthen the Catholic Church, particularly in the face of the Protestant Reformation. The French ambassador informed his king, Henry III, in 1583 that the Jesuits had such influence over leading members of the Venetian government that they could get the government to do whatever they wanted. While this statement was a slight exaggeration – the government did not allow the Jesuits to build a church wherever they wanted in the city – it contained a large grain of truth. The Jesuits mounted a very Jesuitical argument against the theaters, citing the danger that much of the Venetian patriciate would be incinerated should the wooden theaters catch fire.

In 1585 the Council of Ten struck a mortal blow against the two theaters, ordering their demolition within fifteen days. Rarely did the Venetian government bring an end to the business ventures of the patricians who dominated it. The threat of the theaters to public morality and even, perhaps, to the safety of the ruling class caused this highly unusual move. As far as we know, the theaters were immediately dismantled, and there is no further mention of theatrical performances in the records of the Ten for the rest of the century, except for one moment in the 1590s when they ordered bootleg performances of comedies on Murano to be halted. Commedia dell'arte seems almost completely to have disappeared from the city. Only in 1607, when the Jesuits were banished from Venetian territory, did comedies return. When they came back, they did so with an amazing rapidity. We have a report of the performance of a comedy within a month of the Jesuits' expulsion.

Although the two theaters of the 1580s had only a brief life, their historical impact was great. When the first public performance of an opera for a paying audience, anywhere, took place in Venice during the carnival of 1637, it took place in a theater with boxes, the Teatro San Cassiano, owned by the Tron family and erected on the same site that their theater of 1580 had occupied.

6

THEATERS IN THE ANCIENT MANNER AND ANDREA PALLADIO

Although Vitruvius and Alberti described ancient theaters, and later writers on architecture such as Pellegrino Prisciani, Sebastiano Serlio, and Daniele Barbaro expanded on those texts, few theaters in the ancient manner were actually constructed in Italy in the fifteenth, sixteenth, and seventeenth centuries, with the exception of works by Andrea Palladio. The old form did not necessarily fit modern society.

PALAZZO FARNESE, PIACENZA

At least one great masonry theater in the ancient manner was projected, however. In 1558 Giacomo Barozzi da Vignola submitted plans for an enormous new palace with a courtyard dominated by an outdoor theater *all'antica* to be built at Piacenza for the duke and duchess of Parma and Piacenza. The duchess, Margherita d'Austria, seems to have been the moving force behind the construction of the palace. She was the natural daughter of the Emperor Charles V, who had legitimized her, and the half sister of Philip II of Spain. In 1536 Margherita, then the young widow of Alessandro de'Medici, the assassinated Duke of Florence, inherited the Medici property in Rome now called Villa Madama in honor of its new owner. According to Raphael's plan, it was to have included a semicircular theater in the ancient manner (see Chapter 2). Margherita's second husband, Duke Ottavio Farnese, was the grandson of Pope Paul III, whose family had acquired Agostino Chigi's Roman

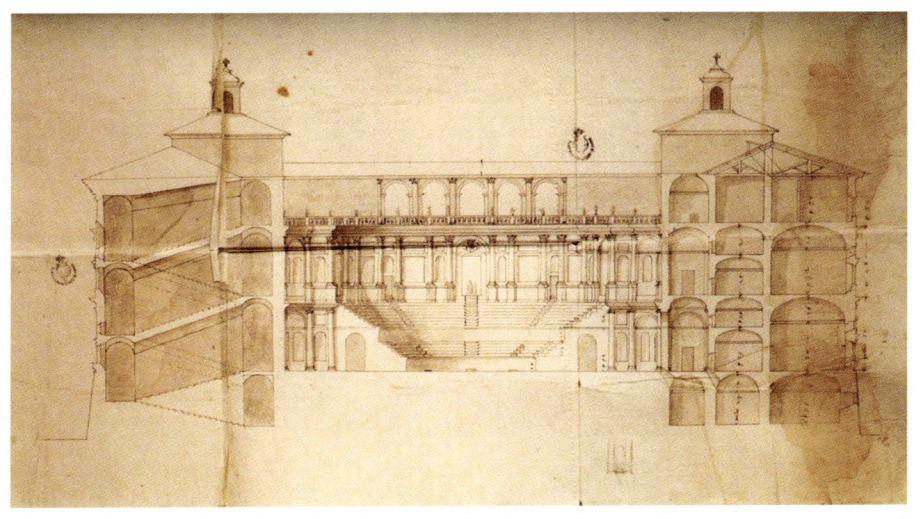

FIG. 73 Giacomo Barozzi da Vignola, project for Palazzo Farnese, Piacenza, cross section of courtyard with elevation of theater. Note two tiny female figures at the tops of the central stairs of the theater (Parma, Archivio di Stato, Gov. farn., Fabbriche duc. e fortif., busta 8)

villa/theater, now called the Farnesina (see Chapter 2). The theater architecture of early sixteenth century Rome, then, was part of both their inheritances.

We know Vignola's plans from drawings (Figs. 73 and 74); only a small part of his design was built.[1] In 1559 Philip II appointed Margherita regent of the Netherlands, then under Spanish control.[2] She went north to assume her new post. Vignola sent her drawings of his project, but because of her absence contruction moved forward only fitfully and came to a halt at the end of the next decade. The fact that Vignola sent her a fairly complex set of drawings suggests that he was confident she would be able to understand them.[3] Few women in the sixteenth century would have had the training to do so.

Vignola's final plan set an outdoor half-oval theater on one long side of the central courtyard, opposite the main entrance (Fig. 74). He used the half-oval, less deep than a semicircle, in order to leave space behind the theater for a loggia that would overlook the palace garden. In Vignola's early schemes, above the seats he placed a Vitruvian colonnade with the shafts set in front of a rear wall, but in the final version the colonnade was replaced by a wall articulated by pairs of engaged half-columns that continued the articulation of the other walls of the courtyard, visually tying the theater into the rest of the palace (Fig. 73). Vignola's theater would have had no *scenae frons*. Instead, the seats would have overlooked the open courtyard, the entrance into which would have appeared to the audience as if it were the "royal door" specified by Vitruvius as the central element of the back wall of a stage. On entering the courtyard, visitors would have confronted the theater seats, putting themselves on stage and reversing the normal role of the spectator. At Piacenza the

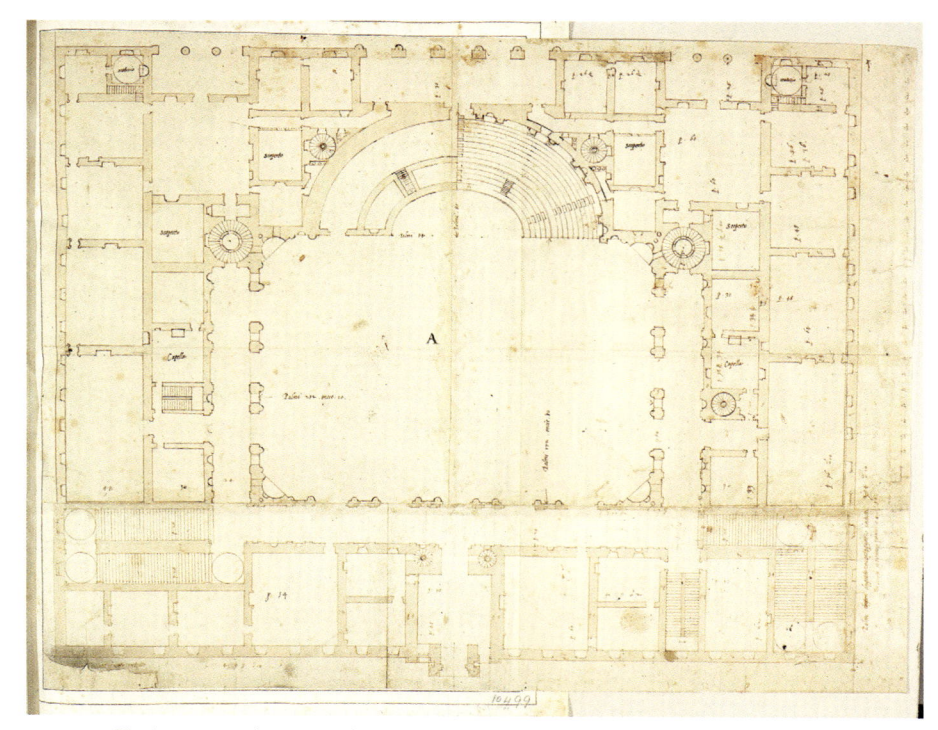

FIG. 74 Giacinto Vignola, copy of project by his father, Giacomo Vignola, for Palazzo Farnese, Piacenza, plan showing two levels (Windsor Castle, RCIN 910499) (Royal Collection Trust / © Her Majesty Queen Elizabeth II 2017)

architecture, once again, would have followed Ovid's definition of a theater as a place to see and be seen.

The theater would have served for jousts and tourneys rather than for the production of ancient or modern plays. Such mock-medieval endeavors, as we have seen, were greatly favored at the time. Analogously, a set of semicircular seats was installed at the lower end of the Belvedere courtyard in the Vatican Palace to accommodate spectators at the tourney held in 1565 to celebrate the marriage of a niece of the Medici pope, Pius IV (Fig. 75). Jakob Binck's view of the tourney shows spectators crowding the windows of the courtyard and the palace, as well as the semicircular seats. Had Vignola's palace been completed, a similar scene would have occurred in Piacenza. Spectators would have lined the open loggias surrounding the courtyard, looking out and down on the whole spectacle of the tourneys on the courtyard floor and of the most important guests watching them from the curved steps.[4] There would have been a spectacle within a spectacle. One cannot fail to note the outrageous anachronisms of a medieval joust taking place in an "ancient" Roman theater built into a contemporary Italian palace. In a drawing Vignola sent to the duchess (Fig. 73), two female figures, probably representing Margherita and a

FIG. 75 Jakob Binck, tournament in the Belvedere Courtyard, engraving, 1565 (Florence, Gabinetto dei Disegni e Stampe degli Uffizi) (Photo: Serge Domingie, Alinari/Art Resources, NY)

lady-in-waiting, appear at the top of the steps in the center of the seats.[5] The figures did not simply give scale to the architecture. They gave the duchess a sense of her commanding presence in the ensemble, where she would have been the center of attention, the focus of the spectacle over which she presided. She was, after all, daughter of an emperor and sister of a king – as well as a very knowledgeable patron of architecture.

ALVISE CORNARO'S THEATER, VENICE

Sometime around 1560 the Paduan enthusiast of theater Alvise Cornaro (see Chapter 3) proposed a theater *all'antica* for Venice that went far beyond the relatively modest structures he had erected on his own Paduan properties.[6] He envisioned enlarging a sandbar located in the Bacino and visible from the Piazzetta (Fig. 33). On this newly created island Cornaro planned to erect a theater in the ancient manner, made of brick to be economical but durable, with semicircular seating and a permanent set.[7] It would have served many purposes. The orchestra would have been large enough to accommodate fights between bears and dogs, men and bulls, and men from different parts of the city. The fights and battles would train Venetian men for war. It could be flooded, to permit the mock-naval battles Romans had enjoyed. Cornaro imagined this theater as a civic amenity to serve all Venetians – to be enjoyed by the "grosso" and the "piccolo," the great and small, of the city. An outsider to the Venetian patriciate, Cornaro disliked the fact that one had to belong to the upper strata of society to enjoy festivals put on by a *compagnia della calza* or performances by professional comedians. Everything on his island would be free. The *compagnie* and *commedia* players would be able to use it. The multi-purpose nature of this theater aligns it with the Mantuan theater of Bertani, with its semicircular seating, permanent set, and an area set aside for combats, although Bertani's theater would have been under princely control.

THEATERS OF ANDREA PALLADIO: THE BARBARO VITRUVIUS, 1556

Andrea Palladio, the major architect of northern Italy in the sixteenth century, designed three theaters in the ancient manner, one of which miraculously survives: the Teatro Olimpico in Vicenza, discussed later. Palladio came to theater design with an intellectual and archaeological background that no architect of the sixteenth century before him possessed. As Pierre Gros noted, he was "the architect of the XVI century who had most exerted himself in the study of Roman theaters and struggled to adapt their structures to the spatial and scenic exigencies of his time."[8] He had collaborated with the aristocratic Venetian humanist and scholar Daniele Barbaro on the publication of a new, illustrated translation of Vitruvius, to which Barbaro appended extensive comments.[9] The book appeared in 1556, with a second edition in 1567;[10]

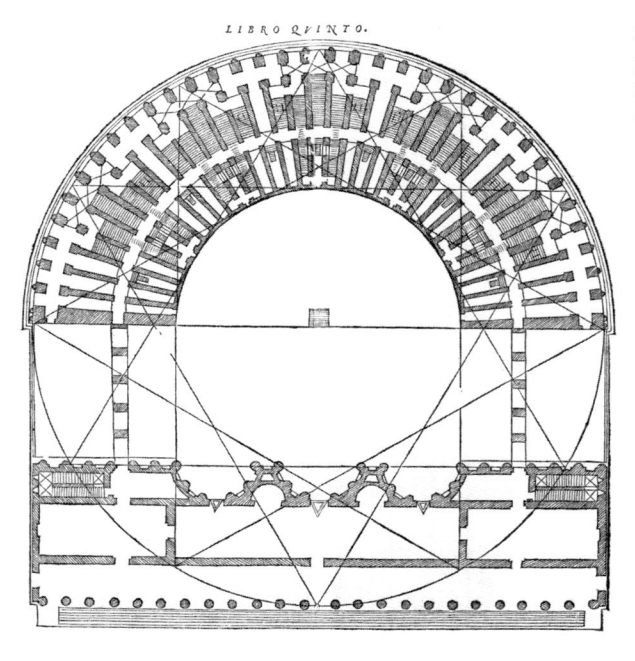

FIG. 76 Andrea Palladio, plan of a Roman theater, from Barbaro Vitruvius, 1567 (Art in the public domain)

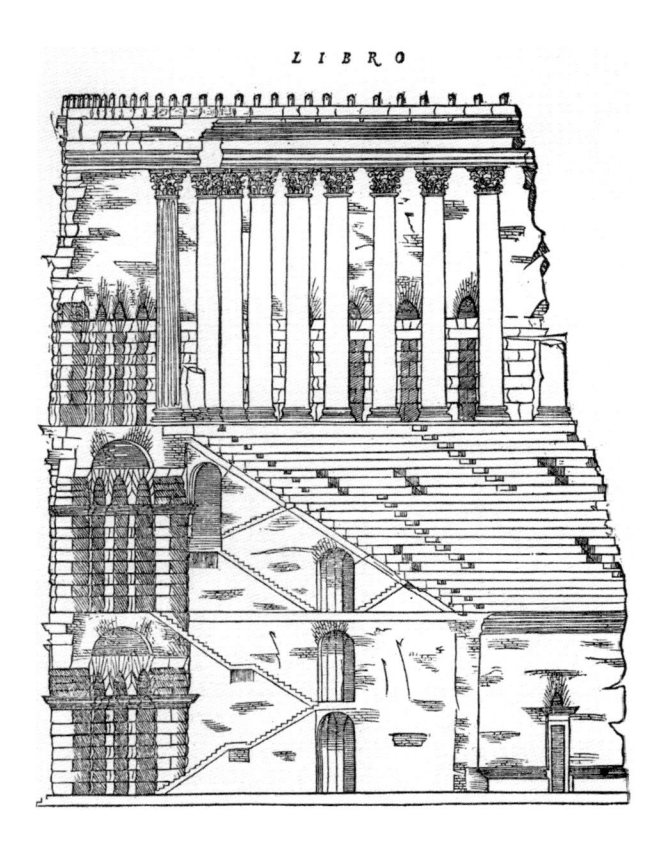

FIG. 77 Andrea Palladio, section through a Roman theater from Barbaro Vitruvius, 1567 (Art in the public domain)

Palladio provided the illustrations, which are among the most elegant to appear in any architectural publication. That the two men worked closely is attested by the fact that Barbaro in his text refers the reader to specific illustrations by "our Palladio." Indeed, in his text Barbaro referred to illustrations already in hand, indicating that at least some of the illustrations were prepared before the text was completed.

Barbaro was concerned with explaining how one could build a theater in the ancient manner that would function for the sixteenth century. To that end he emphasized acoustical clarity, good sight lines, ample passages for circulation, covered spaces to get out of bad weather, places for the performers to dress, and easily changed sets. Acoustics concerned him greatly. Barbaro much preferred a circular form for a theater to the rectangular forms he must frequently have experienced when attending performances in large rooms in private palaces: "Because when the theater may be of angular form, the voice does not come equally to the ears, and some, who are closer, would hear better, and some farther away badly."[11] Barbaro's comments were not innocent of snobbery. "The nobles," he wrote, "will have their seats below, so that the stench that rises on the air, caused by the multitude, will not offend them."[12]

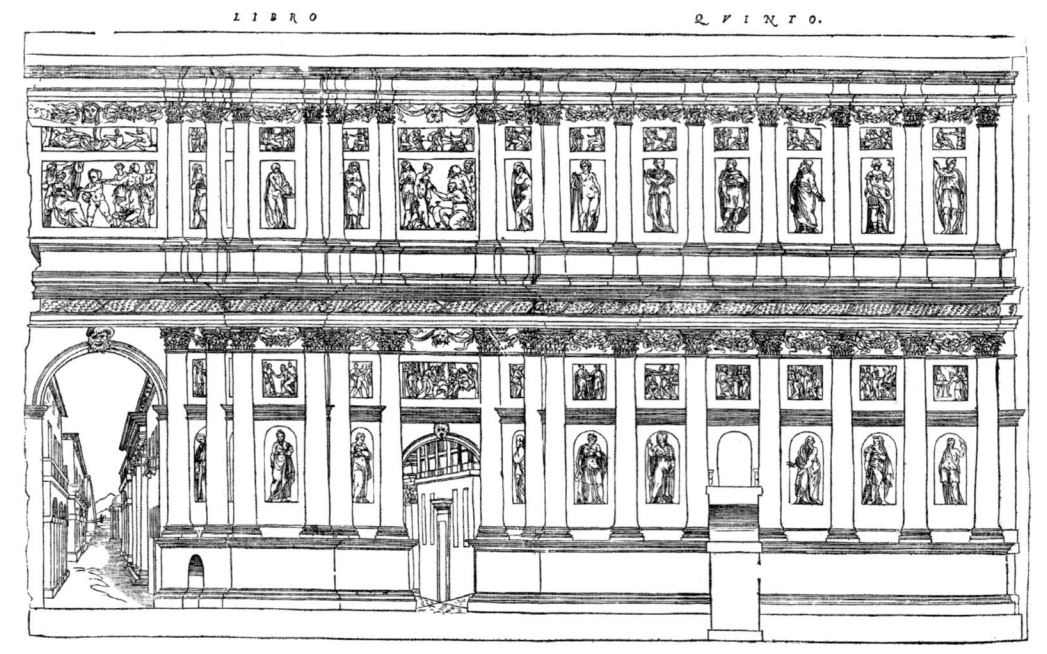

FIG. 78 Andrea Palladio, elevation of *scenae frons* of a Roman theater from Barbaro Vitruvius, 1567 (Art in the public domain)

To Vitruvius's text on theaters, Palladio contributed five architectural drawings: the plan of a Roman theater (Fig. 76), a four-story elevation of part of the exterior of that theater, a section through the seating area of that theater (Fig. 77), an elevation of the *scenae frons* of that theater (Fig. 78), plus a somewhat fanciful plan of a Greek theater. He had studied remains of Roman theaters, but he had never actually seen a Greek example. He only had the Vitruvian text to go on. The purpose of his illustrations was didactic, so that readers "will comprehend many things that we have clarified from the intentions of Vitruvius."[13] Despite the efforts at clarification, the plan of the Roman theater (Fig. 76) is based on a mistake the collaborators made. Palladio drew the circle inscribing four equilateral triangles that Vitruvius calls the "geometric basis" of the plan of a Roman theater so that the circle encompasses the whole of the theater, whereas, according to Vitruvius, the triangles should be contained inside the circle of the walls of the orchestra.[14] For this reason, Palladio's reconstructed Roman stage is too deep. A comparison of Palladio's illustrations for the Barbaro Vitruvius with the theaters he designed makes clear how dependent he was on the forms of Roman theaters.

The *scenae frons* in Palladio's plan of a Roman theater (Fig. 76) has three semicircular niches that each contain a stage door. This detail he and Barbaro based on the remains of the Roman Teatro Barga in Vicenza, which both had

FIG. 79 Basilica, Vicenza, interior of *salone* (Photo: Henry Schmidt)

studied.[15] Inside the doors Palladio drew small triangles, plans of the *periaktoi* mentioned in Vitruvius, that so completely fill the openings that actors would not be able to use them as entrances. Nor could the *periaktoi* be easily rotated: a strange oversight. Barbaro, fascinated both by perspective and quickly changing scenery, commented on the *periaktoi* of the plan:

> The front of the scene had three large niches, as one sees in the plan, in which were placed the triangular machines, which turned on a rotating support, and on each face was painted the scene appropriate to the story to be presented. Thus on one side was the perspective of a comic scene, on another the tragic, and on another the satiric, and according to the occasion they turned the sides.

In his elevation of the *scenae frons* (Fig. 78), Palladio includes not *periaktoi*, but rather perspectival sets. The one behind the central arch shows a street lined with palaces, a loggia, a circular domed temple, and an obelisk; this scene is

FIG. 80 Alessandro Maganza (attrib.), *Amor Cost.*, 1562, fresco, Vicenza, Teatro Olimpico, 1590s (Photo: Ralph Lieberman)

probably for a tragedy. The other shows the lower part of a palace and two columns of a loggia moving off at a sharp angle. Could this be a set for a comedy? What the two men were attempting here was a fusion of their archaeological interest in reconstructing the appearance of an ancient theater with the contemporary taste for perspectival sets for theatrical productions. Barbaro, whose interests were multiple, also wrote a treatise on perspective.

With Barbaro as his guide through the thickets of the Vitruvian text, and given his own firsthand study of the remains of several Roman theaters, Palladio was remarkably well prepared to undertake the design of a theater in the ancient manner when, a few years after the publication of the first edition of the Barbaro Vitruvius, he was called on to create a theater *all'antica* for his hometown, Vicenza. It would not be a stone theater, as described by Vitruvius, but a temporary one of wood, of the type Barbaro had described in his Vitruvius commentaries, based upon Barbaro's copious readings in Roman history.[16]

THEATERS OF ANDREA PALLADIO: VICENZA, 1561–1562

Vicenza in the sixteenth century was controlled by Venice, which sent members of its patriciate to run the city's affairs. Members of the local aristocracy banded together to form the Accademia Olimpica, which promoted the study and enjoyment of things ancient, including drama. Palladio was so respected for his architectural abilities and knowledge of antiquity that he

FIG. 81 Alessandro Maganza (attrib.), *Sofonisba, 1562*, fresco, Vicenza, Teatro Olimpico, 1590s (Photo: Ralph Lieberman)

was invited to become a member of the academy, even though he was not noble. For the carnival seasons of 1561 and 1562, Palladio constructed for the Accademia Olimpica a temporary theater in the enormous main *salone* of the gothic town hall, the Basilica (Fig. 79). His theater was dismantled after its use and then reassembled the following year, "enlarged and much more richly decorated and furnished."[17] As we know from contemporary documents, Palladio's theater was semicircular, with stepped seats and a stage with a *scenae frons*. The *salone* of the Basilica is of such grand proportions that the theater would perhaps have seemed to be outdoors. Two contemporary plays were presented in subsequent years: Alessandro Piccolomini's comedy, *Amor Costante*, and Giangiorgo Trissino's tragedy, *Sofonisba*. Trissino was the noble Vicentine humanist who had "discovered" Palladio, given him his new "ancient" name, and taken him to Rome to study ancient buildings.

Two frescoes in the vestibule of the later Teatro Olimpico, Vicenza, record, at least to some extent, the appearance of Palladio's theaters of 1561–62. Because the paintings date from the 1590s,[18] thirty years or so after the theaters had disappeared and more than a decade after the death of the architect, one has to take their evidence with a caution that is justified when we compare them to a contemporary written description. The frescoes, *en grisaille*, both bear the date of 1562, inaccurate in the case of *Amor Costante*. Attributed to Alessandro Maganza, the quickly painted pictures are not of the highest quality; nor is their state of preservation all one might wish. The misdated painting labeled *Amor Cost* (Fig. 80) shows an oblique view of the stage with two actors posed against rows of sparsely populated curving seats, with a group of women seated below on risers in the orchestra. Based on evidence from the later Teatro Olimpico, these ladies presumably were the wives of members of the Accademia Olimpica. Above the seats rises a Vitruvian colonade into which statues are inserted under swags hanging from the entablature. The *scenae frons* is articulated by pairs of Corinthian columns that flank the central portal and frame statues. Inside the central arch is a partial view of the perspectival set that depicts the houses of a city.

The second and correctly dated painting, labeled *Sofonisba*, (Fig. 81) shows several actors in front of the *scenae frons*, again articulated by pairs of Corinthian columns that support projecting segments of the entablature. A second, shorter level, also with paired columns, rises above the first, and the surface of the *frons* carries numerous small scenes in relief. Between the two actors at center stage one glimpses the perspectival set of a city behind the central arch. From the frescoes we learn nothing of how the stage and the cavea, or seating area, were connected. The paintings also fail to provide a good sense of the size of the theater in relation to human scale. According to contemporary sources, the stage was about 16.7 m wide and 13.6 m tall. The columns of the lower level were approximately 5 m tall and those of the second level 4 m.[19]

Lionello Puppi discovered a written account of the theater as it existed in 1562, composed by Paolo Chiappini, secretary of the Accademia Olimpica.[20] The text, although fragmentary, provides a clear picture of certain aspects of the richly decorated and colorful stage. There were two levels of columns, Corinthian below and Composite above, with gilded capitals and bases and pedestals. On each level were twenty-four half-columns, painted to resemble speckled Numidian marble, which is generally yellow. The two superimposed sets of columns carried two gilded entablatures, the upper of which ran around the entire theater. This detail tells us that Palladio followed the Vitruvian dictum that the top of the cavea behind the seats should be at the same height as the top of the *scenae frons*. Flanking each door of the *scenae frons* were paired columns, and between columns were niches containing life-size statues painted to resemble bronze. Above each statue was a *faux* relief, painted in green to resemble weathered bronze. On each level there were sixteen statues and sixteen reliefs. There were three doors in the back wall, the central larger than the other two, and there was also a door in each of the side walls of the stage. Actors used all these doors. From this information it is possible to make a schematic reconstruction of the theater (Figs. 82 and 83). Each side wall was pierced by one door flanked by pairs of columns with niches between them. Single columns occupied the corners of the stage, or else were located in the *scenae frons* close to the corners. Then, moving toward center stage, came a niche, then two pairs of columns flanking a side door of the *scenae frons*, with a niche between each pair, then another niche, a single column, another niche, and finally the pair of columns flanking the central, larger door, with a niche between those columns as well.[21] Thus twelve columns and eight niches on either side of the central door. That door was given special emphasis by placing above it a painting of life-size figures, made to look like gilded bronze; by inserting painted Victorys alongside the arch; and by hanging the device of the Accademia Olimpico from the center of the arch.

The later fresco of *Sofonisba* (Fig. 81) gives some of these details, but as a whole it does not accord well with the description of Chiappini, and so the

FIG. 82 Andrea Palladio, theater of 1562, Vicenza, schematic digital reconstruction (Drawing: Benjamin Hoyle)

FIG. 83 Andrea Palladio, theater of 1562, Vicenza, schematic digital reconstruction (Drawing: Benjamin Hoyle)

fresco is unreliable. Palladio's illustration of the *scenae frons* from the Barbaro Vitruvius of 1556 (Fig. 78) accords much better with what Chiappini recorded: the two levels of columns with bases and pedestals, the alternation of paired and single columns, statues in niches alternating with columns, relief panels over the statues, a large figurative panel over the central door, perspectival views inside the arches of the doors. The theater in Vicenza lacked the niches into which Palladio inserted the doors in his reconstruction plan of the Vitruvian theater, but otherwise, there seems to be a remarkable concordance between the two designs. Indeed, a later chronicler, a native of Vicenza, stated that Palladio had deliberately recalled the local Teatro Barga, on which he had based his reconstruction in Barbaro's book, in his design for the Teatro Olimpico.[22]

Chiappini described in particular detail the perspectives placed behind the doors. Inside the right door (stage right?) was a view of houses, inside the left a landscape, and inside the doors at the sides more houses. His description of what stood inside the central door is missing from the manuscript, but one can assume with some certainty that there was a perspective view of a city street. These perspectives were not painted, he wrote, but mostly in relief. The floors of the perspective were painted with squares that grew smaller as the perspective narrowed. "They carried the eyes of the spectators into the distance remarkably, and all in the shortest space."[23] That "shortest space" was probably an inclined planar surface enriched with painted squares for the pavement and flanked by buildings rendered in relief.

THEATERS OF ANDREA PALLADIO: VENICE, 1565

In Venice for the carnival of 1565 Palladio designed a temporary theater for the Compagnia degli Accesi, the last of the *compagnie della calza*.[24] The creation of the theater was not without pain for Palladio, who wrote to a Vicentine client, Vincenzo Arnaldi, on February 2: "I have seen to making this blessed Theater, in which I have paid penance for all the sins I have committed and will commit." But Palladio took pride in his design: "Next Tuesday the Tragedy will be performed, when your lordship will be able to see it. I would exhort you to come, because one hopes that it should be a rare thing."[25] The tragedy in question was *Antigono*, written by the Conte da Monte, a gentleman and medical doctor of Vicenza. According to one contemporary, the tragedy, a bloody tale set in ancient Jerusalem, did not "much satisfy."[26]

Where the theater may have been located is not clear;[27] nor do we have preserved visual evidence. Aspects of its appearance, noted by contemporaries, allow us to piece together something of what it looked like, although we do not have a sufficiently detailed description to attempt a schematic reconstruction like the one proposed for the theater of 1562 in Vicenza (Figs. 82 and 83). Vasari, who could have gotten details from Palladio, described the Venetian theater as "a half theater of wood in the manner of a colosseum,"[28] a statement that the astute Nicola Mangini took to mean a semicircular building with stepped seats.[29] Francesco Sansovino, the indefatigable contemporary describer of late sixteenth century Venice, tells us that "the theater was most capacious, able to hold many thousands of persons, in front of whom was the very rich scene, resembling a city, with beautiful orders of columns and other perspectives, which was marvelous to see."[30] Sansovino doubtless exaggerated the size; "many thousands of people" would require a theater as big as the current Metropolitan Opera in New York.[31] A third contemporary observer, the Medici agent Cosimo Bartoli, reported to Florence, "It is true that they had made a theater and scenery of wood very rich with columns, steps and statues."[32] Vasari also says that Palladio had the painter Federigo Zuccaro make for the theater "twelve large histories, seven and a half feet on a side, with infinite other things of the deeds of Ircano, King of Jerusalem, according to the subject of the tragedy."[33] These paintings do not survive.

The theater, then, was wooden, half-round, with steps for seating. In front of the audience was a scene with many columns and perspectives. The scene resembled a city. Statues decorated the theater, as did the twelve large paintings by Federigo Zuccaro. The dimensions of the twelve large paintings provide a starting point for trying to ascertain the theater's size. Mancini, Muraro, and Povoledo sensibly suggested that the paintings were hung on the outer circumference of the half-circle, where they could easily be seen and where they would give the audience a foretaste of the little-known story presented on stage.[34] One might add that covering the exterior with paintings would have saved the time and expense of creating an elaborately articulated exterior in the ancient manner for the theater. They hypothesize, on the basis of a width of 2.6 m per canvas, a theater with a half-circular exterior of perhaps 36 m, which would give a radius of roughly 11.5 m for the depth of the seats. Adding more space for the stage, they believe that the theater would have occupied a rectangular area roughly 25 × 18.5 m. While there is no way to prove this hypothesis, it seems sensible, although one has to leave open the possibility that the theater was half-oval rather than semicircular in plan. Palladio's Teatro Olimpico, of roughly similar size (the *scenae frons* is 25 m wide), has a half-oval plan, as we shall see.

Sansovino's description of the stage is confusing. His "beautiful orders of columns" suggests a columniated *scenae frons* with two levels, like those of Palladio's theaters of 1561–62 or the Olimpico, but "the very rich scene, resembling a city" sounds much more like the kind of perspectival view of an urban space that we know from the illustrations in Serlio. One would seem to exclude the possibility of the other. Palladio, however, had already suggested a way to fuse the two theatrical traditions of the *scenae frons* of antiquity with the perspective urban view of his day. Included, as we know, in the illustrations of the Barbaro/Palladio Vitruvius editions are plans of a Roman theater (Fig. 76) after Vitruvius, and an elevation of a *scenae frons* erected on its plan (Fig. 78). Here we find a two-story wall, articulated by engaged columns and pierced by doors through which one glimpses the streets of a city. The "rich scene" of which Sansovino and Cosimo Bartoli spoke must have looked something like this, just as the *scenae frons* of Palladio's theaters in Vicenza also resembled it. The statues only mentioned by Bartoli quite likely stood in niches, as they did in the printed Vitruvius illustration and the theaters of 1561–62 and 1580.

Daniele Barbaro's comments on and Palladio's graphic reconstructions of Vitruvius's text were hard won. Surely Palladio made use of those achievements in his design for the Venetian theater of 1565. The audience included people who knew both Palladio and Barbaro, and many knew their collaborative publication of Vitruvius, which had been issued in Venice.[35] For both men, the temptation to bring into three dimensions what had been confined to a few pages of text and illustration must have been overwhelming. The presence of the book doubtless influenced the choice of Palladio to design the theater. Unfortunately, it was only a temporary structure, of which no visual traces are known.[36]

THEATERS OF ANDREA PALLADIO: TEATRO OLIMPICO, VICENZA, 1580–1585

Those who have visited the Teatro Olimpico know what a magical place it is (Fig. 84). The survival of the Olimpico is something of a miracle. Palladio's other

FIG. 84 Andrea Palladio, Teatro Olimpico, 1580–85, view of interior from level of peristyle (Photo: Ralph Lieberman)

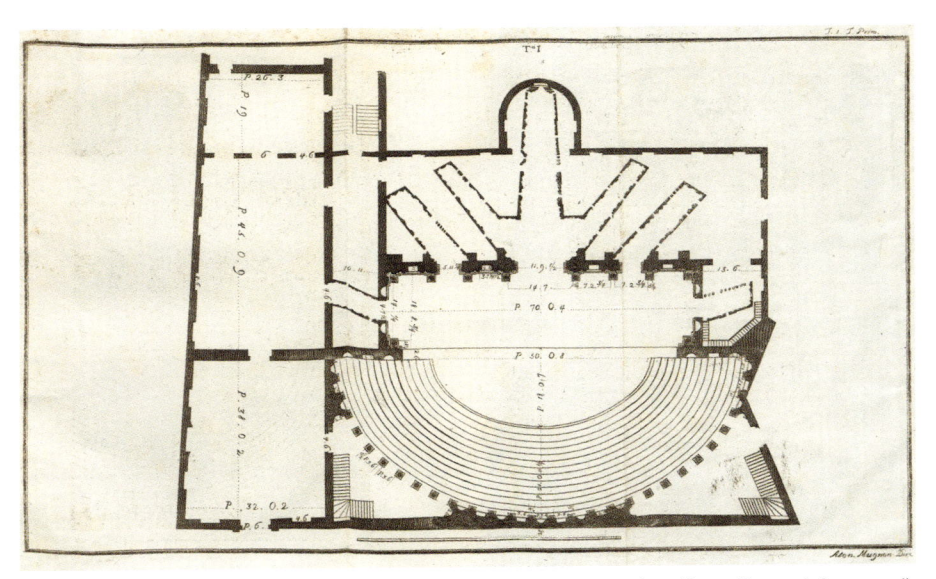

FIG. 85 Andrea Palladio, Teatro Olimpico, Vicenza, 1580–85, plan (from Bertotti Scamozzi) (Photo: Author. Art in the public domain)

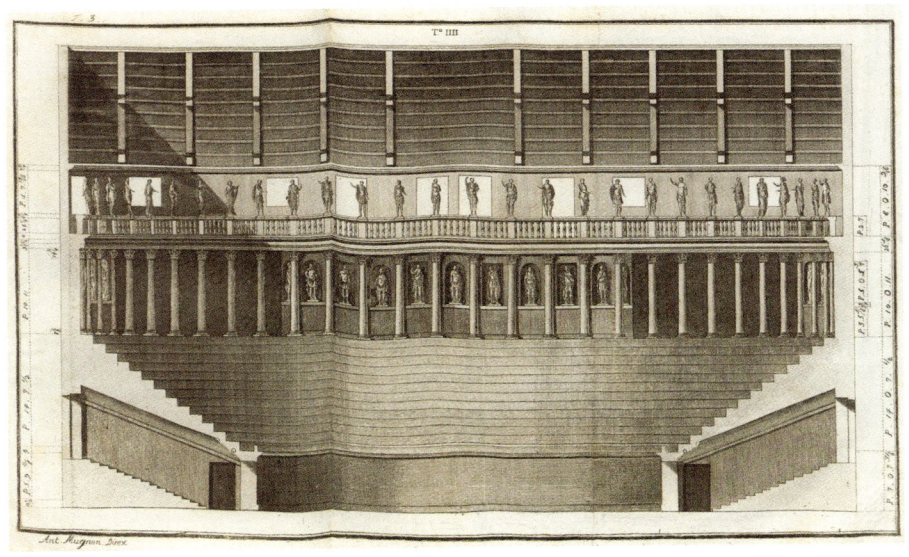

FIG. 86 Andrea Palladio, Teatro Olimpico, view of cavea from stage (from Bertotti Scamozzi) (Photo: Author. Art in the public domain)

theaters were temporary; this one was not. The fact that it was meant to be permanent hardly assured its survival, however. Disuse – it saw performances only rarely until the later nineteenth and twentieth centuries – promoted preservation. The theater also endured as a source of civic pride; important visitors to Vicenza were honored within its walls more frequently than theatrical performances were

FIG. 87 Andrea Palladio, Teatro Olimpico, interior from stage (Photo: Ralph Lieberman)

FIG. 88 Teatro Olimpico, "Pianta del Teatro," detail of Fig. 97

given on its stage.[37] It is wrong, however, to call the Olimpico the first permanent theater since antiquity, as many scholars have done. The theaters of Alfonso I d'Este in Ferrara (see Chapter 1) and of Giovanni Battista Bertani in Mantua (see Chapter 5) preceded it, but both were destroyed by fire.

FIG. 89 Andrea Palladio, Teatro Olimpico, stairs leading from peristyle level to balustrade level (Photo: Ralph Lieberman)

The Accademia Olimpica commissioned the theater from their fellow member, Palladio, in 1580, the year he died; completion fell to other hands. Beset by financial difficulties, construction proceeded fitfully. The hotly contested choice of an opening play was not made until the spring of 1584: Sophocles' *Oedipus Rex* in a new Italian translation.[38] Aristotle considered the play the greatest of all tragedies; that opinion loomed large in the choice. Vincenzo Scamozzi, principal architect of the Veneto after Palladio's death, was hired to complete the perspectival scenery that would extend behind the doors in the *scenae frons*. At Scamozzi's urging, additional land was acquired behind the stage, so that the perspectives of the set could be extended into real space, rather than remain on flat surfaces (Fig. 85). At the last minute, the theater almost did not open. Theatrical events were in bad odor in Venice, where the performance in Vicenza had to be approved and where Jesuits, who had the ears of the old men who ran the city, invariably opposed such entertainments. The Rectors of Vicenza, Venetian patricians appointed to run the city, wrote to the Council of Ten in Venice, asking whether it would

FIG. 90 Andrea Palladio, Teatro Olimpico, balustrade level (Photo: Ralph Lieberman)

be permissible for the performance to go ahead, citing the respectability of the members of the Accademia Olimpica, the great expense that had been faced in preparing a "most sumptuous" theater, and the many foreigners who had come to Vicenza to enjoy the play. The Ten kicked the question upstairs to the Senate, which decided by a large majority that the play should go on.[39] It could have gone either way. At roughly the same time, one recalls, the Ten took the extraordinary step of ordering the total destruction of the two Venetian comedy theaters with boxes (see Chapter 5).

The plan (Fig. 85) of the Olimpico shows it divided into two parts: cavea and stage.[40] Most seating was on thirteen steps arranged in a half-oval, rather than a half-circle, to make the space for the audience fit the restricted site (Figs. 86 and 87). At the top of the steps rises a Corinthian peristyle (Fig. 86), appropriately Vitruvian, with the ten columns in its middle engaged to a wall with niches that are partly carved out of the exterior rear wall (Fig. 85). The legend written on a small plan that accompanies a view of the stage made in 1620 (Fig. 88) notes the acoustical importance of the columns, described as "Loggie per ritener le voci" (loggias to retain the voice). In the niches of the peristyle stand statues of members of the Accademia, dressed in ancient armor (Fig. 87). Stairs lead from the back corners of the peristyle (Figs. 88 and 89) to a final level, at the edge of which is a balustrade with statues that stand over the axes of the columns below and reach toward a flat ceiling, now painted to resemble

FIG. 91 Teatro Olimpico, exterior, southeast façade on Stradella del Teatro Olimpico (Photo: Ralph Lieberman)

the sky (Fig. 90). The direct connection of the upper levels with the exterior wall forced the construction of a balcony outside the building to make possible movement from one side of the balustrade level to the other[41] (Figs. 91 and 92).

Circulation in the theater seems to have been carefully considered. The small plan at the bottom left corner of the print of 1620 (Fig. 88) shows doors at either side of the peristyle level, marked G and labeled "Porte per l'entrate" (doors for entrance), that appear to have been the primary means of entrance for the majority of the audience, who would have descended the steps of the oval seating area or else would have climbed the stairs in the corners to reach the balustrade, or top level. Crossover from one side to the other was only possible along the steps of the cavea or by using the exterior balcony that connected the two sides of the balustrade level. Members of the Accademia, as we will see, had their own separate path to their seats in the orchestra.

FIG. 92 Andrea Palladio, Teatro Olimpico, longitudinal section (from Bertotti Scamozzi) (Photo: Author. Art in the public domain)

The circulation and seating arrangements (Figs. 84 and 86) give a particularly clear sense of how the class structure in a sixteenth century Italian city could be accommodated in a "copy" of an ancient theater – a situation not always noted in writings about the Olimpico. There are striking parallels between the arrangement of the audience by class in the Vicentine theater of 1537 by Serlio and those in Palladio's Olimpico (see Chapter 3). The peristyle and balustrade levels offered spaces for those whose low socioeconomic status barred them from sitting on the steps. The legend for the plan in the lower right corner of the view dated 1620 (Fig. 93) indicates that the area behind the columns of the peristyle was devoted to "Poggi per spettatori" (places for spectators). No seats were provided at these upper levels; presumably those relegated to the heights either brought their own stools or stood. They at least had a better view of the stage than those seated at the far edges of the steps, whose view was partially obsructed by a wall (Fig. 94). Windows at the level of the balustrade (Figs. 86, 87, and 90) ventilated the interior, allowing the noxious body odors that offended Daniele Barbaro to escape, as well as smoke from the oil lamps that illuminated, deliberately dimly, the interior of the cavea.

The stepped seating of the cavea accommodated those whose social status lay midway between the poor and the most important aristocrats and visitors. The steps accommodated the largest part of the audience, which included both citizens of Vicenza and citizens of nearby cities, who apparently flocked to Vicenza to see the play and the new theater. Mazzoni estimates that perhaps 1,500 people were present for the performance. No provision to seat women

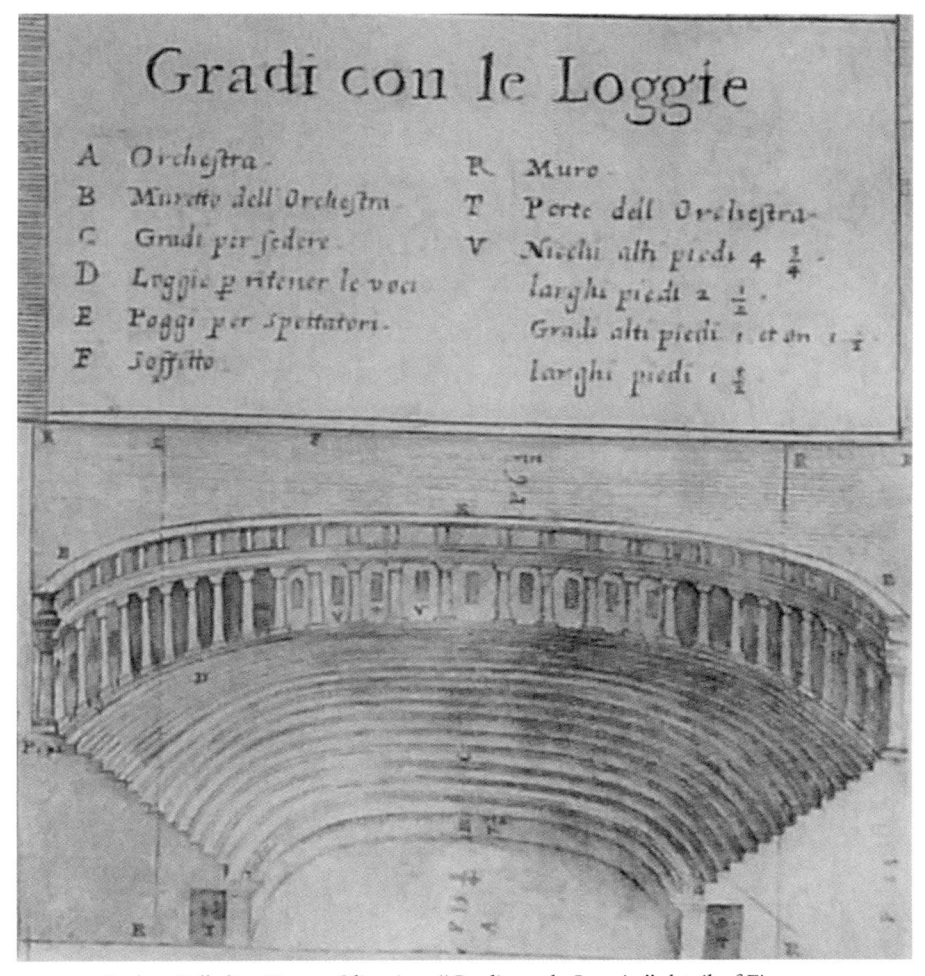

FIG. 93 Andrea Palladio, Teatro Olimpico, "Gradi con le Loggie," detail of Fig. 97

separately on the steps is mentioned in the preserved documentation, but a section must have been set aside for them.

The half-oval orchestra held the most important spectators: members of the Accademia and their wives, the Venetian aristocrats who governed the city, as well as the most important "foreigners" (Figs. 92 and 93). Two separate sets of stairs, visible in Bertotti Scamozzi's view of the cavea (Fig. 86), led directly down to the level of the orchestra to allow the particularly privileged to take their seats without having to make their way through the mob. Risers set at the rear of the orchestra served to seat women, as was the apparent case in Palladio's theater of 1562 (Fig. 80), with the men occupying benches between the women and the stage. No woman was allowed to enter the orchestra until the wife of the prince of the Academy had taken her seat. The Capitana, wife of the Venetian governor, received pride of place on the risers, but she was not

FIG. 94 Palladio, Teatro Olimpico, view of stage right side of interior (Photo: Ralph Lieberman)

granted first entrance. This whole VIP crew arrived only shortly before the performance began, when the curtain fell to reveal the stage, admittedly very different from our practice today. In the following century the physical seating apparently changed (Fig. 95), but the function of the orchestra remained the same.

The stage itself is a rectangle with doors at each narrow end and three doors in the *scenae frons* (Figs. 96 and 97). The wider and taller central, or "royal," door is arched, while the lower side doors are topped by flat entablatures. Scamozzi widened the doors flanking the royal door and extended the side walls (and the depth of the stage) to make room for the doors at the narrow ends and to make his sets behind them more visible.[42] The wall of the *scenae frons* is articulated on the lower level by free-standing columns flanking niches containing sculptures. The columns of the lower level support free-standing statues set in front of bundles of half columns that frame more niches that hold more statues. These present additional members of the Accademia, in ancient armor, each member paying for his own statue. Finally, an attic story, graced by alternating statues and reliefs, intervenes below the ceiling.[43]

As Vitruvius recommended, and Palldio carried out in Vicenza in 1561–62 (Figs. 82 and 83), the upper entablature of the stage runs around the entire interior of the theater. Palladio, however, took this method of unification to a new level by making the three levels of the *scenae frons* correspond to the three levels devoted to the audience. The cornice of the lowest level of the stage set

FIG. 95 G. Ruffoni, Teatro Olimpico, Vicenza, view of cavea and orchestra in 1650. The ceiling, with birds flying, may not be original (Biblioteca Comunale Bertoliana, Vicenza, Acc. O.3[36])

reaches the same height as the top of the seats. The statues with niches and engaged Corinthian columns of the second level are repeated in illusionistic frescoes on the walls at the ends of the seats and then continue into the peristyle level with its niches (Fig. 94). The statues at the top level of the *scenae frons* are also repeated in paint at the tops of the walls at the ends of the seat and then continue in the statues that crown the balustrade. Thus did Palladio create a marvelous unity of space for performance and audience to echo the unity of time and space in the tragedy of *Oedipus*.

The present ceiling above the stage is elaborately coffered, just as it appears in the earliest known view of the stage, dated 1620 (Fig. 97). Although it cannot be demonstrated that this drawing records the ceiling over the stage intended by Palladio, it also cannot be conclusively shown that it is unfaithful to his design. Daniel McReynolds has given us a detailed account of the problems faced by the Academy in the eighteenth century, when it sought to return the ceiling over the stage to its "original" appearance.[44] Those who believed that the drawing recorded that appearance pointed to the usefulness of the coffered ceiling as a sounding board for the actors' voices. Those who denied the reliability of the image pointed to the awkward, unclassically great distance the entablature, separating the ceiling of the stage from that over the audience, had to span. The eighteenth century architect Tomaso Temanza,

FIG. 96 Palladio, Teatro Olimpico, view of stage (Photo: Ralph Lieberman)

citing three madrigals published in 1586 and dedicated to Leonardo Valmarana, prince of the Academy, argued that the whole interior was covered with a cloth that represented the night sky.[45]

Ancient theaters, open to the heavens, had no ceilings over their stages. Palladio's Olimpico, like his other theaters, is an indoor space that conforms to contemporary usage and the north Italian climate at the time of carnival. It is small, in comparison to ancient theaters, and semiprivate, designed to accommodate a select audience. It is a pretend, or "theatrical" ancient theater, where present time and multiple past times overlie each other. To enter the theater today is to slip into a Renaissance fantasy of antiquity – to pass through one distant historical time into an even more remote one. In the production of *Oedipus* actors costumed in a mixture of ancient and contemporary dress, accompanied by contemporary music, performed a contemporary Italian translation of an ancient Greek tragedy in a theater based on Roman examples (but built with cheaper materials) and fitted out with perspective scenery that incorporated the latest Renaissance concepts of the depiction of space. Such play with overlapping historical styles and techniques was common in Renaissance art.[46]

Currently, the tourist entrance to the Teatro Olimpico is through a garden that offers no clue to the location of the interior. The theater was built on the site of an old prison; the sense of how the earlier and later structures may have related to each other is not entirely clear. There is a façade, however (Figs. 91 and 98), that presents a rather blank, planar face to a narrow urban street. The stucco covering of the wall, carefully scored to resemble ashlar, could go back

FIG. 97 Iseppo Scolari (after Ottavio Bruti Revese) proscenium and stage of Teatro Olimpico, 1620, engraving (Vicenza, Pinacoteca Civica di Palazzo Chiericati, inv. B. 2086)

to the sixteenth century, even though it has a certain neoclassical air. Certainly numerous buildings by Palladio have similar surface treatment. A small addition to the theater with a rusticated door, erected to the left of this façade surely in the sixteenth century[47] (Fig. 98), allows entrance into rooms adjoining the theater, indicated on the plan to the left of the oval seating of the interior (Fig. 85). These meeting rooms of the Academy, frescoed in the late sixteenth century (Figs. 80 and 81), served as a public entrance to the auditorium, as, presumably, did the other doors at ground level.

On stage Scamozzi's deep perspectives are warm in color, to contrast with the all-white *scenae frons*[48] (Fig. 99). In Palladio's earlier Vicentine theaters, the architectural elements of the stage were multicolored, to imitate varieties of marble and sculptural materials. One wonders whether the whiteness of the stage walls at the Olimpico was Palladio's original choice, or whether Scamozzi may have decided to make a contrast between the stage and his perspectival sets. These, three-dimensional rather than painted, have the extraordinary effect of transforming people into giants who grow ever larger in relation to the houses as they move toward the ends of the perspectival streets (Fig. 100). Painted *periaktoi* could never have accomplished this visual trick. Behind the central door the perspective splits into three streets, whereas the other doors in the *scenae frons* open onto single streets (Fig. 96). No one in the audience can see the entire effect of all of the streets at once. They are laid out to give partial satisfaction to many, but complete satisfaction to none. Even those sitting in the choicest seats in the very center of the steps cannot look down the total distance of every street. In a court theater, such multiplication of vanishing points would not have occurred. The ruler would have had the choice seat, focused on the single vanishing point, and that would have been that. Other members of the audience would have had views of the sets that became

FIG. 98 Teatro Olimpico, exterior of building with a rusticated portal added to theater (by Scamozzi?) in sixteenth century (Photo: Henry Schmidt)

increasingly distorted as their seats moved farther and farther from the central axis of the theater. Scamozzi's multiple, partial views were an attempt to eliminate this problem created by sets based on a single vanishing point.

In this theater that gave incomplete views to many, only the effigy of the prince of the Academy (not the man himself) had a privileged, fixed position at one end of the central axis (Fig. 96). Mazzoni believes that Leonardo Valmarana's statue, in the central niche of the peristyle (Fig. 87), shows him in the guise of the Hapsburg Emperor Charles V.[49] Valmarana received an annual pension from Philip II of Spain, Charles's son and heir. Although Vicenza had been under Venetian rule since 1404, many of the local aristocrats still felt a strong allegiance to the Hapsburgs of the Holy Roman Empire and Spain. Directly opposite Valmarana's statue, at the far end of the central perspectival street, once rose an equestrian statue atop a triumphal arch, surely a stand-in for the Holy Roman Emperor[50] (Fig. 100). To the observant, the Teatro Olimpico was a thumb in the eye of the ruling Serenissima.

Music, both vocal and instrumental, was by the Venetian composer Andrea Gabrieli. Performed offstage at the beginning of the first act before and after the curtain fell, and at the end of each act, the music was designed to further the meaning of the play rather than to accompany traditional intermedi that contrasted with the action of the drama. The singers and instrumentalists were placed behind the stage-right wall of the *scenae frons*, where they could easily be heard and where they could all see each other (Fig. 85) (no orchestra pit as yet). The director, a Venetian named Angelo Ingengnieri, made a sketch on which he indicated the position of people on stage at an early moment in the first

FIG. 99 Teatro Olimpico, Vincenzo Scamozzi, detail of scenery, 1584–85, viewed through Royal Door (Photo: Ralph Lieberman)

act.[51] Dots indicate their entrance from stage left and their arrangement in a semicircle at center stage. Two altars, surrounded by steps, flanked the central arch. Members of the chorus sat on these steps. Oedipus the King made his entrance through the "royal" arch into the midst of this group. The view of the stage of 1620 (Fig. 97) contains a pavement of geometric shapes that Mazzoni believes Ingegnieri used to remind the large cast where each of them was to stand – an ingenious solution to blocking scenes with many participants, most of whom were amateurs.[52]

Vicenza was crowded with visitors come from afar for the play. It wasn't every day that someone in the sixteenth century could attend a performance of perhaps the most famous play of antiquity in a new theater in the ancient style. Although the play did not begin until 7 p.m., people started arriving as early as 10 in the morning. What they did for nine hours, while they waited, is not clear. Contemporary sources make no mention of sanitary facilities. Lower-class members of the audience, standing or sitting on the levels of the peristyle or balustrade, had only partial views of the already-fragmented views of the

FIG. 100 Teatro Olimpico, central street of set with equestrian statue (of Charles V?) at end, detail of Fig. 97

perspectival sets (Figs. 84 and 101). More privileged members of the audience, seated on the hard wooden steps, encountered serious discomfort from the knees of people behind them. The members of the Accademia, accompanied by their wives and their distinguished guests, made their entrance into the commodious orchestra just before the performance began. Thus the academicians simultaneously put themselves on view in the flesh and, for posterity, in the statues on the *scenae frons* and the peristyle.

FIG. 101 Teatro Olimpico, stage from balustrade level (Photo: Ralph Lieberman)

The *coup du théâtre* of the fall of the curtain was breathtaking. First sweet music and sweet odors filled the house. Trumpets blew, guns fired, and suddenly a curtain that concealed the full width of the stage fell down and disappeared (where it went is not mentioned in the sources). The auditorium had been kept in low light. The stage was revealed brilliantly lit by a dazzling golden light. Oil lamps, with brass reflectors, were arranged above the stage in a hidden line just behind the curtain, at the point where the ceiling over the stage joined the ceiling over the audience. Additional lights were concealed in the perspectival scenes to illuminate the streets of Thebes. Scamozzi seems to have been responsible for the lighting as well as the perspectives. He was only one of the vast group of collaborators who put the performance together: the translator, the costume designer, the director, the composer, the musicians, the actors, the stagehands, the members of the Academy who guarded the doors.

Sadly, Palladio did not live to see the success these collaborators brought to his theater. The triumphant opening of the Teatro Olimpico, however, brought down the curtain on the Renaissance urge to reconstruct an ancient theater almost whole. The immediate innovative future of Italian theater architecture lay in the hands of princely rulers, who were less interested in ancient drama than in creating spectacles of musical performances on stage interspersed with performances of armored knights in combat, all to further their own political ends.

7

DRAMA-TOURNEY THEATERS

FERRARA, *IL CASTELLO DI GORGOFERUSA*, 1561

The courts of northeastern Italy remained hotbeds of theatrical development in the late sixteenth and seventeenth centuries. Alfonso II d'Este, last duke of Ferrara, was an avid promoter of theatrical activities.[1] On March 3, 1561 Ferrara saw the production of a particularly lavish and novel version of the tourney, an aristocratic entertainment that went back in time at least to the twelfth century.[2] Knights in combat traditionally were the central feature of tourneys, but *Il castello di Gorgoferusa*, commissioned by Alfonso, combined battles or jousts with musical interludes set in elaborate scenery. The show started a new taste for hybrid entertainments produced as court spectacles.

This Ferrarese tourney marks the beginning of the most mature phase of what one might call "drama-tourneys."[3] As Elena Povoledo pointed out, such tourneys often shared many or all of certain performative and spatial characteristics: a knightly combat presented as a ballet of horsemen; grand entrances for the combatants; a central, generally rectangular field of combat surrounded by structures that held the audience; separate seating for the judges and authorities; one or two stages at the short ends with perspectival scenery; and dramatic productions with actors, dancers, and musicians.[4] The architectural focus of such arrangements could not have been clear, unless certain elements were suppressed in favor of others. At Ferrara they were.

Presented during the carnival of 1561 to celebrate the elevation of the duke's brother, Luigi, to the cardinalate,[5] the Ferrarese drama-tourney took place in the same courtyard of the Ducal Palace in which Ercole I had presented Plautus' *Menaechmi* in 1487 (see Chapter 1). A stage was built against the north side and seating was arranged in the shape of an ancient semicircular theater, with an open, rectangular space left at ground level between the seating and the stage. That space became a defining characteristic of drama-tourney theaters. The tourney was presented, then, in an updated version of an ancient theater, into which an utterly anachronistic medieval spectacle was inserted, as had already been the case with the Bertani theater in Mantua of a decade earlier. To this mixture of ancient and medieval practices a modern stage with fabulously complex scenery was added. The performance ended with the total simultaneous collapse of the set, largely composed of rocky towers. Action on stage and combats on the theater's floor alternated during the show. Fireworks brought it to a brilliant close.

VINCENZO SCAMOZZI, ODEON, SABBIONETA

Vespasiano Gonzaga, Duke of Sabbioneta, bore the name of a Roman emperor. A member of a cadet branch of the Gonzaga family of Mantua, Vespasiano, with more ambition than means, created for himself on the southwestern border of the Gonzaga realm a major example of Renaissance urban planning: an ideal capital city. He laid out a walled town with a grid plan centered on a piazza dominated by the Ducal Palace and the cathedral (Fig. 102). Inside the west wall of the city he raised a fortress that no longer stands. Between the piazza and the fortress he built, beginning in 1588, the earliest free-standing theater building with an architect-designed exterior that has come down to us, with the possible exception of the façade of the Teatro Olimpico. In contemporary documents Vespasiano's theater is called the Odeon, a Greek term for a building for musical performances and poetry readings.[6] In the design for the theater, Vincenzo Scamozzi, the leading architect of the Veneto after the death of Palladio, faced the challenge of creating an exterior appropriate to a building type developed over the preceding 100 years for performances largely mounted inside already existing structures.[7]

The Odeon, a rectangular solid apparently of two stories, occupies the western end of a block of the regular city plan (Figs. 103 and 104). Relentlessly symmetrical, the block has three bays on the north and south ends and nine on the long western side. The corners and the openings in the ground floor are rusticated, while the *piano nobile* is articulated by pairs of Roman Doric pilasters that flank windows that have alternating triangular and broken segmental pediments. Three doors, one in the center of each façade, provide entrances. The string course that separates the stories bears the repeated motto "ROMA

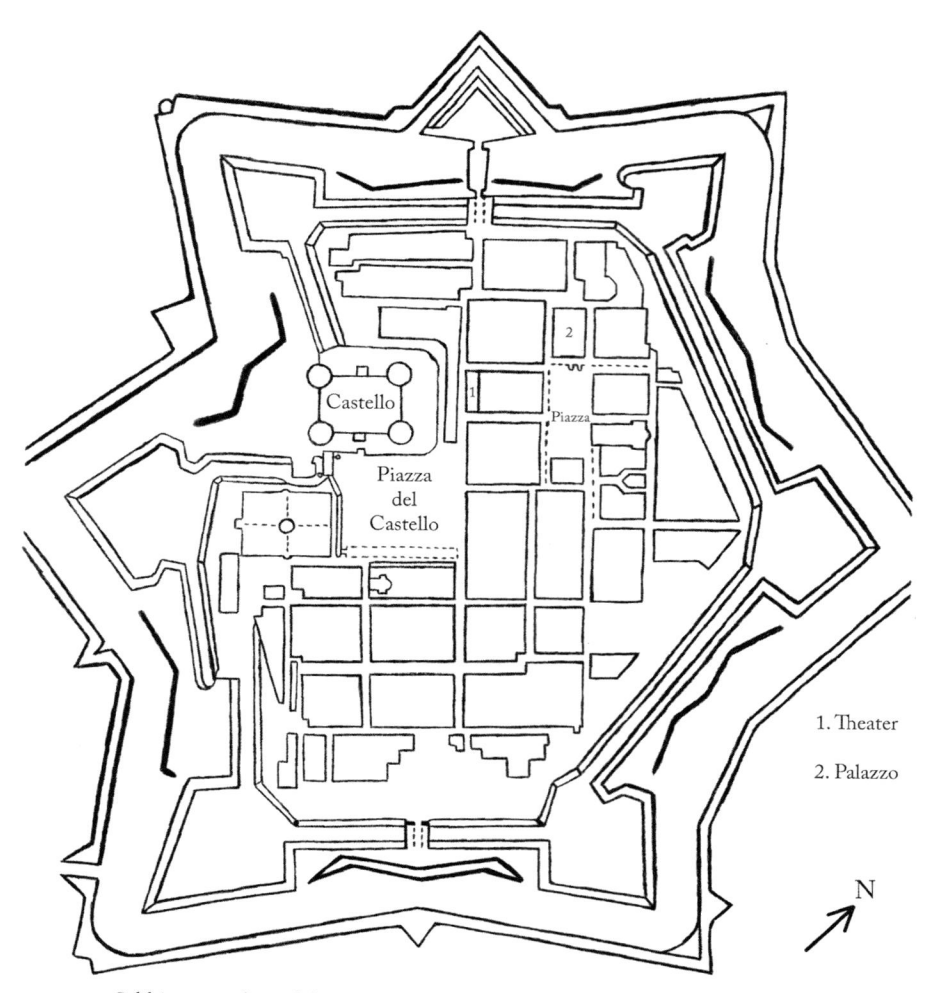

FIG. 102 Sabbioneta, plan of the city (Drawing: Troy Sipprelle)

QUANTA FUIT IPSA RUINA DOCET" ("How great Rome was these ruins demonstrate"). The repeated, albeit enigmatic, inscription insistently connects the building, which bears a Greek name, to ancient Rome.[8]

Having no precedent to work with (at least that we know), Scamozzi based the design on a widely influential Roman palace, Donato Bramante's Palazzo Caprini in Rome of the first decade of the sixteenth century (Fig. 105). Bramante's design, built by a cardinal and then acquired by the famous painter Raphael, had come to be understood as an urban structure of importance.[9] Charles Burroughs has pointed to the importance of Bramante's use of what Vitruvius called the "masculine" Doric order on the Palazzo Caprini.[10] Vespasiano was an avid student of Vitruvius. The masculinity of the order may have been important to a man who took pride in his accomplishments as a *condottiere* and who consistently had himself portrayed in armor. Inside the

FIG. 103 Vincenzo Scamozzi, Odeon, Sabbioneta, exterior from northwest, 1588–90. The small extension to the left of the short façade contains the staircase that leads to the upper level of the interior reserved for the duke and his party (Photo: Ralph Lieberman)

theater, as we will see, Vespasiano surrounded himself with representations of Roman emperors, Hercules, and masculine Olympian deities. The masculine Doric probably also alluded to the contests between knights that took place on the floor of the theater (see later discussion). By occupying the entire side of a city block, the nobly articulated theater announced itself as a singularly important element in Vespasiano's urban scheme. In erecting a separate theater building as part of his new city, Vespasiano was following Vitruvius and

FIG. 104 Odeon, Sabbioneta, exterior from southwest (Photo: Ralph Lieberman)

Alberti, who stressed that theaters were important urban amenities. As far as we know, no theater of modern times had done this before. The exterior of the Teatro Olimpico, which Scamozzi obviously knew, received no such coherent treatment on all sides. The identical northern and southern façades obscure the fact that they served two purposes. The southern door was the entrance into the building for the performers, while the northern door was for the duke and his guests. The door in the middle of the long façade, identical in design to the other two, served as the entrance for knights who would do battle inside. The fourth side of the building, facing a courtyard, provided no entrance.

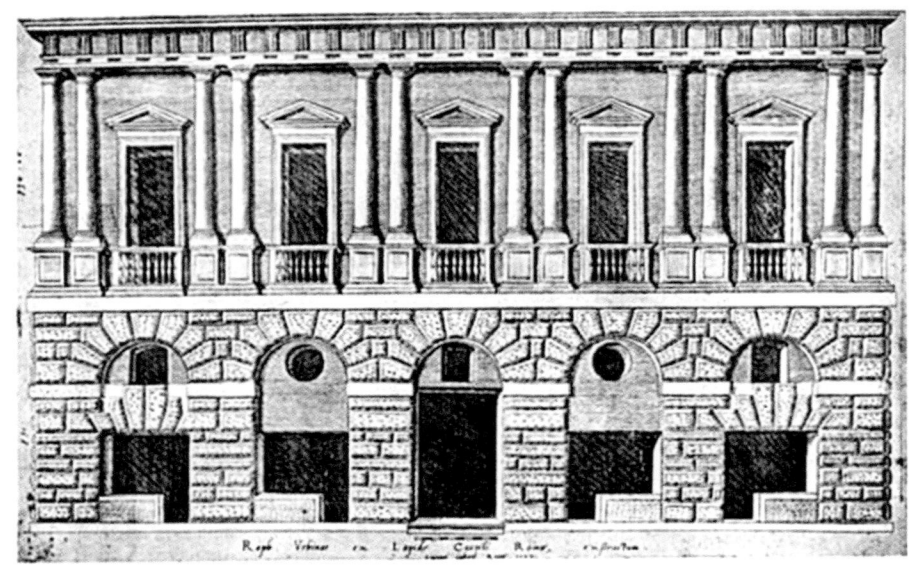

FIG. 105 Antonio Lafrery, elevation of Donato Bramante, Palazzo Caprini, later House of Raphael, Rome, first decade of sixteenth century, engraving (demolished) (Art in the public domain)

In plan, the Odeon is a long rectangle, with smaller spaces at the north and south ends that symmetrically frame the central space for performances (Figs. 106 and 107). The rooms at the north end were for the ruler and members of the audience, while the spaces at the south are designated in the drawing for the "Comici" below and the "Musici" above. There is no indication on the exterior of the disposition of the interior; the smaller rooms at the ends are superimposed into a two-story arrangement, while the central space occupies the full height of the structure. The deep stage, with a flat forestage for the actors laid out in front of a sloping floor that climbed between the buildings of a permanent set designed according to one-point perspective, was modeled on Serlio's stage for his theater in Vicenza of fifty years earlier[11] (Fig. 38).

There is notable correspondence between the articulation of the walls, as shown in Scamozzi's plan and section, and the exterior as built – note particularly the rustication sketched on the exteriors of the north and south walls.[12] But it is also clear that some changes were made in the plan during construction. Of the three doors in the plan that lead from the rooms on the north into the loggia, only the one at the top of the plan was constructed. The other two were replaced by frescos of Roman emperors. No door is shown in the center of the long wall, but that may be the result of taking the level of the plan through the upper story. Or of a later decision to insert a door in the long wall.

Amply lit by windows in the east and west walls, the remarkably well-preserved interior gives us the best experience we will ever have of a

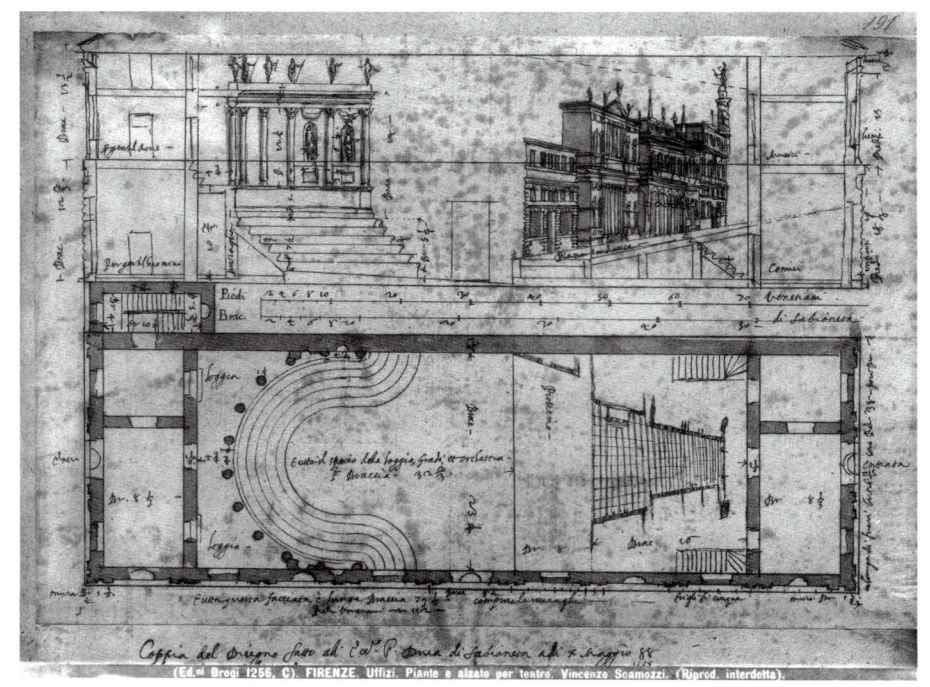

FIG. 106 Vincenzo Scamozzi, Odeon, longitudinal section and plan (Florence, Gabbinetto dei Disegni e Stampe degli Uffizi, UA 191. Signed and dated May 10, 1588) (Photo: Alinari, Art Resources, NY)

FIG. 107 Odeon, Sabbioneta, digital reconstruction of interior, looking west (Drawing: Benjamin Hoyle)

renaissance court theater (Fig. 108). Decorated with brightly colored frescos, the rectangular walls embrace a set of elegantly curved wooden steps that support a Corinthian peristyle over which statues of the Olympian gods rise free in space. Behind the gods, at the top of the walls, frescos of well-dressed contemporary people, standing behind balconies, suggest with their animated gestures the delight the theater offered those lucky enough to be invited (Fig. 109). Similar figures on both side walls surround the entire interior. All

DRAMA-TOURNEY THEATERS 159

FIG. 108 Scamozzi, Odeon, view of interior from stage (Photo: Ralph Lieberman)

together, these paintings of spectators looking down into the space of the theater turn the interior of the theater itself into a spectacle.[13]

The duke and and a small party sat on the upper level of the peristyle, which had its own separate staircase, the anonymous façade of which is attached to the north façade (Figs. 103 and 106). This intimate court theater offered no provision for members of the lower classes. Instead of the unwashed whom Daniele Barbaro, Serlio and Palladio had banished to the upper reaches, the duke and his party occupied the highest point. This arrangement appears to be a novelty in court theaters. Heretofore the ruler and the most important guests had occupied a conspicuous spot at the lowest level. As early as the eighteenth century Tomaso Temanza noted that at Sabbioneta women occupied the upper level, alongside the duke,[14] while male members of the audience sat on the stepped seats below. The peristyle level seems too small, however, to hold perhaps half of the audience. It may be more likely that men and women occupied separate levels of the steps, as they had in Serlio's theater in Vicenza, or opposing sides of the seats, neatly

FIG. 109 Scamozzi, Odeon, peristyle with statues of Olympian gods (Photo: Ralph Lieberman)

bisected by the entrance under the ducal chair (Fig. 108). Most of the audience entered through the north door and then passed through the door situated directly beneath the duke's throne to take their seats on steps that faced each other as well as the relatively large open space in front of the stage (Figs. 106 and 107).

This last detail makes clear that the Odeon was planned to be used for tourneys as well as plays. Bertani's court theater of c. 1550 in nearby Mantua, used in part for tourneys (see Chapter 5), must have been an important precedent for this aspect of the Odeon, because in that theater there apparently was a space between the seating and the stage.[15] (Bertani's theater, one recalls, burned down in 1591, shortly after Scamozzi's opened.) At Sabbioneta, knights would have entered through the door in the long west wall, under a painted triumphal arch (Fig. 110). In later theaters, such as the Teatro Farnese in close-by Parma, knights would also enter through a triumphal arch (see Chapter 8). A subsequent series of theaters of the seventeenth century, designed to accomodate both performancess on stage and jousts on the floor, took up this plan. This aspect of the theater at Sabbioneta does not appear to have been noted in the literature on the building, at least to my knowledge. Apparently Vespasiano made a triumphal entrance into the theater when it opened in February 1590,[16] but this is unlikely to have been the standard way he entered, because there was no way for him to reach his seat in the peristyle without going outside once again. Sadly, he had little time left to deal with this inconvenience; he died the following February.

The painted triumphal arch over the west entrance (Fig. 110) frames a landscape with the Castel Sant'Angelo, Rome, the ancient burial place of

FIG. 110 Odeon, Sabbioneta, fresco of trimphal arch over door in west wall. (Photo: Ralph Lieberman)

FIG. 111 Odeon, Sabbioneta, fresco of triumphal arch on east wall (Photo: Ralph Lieberman)

FIG. 112 Scamozzi, Odeon, view of center of peristyle and wall with Roman emperors (Photo: Ralph Lieberman)

the Emperor Hadrian and the present-day fortress of the popes. The entablature above the arch records the dedication of the building to the current Hapsburg emperor, Rudolf II. At the top of the wall, more painted members of the audience look down on knights entering the door or at actors on the stage. On the east wall across the way, a landscape framed by an identical triumphal arch depicts Michelangelo's still-unfinished Piazza del Campidoglio, the political heart of modern Rome and the point from which all distances were measured in the ancient Roman empire, the *umbilicus mundi* or Navel of the World (Fig. 111). The inscription in the entablature contains a slightly modified version of the motto repeated on the exterior. The deliberate recollections of Rome, and the deliberate conflations of different moments in time, historical and present, could not be clearer.

In Kurt Forster's felicitous view,[17] the frescoes create a cross-axis that links the interior of the theater to the fortress and central piazza of Sabbioneta, between which the theater stands. The fresco of the papal fortress of Castel

FIG. 113 Scamozzi, Odeon, view of stage from ducal throne. The scenery is a modern reconstruction. Note that the backs of the seats are thoughtfully raised above the next floor level up, so that spectators were protected from the feet of those seated above them (Photo: Ralph Lieberman)

Sant'Angelo stands on the side of the duke's fortress (now demolished), while the Capitoline Hill, the political center of Rome, is on the side of the governmental center of Sabbioneta. The theater becomes a microcosm of the world of ducal control, presented as parallel to the larger worlds of papal and ancient imperial control.

At Sabbioneta, the duke sat in the center of the peristyle, framed by columns supporting statues of the Olympian gods (Fig. 108). While the columns derive from Vitruvius, the notion of seating the ruler in such a colonnade does not. On the wall behind the duke painted statues of Roman emperors standing in aedicules lent the modern Vespasian legitimacy (Fig. 112). The image of his namesake stood directly behind him, across a space too narrow to offer anyone else the possibility of occupying the main axis of the theater. Enthroned at the same level as painted Roman emperors, Vespasian placed himself between the gods above and his subjects below. The play-acting that occurred in the Odeon paralleled the play-acting of Vespasiano. When he looked down from his throne on the mock combats in the *platea* (Fig. 113), the namesake of the Roman emperor who had built the Colosseum watched armed struggles in the new theatrical space he had created in his own capital, his own "new Rome."[18]

BOLOGNA, 1628

A great outdoor tourney, *Amore prigioniero in Delo* (*Love Prisoner on Delos*), was produced in Bologna on March 20, 1628 by the Accademia degli Torbidi in honor of the visiting Grand Duke of Tuscany, Ferdinando II. The theater erected in Piazza delle Scuole is recorded in prints by Giovan Battista Coriolano that give us a vivid picture of the entire space, as viewed from the stage through the proscenium arch[19] (Fig. 114). Two lines of opposing knights, mounted on richly caparisoned horses and wearing extravagant headdresses, occupy the central space. The long, narrow structure fuses the shape of a Roman amphitheater with the stage of an indoor theater. One short end of the theater is dominated by the gaping entrance for mounted combatants. Over the entrance, in the prime position, is the box for the cardinal legate, the grand duke, and distinguised guests. To either side of the entrance stepped seats curve to form a semicircle, as they would have in an ancient amphitheater.

Along the sides are four levels of separate compartments supported by vertical posts that extend in depth, as indicated by right-angled cross-hatching, at least on the stage-right side (Fig. 115). These were boxlike spaces, with vertical separations between them, but seemingly without a rear wall with a door. The fronts of the three lower levels of these spaces are decorated with heraldic devices, those on the top exhibiting the single lily of Florence and the three swords of the family of the cardinal legate, Cardinal Spada. At ground level, the enclosing parapet was painted to resemble rusticated masonry to give a visually

FIG. 114 Giovan Battista Coriolano, view of the theater in Bologna of 1628, etching (Bologna, Pinacoteca Nazionale)

firm foundation. The occupants of the enclosed spaces stand, while those on the fourth level at the top are seated in the sun on continuous steps.

The print gives a clear, useful account of the disposition of the sexes at the tourney. Among the spectators, four to six per space, it is possible to distinguish men and women. Men wear broad-brimmed hats and short mantles. Women either are bare-headed and have the high collars of the period, or they wear veils. One veiled woman occupies a place on the second level next to the proscenium on stage right, and two other women appear to accompany her. The fourth compartment from the right on the same level seems to hold one woman and two men. Another woman, bare-headed, stands behind some men in the space second from the proscenium on the third level. In other places women also appear alongside men, although the number of men is much greater. The figures on the top level are drawn with less care, but there may well have been women up there as well. The left-hand side of the print is shown in shadow created by closely spaced vertical lines drawn over the depictions of the spectators (Fig. 114). Although it is hard to distinguish figures, men and women do also appear together on that side.[20]

At the short end of the theater, to stage right of the entrance, the lowest section appears entirely occupied by women, identified again by their tall collars and lack of hats (Fig. 116). Because these seated ladies are not crowded

FIG. 115 Detail of Fig. 114, showing spectators in compartments near the proscenium

together, they are probably the most important women at the tourney.[21] Behind them are three more levels that also appear occupied almost exclusively by women. Two large hats that probably indicate men pop out on the second and third levels – the former at the right edge, the latter close to the left edge. Might these hats indicate immature sons of aristocratic women? Coriolano's print tells us, then, that the sexes were allowed to mingle in the boxlike spaces along the sides, but very rarely in the most privileged seats to the left and right of the legate. There, women were seated to the legate's left, men to his right to make a traditional distinction between genders.

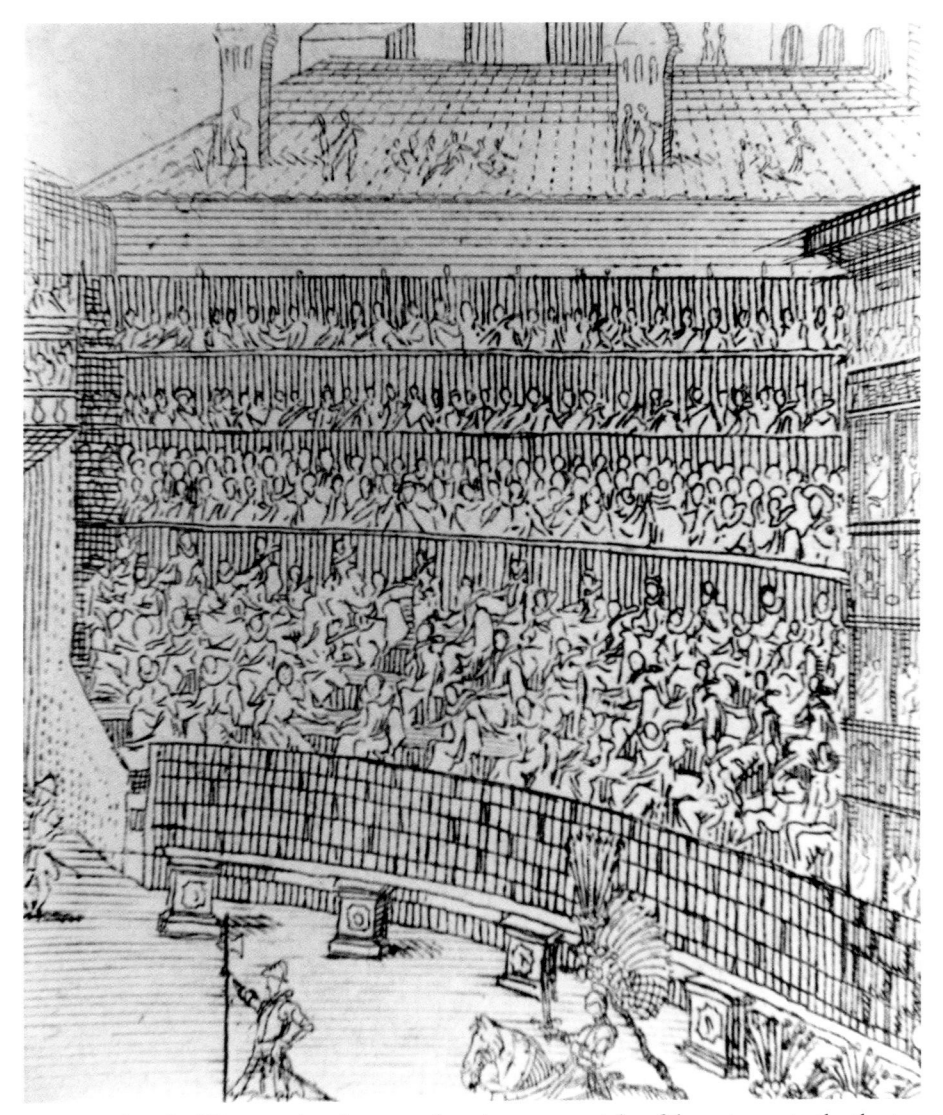

FIG. 116 Detail of Fig. 114, showing curved seating to stage right of the entrance to the theater

The proscenium resembled closely trimmed greenery fashioned into a segmental arch flanked by two oval and two rectangular openings into which allegorical figures were inserted (Fig. 117). The set showed a garden pavilion surround by neatly planted trees drawn in perspective. The legend over the arch tells us that we are looking at the "Garden of Delos, where Amor was chained."[22] Love himself, in chains, is not shown. Coriolano's views of both ends of the theater make clear how divided the vision of the audience must have been in spaces like this that accommodated two diverse types of performance.

FIG. 117 Giovan Battista Coriolano, view of stage of the theater in Bologna of 1628 (Bologna, Pinacoteca Nazionale)

PADUA, 1636

In 1636 the city of Padua saw the production of a tourney intertwined with a musical entertainment entitled *Ermiona*. Of the drama-tourneys of the seventeenth century, *Ermiona* was unusual in that it was not a production ordered by a ruler, but rather an event sponsored by a group of local gentlemen to celebrate no apparent occasion – an earlier instance of that moment in movie musicals when someone says, "Let's put on a show." The unique importance of the event is that it led to the first public performance of an opera, in Venice at the Teatro San Cassiano, less than a year later (see Chapter 9). The gentlemen of Padua were lucky enough to have in their midst an aristocrat of Virgilian name, Marchese Pio Enea II degli Obizzi, to organize the whole affair.[23] Pio Enea (Pius Aeneas in the *Aeneid*) had a way of being present when any number of important musical or dramatic events took place in the seventeenth century.

The precise date of *Ermiona* is not given in the libretto. Scholars have not been able to decide between the spring or the fall. It must have been in the spring, however; in the fall Pio Enea degli Obizzi was a fugitive from Venetian justice. On June 2, 1636 he was accused of having directed an assault on a certain Formica on 11 April on the streets of Padua. On September 4 the rectors of Padua passed a sentence against Pio Enea. Thrown in jail, he escaped the next day. On September 7 he arranged delivery of a supplication to the

Council of Ten in which he proclaimed his innocence and claimed that he had to leave jail in order to gather proof. Finally, in November the marchese turned himself in to the Capi of the Council of Ten. He was put in prison briefly, then on November 13 absolved by the Ten.[24]

The musical performance was based on the Greek myth of Cadmus, the title referring to his bride, Ermiona.[25] The production, featuring some of the best singers and musicians of the day, was followed by a ballet and then by a tourney on foot and on horseback. A theater was created, adjacent to the Pra della Valle, a large oval field in the city. A proscenium stage and a five-story structure that held the audience were specially constructed. The appearance of the stage is recorded in fifteen prints included in the libretto, but unfortunately the structure for the audience is not depicted. The stage opening was framed by pairs of engaged Corinthian columns that flanked statues in niches (Fig. 118). The columns bore an entablature with an image of the winged lion of St. Mark, symbol of the Venetian state, which controlled Padua. According to the libretto, the sets and stage machinery were designed by the Ferrarese engineer Alfonso Chenda, called Rivarolo, "a man worthy of every veneration for his exhalted virtue, and modesty."[26] The free exchange between events on stage and on the floor of the theater is obvious in this particular print, in which knights sprung from dragon's teeth sown on stage as part of the dramatic story

FIG. 118 *Ermiona*, Act II, Scene V, proscenium and stage (General Collection, Beinecke Rare Book and Manuscript Library, Yale University)

break the boundary of the proscenium to engage in real, if mock-, combat in the space of the theater that belongs to the audience. This fusion of story and architecture represents a not-untypical moment of unity between the performance on stage and the tourney in front of the stage in drama-tourney theaters.

Included in the libretto is a clear verbal description of the structure that held the audience, which was divided according to rank. Each of the five levels was separated into bays that held sixteen people seated behind balustrades. On the two top levels sat ordinary citizens, as one might expect, while the third level down was occupied by men from the university and foreign nobles. The fourth level down, or second level up (the most desirable), was reserved for the rectors of Padua – the Venetian patricians who ran the city – and Venetian nobles. At ground level were the ladies and gentlemen of Padua; those gentlemen were the ones who sponsored the event.[27]

This description accords in some ways with what we see in the prints that show the tourney in Bologna of 1628: compartments stacked on top of each other, with men and women together in some cases (Fig. 115). The description of the Paduan theater does not specify that there were separate sections for men and women, but this omission may not represent an oversight. Rather, it may well have been the case that in large compartments that held a dozen people or more, the opportunities for unseemly male/female encounters were minimal, and so the sexes were allowed to sit together.

The shape of this structure, unfortunately, is not described. Was it rectangular? Or was it polygonal or semicircular? The latter may be more likely, to bring the audience closer to the stage than many had been in Bologna in 1628. A semicircular of polygonal shape is suggested by the word used in the description, *girare,* which means to turn on an axis.

BOLOGNA, 1639

As early as 1547 the Sala Grande of the Palazzo del Podestà in Bologna became a venue for both performances of commedia dell'arte and games of court tennis.[28] In 1615 the Sala was remodeled for a tourney at carnival with, at the short ends, stages in front of which the opposing forces of a tourney entered, just as warriors would walk down from the stage in Padua two dozen years later. Seating was along the long sides on three superimposed sets of risers reached by corridors running against the outside walls. These tiers were supported by columns. Women were placed on the side toward the piazza, men opposite. In the middle of the men sat the cardinal legate. The ceiling was painted to resemble a night sky. The Sala also hosted troupes of comedians. In this case it is possible that an additional section of seating would be placed between the seating along the sides to create a

FIG. 119 Giacinto Lodi, Miniature of the Interior of the Sala Grande, Palazzo Del Podestà, Bologna, As Designed by Alfonso Chenda, 1639 (Bologna, Archivio Di Stato, *Anziani Consoli, Insignia*, Vol. VII, C.15a, 1639)

theater focused on one stage. This theater burned in 1623 and then was replaced by one with essentially the same design, with the addition of more advanced machinery that could raise live horses, mounted by armed knights, into the air!

In 1639 the Bolognese Sala was completely remodeled to house a drama-tourney in honor of Cardinal Sacchetti, the legate. Pio Enea degli Obizzi supplied a theme for the tourney, and Alfonso Chenda designed the stage machines and sets. This pair had collaborated three years earlier on *Ermiona* in Padua. Chenda was surely responsible for the remarkable transformation of the auditorium as well. A miniature by Giacinto Lodi preserves the appearance of Chenda's Sala, with the separate parts identified in a legend below the view of the interior (Fig. 119). At either end were stages (A and F) framed by pairs of Corinthian columns that flanked niches holding statues, all much like what Chenda had designed for Padua. A ramp (C) leading down from the stage to the floor of the room (F) served as the entrance for knights on horseback. On the stage, a deity supported on cloud machines (B) hovered over the landscape, which represented Sicily, while Iris (E) descended on a rainbow over the center of the room, under a painted sky. Along the walls were five orders of boxes (I) that numbered 160; the boxes at ground level at left were reserved for cardinals, dukes, and princes (G), while those at right (H) were for the Gonfaloniere of the city and members of the Accademia degli Anziani.[29]

Chenda, architect of the remodeling, was fresh from working in Venice, first in 1637 at the Teatro San Cassiano and then in 1639 at the Grimani theater, SS. Giovanni e Paolo. As we will see in Chapter 9, theaters with boxes had become the rule in Venetian theaters of the early seventeenth century, building on the Venetian invention of theater boxes in 1580. The Bolognese boxes, therefore, were an immediate and direct import by Chenda from the theaters of the Serenissima. As well, the painted sky made the theater recall outdoor tourneys of the kind that had taken place in Bologna in 1628. The tourney theaters in Bologna and Padua had incipient boxes, but Chenda's Venetian experience led him to fuse the Venetian tradition of smaller boxes with the opera-tourney theaters of earlier years of the seventeenth century to create a hybrid, or perhaps a hybrid of hybrids.

8

FERRARA, PARMA, PESARO, AND THEATERS OF GIOVANNI BATTISTA ALEOTTI

Ferrara was lost to the d'Este family in 1597, when the last duke, Alfonso II, died without a direct heir, and Pope Clement VIII Aldobrandini, the feudal lord, took over the city. Cesare d'Este, cousin of the last duke, moved the family and its possessions to Modena, a fief of the Holy Roman Emperor, and established his ducal court there. Despite the fact that Ferrara no longer enjoyed the presence of a d'Este court, the city continued well into the seventeenth century to be a major center of theatrical innovation. Partly this fact was due to the presence of Giovanni Battista Aleotti, a polymath with important interests in hydrology and mapmaking who numbered among his talents designing theatrical architecture and machinery. In Aleotti's hands, the drama-tourney theater reached its zenith in the Teatro Farnese in Parma.

FERRARA: TEATRO DEGLI INTREPIDI

Aleotti, just before 1606, designed a theater in Ferrara for the Accademia degli Intrepidi, one of those local societies of aristocrats who interested themselves in artistic and chivalrous endeavors. The prince of the academy, Marchese Enzo Bentivoglio, had a long history of producing entertainments in the city, particularly in the Sala Grande of Palazzo Ducale for Alfonso II d'Este. In 1604 for his Accademia, Bentivoglio rented a large unused granary that belonged to the departed d'Este. Into this empty space Aleotti inserted his new theater. It appears in a rough sketch on the map of Ferrara published by

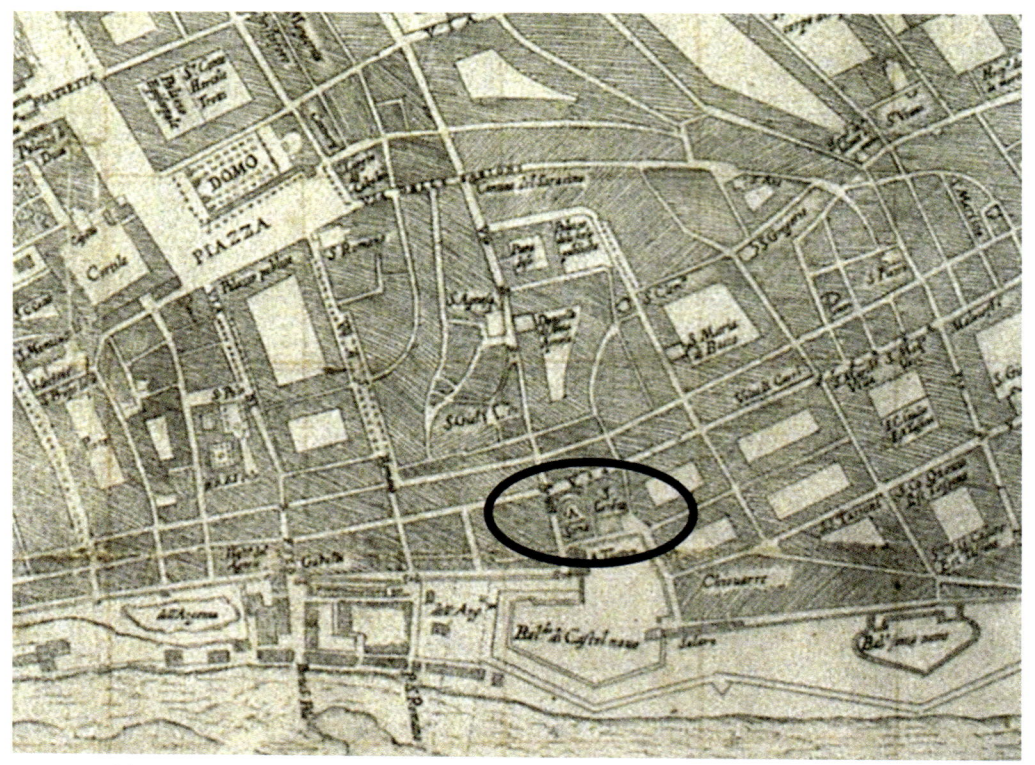

FIG. 120 Giovanni Battista Aleotti, map of Ferrara, 1605, detail showing location of Teatro degli Intrepidi at letter A (Ferrara, Bliblioteca Comunale Ariostea)

Aleotti in 1605 (Fig. 120), and in a (probably) autograph plan by the architect[1] (Fig. 121). An acoustical study of the theater, using digital technology, has demonstrated that the acoustics were first-rate.[2] Seating was in a U on steps which turned at the ends of the U to run parallel to the front of the stage (Fig. 122). A row of columns, straight out of Vitruvius, encircled the seats toward the top. The relatively deep stage was fitted with a perspectival set with moving parts that were intended to hold the types of scenery that Serlio had specified more than half a century earlier: a tragic, a comic, and a pastoral set. In 1618 Aleotti published an engraving of his tragic set, dedicated to Ranuccio I Farnese, Fourth Duke of Parma and Piacenza, then his employer[3] (Fig. 123). Aleotti noted that only the tragic set had been completed.[4] The print shows that the stage had a fixed proscenium, flanked by pairs of columns that framed niches holding statues. Although Aleotti did not invent this type of proscenium – as we saw in Chapter 4, a similar proscenium had been constructed in Siena as early as 1560 (Fig. 60) – it became standard in his work and in that of other Ferrarese theater architects like Chenda, and it enjoyed widespread use thereafter.

Between the stage and the seating was an open area, an extension of the flat floor embraced by the seats. The parallels with Scamozzi's theater in

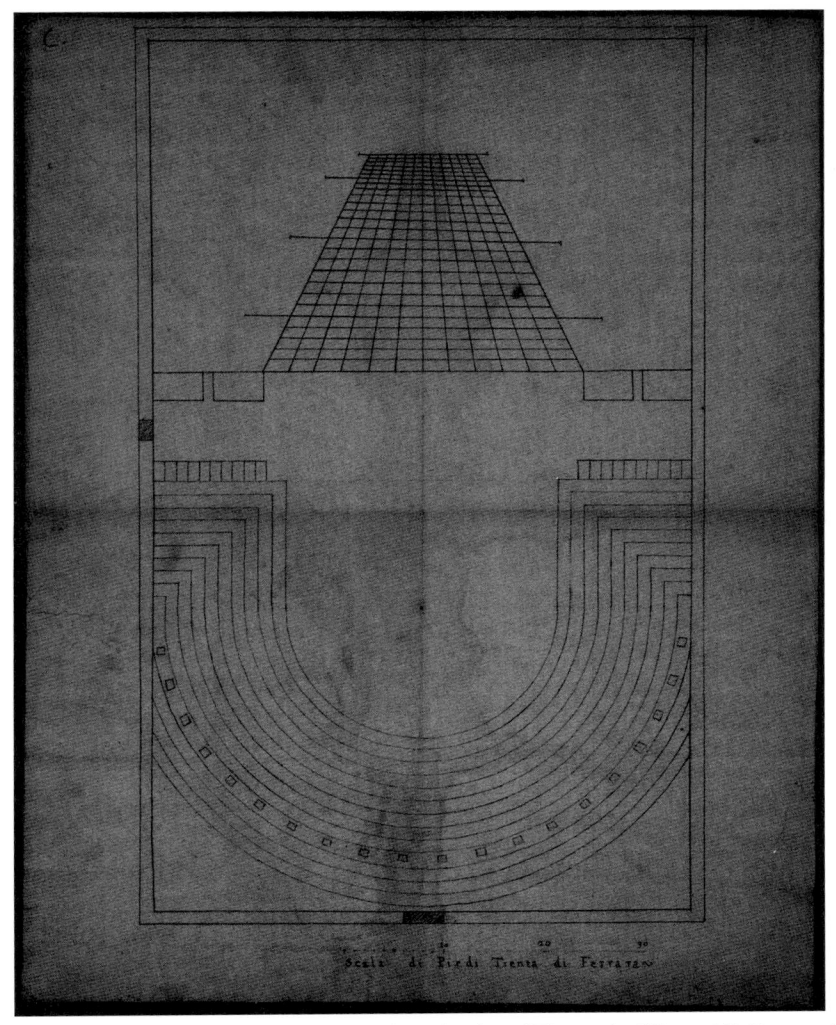

FIG. 121 Giovanni Battista Aleotti (attributed), plan of Teatro degli Intrepidi, Ferrara, drawing, c. 1605 (Modena, Archivio di Stato, Mappario Estense, Fabbriche 15, IMG 5721bis)

Sabbioneta are striking (Fig. 106). In 1598, when Aleotti worked in Mantua on the production of the pastorale *Il pastor fido*, he could easily have visited Sabbioneta. He also may have owned a set of drawings of the Teatro Olimpico, which he requested in December 1595.[5]

PARMA, 1617–1619, TEATRO FARNESE

The Teatro Farnese in Parma, as it has come to be known,[6] is one of the most studied theaters in Europe, in part because it has been preserved (at least roughly) and in part because it is a spellbinding work of architecture.[7] Of the three

FIG. 122 Teatro degli Intrepidi, Ferrara, digital reconstruction (Drawing: Benjamin Hoyle)

pre–eighteenth century theaters in Italy that have survived, it is the largest and most lavish, and the prime, most mature example of the drama-tourney theater. In many ways it is a Ferrarese theater transported to Parma: a much enlarged version of Aleotti's Teatro degli Intrepidi of a dozen years earlier and a descendant of the elaborate combination of scenic effects and tourney that characterized the production of *Il Castello di Gorgoferusa* in 1561. Heavily damaged toward the end of World War II during an American air raid, the Teatro Farnese today is largely a reconstruction made of unpainted wood (Fig. 124). There was no attempt to reproduce the original architectural finishes nor the illusionistic ceiling painting, filled with ancient gods floating in a blue sky, that had already been dismantled in the ninettenth century.

In 1617 Duke Ranuccio I Farnese ordered the construction of this enormous permanent theater to entertain Cosimo II, Grand Duke of Tuscany, a guest whose appearance in Parma was deemed probably imminent, but not entirely sure. Stricken with tuberculosis, Cosimo hoped to make a pilgrimage to Milan to pray for his health at the tomb of San Carlo Borromeo, the sixteenth century Milanese archbishop canonized in 1610. Neither a date nor a route for the voyage to Milan had been established, however.[8] Usually such an extravagant theater would be built only to celebrate a dynastic marriage, not just to delight a guest passing through, unless that guest were a king or a member of the imperial Hapsburg family.

Ranuccio had good reason to treat Cosimo royally. He wanted to arrange a marriage between his son and heir, Odoardo Farnese, and a Medici princess to help secure the position of his state in the world. As a ducal family, the Farnese were arrivistes. His great-great-grandfather, Pope Paul III, had assigned the papal fiefs of the Duchies of Parma and Piacenza to his oldest son, Pier Luigi Farnese, in order to establish a hereditary state for his family. Pier Luigi, hated by his subjects, was assassinated in Piacenza in 1547. The duchies then fell to Pier Luigi's son, Ottavio, who had married Margherita d'Austria – they of the unfinished palace at Piacenza that Vignola designed[9] (see Chapter 6).

The Duchies of Parma and Piacenza occupied a strategic position on the plain of the Po valley. They butted up against Milan, controlled by Spain; the Duchy of Mantua, ruled by the Gonzaga; and the Duchy of Modena, ruled by the d'Este. Tuscany could be a powerful ally in the risky games of diplomacy small Italian states had to play. In 1615, when the ducal heir, Odoardo, was only three, Ranuccio approched Cosimo II to arrange an alliance through marriage between the two states.[10] Ranuccio had in mind a triple accord among Parma, Tuscany, and Urbino, whose more or less contiguous territories would form a barrier across the Italian peninsula to papal expansion from the south or Spanish expansion from the north, via Milan. (He must have counted on cooperation from the d'Este of Modena, whose lands separated Parma from Tuscany.) Ranuccio even assured Cosimo that he would be happy with whichever daughter the grand duke might choose as

FIG. 123 Oliviero Gatti, engraving of Giovanni Battista Aleotti's proscenium and tragic set, Teatro degli Intrepdi, 1618 (Macerata, Archivio privato Compagnoni Floriani)

Odoardo's bride.[11] In 1611 Ranuccio had faced a conspiracy to overthrow him by a group of Parmesan nobles. The conspiracy had been known to, and perhaps approved by, the Gonzaga and Medici. Ranuccio wanted to cancel the adversarial stance of the latter.[12] With marriage negotiations between Parma and Florence ongoing, Ranuccio sought to impress Cosimo with the most lavish theater he could create. Perhaps its purpose was to suggest the grand celebration that would accompany a future marriage. It would outshine by far the theater that Vasari and Buontalenti had created in the Uffizi. Indeed, the Teatro Farnese would become the most lavish theater in the Europe of its day.

To design the theater, Ranuccio, advised by the Ferrarese nobleman Enzo Bentivoglio, called in Bentivoglio's theater architect, Giovanni Battista Aleotti. As Marzio Dall'Acqua has shown, Aleotti had already worked in Parma in 1616, designing a tourney sponsored by Ranuccio held in the courtyard of the bishop's palace, which the Farnese had taken over.[13] Back in Parma in 1618 to design a much more ambitious theater, Aleotti confronted a remarkable existing architectural situation. The palace of the Farnese, typical of princely residences in northern Italy, was a roughly coordinated affair built over time (Fig. 125). In the first decade of the seventeenth century Ranuccio had partly constructed a large multipurpose addition, the Palazzo della Pilotta, so-called from its courtyard, where a ball game was played. The courtyard had been left in an unfinished L shape, because to complete it required razing part of the church of S. Pietro Martire, whose monks were loath to give ground. The *piano nobile* of one wing of the Pilotta was devoted to an enormous room intended to display armor in glorification of the Farnese history of notable military men, especially Ranuccio's father, Alessandro, who had been regent of the Netherlands for the Spanish crown and had even planned an invasion of Protestant England under the cover of the Spanish Armada. Into the still-empty and available armory Ranuccio chose to insert his theater.

The importance of this armory to Ranuccio's intention to celebrate his family's military prowess is made clear by the innovative, monumental, multi-ramped staircase he ordered constructed to conduct visitors from the courtyard to the armory (Fig. 126, lower left). Visitors entering the courtyard, in a carriage, on horseback, or on foot, confronted the brick walls of the Pilotta, supported on sturdy piers (Fig. 127). From beneath the great vaults that hold up the armory/theater (Fig. 128) they would mount the single ramp of the lower part of the stairs, with a thoughtfully placed landing to ease the climb (Fig. 129). At a second landing they would emerge into light and find themselves obliged to turn 180 degrees and choose one of two ramps (Fig. 130). The latter lead through a screen of piers to the door to the theater. The piers support diagonal arches (Fig. 131). Above them soars a dome worthy to crown a church crossing, the long axis of its irregular octagonal shape placed athwart the visitor's path (Fig. 132). A more imposing staircase could not be found in any Italian palace of the day.[14] Thanks to the transformation of the armory at the top of the stairs into a theater, the staircase became the ancestor of such extravaganzas as Charles Garnier's famous stair hall at the Paris Opéra. At the top of the stairs, a triumphal-arch door frame, later embellished by the addition of a riotous late Baroque crown, leads into the theater (Fig. 133).

In Aleotti's Teatro Farnese seating is on rows of steps arranged in an elongated U (Fig. 134). Above the seats rises a two-story arcade, a more complex version of the Vitruvian colonnade at the top of the seats of the Intrepidi (Figs. 122 and 123). Between the seating and the stage is an open area contiguous with the flat floor surrounded by the seats. Flanking the area in front of the stage are two triumphal arches graced by statues of the second and third Farnese dukes, Ottavio (stage left) and Alessandro, on horseback (Fig. 134). They announce the theme of tourneys and jousts for which the theater was intended, while celebrating the memory of great military men of the family to recall the original function of the room. The inscription over the proscenium, BELLONAE E MUSIS THEATRUM RAINUTIUS FARNESIUS PARMAE ET PLACENTIAE DUX IV CASTRI V AGUSTA MAGNIFICENTIA APERUIT ANNO MDCXVIII,[15] begins with words indicating that the room belongs both to Bellona, goddess of war, and to the Muses. As such, it reprises the message of the Urbino theater of 1513: good rulers wage war and peace. Under the statue of Alessandro at stage right is the door through which participants in tourneys entered.[16] A monumental

FIG. 124 Giovanni Battista Aleotti, Teatro Farnese, Parma, 1617–18, interior from stage (Photo: Ralph Lieberman)

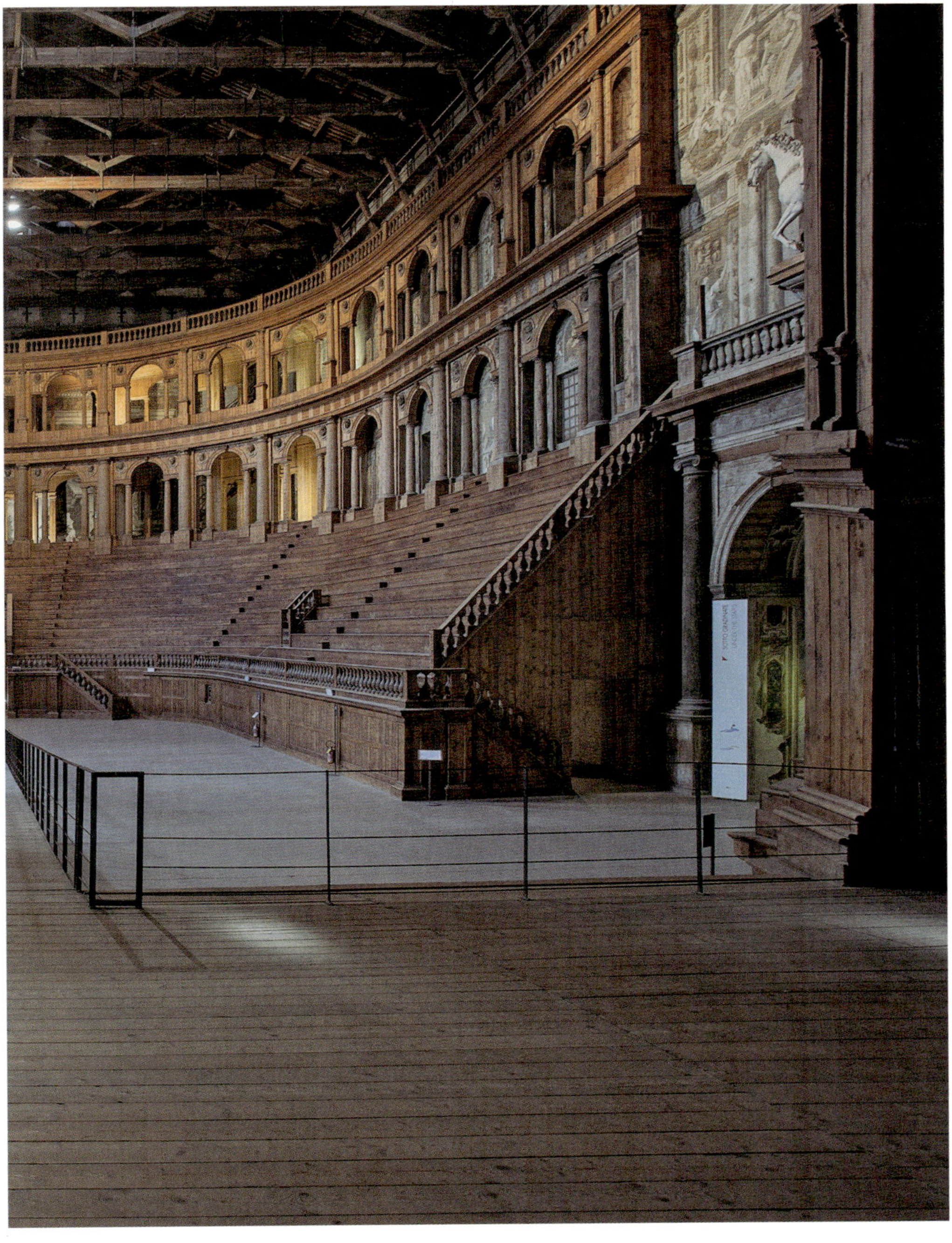

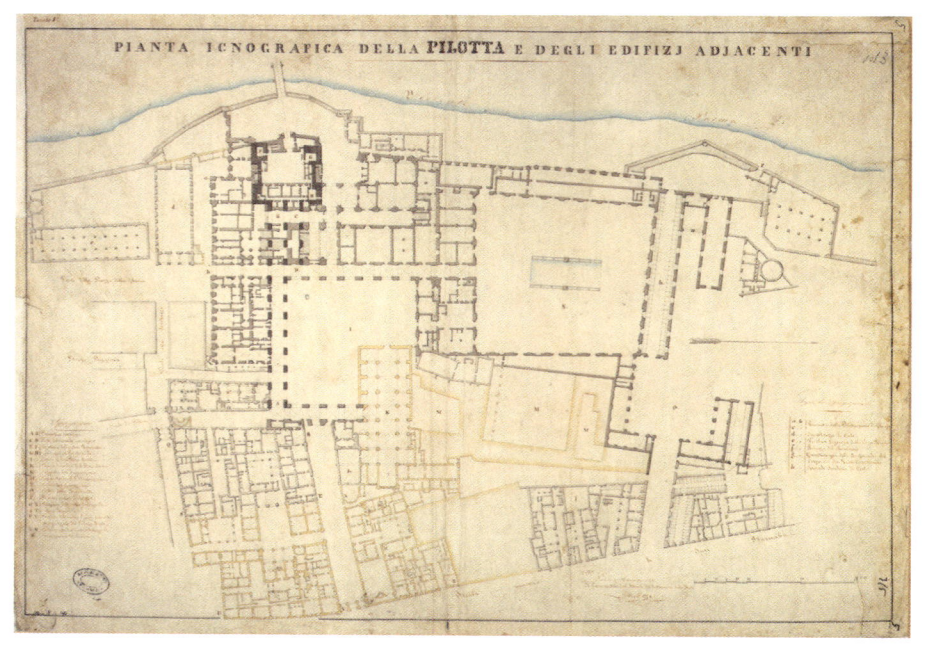

FIG. 125 P. Mazza, plan of Palazzo della Pilotta, Parma, nineteenth century (Parma, Archivio di Stato, mappe e disegni, vol. 3, n. 5)

proscenium, with an engaged giant order of Corinthian columns flanking niches with statues, frames the stage, which is endowed with ample depth and height to house the machinery Aleotti designed to create fabulous stage effects (Fig. 126).

From the earliest decades of the construction of theaters during the Renaissance, indoor theaters masqueraded as outdoor spaces, often palace courtyards. Recall, for instance, the theater of 1548 at Lyon designed by Serlio, with its courtyardlike walls and heavenly painted-cloth ceiling (Fig. 50). The Teatro Farnese, however, aspires to appear to be the central piazza of a city. The two-story arcade that surmounts the seats (Fig. 135) is copied, almost line for line, from the exterior of Andrea Palladio's Basilica in Vicenza (Fig. 135), which Aleotti apparently considered the last word in the design of a porticoed building facing a city square. A late seventeenth century view of Palladio's Basilica shows it used by spectators at a tourney in the piazza (Fig. 137).[17] The make-believe character of the "outdoor" Farnese theater was pushed even further by an illusionistic ceiling painting by Lionello Spada and assistants. There two additional levels of painted arcades, filled with spectators, were oversoared by airborne ancient gods, with Jupiter on his eagle at the center (Fig. 138). Aleotti at one point proposed that the stage curtain be decorated with a view of Parma as seen from the northwest, to create the effect of sitting outside looking at the local landscape. As Dall'Acqua has noted, the spectators' view of the painted landscape would have been from inside the city, a point actually opposite from the actual suburban site from which the scene was taken, thus simultaneously presenting and confounding a sense of spatial reality.[18] The curtain was never executed, and the ceiling, as noted, is no more.

The theater was carefully placed inside the existing walls of the armory, so that the openings in the Palladian arcades along the sides lined up with the existing windows in the south wall, to allow the maximum amount of natural light to enter[19] (Fig. 139). Entrance for the audience from the great domed staircase was through a narrow, low compression space that passed under the seats and made the vastness of the interior all the more surprising (Fig. 124). As one mounted the stairs and passed through the tunnellike corridor, there was no way to tell what lay ahead; Aleotti's control of the act of entering produced a *coup de théâtre*. Architecture, painting, and sculpture united to form an ensemble of illusion and reality that doubled the height of the room and dissolved the ceiling into a vision of the heavens decades before Andrea Pozzo, beginning in 1684, famously painted away the vault of the nave of the church of Sant'Ignazio in Rome to heighten the nave and reveal a heavenly vision.

Aleotti was only in Parma for four months, arriving in November 1617, and returning to Ferrara in March. During that brief stay, he worked his way through several designs for the theater that are preserved in drawings — some from his own hand — too numerous to consider here.[20] An undated plan in Parma (Fig. 140) shows seating on thirteen steps surrounded by a wide corridor set between the steps and the existing walls, but does not show the existing windows; nor does it indicate a door for the knights to enter. The corridor is in the right place to accommodate spectators whose socioeconomic status denied them places on the steps. Such spectators may also have been accommodated on higher levels; the stairs drawn at the upper left corner of the plan are certainly reminiscent of the steps that led to the upper levels of the Teatro Olimpico (Fig. 89). This drawing also contains the outline of an ample concave forestage in front of the proscenium (the area is much too large for the small orchestras of the day).[21]

A later (?) plan conserved in Ferrara (Fig. 141) enlarges the seating area by eliminating the wide corridor and extending the steps to the outer walls. The corridor persists around the curved end of the seats, as it does in the final version of the theater (Fig. 142). In this drawing the opening in the proscenium remains in the same place, but is widened to accord with the width of the floor embraced by the U-shaped amphitheater seating. The windows, now shown, are however partly blocked by the arcades set close to the outer wall. There are fifteen steps, separated by a walkway located in the middle of the risers; the

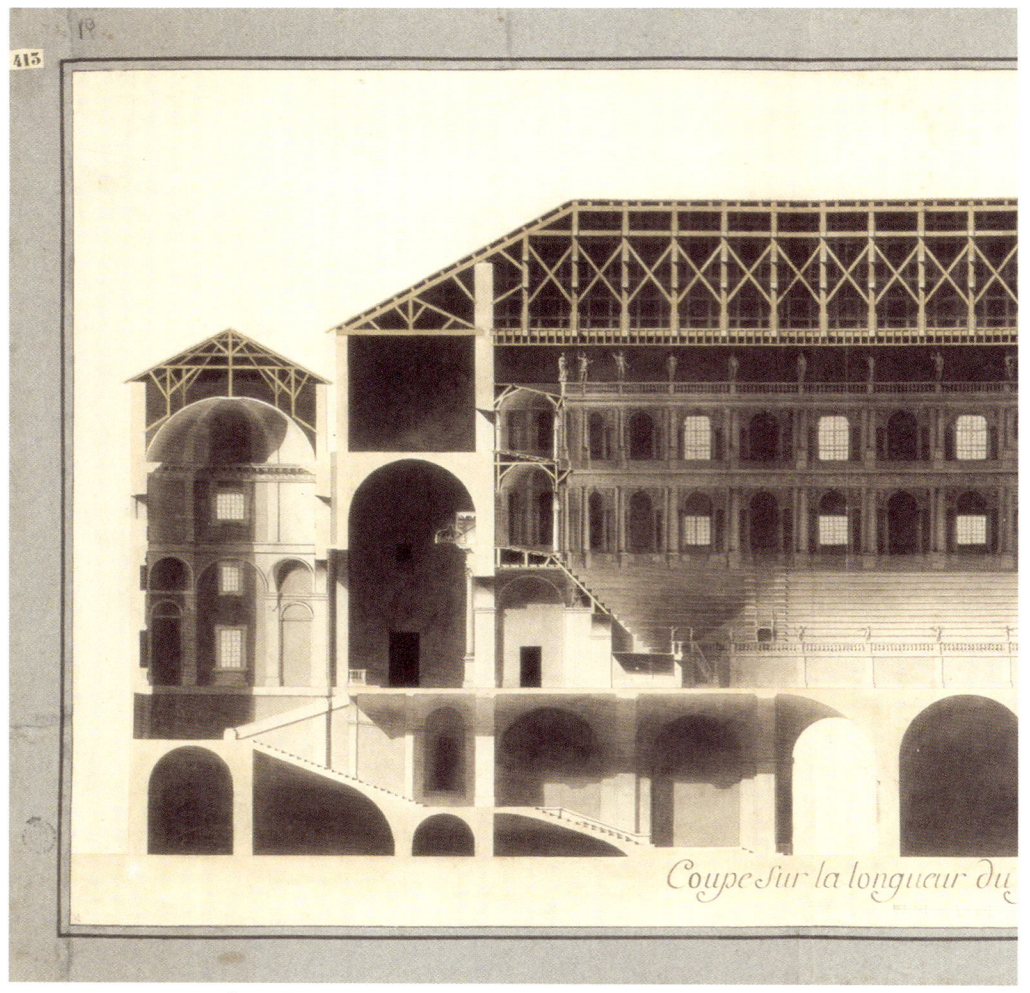

FIG. 126 L. A. Feneulle, Palazzo della Pilotta, Parma, longitudinal section through staircase and Teatro Farnese, c. 1780 (Parma, Archivio di Stato, Mappe e Disegni, vol. 4, 18)

steps turn 90 degrees to run parallel to the stage, a generally accepted practice in drama-tourney theaters. The forestage is eliminated, so that the wide opening for the stage is not set back from the front wall of the proscenium, as it is in the final version.

A longitudinal section (Fig. 143), generally recognized as an autograph drawing by Aleotti, exhibits a different scheme still. Seven rows of risers that turn parallel to the stage are surmounted by the two-story arcade. Behind the arcades are more risers, five below and four above, with a fourth and final set atop the upper arcade.[22] The visual effect of audience members stacked on top of each other and seated behind arches is not unlike that of audience members seated in superimposed rows of boxes. One wonders whether Aleotti may have known the Venetian theaters with boxes that had reopened as early as 1610 (see Chapter 9). The entrance to the theater (lower left) is through a low passage lined by columns and sculpture. The end of the passage toward the stage supports a seating area for the ducal couple. In this drawing, no triumphal arch set into the side walls intervenes between seats and proscenium, although there is a door for knights at the level of the floor. The elaborate and expensive nature of this project suggests it was doomed because it was overly ambitious. Planning and execution of the theater moved swiftly, because Aleotti could report on January 18, 1618 to Ranuccio Farnese that the time had arrived to construct the last steps for seating.[23]

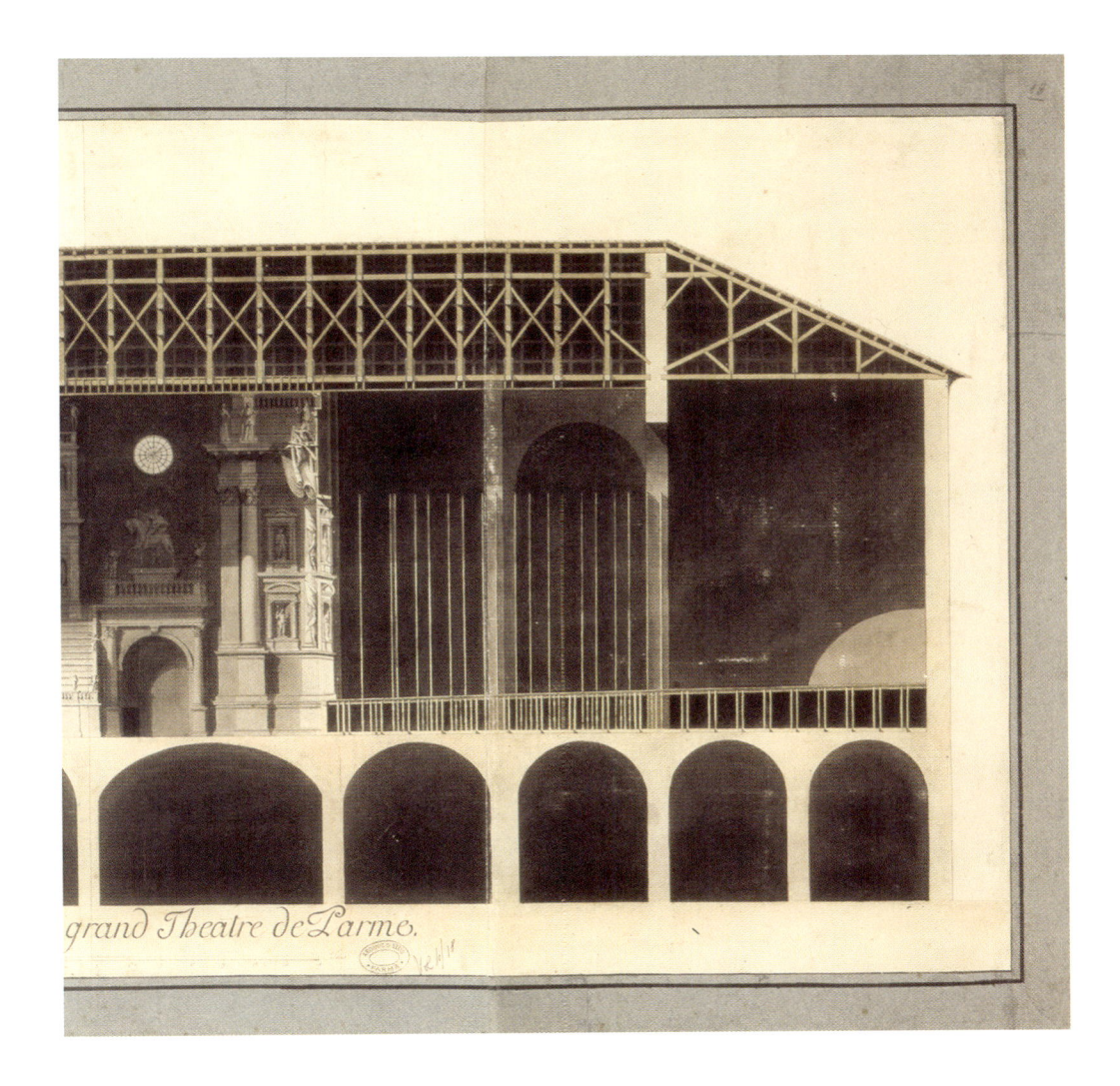

FIG. 127 Palazzo della Pilotta, Parma, exterior. The theater is in the wing in the center of the photo (Photo: Henry Schmidt)

FIG. 128 Palazzo della Pilotta, Parma, ground floor vaults and entrance to staircase (Photo: Henry Schmidt)

FIG. 129 Palazzo della Pilotta, Parma, single ramp staircase leading up from ground level (Photo: Ralph Lieberman)

The lack of an imposing entrance for knights in this drawing is solved in the theater as built by the introduction of triumphal arches between seats and stage. The juxtaposition of the three parts of the theater — seating area, triumphal arch, and proscenium — is awkward, but understandably so (Fig. 144). All three

FIG. 130 Palazzo della Pilotta, Parma, view from second landing down single ramp stair (Photo: Ralph Lieberman)

FIG. 131 Palazzo della Pilotta, Parma, view from second landing up toward door of theater (Photo: Ralph Lieberman)

FIG. 132 Palazzo della Pilotta, Parma, dome over staircase (Photo: Ralph Lieberman)

are necessary for the whole. In shifting to a giant order for the proscenium, Aleotti tried to focus attention on the stage area, but the competition among elements remains keen.

Perhaps the most amazing part of the planned entertainment of 1618 to impress (stupefy?) Cosimo II was a mock-naval battle, or *naumachia*. One of Aleotti's primary skills was hydrology. Taking advantage of the fact that the floor of the theater is supported on stout piers that sustain strong vaults (Fig. 128), he designed a system of pumps that raised water to storage tanks under the stage. The water would flood the floor of the theater to a depth of around 30 centimeters. The Medici could not do the same in the Uffizi. There were also, just outside the Farnese theater, special stairs to bring horses up to theater level for jousts and horse ballets. Horses could not be brought into the Uffizi theater. Word of the superiority of the Teatro Farnese got back to Florence. Count Alfonso Pozzo reported to Ranuccio in an undated letter that the engineer of the Grand Duke had visited the Farnese theater in Pozzo's company and praised it: "He liked the *Salone* extremely, and said that he has never seen a more magnificent or superb theater, much larger than theirs in Florence. The opening of the stage is smaller than theirs: the space we have inside he says is such that they do not have one sixth of it." [24] Even if the Medici duke should not visit Parma, he would learn that his theater had been bested.

A libretto, *La difesa della bellezza* (*The Defense of Beauty*), was prepared for the musical entertainment that would accompany the tourney to entertain Cosimo II. For this production Aleotti designed elaborate stage machinery to

FIG. 133 Palazzo della Pilotta, Parma, monumental entrance to theater (Photo: Ralph Lieberman)

transport gods across the sky, bring up demons from below, imitate ocean waves, and change locations several times. The libretto, by Count Pozzo, had as its ultimate purpose the glorification of peace, a message aimed at Cosimo II, whose name is mentioned several times at the close of the performance. Musical interludes were to alternate with chivalrous combats. At the beginning Aurora (Dawn) was to appear on a cloud to sing sweetly; at the end Night would conclude the performance.[25] The combats were to

FIG. 134 Giovanni Battista Aleotti, Teatro Farnese, Parma, stage (Photo: Ralph Lieberman)

FIG. 135 Giovanni Battista Aleotti, Teatro Farnese, Parma, north side wall (Photo: Ralph Lieberman)

appear in a crescendo of marvels: first on foot, then on horseback, and finally amid the flood on the floor. It would have been quite a show. The impresario, Enzo Bentivoglio, wrote to his brother, "I hope to have made for His Highness the most beautiful celebration that has ever been made in Europe."[26]

FIG. 136 Andrea Palladio, Basilica, Vicenza, exterior, designed 1546 (Photo: Ralph Lieberman)

In early 1619 Cosimo II, too ill to travel, cancelled his trip to Milan. The enormous, costly Teatro Farnese sat unused for a decade, until it opened for the celebration of the wedding of Ranuccio's son, Odoardo, now duke, to Cosimo's daughter, Margherita, in the fall of 1628.[27] In the course of the next 200 years, the theater was used only seven more times. Mounting regular performances there was too expensive.

Aleotti moved on to design a theater in Pesaro.

PESARO, 1621, THEATER IN THE DUCAL PALACE

The most immediate progeny of the idle Teatro Farnese was the theater erected in Pesaro in 1621 to celebrate the marriage of the heir to the Duchy of Urbino, Federigo Ubaldo della Rovere, to Claudia de' Medici. She was the sister of Cosimo II and the youngest child of Grand Duke Ferdinando and Christine of Lorraine, the focus of the fabulous Medici wedding of 1589[28] (see Chapter 4). Preserved in the Biblioteca Oliveriana, Pesaro, in an eighteenth century album of documents of diverse dates, is a drawing for the temporary theater erected in the Sala Magna (Great Room) of the Ducal Palace for the

FIG. 137 Tourney in the Piazza Maggiore, Vicenza, engraving, 1680, from *Charles Patin, Le pompose feste di Vicenza fatte nel mese di giugno 1680. Padova, Pasquati, 1680* (Biblioteca comunale Bertoliana, Vicenza, Biblioteca Gonz 21.7.22)

FIG. 138 Teatro Farnese, anonymous nineteenth century painted view of interior, showing ceiling painting demolished in nineteenth-century (Teatro Farnese, Parma) (Photo: Ralph Lieberman)

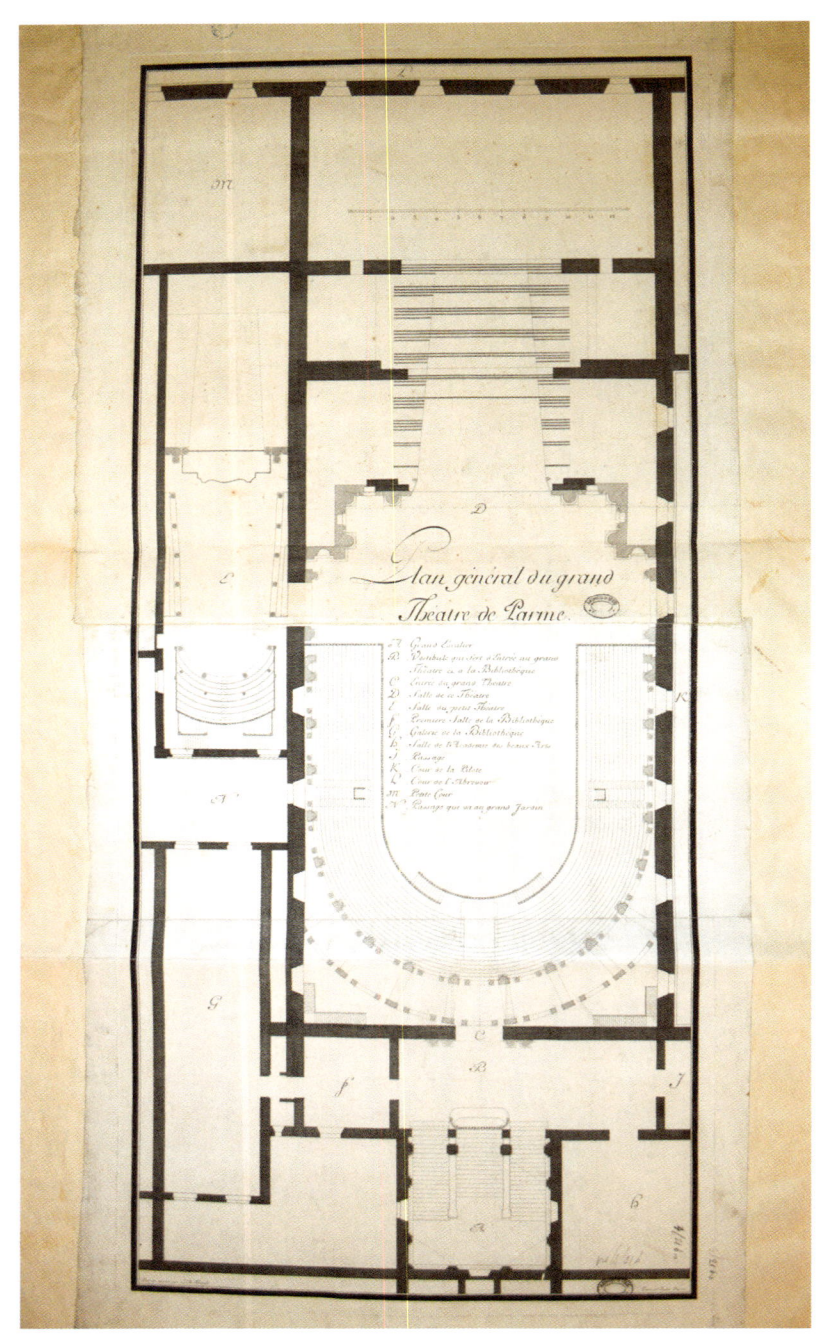

FIG. 139 L. A. Feneulle, Teatro Farnese, Parma, plan of theater and staircase, c. 1780 (Parma, Archivio di Stato, Mappe e Disegni, vol. 4, 21bis)

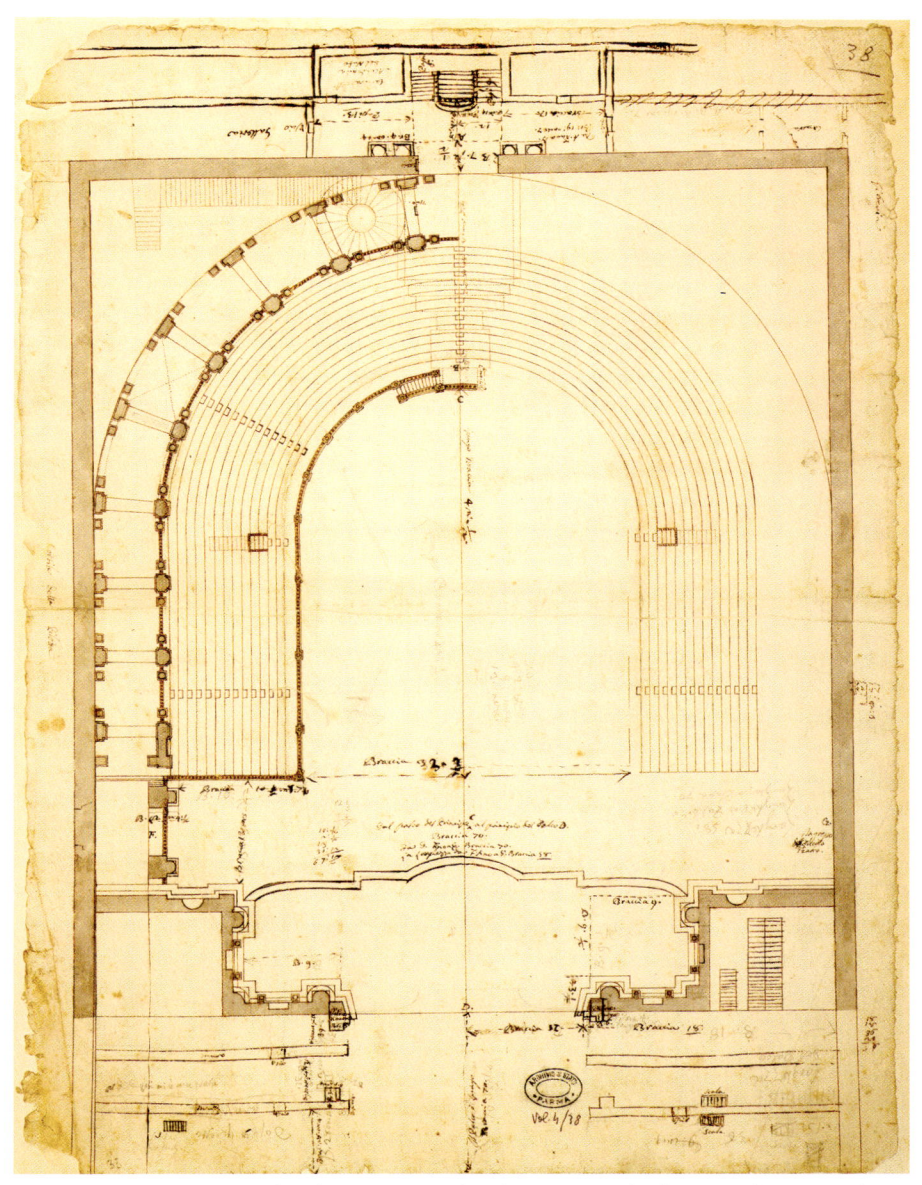

FIG. 140 Teatro Farnese, plan showing a corridor above seats and a forestage (Parma, Archivio di Stato, Mappe e Disegni, vol. 4, 38)

wedding festivities.[29] The drawing (Fig. 145) has two parts: a perspective view of one side of the seating area occupies most of the sheet, while a small plan of the theater is inserted in the lower right corner (Fig. 146). The drawing includes a legend that identifies the parts: 1. Portico that runs around the steps; 2. Steps where the people sit; 3. Floor; 4. Orchestra for Musicians; 5. Stage;

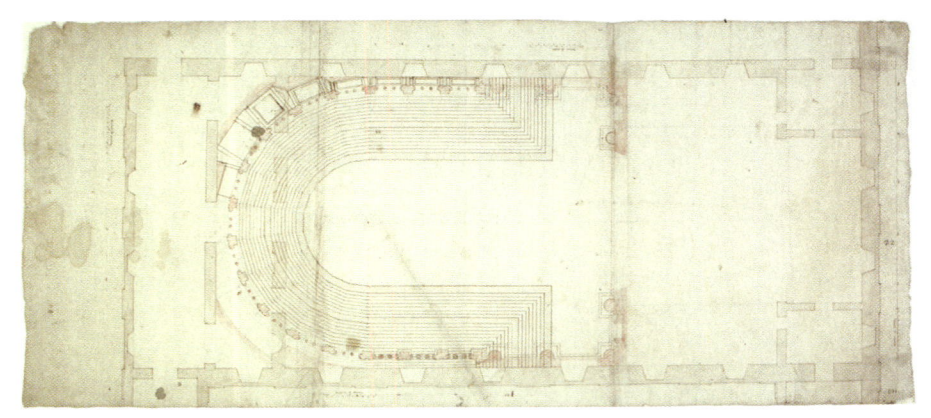

FIG. 141 Teatro Farnese, plan showing existing windows and seats turned to face stage (Biblioteca Comunale Ariostea, Ferrara, Aleotti, Disegni, ms. cl. I, n. 162)

FIG. 142 Giovanni Battista Aleotti, Teatro Farnese, Parma, vaulted corridor above stepped seats (Photo: Ralph Lieberman)

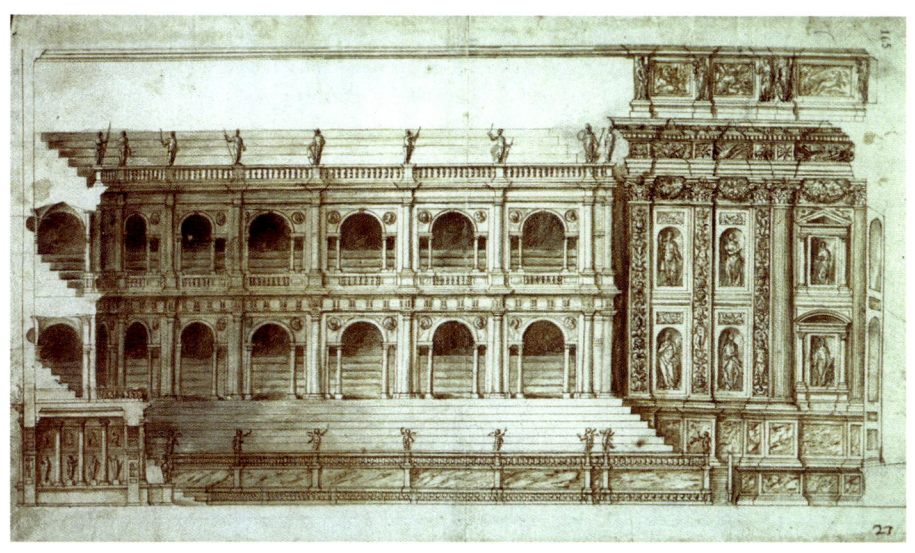

FIG. 143 Giovanni Battista Aleotti, project for the Teatro Farnese with four levels of seating, a royal box, and deep proscenium (Biblioteca Communale Ariostea, Ferrara, Ms. C1.I.763, f. 165)

6. Proscenium; A. Plan of the Theater. Adriano Cavicchi has convincingly attributed the drawing to Aleotti.[30]

The view of the side of the room shows an arcade of piers with engaged columns (of an indeterminate order, but not Doric) supporting a balustrade. Below the level of the arcade are five steps for the audience. Separated by some distance from the proscenium, the steps rest on a podium and turn to run parallel to the stage, as they do in the Teatro degli Intrepidi (Fig. 122). On the basis of this sketch it has been possible to make a digital reconstruction of what the room looked like (Fig. 147). Not surprisingly, it looked much like the Teatro Farnese. The arcade, however, was based on the ancient Roman Theater of Marcellus, rather than on the modern Basilica in Vicenza. Indeed, the Pesaro theater has a more strictly classical air than the one in Parma, and Cavicchi has compared it to the reconstruction by Pirro Ligorio of the ancient Theater of Marcellus in Rome published in an engraving of 1558.[31] In Pesaro Aleotti once again followed the long Ferrarese tradition of putting a Vitruvian row of columns at the top of a theater to improve acoustics. The slightly U-shaped plan of the theater and the distance of the seats from the stage suggest that action took place on the floor below the spectators: a tourney, a ballet, or both.[32] There was no provision to get horses up to the floor of the theater, however. As in Parma, no obvious place was set aside for the ruling family and important guests – no royal podium in the middle of the floor, or platform set on axis into the steps. The lack of a princely platform on the floor also makes clear that that level was used for part of the entertainment.

FIG. 144 Giovanni Battista Aleotti, Teatro Farnese, detail of seats, triumphal arch, and proscenium (Photo: Ralph Lieberman)

The tiny sketch plan of the proscenium and stage (Fig. 146) provides important information. The pairs of half-circles to either side of the stage opening represent half-columns that rose from robust bases to flank semicircular niches. They surely carried an architrave across the top of the stage opening to create the same type of Ferrarese proscenium that appears in the print of Aleotti's tragic scene at the Teatro degli Intrepidi (Fig. 123).

The most novel element of the plan is the semicircular orchestra pit in front of the stage: a tiny theater within the theater, with steps facing the stage for the musicians. In this thoughtful configuration, instrumentalists could simultaneously see each other and the singers, and the singers could see the musicians, so that everyone had a good chance of staying together. There would have been no conductor. Because the back wall of the pit shielded the players from the audience, their movements would not have detracted from the action on stage. This drawing demonstrates how well Aleotti understood the needs of

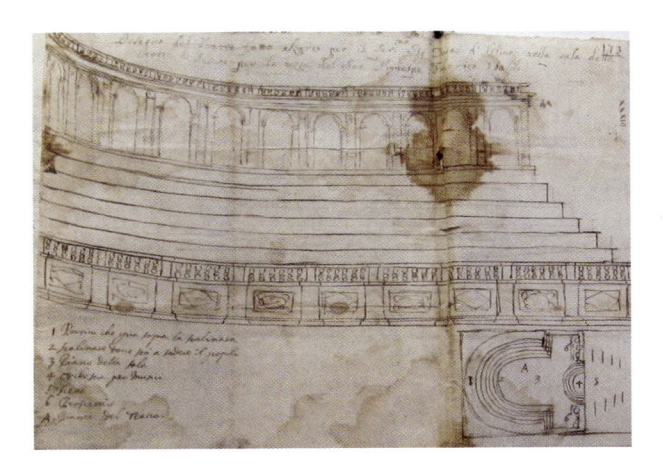

FIG. 145 Giovanni Battista Aleotti (attrib.), sketches for Pesaro theater of 1621 (Biblioteca Oliveriana, Pesaro, Ms. 387, XXXIII, 173) (Photo: Author)

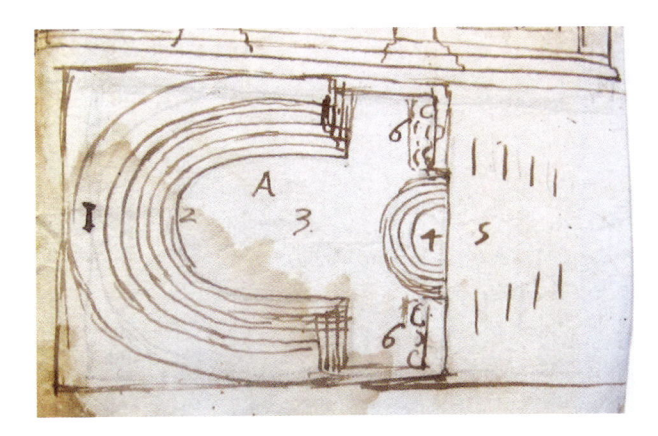

FIG. 146 Giovanni Battista Aleotti (attrib.), detail of Fig. 144

performers and audience. His orchestra pit for Pesaro predates any other that we know, particularly the one designed by Francesco Guitti in 1628 for the Teatro Farnese (discussed later), which had been thought to be the earliest orchestra pit for which we have visual evidence.[33] That distinction now belongs to Aleotti. Previously, musicians had been placed, sometimes haphazardly, behind the scenery, or on top of buildings that formed part of the sets.[34] Often the singers and instrumentalists could not see each other. Only if both were simultaneously off-stage, as the chorus and instrumentalists were in Palladio's Teatro Olimpico, could they be together in one space where they were able to coordinate their performance. The orchestra pit was an invention crying to be made, and Aleotti appears to be the person who made it.

The Pesaro theater of 1621 and the Farnese theater in Parma of three years earlier, designed by the peripatetic Aleotti, can be understood as architectural symbols of the alliance among Parma, Tuscany, and Urbino that Ranuccio I Farnese sought and that the rulers of Florence and Urbino surely understood. Tuscany, the geographic center of the alliance, eventually married two

FIG. 147 Digital reconstruction of Pesaro theater of 1621 (Drawing: Benjamin Hoyle)

princesses to the heirs of flanking Urbino and Parma. Visually similar, Aleotti's two theaters served similar political ends.

PARMA, 1628

Finally, in 1628, a Farnese/Medici wedding was celebrated in Aleotti's great theater in Parma. Ranuccio I Farnese died in 1622, before his ten-year-old heir was of age to take a bride. Once turned sixteen, Odoardo carried out his father's plan by marrying Margherita de' Medici, daughter of Cosimo II. The celebration in Parma was extravagant. Not only was the great theater of 1618 finally opened, but Odoardo also built a second theater in the courtyard of the Palazzo della Pilotta to stage a production of Torquato Tasso's pastorale *Aminta*. The vastness of the Teatro Farnese, upstairs in the ex-armory, was ill suited to a work that depended largely on the spoken word for its effect. Also, the machinery that Aleotti had designed a decade earlier could not easily be removed to make way for the scenery for a second production. Thus the necessity for a double-theater wedding.[35]

In the Teatro Farnese, as the guests assembled, their attention was directed to the princely couple, seated on the central axis under a structure of sufficient size to block the view of spectators behind them.[36] The newly composed "drama-tourney," with music (now-lost) by Claudio Monteverdi, integrated musical and scenic effects with symbolic combats in which a peripatetic young duke was the principal actor, sometimes appearing on stage, sometimes dueling on the floor, sometimes fetched by a performer from his seat.[37] A new libretto, with the title *Mercurio, e Marte*, was crafted to make use of the existing machinery designed ten years earlier by Aleotti. Once again that master impresario, Enzo Bentivoglio, was called on to supervise the production, although he was not much in Parma this time around. The duke's mother, the dowager duchess Margherita Aldobrandini, also played an important supervisory role for her teenage son.

In the libretto, Mercury, representing commerce and literacy, was opposed to Mars, representing military valor. In the end the audience came to understand that Odoardo, star of the show, combined the virtues represented by the two gods. Another theme of the celebration pointed to the union of the military history of the Farnese with the Medici history of great patronage of art and learning, now joined together in one happy couple. In four combats Odoardo proved his valor over the four elements: earth, air, water, and fire. Before the last combat, the floor of the theater was suddenly flooded, to the astonishment of all, even of the performer portraying the nymph Galatea. (Aleotti, in his eighties, was not able to attend the opening performance in his masterpiece and witness the shock registered by the audience at his aquatic extravaganza.) Galatea appeared on a rock that moved through the water toward the ducal seats, pulling behind her a second rock onto which Odoardo stepped to vanquish his last knightly foes. One doubts that there had been a rehearsal of the flood. At the end, Jupiter, seated amid the gods on a cloud above the stage, brought the symbolic drama to a close, with the words "Let sword and pen, pen and sword / Each share part of its glory / With the other."[38] United once again were symbols of war and peace, as the original inscription over the proscenium had specified.

Francesco Guitti protected the musicians in the orchestra pit with a waterproof wall. Guitti's orchestra pit remains of historical importance.[39] Its presence in the Teatro Farnese signals a moment in which a great composer, Monteverdi, collaborated with an architect to improve the arrangements for musicians in a theater. Guitti's design is preserved in a drawing that he included in a letter of February 18, 1628 to Enzo Bentivoglio in Ferrara.[40] The drawing (Fig. 148), which Guitti notes is without measurements, shows a half-oval space, marked A, set inside stairs attached to the front of the stage. The floor of A is at the level of the floor of the theater. The musicians would sit in this area, hidden from the audience by the wall that protected them from the water of the *naumachia*. The stairs were movable, so that they could be extended or retracted as needed to allow movement between stage and floor; Odoardo used these stairs at least once to enter a combat. On top of the wall, C, was a balustrade that supported lamps that illuminated the stage and the musicians' scores. Monteverdi, according to Guitti, was very pleased with this arrangement for his players, perhaps his first experience of an orchestra pit. Guitti states, "Monteverdi has finally found the Harmony, because I have accommodated him with a place for his benefit, which works well for him."[41] Clearly Monteverdi had been searching for solutions to at least two problems he faced in creating a successful performance in the theater. In its vast space, his compositions, played by small ensembles, might be difficult to hear; before going to Parma he had said that he needed to study the large hall in order to compose for it.[42] Second, his musicians needed to coordinate with each other and with the singers on stage. He expressed his dissatisfaction with the arrangements for musicians[43] and turned to Guitti for a solution. According

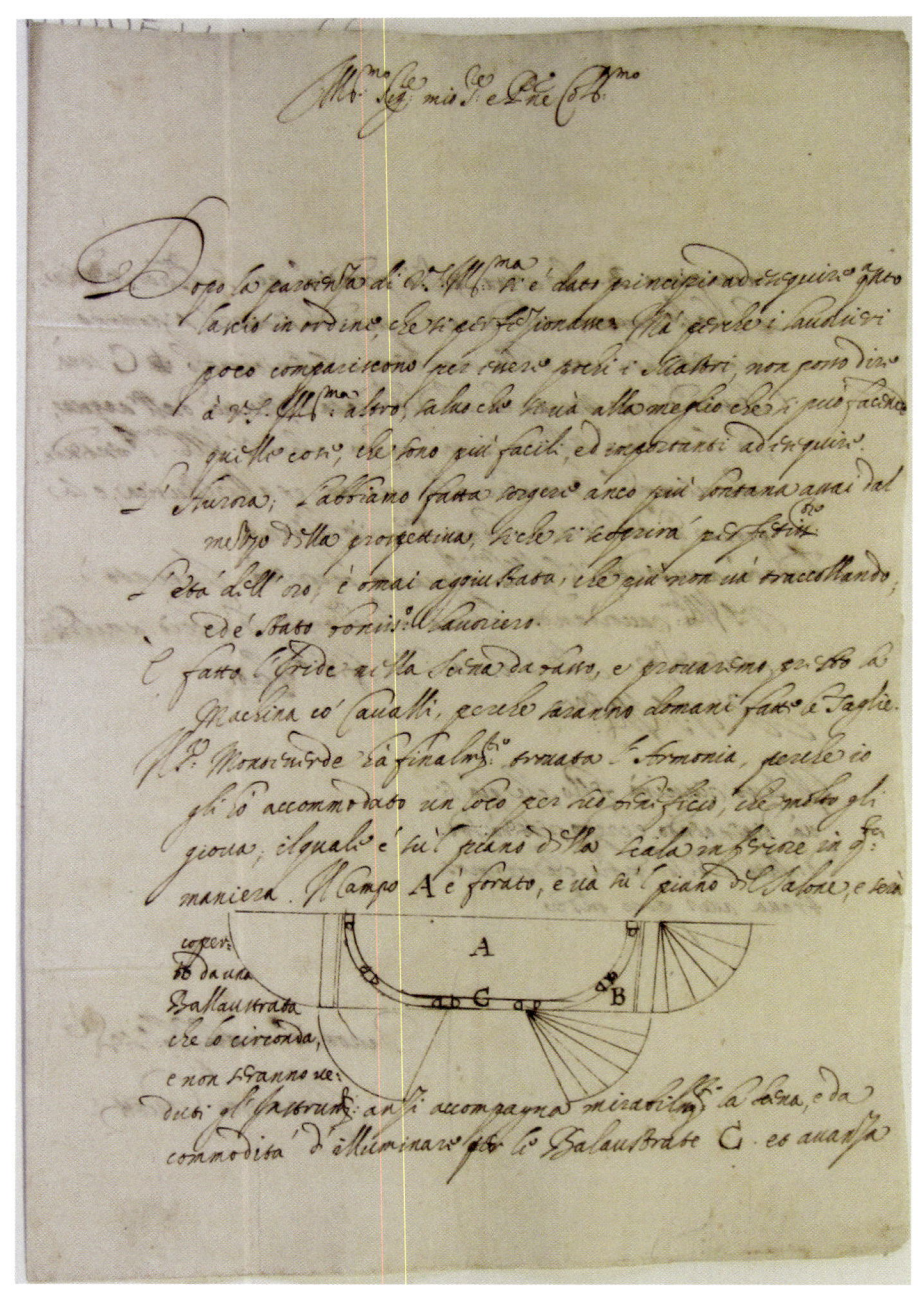

FIG. 148 Francesco Guitti, letter of February 18, 1628 to Enzo Bentivoglio (Biblioteca Comunale Ariostea, Ferrara, Manoscritti Antonelli, ms. 660)

to Guitti, the pit had worked well in a trial both in terms of hiding the musicians from the audience and in terms of the quality of the sound projected into the space. In Parma Monteverdi placed his musicians in five locations in the theater – the pit, the balconies below the two equestrian statues, and on both sides of the stage (presumably behind the scenery). Guitti's pit did not completely solve the problem of allowing all the musicians to see each other all the time; nor did it entirely solve the problem of the coordination of music with the movement of the scenery, an issue that was still troubling as late as a month before the performance of December 21.[44] It would seem that Monteverdi placed his instrumentalists in several places in the large theater, much as he famously placed his choirs around the vast interior of the church of San Marco in Venice, where he was choirmaster. Monteverdi did not, in the end, entirely find his Harmony in Guitti's pit.

Far less care was taken with the locations for musicians in Guitti's theater outside in the courtyard of the Pilotta. Monteverdi's associate, Antonio Goretti, complained bitterly about the arrangements for musicians in a letter of November 16, 1627 to Enzo Bentivoglio:

> We have had a lot of trouble because the space assigned us for this blessed music is too small, as if it were not an essential part of the performance. But no one ever thinks about the place where the music will be played, even though it is a vital problem. I had hoped we would have a better arrangement in this new theater, but just the opposite is true.[45]

FERRARA, TEATRO DEGLI OBIZZI, 1660

In 1660 a coda to the grand architectural composition of the Teatro Farnese was built in Ferrara. A fire in that year destroyed Aleotti's Teatro degli Intronati, which had been purchased and restored in 1640 by Pio Enea degli Obizzi's father, Roberto.[46] Pio Enea rebuilt the theater immediately, giving the architectural commission to Carlo Pasetti, who had worked in the theater in the previous decade. Luckily, a contemporary description of the theater and a view of its interior have come down to us[47] (Fig. 149).

A major purpose of the theater was to offer a space where tourneys could still be held. Although the vogue for such entertainments was waning, Ferrara still had a taste for them, and locals decried the loss of the old theater of the Accademia degli Intrepidi, because it was the only one remaining that was capable of presenting such spectacles. Pio Enea rushed to fill the void. The seating was arranged in a U, with a slight widening of the central space at the fourth box toward the stage. The seating arrangement was rather complex: a combination of risers, with only slender columns as vertical separations, in the lower three levels, and boxes in the fourth and fifth. At each level the seating areas retreated slightly from the center of the theater, so that the boxes on the fourth and fifth levels were shallow. The purpose of the receding seats was to enhance the sight lines of action on the floor. The two top rows received the most elaborate architectural treatment. In the central group of nine boxes, herms poised on extremely slender shafts rose through both levels to support the cornice under the ceiling, while the convex fronts of the boxes at the top

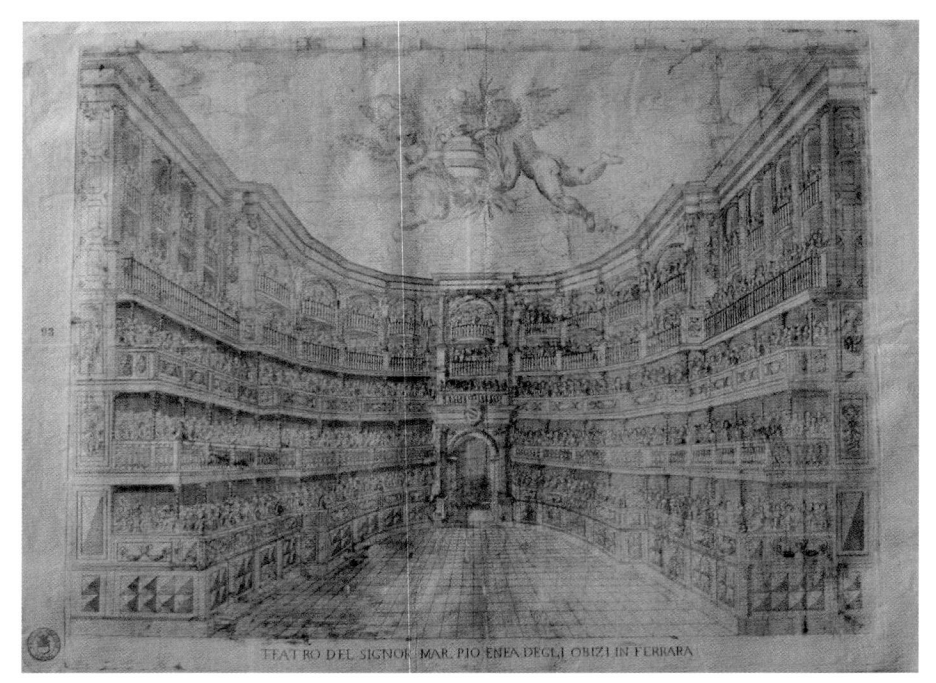

FIG. 149 Teatro degli Obizzi, Ferrara, view of interior, engraving, 1660 (Biblioteca Comunale Ariostea, Ferrara, Raccolta Iconografica ferrarese, H 5.1, n. 93)

undulated in a vigorously Baroque fashion. Where the sides of the theater became straight, toward the stage, the herms gave way to a giant order of flat pilasters. On the central axis were two tall arches, the lower sheltering the entrance for knights, the upper arch rising above the projecting box on the third level reserved for the cardinal-legate. The legate, however, had to endure two more boxes over his head.

The elaborate architecture of the upper levels suggests that only members of the more fortunate classes attended this theater.

The architecture was busy – note the Ferrarese diamond patterns at floor level – perhaps appropriately so for a theater in which the attention of the audience would be focused more on the central space than on the stage. Heraldic devices of the Obizzi were sprinkled around the interior. The ceiling appears to have been painted to resemble a cloud-filled sky, and the two oversized flying putti bearing Obizzi arms in the print (Fig. 149) may actually have been part of the ceiling decoration. The stage was deep, with space for long perspectives in the scenery, and of course, since we are in Ferrara, the stage opening was framed by paired columns flanking niches with statues. In its nervous complexity, this theater, without the clarity of form of its predecessor by Aleotti, represents the twilight of the drama-tourney theater. That twilight had been hastened by the dawn of publicly performed opera.

9

SEVENTEENTH-CENTURY THEATERS IN VENICE, THE INVENTION OF THE OPERA HOUSE

REOPENING THE COMEDY THEATERS

With the expulsion of the Jesuits from Venetian territory in 1607 and a younger generation of Venetians in power, comedies returned within a month of the settlement between the republic and the papacy. By the summer of 1608 the English traveler Thomas Coryat could go to a play in a modest theater, which had a ground floor for the all-male audience and an upper level where masked courtesans sat (see Chapter 5). Coryat's description, one recalls, seems to be of an interior hastily arranged to catch the first economic fruits of the return of comedies.[1]

Quickly the Tron family, which had built one of the theaters that opened in 1580 (see Chapter 5), got back into the business of being impresarios, probably in 1610, or perhaps even earlier.[2] In that year G. B. Andreini, a member of a commedia dell'arte troupe, wrote to the duke of Mantua that he did not think his company would play carnival in Venice that year because of the "great controversies that have arisen, the fault of everyone wanting boxes, for which many nobles have become enemies."[3] This language suggests that boxes may have just become available for the coming carnival, and it makes clear that there were not enough to go around. Because we know that the other two Venetian theaters for commedia dell'arte that date from the first decades of the seventeenth century did not exist in 1610, Andreini's letter likely referred to the Tron theater, known as the Teatro San Cassiano after the parish in which it stood. A second theater, the Teatro San Moisè, built by two brothers of the Giustiniani family, opened for business during the 1613–14 carnival season. According to a letter of January 18, 1614, written to the majordomo of Don Giovanni de' Medici (natural son of Cosimo I), "There has been built in this city a theater to perform comedies better, more capacious and more beautiful than the one your lordship knows at San Cassiano."[4] Within six years of the return of comedies to Venice, then, two theaters had been erected to house them. The first of these clearly had boxes over which noble families were squabbling in 1610.

The Teatro San Cassiano had a direct relation to the Tron theater of 1580. When the Council of Ten ordered the demolition of that theater, it did not order the destruction of the materials that had been used to build it. The Tron, hoping for an eventual change in governmental policy, may have stored the pieces, available for reassembly once the ban on comedies were lifted. The clear mention of the controversy over boxes in Andreini's letter of 1610 suggests that the new theater had a similar disposition of spaces to that of its predecessor. That theater had been a great success when it opened in 1580. In that year Ettore Tron (1535–99), one of the brothers who had invested in the theater, wrote to the duke of Ferrara that the boxes of his theater were rented to many nobles.[5] It would seem that history repeated itself in 1610.

A younger Ettore Tron (1573–1646), nephew of Ettore Tron who opened the theater in 1580, ran the theater in the early seventeenth century. The second Ettore was the son of Andrea Tron (1543–83), who had died leaving a number of very young children. In their name a pleading letter had been written to the Council of Ten, just before the theater was ordered demolished, begging that the theater be allowed to operate so that Andrea's fatherless children might be supported by its receipts.[6] The second Ettore, Andrea's oldest son, was one of those orphans. He had been twelve when his family's theater was ordered demolished, old enough to remember the humiliation and financial loss. That alone would have been reason for him to rebuild the theater quickly, once the chance presented itself. He had also been old enough to remember that the theater had been composed of boxes, and one can imagine that his uncle Ettore had told him the story of the early success of the family enterprise.

In 1619 in a series of letters written between June and December we hear something quite specific about the Tron theater.[7] Ettore was trying to chisel the actors out of their share of the rent of the boxes. A letter of October 20 states that Tron had previously given the actors a fourth of that rent. Now, the correspondent states, he does not intend to give the comedians anything from the boxes, "something that has never happened before."[8] In comparison, a second theater owner, Lorenzo Giustiniani, had been giving the actors half of the receipts from the boxes in his theater, the Teatro San Moisè.[9] Lorenzo and his brother Alvise were newcomers to the theater game. Although their San Moisè seems to have been rather small, it apparently imitated the Tron theater in having boxes. That would have been smart business, given the eagerness the Venetian nobility had shown to possess them. Lorenzo Giustiniani wrote to Don Giovanni de' Medici in 1613 that he would give the Confidenti, the commedia dell'arte troupe he hoped to have in his theater at carnival, the rent from the chairs and stools in the platea as well as a "reasonable" portion of the rent from the boxes.[10] That reasonable portion would seem to have been half.

In 1622 a third great Venetian family, the Vendramin, opened the Teatro San Luca or San Salvador.[11] In January of that year Alvise Vendramin promised to erect a theater for comedies at a cost of roughly three thousand ducats, and to have it ready by Christmas.[12] This theater persists, in quite altered form, as the Teatro Goldoni, the main venue for legitimate theater in Venice today. (The San Cassiano and San Moisè have long disappeared. The site of the former is now the garden of Palazzo Albrizzi.) It seems to have been slightly smaller than the Giustiniani theater, in that in 1635 it was evaluated for tax purposes at four hundred ducats, whereas the San Moisè was evaluated at five hundred.[13] It too had boxes, because they are mentioned in a contract of 1622 between the Accesi, the resident troupe, and the owners.[14]

Probably after 1633, a young man from a particularly rich and powerful noble family, Giovanni Grimani, opened a small wooden theater for comedies. We know almost nothing about this theater, but Giovanni Grimani was to play a major role in the history of theaters for opera.

For reasons that are not clear, the records of the Council of Ten bear no trace of these theaters. That body seems, after 1607, to have lost almost all interest in controlling theatrical production in Venice. The decree of 1508 that gave the Ten the power to regulate theater was never repealed, and on rare occasions it was reinvoked in subsequent centuries. But during the revival of comedies in Venice in the early decades of the seventeenth century, the government kept a hands-off attitude. That can only have been a relief for the owners of the theaters.

Lack of supervision by the Council of Ten did not signal that going to these theaters was entirely safe. On the night of November 28–29, 1621, a nobleman, Benetto Bembo, was assaulted by four armed men as he entered the Teatro San Moisè. The assailants were thrown out of the theater, but they lay in wait near the main entrance. When Bembo left the theater, accompanied by another noble, Bernardo Marcello, and Zuane di Benedetti, the three were attacked mercilessly. Zuane was killed instantly and Bembo died later from mortal wounds. Marcello miraculously escaped, his cloak having protected him.[15]

Murder inside a theater was not unknown. During the carnival of 1632–33, on the night of January 15 in the Teatro San Luca, one noble, Francesco Foscolo, attacked two other nobles, Donà Pisani and Gerolamo Marin, wounding the first and killing the second. Others were involved, including a musician named Marte.[16] Foscolo and Marte were absolved of the crime.[17]

On December 18, 1633 Piero Gritti, who had gone to the Teatro San Luca unarmed and accompanied by his sons, was murdered by Zuanne Morosini with many blows of a dagger. Gritti, whose sons ranged in age from ten to seven, died on December 24. His mother and his widow petitioned the Council of Ten to bring the murderer to justice. Morosini was banished in perpetuity, or he could surrender himself to the Ten and be exiled to Marano (a town at the northern end of the Adriatic Sea just west of Trieste) for five years.[18]

In 1670 Nicolò Foscarini was murdered by Giovanni Mocenigo in the Teatro San Luca,[19] and ten years later two senators of the Contarini and Grimani families got into an argument over a seat in a box and Grimani was stabbed in the shoulder with a knife.[20]

The Teatro San Cassiano flourished until 1629, when, according to an entry in a manuscript in the Museo Correr: "Tron theater reduced to ashes."[21] Because a great plague swept Venice in 1630, the theater was not rebuilt immediately. But it was up and running by 1633, when on December 16 the ambassador of the Holy Roman Emperor requested a box. Giving the ambassador a box meant taking one away from a Venetian. The ambassador generously stated that he did not want to inconvenience a noble. Rather, a box should be taken from a merchant, since merchants had the lion's share of the best boxes anyway.[22] One wonders whether indeed that was the case. The *cittadini* class, the group next down the social scale from the nobles, was composed of rich merchants, but nobles considerably outnumbered *cittadini*. Before a merchant could be thrown out, the theater burned down again on the night of December 19.[23] Constructed almost entirely of wood and lit by the flames of oil lamps and candles, theaters like the San Cassiano were all too susceptible to fire. Fortunately, we have no accounts of audiences being trapped inside them. The San Cassiano was rebuilt again within a year or two, and in this fourth version (the four versions dating from 1580, c. 1610, 1629ff., 1634ff.) it once again played a very important role in theater history. In 1637 it was the first theater, anywhere, in which a public performance of an opera to a paying audience took place.

TEATRO SAN CASSIANO AND THE FIRST PUBLIC PERFORMANCE OF OPERA

Since the San Cassiano IV holds such a crucial place in the history of opera, one would very much like to know all the architectural particulars. Unfortunately, we have almost no evidence. There is no visual record, nor is there a verbal description. Even the historical documentation that has been published about its first moment as an opera house cannot be retraced. Remo Giazotto, in a famous series of articles called "La Guerra dei Palchi" (The War of the Boxes) cited a document of May 1636, in which the Council of Ten gave permission to the Tron to "open a theater of music," but the document does not exist in the place Giazotto cited.[24]

Given the history of this Tron theater – in 1580 it was one of the first two with boxes in Europe and consistently rebuilt with boxes after 1607 – it seems safe to assume that San Cassiano IV had boxes like its predecessors'. There seems no reason for the Tron to have changed a profitable architectural situation. In terms of seating it continued to be the type of theater the Venetians had invented for commedia dell'arte. But to mount an opera such as *Andromeda*, the production for the carnival of 1537, a stage that had been sufficient for the needs of a commedia dell'arte troupe would not have been adequate for the new stage effects. We have the printed libretto for *Andromeda*, and so we know what scenic effects were required: a water scene, a forest, a palace, and another sea scene with Andromeda chained to a rock and guarded by a sea monster. These scenes apparently changed in view of the audience. The hero Perseus flew down from the sky to kill the monster and save the girl. There were several flying gods, and at the end Jupiter and Juno and other gods descended on clouds from the heavens. Hidden machinery was needed for all these airborne effects. The typical, unchanging sets on which comedies were played, composed of a few houses and a painted backdrop, required only a shallow stage and no hidden machinery. San Cassiano IV must have been fitted out with a deeper stage than its predecessors, and complex machinery must have been installed in the areas above, behind, and even below the stage.

Mancini, Muraro, and Povoledo argue convincingly that Alfonso Chenda was probably the person who designed the scenery and remodeled the stage. They make the compelling point that once *Ermiona* had been performed in Padua, the stage machinery that Chenda had designed for it was no longer needed there. Pio Enea degli Obizzi could have turned it over to the people involved in the Paduan production to use in Venice. Basically the same types of scenes occur in *Ermiona* and *Andromeda*, and so it would have been economical to adapt the machines to a new libretto. Mancini, Muraro, and Povoledo even suggest that the same scenery and machines were used in the opera *La Maga Fulminata*, produced the next year by the same crew at San Cassiano. The artists involved in the two operas footed the bills for the productions. They were not rich, and the libretto of the second tells us that they had spent less than two thousand ducats, a sum that suggests the maximum reuse of existing stage effects possible.[25]

At San Cassiano, there also had to be a place for the musicians who accompanied the opera. Even though their numbers were few, they still needed a place to sit together and play, where they could see the singers and the singers could see them. The orchestra pit had come into being in the preceding decade (see Chapter 8), and so one has to posit that this theater had some such arrangement for the instrumentalists.

The great shift that took place at the San Cassiano in 1637 replaced the simple, static sets of comedies with the effects of illusion and movement developed in court theaters, particularly in the wake of the achievements of Buontalenti for the Medici wedding of 1589 or of the artists associated with the Teatro Farnese of 1618–28. That kind of spectacle, heretofore reserved for audiences invited to great dynastic celebrations, was now made available to a paying public as part of the entertainment afforded by the new art form of opera, which combined the delights of music, singing, dancing, acting, rich costumes, and fantastic stage effects. The libretto of *La Maga Fulminata* made a pointed comparison between that thriftily but lavishly staged opera and court extravaganzas: "similar by princes cost an infinite amount of money."[26] Although the box holders at the opera were nobles or wealthy merchants or foreign ambassadors, others of far more modest means could attend the theater in the platea, from which they had as good a view of the stage – indeed, an even better view than some of the rich folks who had boxes far along the side toward the stage.

The success of opera at carnival was so remarkable that by 1639, only two years after *Andromeda* had gone on the boards, three theaters were offering opera to Venetians and to the foreigners who quickly began to come to Venice for the new musical entertainment. It is hard to imagine another innovation in theatrical entertainment that caught public fancy so rapidly, and so quickly caused the modification of theater design to accommodate it.

Before 1637, the Teatro San Moisè had changed hands. Its owners, the Giustiniani brothers, died childless and left the theater to relatives of their mother, the brothers Almorò and Marin Zane. The new owners remodeled the theater in 1629; in 1639 they remodeled it again, to enlarge the stage to accommodate the production of opera. The work with which they opened their enlarged theater was not new, but it was choice: Claudio Monteverdi's *Arianna*, originally produced at the Mantuan court for a Gonzaga wedding in 1608 (see Chapter 10). Court opera here made its first appearance on a public stage for a paying audience. In that same year another nobleman, Giovanni Grimani, abandoned his small theater for comedies and constructed a large new theater, the SS. Giovanni e Paolo, the first theater designed from scratch to present opera. Of this house, more later.

Some theater owners had violent pasts. Both Almorò Zane and Giovanni Grimani had been in serious trouble with the authorities. In 1614 Zane, age twenty, had a falling out with a prostitute, Chiara Gruata, who refused to take him back after he had abandoned her bed for many months. He began his revenge by throwing rocks at her window. Next he and a friend climbed up on her balcony and broke into her house; several days later he and a crowd of friends assaulted the house with stones, interrupting Chiara's dinner with gentlemen callers. The Council of Ten threw him into a cell without light for two years.[27] On May 5, 1621, Zane and a companion were attacked near the Ponte Tre Archi by Giacomo Priuli, son of the doge, and Zuanne Capello. Zane was seriously wounded, but Priuli and Capello were exonerated.[28] In 1630 Zane and the famous courtesan Perina Nave, accompanied by a *bravo* (sword for hire) in Zane's service, broke into a house where Nave's servant had sought refuge. They badly injured the wife and a servant of the owner of the house and mortally wounded the owner's son-in-law. The Council of Ten banned the *bravo* from Venice in perpetuity, but they found it difficult to agree on a punishment for Zane and Nave. While the debate on his fate stretched on, Zane broke out of prison. Enraged, the Ten banished him from the city for fifteen years. Nave ended up with a six-month stay in prison.[29] Zane apparently did not suffer banishment for long. Justice, the virtue on which Venice prided itself, could be flexible for nobles.

In 1632 Giovanni Grimani, age twenty-five, lay in waiting for several days with his *bravi* and servants to ambush the captain of the ships of the *capi* of the Council of Ten, who was seriously injured by a blow with a sharp weapon. Since the *capi* of the Ten were among the most powerful men in Venice, this was not a smart thing to do, unless arrogance led someone to consider his family's power all-reaching. Grimani was banished in perpetuity and fined five hundred ducats, to be given to the captain. If, however, he presented himself to the prison within a month, his fine would be reduced to three hundred ducats and he would be exiled to Zara for three years.[30] These dates suggest that, if he served his three years at Zara, he could not have opened his little comedy theater in Venice much before 1635.

TEATRO SS. GIOVANNI E PAOLO

Particularly significant for opera in Venice was the entry of the rich and powerful Grimani of Santa Maria Formosa. In 1639 Giovanni Grimani, now a mature thirty-two, suddenly decided to abandon his small comedy theater and build a new, larger theater of masonry, all in a remarkably short time, to jump on the opera bandwagon. Giovanni and his descendants – rich, powerful, ruthless – became the single most potent theater owners in seventeenth-century Venice. His theater opened during the carnival of 1639 with a new opera, *Delia osia la sera sposa del sole* (*Delia, or Evening Bride of the Sun*). In the printed libretto for *Delia*, the composer, Giulio Strozzi, praised:

> that most noble theater which [Giovanni Grimani] in this city of Venice, in the space of a few days has with such greatness of spirit caused to be born, to endure many year for the sole benefit of music. And it is true that it seems to me that the stones came together by themselves, as if

invited by by the harmony of new Anfioni, that ample and sturdy theater with so little effort rose from the foundations.[31]

This "ample" new theater, called the Teatro SS. Giovanni e Paolo after the nearby Dominican church, was considerably larger than the theaters it set out to overtake.[32] Indeed, Grimani in 1645 admitted to the Florentine ambassador to Venice that the theater was a bit too long for the best acoustics. Had he to do it over again, he would remove the two vertical tiers of boxes next to the stage, where the sound was not very good, and replace them with a column to either side.[33] The ambassador called the theater the most spacious and beautiful in Venice. The fact that it was built of masonry suggests that Grimani wanted to protect his investment from loss by fire, to avoid the fate of the wooden San Cassiano that had burned all too frequently.

We have no name for Grimani's architect. We know, however, from the published libretto of *Delia* that its scenery was designed by Alfonso Chenda.[34] He was, in all likelihood, also the architect. Because the SS. Giovanni e Paolo was the first theater built *ex novo* to house opera, Chenda was, in all probability, the first architect to design a purpose-built opera house.[35] In his statement in the libretto, Giulio Strozzi seemed to note the unique function of the theater when he stated that the house was for the benefit of music alone. No comedies intended.

Chenda was the scene designer and architect most closely associated with the earliest public performances of opera in Venice (see Chapter 7). He planned the temporary theater in Padua in 1636 for *Ermiona*, the tourney cum musical entertainment that became the catalyst for the first public opera performance a year later at the San Cassiano. Because the same troupe of singers and musicians who performed *Ermiona* in Padua was responsible for *Andromeda* in Venice, Chenda may well have remained part of that creative team and designed the sets for *Andromeda*. Or he may have adapted the sets for *Ermiona* to the new purpose of *Andromeda*. If he did either, then he would have been consulted on the modifications to the stage. Three years later, in 1639, Chenda was busy not only at the Teatro SS. Giovanni e Paolo in Venice, but also in Bologna, where, as we saw, he designed a new interior arrangement for the Teatro Salone in the Palazzo del Podestà. For Chenda's Bolognese theater we have a contemporary miniature that shows its appearance (Fig. 113). The two parallel sides of the theater are composed of superimposed rows of boxes for the spectators, while the far wall consists of a proscenium articulated by two columns that frame a landscape set. The sky of the landscape continues above the proscenium into a painted ceiling that turns the "Salone" into an outdoor space. This view may well give us a sense of what the Teatro SS. Giovanni e Paolo looked like in 1639.

The Grimani theater underwent remodeling at unspecified times. Twenty years or more after Giovanni first built the theater, perhaps in 1663, it was reconfigured.[36] At that point the ranks of boxes were likely increased to the remarkable number of seven, to produce the very tall house that was visited in 1663–64 by the Englishman Philip Skippon, who noted the seven levels.[37] A drawing of the theater, discussed later, shows five rows of boxes, but it was made in the 1690s, long after Skippon's visit. The theater shown in this drawing must be the result of another remodeling post 1664 that decreased the height of the house. Or perhaps the Englishman miscounted.

TEATRO NOVISSIMO

The Tron, Zane, and Grimani theaters all presented operas in 1639; only the Vendramins' Teatro San Salvador stuck with comedies. The financial success that the three opera-producing houses enjoyed led a group of "diversi Cavalieri" to band together to construct a fourth opera theater, the Teatro Novissimo, which opened in January, 1641, with a production of *La Finta Pazza* (*The Pretended Crazy Woman*), music by Francesco Sacrati, libretto by Giulio Strozzi, and a spectacular production designed by Giacomo Torelli, who also designed the theater.[38] The Novissimo, which rose on land rented from the monks of the nearby church of SS. Giovanni e Paolo, lasted only five seasons, collapsing for financial reasons. It was a brave attempt to create a different kind of house, one in part run by artists themselves rather than by noble entrepreneurs, although the original expenses were underwritten by three noblemen. Most scholars now believe that Torelli was the moving force behind the endeavor. When the theater failed, Torelli went to Paris to work for the French court. (For his later Italian career back in his hometown of Fano see Chapter 10.)

The Novissimo was located north of the church, toward the lagoon on the fringes of the city. One passed behind the noble Gothic apse to reach the land on which it stood, or else one arrived by gondola on the Fondamenta Nove, just adjacent to the north. The site is now incorporated into the Ospedale Civile. On the land stood two *tezze*, or storage buildings, that became the structures that housed the new theater, largely constructed inside them. The roof of one of the structures was not high enough to accommodate the boxes, of which there must have been at least three rows, and so it was raised.[39] According to a contract of October 2, 1640, the first part of the construction of the boxes consisted of an armature or frame that held them up.[40]

Torelli himself apologized to the audience of *Bellerofonte*, the opera presented in 1642, for the narrowness of the theater, caused by the shape of the site. "The site of the Teatro Novissimo is quite restricted, and for that reason not everything could be made to work together; the narrowness would make it hard for even a singular architect to make something perfect," Torelli wrote, with perhaps excessive modesty.[41] To fuse the spaces of the two *tezze,* the party wall or walls between them were removed. The stage itself was built *ex novo* on open ground, and the monks jealously stipulated that only that portion of the ground designated in a drawing for the theater could actually be used for the stage and the *sfondri,* a small structure tacked on to the rear of the stage to give an added illusion of depth to the scenery.[42] The monks did not want the theater to take up one more inch of their land than they had agreed to permit. There is no sense that money was spent on the exterior of the existing structures to give them visual unity or elegance. Indeed, the doors of both old buildings were maintained.

The monks had no intention of allowing the theater to persist for an extended period. The original contract stipulated that the theater would be in use for only two seasons, although the contract was renewed. The monks were also dead set against comedies and other buffooneries being played in the theater. The contract states that "nothing could be performed in the theater except *opere in musica,*[43] ... only the above mentioned heroic operas in song."[44]

In this narrow, hastily constructed theater some of the most important early public performances of operas took place. Part of their importance lay in the remarkable sets that Torelli designed and the new stage machinery he created to make his set changes work in a trice. Torelli was a gentleman from Fano, a city south of Venice on the Adriatic coast, who had been educated in Florence.[45] He came to Venice as a kind of naval architect attached to the Arsenale, that great factory for ships where the Venetian fleet was constructed in an early version of mass production. His experience with the outfitting of ships, specifically with the use of rope and tackle, played a major role in his creating machinery that moved sets with utmost ease. All it took to move a Torelli set was one man turning one wheel, instead of many men moving many separate parts simultaneously. We are told that when Torelli made the city of Venice appear to rise from the sea during the prologue of *Bellerofonte,* the audience was stupefied by the fool-the-eye effect[46] (Fig. 150).

Although we have no visual record of the interior of the Novissimo, we do have engravings of Torelli's sets for *Bellerofonte* and *Venere Gelosa* (*Jealous Venus*) (Fig. 151), the opera presented during the third season in 1643.[47] These engravings not only show the remarkable spatial effects Torelli achieved on stage, but also the different proscenia he designed for the two productions. For both, one architectural frame encloses all of the different sets. Each frame makes use of a different classical order: for *Bellerofonte* the Doric, for *Venere Gelosa* the Ionic. In the case of the former, the stage opening is marked at the sides by channeled Doric pilasters that carry an entablature divided into the requisite triglyphs and metopes (Fig. 150). The impression is of an orderly and rather severe architectural frame, an impression furthered by the geometric

FIG. 150 Giacomo Torelli, set for prologue of *Bellerofonte*, with view of Venice just risen from the sea (by concession of the Ministry of Cultural Resources and Activities and Tourism – Biblioteca Nazionale Marciana, Venice) (Photo: Shylock, Venice)

panels that decorate the wall beneath the stage. Only a couple of oval panels suggest anything even vaguely playful. Not so the proscenium for *Venere Gelosa*, where single Ionic columns rise above bases decorated with elaborate cartouches that contain masks (Fig. 151). The columns are banded and then wrapped with looping swags. The entablature that the columns carry breaks forward above them, and then recedes in the middle to make room for an elaborate cartouche, complete with curving borders, a motto on drooping swags, and figural decoration. The frieze has a bulbous rinceau decoration, while the wall below the stage has more swags, a projecting pedestal, and a lot of delicate strapwork that echoes the forms that encrust the surfaces of the columns. Deliberately excessive, it subscribes to the Mae West theory of aesthetics: "Too much of a good thing is wonderful."

The point of the difference between the two proscenia is clear. As far back as Vitruvius, the orders were thought to denote genders. The hefty Doric was considered masculine, the slender Ionic feminine. Bellerophon is a heroic male

FIG. 151 Giacomo Torelli, proscenium and set for prologue of *Venere Gelosa* (by concession of the Ministry of Cultural Resources and Activities and Tourism – Biblioteca Nazionale Marciana, Venice – reproduction prohibited) (Photo: Shylock, Venice)

figure who comes to the rescue of a helpless maiden. His acts must be framed by the Doric. Jealous Venus, the central figure of the second opera, is an exceedingly stereotypical, changeable female, whose characteristics are ridiculed both in the plot and in the outrageously "feminized" frame through which the audience viewed the opera. The same proscenium was used the following year for *Deidamia*, an opera also named for its female protagonist. If its proscenium could be changed to fit the nature of each opera, then the Novissimo was an empty vessel whose architecture could be manipulated to accord with the character of each new work. One suspects that the architecture of the proscenium was painted on the wall around the stage opening – cheap and easy to execute and change. The channels in the Doric pilasters of *Bellerofonte* cast illusionistic shadows that appear created by light that comes from a chandelier in the center of the auditorium and throws shadows to either side of the channels.[48] The Ionic columns of *Venere Gelosa* do the same.

The libretto of the first opera produced in the Teatro Novissimo played a knowing game with the audience, suggesting that the librettist was keenly aware of the levels of illusion that confronted viewers in the theater. As Ellen Rosand, who has beautifully analyzed the libretto, put it,[49] the opera wove "a complex and seductive web of connections with the audience."[50] The proscenium presented an illusion of architectural forms illuminated by the actual central chandelier. The sets would have been designed according to one-point perspective to give the illusion of being real spaces. The title, *La Finta Pazza*, refers to feigned insanity on the part of Deidamia, who is in love with Achilles, who is disguised as a girl by his mother to save him from death in the Trojan War (Deidamia knows he's a man). In the opera, there are plays within the play. Characters on stage, watching the inner play, self-consciously recognize that they are representatives of (or intermediaries for) the audience watching them. The architecture itself was part of the complex overlays of illusion and reality. The illusionistic proscenium was the frame through which awareness of these illusions passed.

THE SOANE MUSEUM DRAWING OF TEATRO SS. GIOVANNI E PAOLO

For all of these Venetian theaters of the seventeenth century we know only one drawing, a plan and section of the Teatro SS. Giovanni e Paolo, now in Sir John Soane's Museum, London, signed by Tommaso Bezzi[51] (Fig. 152). The drawing is bound into a volume of drawings that have to do with the construction of the Teatro Tordinona in Rome by the architect Carlo Fontana (see Chapter 11). The fact that an inscription on the drawing explains how to use the provided scale in Venetian feet suggests that the drawing was made for Fontana so that he could have a clear idea of one of the most important theaters in Italy to aid him in designing his own theater. He would have had no such precedent available in Rome, and it would have been natural for him to turn to Venice to learn how to lay out a modern house for opera. Bezzi identifies himself on the drawing as *ingegnero* of the Teatro S. Giovanni Grisostomo in Venice. Fontana's first version of the Tordinona opened in 1671, seven years before the S. Giovanni Grisostomo, and so the drawing cannot have been made to help in the design of that version. Fontana built a second, larger version of the theater in the 1690s, and so the state of the SS. Giovanni e Paolo that Bezzi's drawing shows must date from that time.[52]

Because this is the only piece of visual evidence we have from the seventeenth century that shows us a Venetian theater, we need to examine it carefully. The oblong sheet contains two drawings of the theater: to one side a plan and to the other a longitudinal section. There are several inscriptions that aid in identifying the parts and give their measurements, all in Venetian feet. A note at the top of the section says that the overall length is 120 feet. At almost precisely its middle the theater is divided into two parts, the auditorium and the stage.

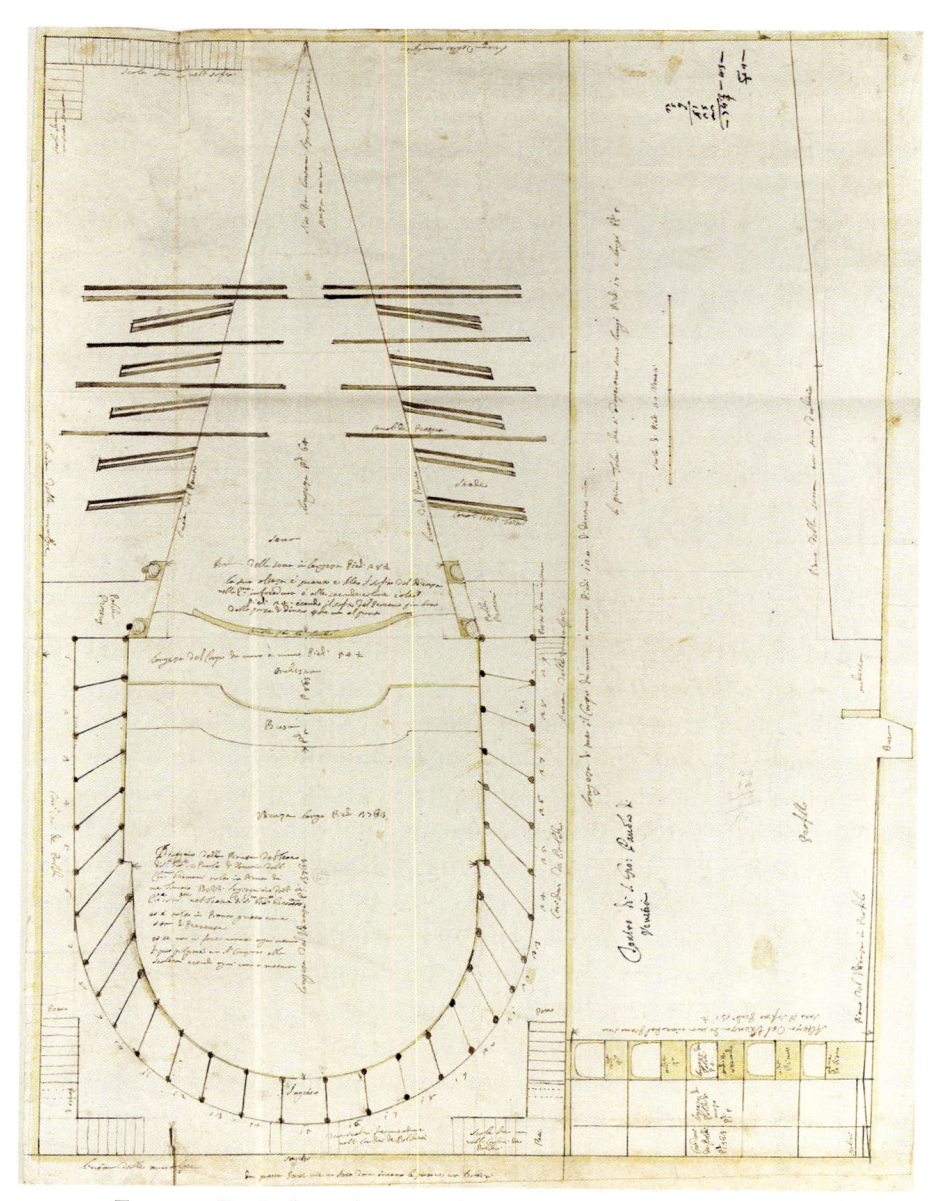

FIG. 152 Tommaso Bezzi, plan and section of Teatro SS. Giovanni e Paolo, Venice, 1691–95
(© Sir John Soane's Museum, London, 117, 34)

The plan shows ground level, with the platea surrounded by thirty-one boxes, numbered clockwise, laid out in the form of a semicircle extended by straight lines toward the stage. Where the curve and the straight lines join there is a small projection. The boxes are surrounded by an access corridor, and their party walls are set in an irregular radial pattern roughly centered on the center of the curved apron of the stage. The ends of the party walls between the boxes are marked by dark dots that indicate the vertical supports for the boxes. The segmentally curved, arched openings of the boxes into the auditorium are shown in elevation in the section drawing. According to an inscription, the boxes were four feet wide and five feet deep, at least in the boxes opposite the stage. Others halfway along the sides were deeper. No doors are indicated on the plan, but surely there were doors. At the corners of the building were two matching sets of stairs that led from the ground floor up to the other four rows of boxes. We can assume that the stairs on the upper level followed the same pattern. The entrance to the theater seems to have been on the central axis, but the plan is quite vague about the appearance of the exterior. The entrance seems to have been flanked by two steps to either side that led up to the level of the *pepian*, or bottom rank of boxes. Straight ahead was an empty space, instead of a box, that allowed access to the platea. At the end of the corridor on the stage-left side of the plan five steps led up to the level of the proscenium box and the stage. On the opposite side matching steps are not shown.

The section shows the ways the level of the ground floor changes. A digital reconstruction aids in reading this part of the drawing (Fig. 153). From the entrance there is a slight slope upward toward the floor of the platea, which in turn slopes down toward the stage to improve visibility. At the end of the sloping floor of the platea a deep channel is abruptly cut into the ground. On the plan, we can see that this channel had a curved edge at its center and a fairly constant width as it stretched across the house from one row of boxes to the other. The purpose of this "dry moat" was to protect the musicians and singers from the audience. Such a defensive feature attests to the unruly nature of seventeenth-century audiences, who often shouted, clapped, stomped their feet, and threw furniture and food at the stage and the boxes.[53] The elevation of the fronts of the boxes tells us that the wall below the box openings at the *pepian* level was higher than the walls of the upper boxes. This added height was probably designed to make jumping in or out of the *pepian* boxes during a performance more difficult. We know that the boxes on the lowest level were the favorites of young nobles, who liked to exchange bawdy remarks with gondoliers and others of the lower classes gathered in the platea. Sometimes fights broke out, if a young nobleman chose to leap into the platea to challenge a man who had spoken rudely to him. A general melee could result in pistols being fired, followed by pandemonium.[54] Beyond the moat was the area reserved for the musicians who accompanied the opera. They were concealed by a wall that separated them from the moat, but this wall was low enough not to block the view of the stage. The front of the orchestra pit curved in the same way the front of the moat curved, so that it appears that the shape of the moat simply followed the shape of the orchestra, which in turn responded to the curve of the apron of the stage.

The Teatro SS. Giovanni e Paolo was the largest in Venice for several decades. The other theaters got by on audiences that were smaller. If there

FIG. 153 Teatro SS. Giovanni e Paolo, Venice, digital reconstruction of longitudinal section (Drawing: Benjamin Hoyle)

were 31 boxes on five levels, minus one for the entrance to the platea at ground level, then there was a total of 154 boxes, each capable of holding four people, for a grand total of 616 in the boxes at each performance. The proscenium boxes could hold another 16–20 per side, depending on whether there were four or five levels of proscenium boxes. They would bring the total of people in boxes to slightly fewer than 650. It is difficult to estimate the number the platea could accommodate. If 250 could be squeezed into that area, assuming something like 5 square feet per person, then the theater may have held about 900. The moat took up about 150 square feet of floor space, or enough room for roughly 30 paying members of the audience. That is a reduction of only about 3 percent of the audience, but it still signifies a loss in box office receipts for the sake of security.

A goodly percentage of the audience, then, was made up of people who did not belong to the nobility or the *cittadini*. Contemporary sources tell us that anyone who had a just a little money for a ticket could go to the opera. A Roman nobleman reported at midcentury: "The cost to anyone who wants to see [the opera] does not exceed half a scudo, and almost everyone in Venice, without great inconvenience, can afford it, because money is abundant here."[55] As a French observer, Alexandre de Saint-Didier, pointed out in 1680, this made the people of Venice happy. "Nothing renders subjection sweeter to the people," he wrote, "than to see that they enjoy every pleasure in Venice in common with the nobles."[56] Foreigners found the opera useful for the conduct of discourse with Venetians, banned by law from talking to foreign ambassadors. The French ambassador noted that it was important for all the representatives of other states in Venice to go to the opera, where they could exchange signs with Venetians.[57] The corridors surrounding the boxes certainly provided places for encounters that may only have seemed to happen by chance. There a quick smile or nod or wave of the hand could go unobserved by the authorities, or two men in masks could exchange a word or two without being recognized. Boxes, as ever, could serve love as well as politics.

Giving slightly more than half of the area of the theater over to the stage makes clear how important scenic effects were for the success of public performances of opera in Venice. (The stage occupied 64 of the 120-foot length of the entire interior.) The stage effects in these performances were the seventeenth-century equivalent of the special effects in a film like *Star Wars*, which ushered in the era of flashy, computer-generated film imagery. Audiences went to the theater to be stunned by the cleverness of the illusions the scene designers had created. At the Teatro SS. Giovanni e Paolo the stage was framed by pairs of half-columns set along the two diagonal lines that controlled the placement of scenery farther upstage. The front of the stage bowed out in an elegant segmental curve that must have seemed to project the players at center stage toward the audience. The floor of the stage sloped up as it moved toward the back, a fact clearly shown in the section, so that the level of the stage at the rear wall of the theater was even slightly above the level of the floor of the second circle of boxes. The slope of the floor was part of the perspectival illusion built into the architecture itself, so that as the floor sloped upward, so did the wings at the sides of the stage come closer to each other to create the effect of a vanishing point in the distance. In the upper left corner of the plan are the indications of the stairs that led below the stage and up into the fly space, where the machinery was concealed. The slope of the stage floor created space beneath it to accommodate machinery.

Circulation for the audience was well handled by the pairs of stairs that connected each level of boxes. The boxes themselves were so divided as to point their interior spaces toward the stage for optimum viewing, while the openings into the boxes created frames around the box holders, on view from inside the theater. The boxes worked as places both to see and to be seen. There were serious problems of viewing for the box holders on the sides, however. Some of them had only the most fragmentary views of the visual spectacles on stage. Public opera had taken over the lavish stage effects of court *intermedi* and court opera, which depended on a single vanishing point to create scenery that worked best from the very center of the house. When the ruling prince and his party sat on a dais right in the center of the theater, they not only were the focus of the attention of the audience, but were also placed where they could enjoy the full delight of the sets, a delight from which almost all the rest of the audience was excluded. The theater with boxes, arranged in some kind of curve, was invented for performances of commedia dell'arte, which used only simple scenery on a shallow stage. Viewing such a stage is no problem from almost any box in the house. When the commedia dell'arte auditorium was joined to the court stage, however, no provision was made to improve the view of the deep stage for box holders on the side. The theater we see here is a hybrid that worked economically for the owners and socially for the box holders to display themselves, but not visually for those insufficiently important or rich to acquire a box toward the center of the curve. For those along the sides it must have been enough to be part of the spectacle, in an interior gussied up to give it something of the sumptuous quality of a palace. So it would seem from the description of a visiting Frenchman, Jacques de Chassebras de Cremailles, who wrote a long piece on Venetian opera houses for the *Mercure Galant*, a tony French journal, in 1683. While he devoted only a few words to the SS. Giovanni e Paolo (saving his most fulsome description for the S. Giovanni Grisostomo), he noted that it was beautiful, extremely deep, and painted and gilded.[58]

TEATRO SAN GIOVANNI GRISOSTOMO

Opened in 1678, the Teatro San Giovanni Grisostomo became the largest and by far the most elegant in the city.[59] With this theater, the Grimani put their own SS. Giovanni e Paolo in the shade, even though the latter continued to flourish until the early years of the next century.[60] Centrally located near the Rialto Bridge, the Teatro San Giovanni Grisostomo was erected on a largely rectangular plot that had once been the site of the houses of the family of Marco Polo.[61] A fire in 1595 had destroyed the medieval buildings; the few simple structures that stood on the site were easily removed. On two sides of the site were canals to bring well-to-do patrons to the theater. The theater takes its name from the nearby church dedicated to Saint John Chrysostom, an early church father who, ironically, fulminated against the sinfulness of the theater. The present-day Teatro Malibran, named for the great nineteenth-century soprano, Maria Malibran, who once sang Bellini's *La Sonnambula* there, rises on the same spot.

Of this theater we have two firsthand accounts and a view of its interior in a mediocre etching of 1709 (Fig. 154). The print shows a theater with five ranges of boxes supported by carved human figures, an orchestra pit with proscenium boxes to either side, and a stage with a presumably slanted floor and scenery that forms a deep perspective. There are a dozen musicians in the pit and two costumed performers on stage, but no one in the empty house to enjoy their skills. Above the proscenium arch is an enormous Grimani coat of arms.

The two written accounts, far more helpful, were made by a French opera enthusiast, Jacques de Chassebras de Cremailles, and a Swedish architect, Nicodemus Tessin, in Venice, respectively, in 1683 and 1688, within a decade of the opening.

Tessin's handwritten account in his journal contains loose sketches of details of the theater. He wrote in the German dialect spoken in Sweden in his day, a language that presents considerable difficulties for contemporary translators. Mancini, Muraro, and Povoledo published a "free adaptation in Italian, more comprehensible but not arbitrary," using seventeenth-century Venetian and

FIG. 154 Interior of Teatro S. Giovanni Grisostomo, Venice, etching, 1709 (Venice, Museo Civico Correr)

modern terminology.[62] Their indeed more comprehensible version of Tessin's text is followed here.

From Tessin we learn much that is not shown in the etching of 1709. There are 165 boxes in five ranges. Between the platea and the orchestra was a dry moat, similar to the one at SS. Giovanni e Paolo. Tessin describes some colors. The pairs of columns at the opening of the stage, barely visible in the print, were painted a light gray; their base a golden yellow. The white statues between the openings of the boxes were displayed against a green ground decorated with gilded foliage. There was a brilliant red curtain shot through with gold. An opening above the proscenium allowed performers to fly down from the stage toward the audience. Perhaps the most remarkable architectural detail has to do with the configuration of the nine boxes opposite the stage. They are arranged almost in a straight line, to give them better views of the stage, despite the fact, as Tessin notes, that a curved end of the theater opposite the stage is better for acoustics.[63] The central box projects forward into the theater, something that Tessin showed in a sketch (Fig. 155). Unfortunately, Tessin did not draw the entire theater.

The description of Chassebras de Cremailles of the Teatro San Giovanni Grisostomo is the most elaborate we have of any Venetian theater of the seventeenth century. Written only five years after the opening, it gives us the theater in its heyday. The description should be read with an eye on the view

FIG. 155 After Nicodemus Tessin, sketch plan of nine central boxes of Teatro S. Giovanni Grisostomo, Venice (Drawing; Troy Siprelle)

of the interior of 1709 (Fig. 154). Here translated is the passage almost in its entirety (a few remarks are deleted, where they have no bearing on the architecture), with explanatory comments inserted between the paragraphs:[64]

> Of the six other theaters that are used for Opera, I will begin with that of Teatro S. Giovanni Grisogono [Saint John Chrysostom]. This is the one most talked about, and which one could call a Royal Theater for its magnificence. It belongs to the same two brothers, Messieurs de Grimani, who built it in 1677 with a marveolous swiftness, only three or four months being necessary for its construction.
>
> This family is originally from Lombardy, and they moved from Vicenza to Venice in the 8th century. They have given two Doges to the Republic, Antonio in 1521 and Marin in 1595. There have been three Cardinals, Domenico under Alexander VI who left his library to the Republic, Marin, under Clement VII and Giovanni under Pius IV, and also three Patriarchs of Aquilea, and many great officers, and they have still at present two Procurators of Saint Mark, Antonio and Francesco, who are among the first dignitaries of Venice and the office is awarded for merit.

The opening of the passage stresses the historical importance of the Grimani family in Venice. The point was to assure the readers of the *Mercure Galant* that opera in Venice was under the highest possible patronage. The author's statement that the theater was magnificent enough to be called a royal theater is justified by pointing to the distinguished family history of its noble patrons.

> This Teatro S. Giovanni Grisogono is the largest, most beautiful and richest of the city. The room for the audience is surrounded by five rows of boxes, one above the other, with thirty one in each row. They are enriched with ornaments of sculpture in the round and in relief, all gilded, representing different sorts of ancient vases, shells, animal heads, roses, rosettes, florettes, leaves and other enrichments. Below and between each of these boxes are also human figures painted to resemble white marble, also in relief, and life-size, holding up the boxes which they also separate. These are men with clubs, slaves, terms of both sexes, and groups of little children, all disposed so that the heaviest and most massive are below and the lightest above.

This part of the description stresses the richness of the decorations. No surface had been left undisturbed, so that the effect of all the gilded ornaments must have been dazzling. These ornaments framed the figures of the boxholders looking into the auditorium and at each other, surrounded by splendor.

Particularly interesting is the description of the marbleized figures that seemed to hold up the rows of boxes. They were arranged in the following order, from bottom to top: males with clubs, who obviously represented muscular Hercules; then slaves, also strong men who refererred to the famous figures by Michelangelo; then herms, first the stronger male and then the weaker female; finally, groups of children.[65] Once we know this cast of characters, it is fairly easy to descry their presence in the engraving of the interior. Each group of figures had increasingly less to support as the building rose vertically, so that the apparent strength of each was diminished in a logical fashion, from Hercules, the strongest of the ancient heroes, to children at the top. The herms served as boundaries between the interiors of the boxes and the center of the house, and as framing elements for members of the audience. All in all, the rows of figures gave the interior a wonderful sense of richness and fantasy that the apparently more severe earlier theaters of the city had lacked. In the drawing of the SS. Giovanni e Paolo, made by the same Bezzi who may have designed this theater, the fronts of the boxes were quite plain. The San Giovanni Grisostomo seems to represent a quantum leap in elaborate decorations for Venetian theaters.

> The upper walls and ceiling of the room are painted with a fictive architecture in the form of a gallery, at one of the ends of which and on the sides of the theater are the arms of the Grimani, and above a glory of some mythical divinity, with a quantity of little winged children, who carry garlands of flowers.
>
> The stage is thirteen toises [the toise equaled 5 to 5 1/2 ft.] and three feet long, by ten toises and two feet wide, raised up in proportion.[66] It opens through a great arch [Portique] of the height of the room, in the thickness of which are four more boxes on each side of the same symmetry as the others, but much more ornate and enriched; and in the vault or arcade two Fames with their trumpets appear suspended in air, and a Venus in the middle who caresses a little Amor.
>
> An hour before the opening of the theater, the picture of this Venus disappears and reveals a great opening, from which descends a chandelier with four silver and gold branches, twelve or fourteen feet tall, of which the main body is a great cartouche of the arms of the Grimani, with a crown of Fleur de Lys, and of rays surmounted by pearls. This chandelier carries four great flambeaux of white wax, which light the room, and remain lit until the curtain is raised, and then it all vanishes, and goes back to its original state. When the performance is over, this machine appears anew to light the audience, and to make it easy for them to exit, without confusion. The arms have eight vertical stripes of silver and red, the third stripe charged with a small cross with two red crossarms. This cross distinguishes one of the branches of the family. It was given to their ancestors as proof of their valor in the holy wars at the time of Godefroy de Bouillon.

The last part of the description dwells on the upper part of the house. Above the tiers of boxes, with their figural decorations, was a level of painted architecture, a gallery that suggested that the interior of the theater opened to the sky. In this sky were painted the representation of an ancient god the Frenchman did not recognize, along with flights of putti bearing flowers. The children sound particularly Venetian, the descendants of the glorious putti of Titian and Veronese. In the center of the ceiling two figures of Fame were painted as if in flight. (Probably they were not sculpture suspended from the ceiling, although one could read the text to say that.) They flanked a painting of Venus caressing her son, Amor. The fame of Love is trumpeted from the center of the house, an appropriate image to rise over a stage on which tales of love will unfold. Then, wonder of wonders, we learn that the painting of Venus and Cupid can slide away, to allow a huge chandelier to descend into the theater an hour before the curtain rose, to light the way for the arriving audience. The chandelier would disappear at the beginning of the performance, and return to light the departure of the spectators at the end of the evening. Its descent and ascent must have been a remarkable sight.

The shape of the chandelier is equally startling – the central section was a great coat of arms of the Grimani family, whose arms were also rendered in paint on three sides of the ceiling. De Chassebras de Cremailles even gives us the colors of the arms, silver and red, which allows us to color in the arms visible above the stage in the engraved view. At the end of the performance, then, the space of the theater changed from one in which Venus was triumphant to one on which the Grimani triumphed. The figures of fame that had once flanked Venus now flanked the arms of the Grimani. If we think back to the careful arrangement of the arms of greater powers in the Gonzaga theater in Mantua of 1501 (see Chapter 1), or to the crown-shaped chandeliers representing popes and emperors at the Medici wedding of 1565 (see Chapter 4), the contrast is striking. No higher power soars over the arms of these Venetian nobles, who can create a theater that might be called royal. The theater trumpets their fame.

10

SEVENTEENTH-CENTURY THEATERS FOR COMEDY AND OPERA

Around the turn of the seventeenth century, one recalls, opera as an art form emerged in Florence and then Mantua. There is little of architectural interest about the spaces in which opera was first performed in Florence, but the presentation of Claudio Monteverdi's *Arianna* in Mantua in 1608 marked the beginning of the construction of grand spaces for the performance of operas. Thirty years later, commercial opera theaters came into existence in Venice, described in Chapter 9. Quickly theaters for the new art form began to rise all around the Italian peninsula.

MANTUA, 1607 AND 1608

Duke Vincenzo I Gonzaga (r. 1587–1612) devoted much of his energy and fortune to the patronage of theatricals. In 1598 Vincenzo staged Giovanni Battista Guarini's pastorale, *Il Pastor Fido*, a complex undertaking that required years to bring to fruition, in a theater designed by the court architect, Antonio Maria Viani. Sadly, we have no visual evidence for Viani's theater, nor do we know what the stage machinery invented by the young Giovanni Battista Aleotti from Ferrara looked like.

During Vincenzo's years *Orfeo* and *Arianna,* the two earliest operas of his court composer, Monteverdi, were first performed. *Orfeo* was given a modest premier on February 24, 1607, the last day of carnival, in a room which is described as "angusta" (narrow and cramped). Probably the performance took place in the Gonzaga palace in the suite occupied by Vincenzo's sister, Margherita Gonzaga, last wife of Alfonso II d'Este and last duchess of Ferrara, who returned to Mantua after her husband's death.[1] The opera, sponsored by Vincenzo's sons, Francesco and Ferdinando Gonzaga, could not be presented in the permanent theater of the court, because the duke had already scheduled a comedy for that venue that day. This landmark in the history of music hardly had its first outing in a landmark in the history of architecture.

Arianna, on the other hand, was performed in front of a vast public in 1608 as part of the celebration of the marriage of Francesco Gonzaga, heir to the duchy, to the Infanta Margherita of Savoy. A large outdoor theater, overlooking the lakes that encircle Mantua, was constructed by Viani. A contemporary said it held five thousand people, a figure deserving suspicion. No visual representation of Viani's theater is known, but there were contemporary verbal descriptions. From these Nino Pirotta has reconstructed certain aspects of the theater,[2] which had a wide stage hidden by a curtain that, at the sound of trumpets, rose to disappear in an instant.[3] In front of the stage, at a lower level, was a space with a flat floor on which performers danced. To either side of this space were large raised areas given over to seats for ambassadors or to musicians, who were able to see the performers on stage or on the floor. The seating may have been semicircular, or it may have been polygonal. No proscenium is mentioned, but it is hard to believe that none existed. Viani's theater hosted three different productions as part of the marriage celebration: *Arriana*, *Idropica*, a comedy by Guarini that lasted well over five hours, and the *Ballo delle Ingrate*, a ballet.[4] (Seemingly there were no chivalric jousts.) The scenic effects were apparently marvelous. At the end of *Arriana* Bacchus and Ariadne appeared center stage, Venus rose from the sea alongside the large rock that dominated center stage, Jupiter floated in on a cloud, and soldiers of Bacchus danced in the orchestra. There must have been machinery both below and above the stage. Opera, in its infancy as an art form, became the offspring of court patronage, with all of the tricks that patronage had come to require of theatrical presentations.

Around 1640, variations on the public opera houses that had developed in Venice began to spread throughout Italy, sometimes accompanying the new art form of opera as a shell travels with its turtle. Operas first produced publicly in Venice were taken – sometimes by all or part of the original company, sometimes by groups of traveling musicians – to other centers, which had to erect or modify theaters to accommodate the combined spectacle of music, drama, dance, costumes, and scenery. Three types of patrons assumed responsibility for creating appropriate theaters. In cities under direct princely or vice-regal control, a new theater generally rose under the auspices of the ruler, who used it for his own political purposes. In cities where the local upper classes controlled cultural affairs, an academy or a similar organization of educated gentlemen usually sponsored the theater's construction. Some cities, such as Florence, saw a combination of both types of patronage. Sometimes traveling players built their own theaters for profit, as in Naples.[5] The variety of solutions to the same basic problem – housing opera – is striking. It was a period of experimentation.

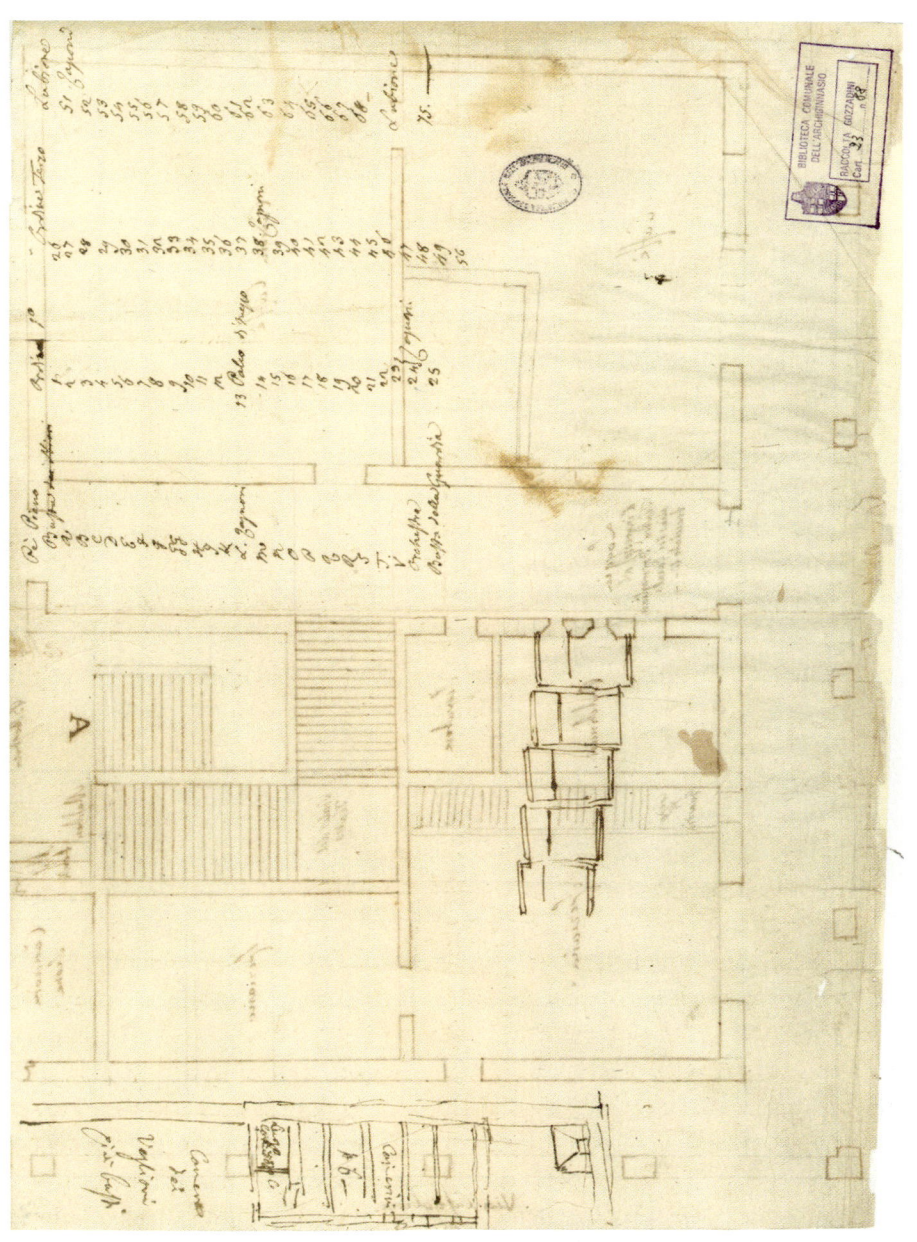

FIG. 156 Teatro Formagliari, Bologna, 1641, plan in 1802 with sketch of stepped boxes (Bologna, Biblioteca Comunale dell'Archiginnasio, Raccolta Gozzadini, cart. 23, n. 88)

BOLOGNA, 1641 AND 1653

The use of theaters with boxes for opera in Venice quickly set off a copycat process in relatively nearby Bologna, where the ruling papal legate left decisions about culture up to the local aristocracy to keep that group content. In 1641 the gentlemen of the Accademia dei Riaccesi constructed in Palazzo Formagliari a new theater designed by the local architect Andrea Sighizzi. These gentlemen were disdainful of the lower classes who flocked to Alfonso Chenda's Teatro della Sala in the Palazzo del Podestà, with which we are familiar (Fig. 113). Teatro Formagliari, to distinguish itself architecturally, had a U-shaped plan with orders of boxes to which Sighizzi gave a novel conformation by stepping each level down in a regular manner toward the stage (Fig. 156). A contemporary chronicler described the theater in reverse terms: "the boxes, as they move from the stage toward the center of the theater, rise by a few inches one above the other, and similarly they also project a few inches into the space. In that way each box better faces the stage, and the one does not impede the view of the other."[6] Thus were the aristocrats of Bologna given better views of the stage. A clear improvement on the Venetian prototype, this scheme was picked up in the eighteenth century by the Bolognese Francesco Galli Bibbiena for his Teatro Filarmonico in Verona of 1716. A drawing of Bibbiena's Veronese theater (Fig. 157) shows the nature of

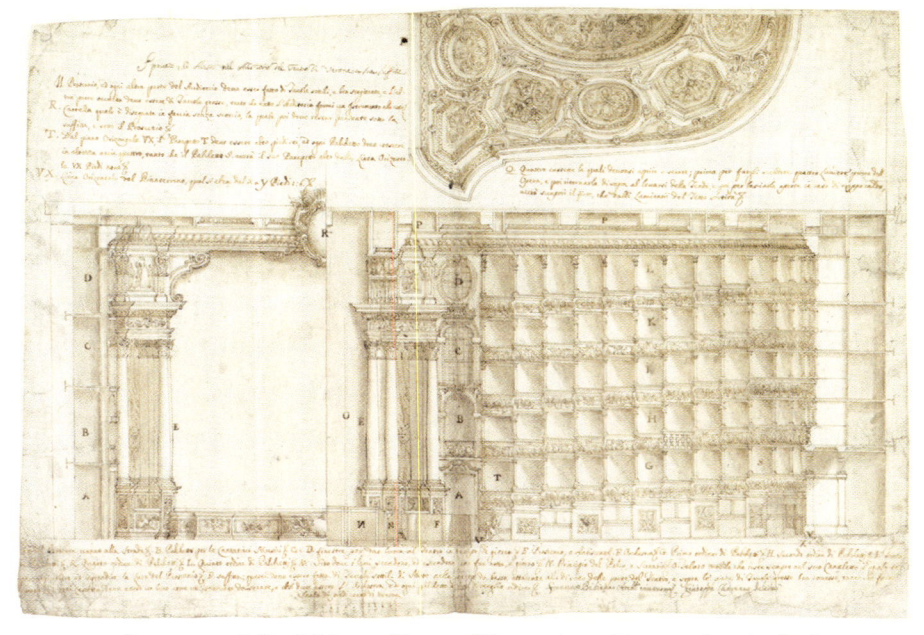

FIG. 157 Francesco Galli Bibiena, Teatro Filarmonico, Verona, longitudinal section, drawing, 1716 (Cooper-Hewitt, Smithsonian Design Museum, New York. Art in the public domain)

Sighizzi's invention for the Formagliari, which no longer stands. At Teatro Formagliari the ends of the boxes slightly contracted toward the stage. There were a forestage and an orchestra pit, and perhaps proscenium boxes.[7] Sighizzi himself used his scheme again in Bologna for his Teatro Malvezzi of 1653, a house that, although less exclusive socially, was also built by upper class subscribers. Why this type of theater, with its improved sight lines, did not enjoy a wider success is not clear.[8] Perhaps the added cost of constructing multiple levels was its downfall. The lack of enthusiasm for Sighizzi's clever scheme suggests that sight lines were not the most important issue for audiences. Being seen counted more than what one saw.

NAPLES, 1650 AND 1652

In September 1650, the ambassador of the duke of Modena reported from his post in Naples on theatrical events in the palace of the Spanish viceroy, Count Oñate. The count had invited a group of players and musicians, from "diverse parts of Italy," to perform at his court. According to the ambassador, "the musicians have made at their expense a sumptuous theater with boxes and superb costumes at a cost of 2,500 ducats."[9] That was no mean sum. Three weeks later the ambassador reported that the theater erected by the musicians was in a room in the vice-regal palace called the Stanza del Pallonetto, a name that indicates a space for court tennis, or some other type of indoor ball game. The production of the opera, *Dido, or the Burning of Troy*, had been a great success. The spectators had to pay to enter the theater: five carlini at the door, two carlini to rent a stool, and four ducats to rent a box. Even the viceroy himself had to pay for his box.[10] *Dido* originally had been presented in Venice during the carnival of 1641 at the Trons' Teatro San Cassiano. The printed Neapolitan libretto of *Dido*, dated October 10, 1650, was signed by one Curzio Manara, who styled himself "Pellegrino Architect."[11] We may assume that Manara had designed the theater erected by the troupe, as well as the scenery for the production, which the Modenese ambassador praised for its great variety.

If the theater was like a typical Venetian house, with five rows of 31 boxes each, or approximately 150 boxes, then a full house would have brought in roughly 600 ducats from box rentals. Five performances with a full house would have paid back the investment of 2500 ducats and produced a profit for the troupe. We do not know, however, whether the house was that big, nor do we know how many performances took place. It is likely that there may not have been enough vertical space for five rows of boxes. A theater with four rows might have brought in 480 ducats a performance, one with three rows 360. In a three-level theater five performances would have meant losing money, but seven performances would have achieved the break-even point.

Before the arrival of these players and musicians, there had been considerable theatrical activity in Naples for at least a century, supported both by the vice-regal court and by rich nobles who paid for performances in their own palaces.[12] What we know about the architectural character of the earlier theatrical space in the viceroy's palace suggests that it was a typical court theater, with a twist. In 1632 a Genoese visitor to Naples, Giovanni Vincenzo Imperiale, went to the palace, where every Monday a comedy was performed, in the company of Cardinal Savelli. Imperiale and the cardinal sat in "a raised box, completely surrounded by shutters, constructed for the use of the cardinal." From there Imperiale could look out on the "spacious and noble room" brilliantly lit by candelabra, but even more brilliantly lit by the "most beautiful glowing women, a theater no less of the battles of the spectators than of the fool-the-eye visual effects of the spectacles."[13] This description must be of a typical court theater, with the competitively dressed women displayed on raised benches, probably set against the side walls, and lit to the glowing point by lights hanging above them. Only the cardinal had a private box, from which he could see but not be seen. This theater had probably been constructed or outfitted around 1632 by the recently arrived viceroy, the count of Monterey, who was passionate about the theater, so much so that he even began to go to public comedy theaters, shunned by the Neapolitan aristocracy. In the public theater, he had a box built for himself, to which he also took his wife, as a scandalized contemporary noted.[14] These earlier Neapolitan comedy theaters, with boxes probably in the Venetian manner, would have been inadequate for the purposes of the opera troupe invited by Oñate to perform in 1650. Moreover, the old theaters also bore the stigma the Neapolitan nobility attached to comedies performed in public. Oñate wanted a new, untarnished theater in the palace itself to which he could draw the nobles and the citizens of Naples.

The new palace theater built by the opera troupe was immensely successful, for in November of 1650, a month after he had reported the success of *Dido*, the Modenese ambassador wrote that the viceroy "has ordered constructed in the palace in the part toward the park a large theater to present tragedies much more comfortable for the audience that the one in the ball court."[15] It seems that the viceroy had cleverly used the capital of the players to try out his idea of building a new theater in the palace. Once he discovered that the idea worked, he embarked on building an even better theater himself. While the new theater was under construction, the theater in the Pallonetto continued to be used, until the new theater opened. Other operas of Venetian origin followed in the Pallonetto through July 1652, when a famous traveling group, the Febiarmonici, presented *La Finta Pazza*. The first great success of the Venetian Teatro Novissimo in 1641 became the last opera given in the ball court.

The viceroy's larger and more comfortable theater opened in December 1652, with a production of *Veremonda, The Amazon of Aragon*, with music by

Francesco Cavalli and scenery, stage machinery, and choreography by Giovanni Battista Balbi, both of whom had already made names for themselves in Venice. Although Curzio Manara was still in Naples,[16] Balbi seems to have been the designer of the theater. By September 1651, the Febiarmonici had been performing in the vice-regal palace, with Balbi the head of the troupe. Although Balbi was particularly well known as a choreographer, he had worked in Paris alongside Giacomo Torelli, from whom he surely could have learned techniques of scene design and architecture. The libretto of the opera was dedicated to the viceroy Oñate by Balbi, whose words suggest that he claimed architecture as his forte: "[in the theater there] will conspire to the learned leisure of Your Excellency Poetry, Music and Architecture, this last, however, signaling my devotion to Your Most Excellent Person."[17] Perhaps the two years required to build the new theater, when theaters could go up in a matter of months, can partly be explained by the arrival of the Febiarmonici in Naples in 1651, with a subsequent change in architectural plans at their suggestion that lengthened the construction time. What that theater actually looked like we do not know, since no visual or verbal description has come down to us. Given the Venetian background of Balbi and Cavalli, it seems fair to assume that the theater was in the Venetian manner, with boxes.

Oñate's construction of this theater was politically motivated, as Lorenzo Bianconi and Thomas Walker have shown.[18] He had ruthlessly suppressed a rebellion of Neapolitan nobles against Spanish rule in 1647–48. Almost immediately thereafter, in June 1649, for the feast of St. John Baptist, the viceroy organized a series of public spectacles with the clear propagandistic intent of enforcing a sense of his victory. Included in this sequence of events was a musical performance, with elaborate scenery, that took place in the vice-regal palace. Entitled *The Triumph of Partenope Liberated*, it was an allegorical representation of the salvation of Naples from chaos by the Spanish, to which the flower of the nobility were invited. In August Oñate began the execution of rebellious nobles.

Bringing Venetian opera to Naples also seems to have been part of the count's cultural politics, in that by entertaining the upper classes, he sought to impress them with his munificence and power. *Veremonda*, however, had a much clearer political point to make. The opera was given in celebration of the Spanish victory over a rebellion in Barcelona, a rebellion that had been harder to put down than the one in Naples. The subject of the opera was ostensibly the victory of the Aragonese over the Moors. That, of course, could be interpreted as the victory of the current Spanish government over the rebellions in Naples or Barcelona. The theater served the viceroy's purpose of assembling the nobles of Naples in his court to remind them who was boss. If he controlled the assignment of boxes to the nobles, then he could reward the faithful with nearness to his own box and punish the recalcitrant by placing them at the far reaches of the theater. We do not know that this is what he did, but one can easily imagine that he used the seating in his theater for his own purposes. That those purposes included glorifying his own office and Spanish rule is made clear by the fact that immediately after the opening performances of *Veremonda*, the Neapolitan painter Massimo Stanzione began to decorate the theater with a hardly subtle series of portraits of the forty-three viceroys who had reigned in Naples.

Oñate left Naples at the end of 1653, and with him departed opera performed in the vice-regal palace. The Teatro San Bartolomeo was refitted to house the performance of opera, and it continued to be the main venue for that musical genre until the construction of the Teatro San Carlo, built as an adjunct to the royal palace by Carlo di Borbone, the new king of Naples. He came to that realm from the Duchy of Parma, which he had inherited from his mother, Elisabetta, Queen of Spain and the last of the Farnese. Carlo had the Teatro San Bartolomeo dismantled, so that its wood could be used in the San Carlo. That great theater, opened in 1737, continued Oñate's policy of associating the performance of opera with royal power. From being the heir to the grand Teatro Farnese in Parma Carlo became impresario of one of the most splendid opera houses of Europe.

MODENA, DUCAL THEATER

As part of his use of the arts for political ends, Francesco d'Este, Duke of Modena, erected inside the city hall of Modena a theater for the performance of opera.[19] He had attended performances of opera in Venice during the carnival of 1644, just in time to catch the fervor that accompanied the unveiling of the new public art form. As his interest in opera grew, in 1648 he staged a Venetian opera, Faustini's *Ersilia*, in a small existing theater in his castle – the first performance of an opera in Modena. In 1650 he ordered drawings (sadly now lost) of four Venetian theaters, S. Cassiano, S. Luca, S. Moisè, and SS. Giovanni e Paolo. Perhaps inspired by the accounts he had received from his ambassador in Naples, in 1654 he ordered his architect, Gaspare Vigarani, to design an opera theater inside the city hall. Choosing the city hall rather than the ducal palace as the location of the theater suggested at least two things: a closer collaboration between the duke and the city than the one that existed, and a desire to make this entertainment readily available to his subjects. Taking over a space in the city hall, however, recalls vividly what the Medici had done in Florence and Siena a century earlier. Then, as we saw, Cosimo I turned the meeting halls of the city governments into places of entertainment, thus making clear his complete takeover as ruler. Francesco had a dicier relationship with the government of Modena, and so his move into their space appears rather aimed at conciliation.

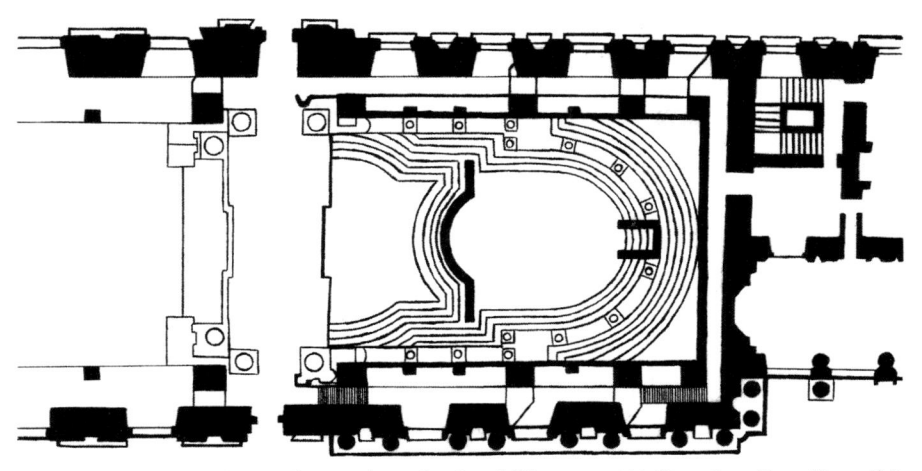

FIG. 158 Paris, Salle des Machines, plan, after Israel Silvestre, 1668 (Drawing: Troy Sipprelle)

An architect of considerable invention, Vigarani did not copy the Venetian opera houses depicted in the drawings sent to Modena four years earlier. Instead, he rethought the idea of the theater, doubtless at the behest of Francesco, who intended the theater as a site in which he would display his own taste, not that of moneymaking Venetian impresarios. Alice Jarrard has made a compelling case for the innovative nature of this design, of which almost all visual traces have disappeared. It was a noble classical hall, with two levels of Corinthian columns supporting galleries. It is not clear whether the galleries were divided into Venetian boxes or not. Vigarani's design of 1659 of the Salle des Machines in the Tuileries Palace in Paris for Louis XIV, which had two rows of square columns holding up galleries with boxes, may well give us an idea of what his theater in Modena looked like.[20] A coffered ceiling, instead of the standard theater ceiling that alluded to the outdoors, covered the interior, giving the space something of the dignity of a church, with which it was clearly intended to compete architecturally. It must also have had a sense of classical grandeur, since Vigarani was a master of deploying the classical orders to vigorous monumental effects, even in small spaces.

Most innovative was the seating in the platea, which was stepped down toward the stage in order to place the ducal seat at the optimum point for viewing the perspective sets. In this way he both held the place of honor and focused his attention and that of the audience on the stage.[21] The spectacles that happened on the stage, which was essentially twice as deep as the auditorium and half again as tall, were the gift of the duke to his citizens. They represented his munificence, which, however, he was able to enjoy to a degree afforded to no one else in the house, save his duchess. In this sense, the duke's decision to place himself at the most advantageous place for viewing the

FIG. 159 Bartolommeo Feris, "Francesco d'Este, Duke of Modena, inspects his theater," etching, 1659, from *L'idea di vn prencipe et eroe christiano in Francesco 1. d'Este di Modona, e Reggio duca 8. ... Composto, e di poi descritto, per ordine della medesima altezza dal p. Domenico Gamberti della Compagnia di Gesù*, In Modona: per Bartolomeo Soliani stampator ducale, 1659 (Modena, Biblioteca Estense Universitaria, Bibl. Forni XII 385)

stage, in the middle of the audience, reflected a desire to maintain the tradition of court theaters. Vigarani continued that tradition in Paris, where he gave Louis XIV a long raised promenade through the orchestra to his royal box, surrounded by an elegant curved balustrade, all of which allowed Louis to play a role in the Salle des Machines that suggests a punning paraphrase of one of his famous remarks: "Le théâtre, c'est moi." ("The theater, it's me.") (Fig. 158). Unlike Louis's theater in a royal palace, Francesco's was a palace theater in a public building, an insertion of princely prerogative and largesse in a structure built for municipal government. Absolutism vs. government by hard-won consent.

The duke's role as moving force behind the theater is preserved in an etching of 1659 by Bartolommeo Feris, part of a suite of prints showing the duke in his multiple roles as ruler (Figs. 159 and 160). In this haunting image, Francesco, the only one wearing a hat, stands, dwarfed by the space he has created, to confer with his architect and others in a room still under construction. The lord advises at the birth of his grandiose cultural monument.

FIG. 160 Detail of Fig. 159

Vigarani's monumental Corinthian columns rise to either side of the low proscenium arch, surmounted by the d'Este arms watched over by two larger-than-life-size allegorical figures reclining on a pediment of rigorously pure geometric form. The sobriety of the classical architecture is striking. Francesco must have willed it that way – his personal taste as an expression of his power. The style of the theater could hardly be more different from the visually riotous interior of Ferdinando Tacca's Teatro della Pergola (discussed in the following section), rising under Medici patronage in Florence at almost precisely the same time. At Modena, the sobriety even extended to the set, presumably also by Vigarani, so that architecture and scenery were fused in a way not often encountered.

Inserted in the spectacular Baroque frame that encloses the scene is an inscription in not entirely correct Latin: UT SCENARUM MENDACIA SINT VERAE SIMULACRA MAGNIFICENTIAE FRANCISCUS CONFECTO THEATRO, SPECTACULA FACIT PRINCIPUM ADMIRATIONI. (So that the falsehoods of the scenery may be the simulacra of true magnificence Francesco having built the theater made the spectacle for the admiration of important people [or princes].) In other words, the duke made the deception of the stage effects to impress (and delight?) either his subjects who came to the theater, or his fellow rulers, or both, depending on how one chooses to understand *principum*.[22] The apparently deliberate ambiguity of the inscription fit Francesco's policies at home and abroad.

FLORENCE, TEATRO DELLA PERGOLA

Faced with the rising popularity of opera, the grand dukes of Tuscany, like the duke of Modena, found themselves without a theater in which the new form could be readily presented; no space in the city was sufficient for the grandiose spectacles seventeenth-century rulers were increasingly expected to provide.[23] The Medici also suffered from Farnese envy. When Margherita de' Medici married the young duke of Parma, Odoardo Farnese, in 1628, Odoardo finally opened the grandiose Teatro Farnese to honor his bride and entertain his guests (see Chapter 8) An honored guest at the wedding was Gian Carlo de' Medici, brother both of the bride and of Grand Duke Ferdinando II. In 1644 Gian Carlo achieved his own title, when Innocent X gave him a cardinal's hat – a garment for which his love of the good life did little to qualify him.

The Accademia degli Immobili, a learned aristocratic society, invited the cardinal to be their patron in 1649, and in 1650 they opened a small theater in a house in Via del Cocomero for the production of comedies – performances in which the cardinal took delight.[24] When that theater quickly became too small, the cardinal rented from the Arte della Lana an unused warehouse in Via della Pergola, therein to construct a new, larger theater, whose cornerstone was laid on July 12, 1652, in the cardinal's presence. Designed by Ferdinando Tacca, son of the sculptor Pietro Tacca, the Teatro della Pergola finally opened for the carnival of 1657, although it was not completely finished until 1661. Tacca took pains to design a highly functional theater, and, in particular, to make the theater convenient for Gian Carlo and his kinfolk. The cardinal and other Medici paid for half of its cost, while the members of the academy picked up the other part. But Gian Carlo never paid the rent for the land due to the Arte della Lana. That ballooning bill was only settled in 1713 (sixty-one years later) in an arrangement brokered by Grand Duke Cosimo III, who arranged for the Accademia to take permanent ownership of the entire property. At that point, for the first time, a paying audience was admitted. Until then, the Pergola had been reserved for the entertainment of the Medici, their court, their visitors, and the members of the Accademia.[25] The Pergola was a court theater, then, even though it rose at a considerable distance from the palace. The Via della Pergola, a few blocks northeast of the cathedral, had to be reached by carriage. In 1683 an additional piece of land was purchased to provide space for courtiers' carriages to disgorge passengers – an early instance of the effect of wheeled transport on the layout of a theater. In 1689, on the occasion of the marriage of Cosimo III, the interior of the theater was remodeled by Filippo Sengher – another instance of the fact that the Medici treated it as a court theater.

We know the appearance of the original interior of the 1650s from prints published on the occasion of an opera performance given on June 18, 1658 at the behest of the cardinal to celebrate the birth of a son to Philip IV of Spain (Figs. 161 and 162). (The cardinal bore the titles of Generalissimo del Mare and Cardinal Protector of that country.) One etching shows the interior from the stage, with the half at stage left filled with spectators and that at stage right empty (Fig. 161). The rendering does not provide a full view of the auditorium, because the proscenium cuts off the parts closest to the stage. At the time of the production in 1658 a printed account of the plot of the opera was published that included a description of the theater.[26] Taken together, the visual and written sources give a rather clear picture. We know no plan of the original theater, but a plan made after it was remodeled in 1689 is preserved in Sir John Soane's Museum, London[27] (Fig. 163).

What we see in the view of the original interior is a conjunction of court and commercial theater forms (Fig. 161). Three levels of boxes surround an

FIG. 161 Silvio degli Atti, Teatro della Pergola, Florence, view from the stage, etching, 1658, in Hipermestra festa teatrale rappresentata dal sereniss. principe cardinale Gio. Carlo di Toscana per celebrare il giorno natalizio del real principe di Spagna. Florence, "Nella stamperia di S.A.S.," 1658, pl. 1 (General Collection, Beinecke Rare Book and Manuscript Library, Yale University)

FIG. 162 Silvio degli Atti, Teatro della Pergola, Florence, view of proscenium, etching, 1658, Hipermestra festa teatrale rappresentata dal sereniss. principe cardinale Gio. Carlo di Toscana per celebrare il giorno natalizio del real principe di Spagna. Florence, "Nella stamperia di S.A.S.," 1658, pl. 1 (General Collection, Beinecke Rare Book and Manuscript Library, Yale University)

auditorium with an oval shape.[28] The boxes are supported by rows of columns that separate seats on the floor in the center from risers for spectators that line the outer walls. Rows of benches line both sides of the center aisle. Toward the stage curving balustrades separate the benches from a section in which more important people sat. The written description tells us that men and women occupied opposite sides. Dominating the interior was a baldacchino that rose over the seats of the Medici, placed on axis and opposite the stage at ground level. The upper rows of boxes represent the new form of the commercial theater, while the seating on the main floor continues practices long established in court theaters. The theater is a hybrid, part old-fashioned court theater, part new theater with boxes. The columns raise the new typology above the old.

Recorded in a second etching is the proscenium (Fig. 162), with its broad arched opening onto the stage. Flanking the opening are pairs of free-standing composite columns with free-standing statues on pedestals set inside each pair – a more three-dimensional variant on the Ferrarese proscenium scheme. The projecting columns support an entablature that steps back and runs across the opening, with a coat of arms in the center that sports the windmill device of

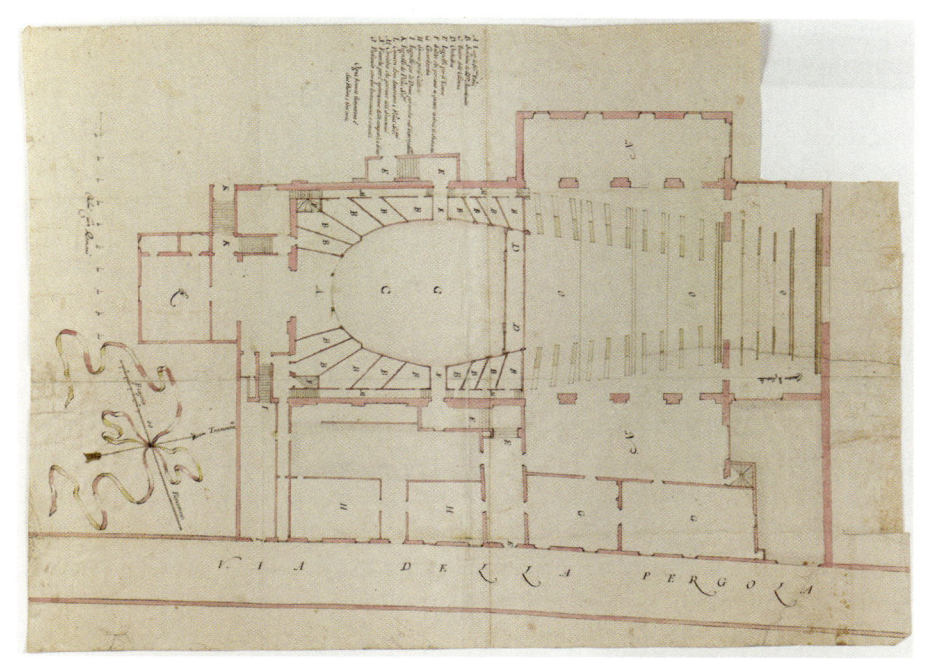

FIG. 163 Teatro della Pergola, Florence, plan, early 1690s (© Sir John Soane's Museum, London, 117, 32)

the Immobili. Over the center of the theater hung a large Medici coat of arms. That arrangement signaled the dual patronage of the theater.

For the cardinal, according to the written description, special architectural arrangements were made. Not only was his place in the audience marked by the baldacchino, but he also had a large room behind the baldacchino to which he could retire to avoid the heat and odors created by the audience. From there he could see and hear just as well as he could from his "throne" in the auditorium. Should he so choose, a subterranean passage allowed him to go backstage and then return to his seat unobserved. The cardinal's "throne" was the only seat on the central axis; no one else enjoyed that privilege. As far as we know, other theaters with boxes always had a box placed on the center line of the house. The central box on the second tier, the most desirable place of all, was invariably occupied by the ruler. If one looks carefully at the view of the interior of the Pergola (Fig. 161), one realizes that in the three levels of boxes above the Medici baldacchino, there is no central box. Instead there are eight boxes in each range rather than the expected odd number. One assumes that the cardinal specified this arrangement in order to stress his and his family's importance. The libretto of 1658 tells us that in his design for the Pergola Tacca incorporated the best features of the best theaters in Italy; it would seem that he also invented a new feature. The prominence of the Medici at this end of the theater is (perhaps modestly) offset by the placement of the arms of the Immobili above the stage opening at the opposite end (Fig. 162).

Tacca had been sent by the cardinal to study theaters in three capitals that had or once had similar ducal rule: Ferrara, Mantua, and Parma, and in Bologna and Venice.[29] His first stop was Bologna, where he was shown "the theaters of this city," according to a letter of June 2, 1654, written by Lucio Malvezzi to Gian Carlo.[30] The Teatro Malvezzi was only a year old; thus, presumably, the cardinal had sent a letter of introduction to Malvezzi in Tacca's behalf.[31] In Bologna, he must also have visited Chenda's Teatro della Sala (Fig. 113), with its five orders of boxes, and Sighizzi's Teatro Formagliari, with its boxes descending gradually toward the stage (Fig. 156). On June 5 the cardinal's sister, the duchess of Parma, wrote to her brother that Tacca was "immediately allowed to see the theater and to study everything in it that he showed a desire to see."[32] That theater must have been the Teatro Farnese (Figs. 124 and 134), where the duchess as a new bride had been honored in 1628. Tacca sped through northern Italy. On June 6 the duke of Mantua, Carlo II Gonzaga, wrote that although he had not been in Mantua when Tacca arrived, his people had shown Tacca "my theaters."[33] Later, when Tacca visited the duke at his villa in Revere, Gonzaga found him impressive.[34] Cardinal Cibo, the papal legate in Ferrara, reported on June 8 to his relative Gian Carlo that Tacca had been taken to the two theaters in that city, where he had also been shown all the machinery in them, as Gian Carlo had instructed.[35]

Then on to Venice, whence on June 13 both the Venetian Abbot Vittorio Grimani Calergi and the Florentine Giovan Battista Rucellai wrote to the Medici cardinal that they had assisted Tacca in inspecting the theaters of that city.[36] No buildings were specified, but Venice provided a head-spinning variety of functioning commercial theaters – most likely seven in all. Of those, the Teatro Vendramin, or San Luca, was probably the most recent, having been rebuilt after a fire of 1652 with five orders of boxes, twenty-one on the ground level and thirty-three in each of the other orders. The state of the Grimani theater, SS. Giovanni e Paolo, in 1654 is not entirely clear. Since it was the largest in Venice, Tacca surely would have seen it. Others he could have observed were the Tron theater, San Cassiano; the Giustiniani theater, San Moisè; and SS. Apostoli, opened in 1649. The small Sant'Aponal, built in 1659 with only three orders of fifteen *palchi* each, had an elliptical plan that may well have influenced the shape of the Pergola. The even smaller Teatro San Gregorio, or Teatro alli Saloni, offered interesting parallels to Tacca's eventual plan for Florence; it had no ring of boxes, but a few "in faccia alla scena" (in front of the stage) that were occupied by a group of academicians. Others in the audience presumably sat on benches or chairs on the floor. Would that we still possessed the drawings that Tacca surely made of all these theaters of northern Italy.

As noted, the plan of the Pergola preserved at the Soane Museum (Fig. 163) shows the building after modifications were made in 1689, but only to the interior. As Françoise Decroisette has pointed out, Tacca designed a theater that beautifully fit into the site and existing buildings, while serving its functional needs as well. The west side of the property, facing Via della Pergola, was occupied by four houses that were retained and turned into entrances, *guardarobe*, and quarters for the custodian. Open spaces surrounding the warehouse were kept to envelope the theater in a cushion of silence. The theater itself was inserted into the former warehouse, a long rectangular structure.[37] At the northern end of the building was the space for the audience, with the southern end given over to the stage and its service spaces. To either side of the stage were capacious wings for the storage and movement of scenery, and at the south end a space was added for the extension of perspectival effects. The contemporary description notes the presence of many entrances and exits, so that the theater could empty and fill quickly. Women and the Medici had their own separate entrances at the north end, while men came in through doors on the sides of the auditorium. The Medici entrance on the northeast corner led into a separate, spacious apartment. In the remodeling of 1678 the seating on risers beneath the boxes and behind the columns was replaced by boxes held by members of the Accademia. Why these boxes were of different sizes is not clear. Perhaps there was a sliding scale of rents; perhaps some academicians had larger families than others. The Medici baldacchino was removed and replaced by a central box equal in width to the four central boxes directly above it.

The Pergola was an architectural experiment that satisfied the particular set of needs of its patrons, the Medici court and the members of the Accademia, while it handsomely accommodated the elaborate production values of the new art form of opera. Because the Pergola served such specific needs, it had no direct descendants, except perhaps for the oval form that came to dominate the design of opera houses in the next century. Although it was a physical extension of the Medici court, it made no architectural statement in the cityscape of Florence. No one seems to have thought that there was a need for the theater to do so. The anonymous houses in Via della Pergola that screened it were retained; indeed, their nondescript façades still mark the exterior of the theater, although a somewhat more imposing entrance was added much later.[38]

SIENA, TEATRO DEGLI INTRONATI

The theater that opened in 1560 in Siena in the Sala del Consiglio Generale in Palazzo Pubblico for the visit of Duke Cosimo de'Medici (see Chapter 4) was remodeled at least twice in the seventeenth century: first by Mattias de'

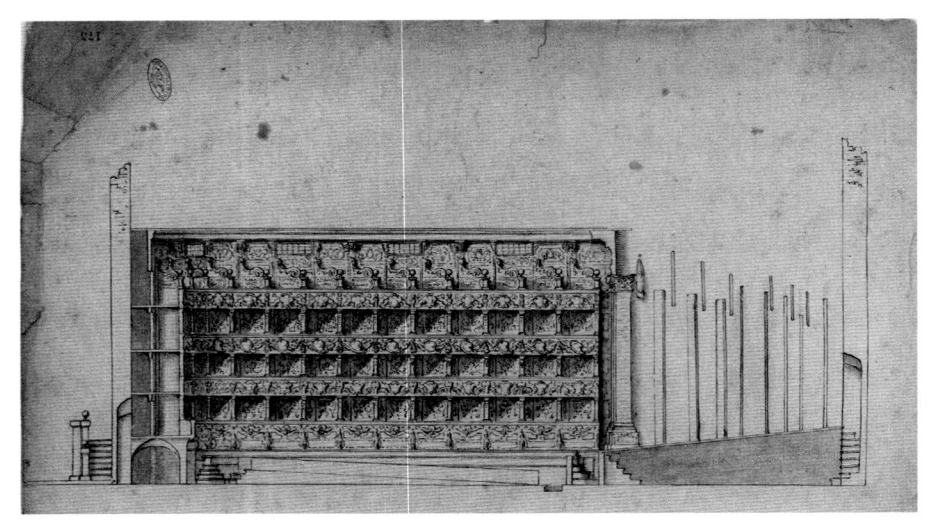

FIG. 164 Teatro degli Intronati, Siena, longitudinal section (Rome, Vatican Archive, Fondo Chigi P.VIII.17,0368,fa,0175r)

Medici, governor of the city and brother of the grand duke and of Cardinal Gian Carlo; and then by Cardinal Leopoldo de' Medici and the Accademia degli Intronati in 1668–69 into what must have been considered one of the most important theaters of the later seventeenth century in Italy.[39] Mattias was an enthusiast of Venetian opera, which he encountered firsthand in 1641. In 1645 the Florentine ambassador procured for him drawings of the SS. Giovanni e Paolo, together with the advice of Giovanni Grimani that, were he to rebuild his theater, he would make it shorter for acoustical reasons. In 1646 on the order of Mattias the Sienese theater was reconstructed "in wood and remade in better form."[40] The opening production, in 1647, was the last, because the vast sums that the opera-loving Mattias committed to the project exhausted available funds.[41]

We know the plan of the later theater from two almost identical drawings, one in the Vatican and one in Sir John Soane's Museum in London (Fig. 165). The section is preserved in another drawing in the Vatican (Fig. 164). We do not know how much of the rebuilding under Mattias was retained in this version, nor is the architect of the theater known. Michele Cordaro has attributed it to Carlo Fontana, but the attribution is questionable on both stylistic and historical grounds.[42] The willfully wavy steps that lead into the theater and the equally curvaceous steps at the ends of the rows of risers in front of the boxes do not seem to come from the more sober hand of Fontana. The fact that the London drawing is included in an album of drawings assembled by Carlo Fontana also speaks against his having been the architect of the Sienese house. The Soane album consists largely of drawings related to Fontana's designs for the Teatro Tordinona in Rome. When he designed his second

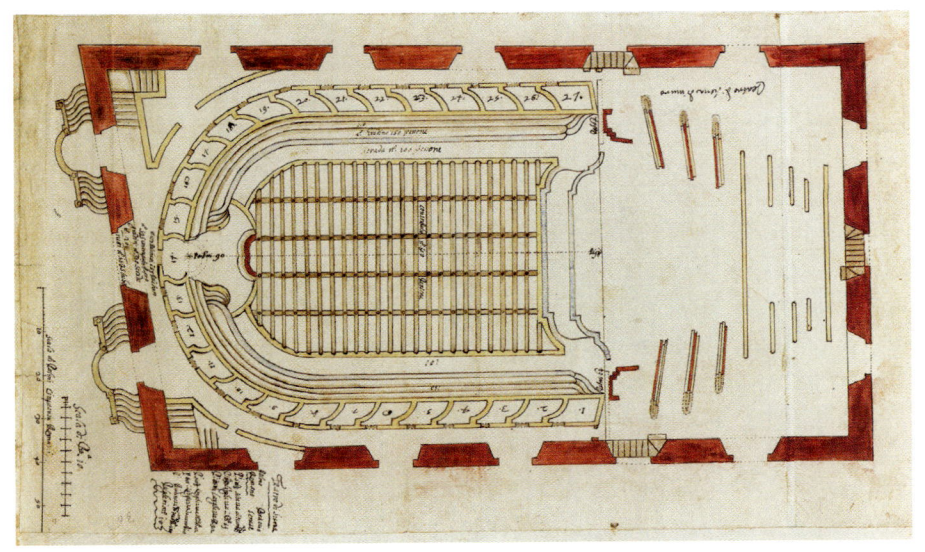

FIG. 165 Teatro degli Intronati, Siena, plan, early 1690s (© Sir John Soane's Museum, London, 117, 36)

version of that theater in the 1690s (see Chapter 11), he sent away for drawings of three important theaters in Italy: Teatro della Pergola, Florence; Teatro degli Intronati, Siena; and Teatro SS. Giovanni e Paolo, Venice. Each of these plans arrived in Rome with a scale in the unit of measure of its city and accompanying instructions on how to translate those measurements into *palmi romani*. Each drawing is identified in Fontana's own hand with the appropriate name of the theater – in the case of Siena "Teatro di Siena di nuovo."[43] Had he designed the Sienese theater, he would hardly have needed to have this drawing sent to him.

The Soane plan (Fig. 165) contains written information lacking in the Vatican version. The number of spectators it could hold, 1,535, is clearly enumerated: 107 boxes in 4 orders of 27 at 5 per box for 535 (no box in the center in the bottom order); 500 on the floor of the auditorium, 300 on the benches in the platea, and 200 in the *strade*, which must mean the aisles. The walls separating the boxes were curved, to produce better sight lines for those seated toward the rear. Stairs in the corners of the irregularly shaped medieval walls led to the upper boxes. On stage the first three rows of flats were angled to prevent those in the boxes closer to the stage from looking behind the scenes.

The section is filled with valuable information that helps to interpret the plan (Fig. 164). The section tells us that the paired, curvaceous stairs led to the level of the first order of boxes, including the central *palco* that bowed slightly toward the stage. Dotted lines on the plan seem to indicate that the platea was entered on a lower level, through the central door that originally had given access to the Sala del Consiglio Generale. In the section, the steps shown immediately inside the auditorium are those that lead up to the *gradi*, or risers. To either side of the entrance, one step leads down to the level of the platea, while the three convex steps facing the entrance allow access to the rear of the raked floor on which the central benches are set. In front of the wall enclosing the orchestra is a single step that lowers the floor in front of that wall, perhaps an indication of the presence of a vestigial protective "moat" separating musicians from audience. All in all, the changes in levels are handled with less clarity than one might hope. Doors beside the pit give access to the area under the stage, while doors at the end of the corridors behind the boxes of the first tier open onto the stage. Steps in the orchestra pit allow the musicians to face the stage, while stairs carved out of the thickness of the exterior walls allow access to the important area under the raked stage where scenery and machinery would have been stored. The interior is richly decorated, and the boxes of the top tier are separated by low walls terminating in posts capped by balls or globes. Windows let in light immediately below the ceiling and provide ventilation. The giant order of Corinthian (?) pilasters that formed the proscenium are basically just stage flats; they have almost no depth. Whoever designed this theater suffered from *horror vacui*.

The only hint that this theater was not just another theater built by a learned aristocratic academy is the curved front of the central box in the second range of boxes. That box must have been reserved for the man sent from Florence to govern the city. Should the grand duke visit, he and his party would occupy that prime spot in the theater. Thus did an academic theater receive a court theater inflection.

FANO, TEATRO DELLA FORTUNA

Giacomo Torelli, the scenic genius who enjoyed a great success between 1641 and 1644 in Venice at the Teatro Novissimo, was called to Paris in 1645 by Anne of Austria, widow of Louis XIII and regent for the young Louis XIV. The summons was instigated by a cousin of the French queen, Odoardo Farnese, that duke of Parma whose wedding inaugurated the Teatro Farnese in 1628.[44] Such high patronage assured Torelli of instant employment in Paris, where his sets were as successful as they had been in Venice. The young Louis loved his work, and the powerful Cardinal Mazzarin became his protector. His success continued unabated until 1661, when he incurred the displeasure of the now-mature Louis. Torelli became close to Louis's minister, Nicolas Fouquet (1615–80), who was famously thrown in jail by the jealous king after being entertained all too lavishly at Fouquet's just-completed château of Vaux-le-Vicomte. Part of that entertainment was designed by Torelli. With Fouquet's fall, Torelli had to leave France. He returned to his native city of Fano, on the Adriatic coast, where as a young nobleman in his early thirties

FIG. 166 Luigi Vanvitelli, project for tower added to Palazzo della Ragione, Fano, drawing (Fano, Biblioteca Comunale Federiciana, Collection of prints and drawings, SM B/1/4, by concession of the Library Commission of the Comune of Fano)

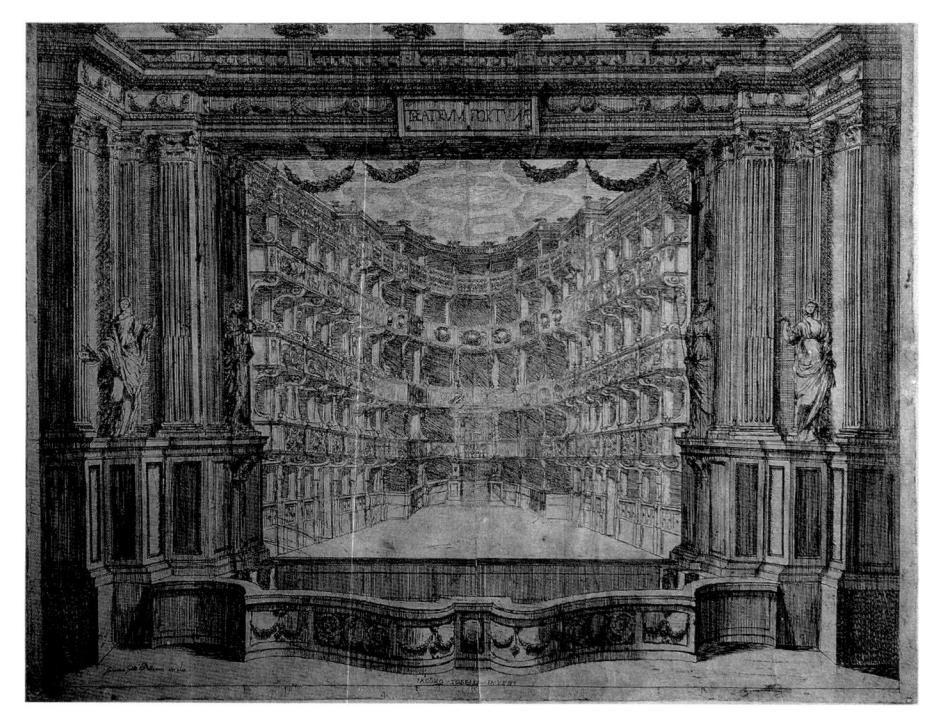

FIG. 167 Fernando Galli Bibiena, view of proscenium and interior of Teatro della Fortuna, Fano, engraving, c. 1719 (Jesi, Biblioteca comunale Planettiana, Fondo stampe Honorati, Coll.: St. varie 1)

he had first exhibited an interest in the theater by helping to produce comedies in the Sala Grande della Comedia in the Palazzo della Ragione. Repeated in Fano was the devolution of a medieval city hall into a place of entertainment, just as we have seen in Bologna, Florence, and Siena. (Like Bologna, Fano was under papal control.) In 1556 the meeting room of the town fathers of Fano received the new name of Sala delle Comedie. An eighteenth-century drawing shows the exterior of the town hall of Fano, with an arched portico at ground level and large, round-arched windows in the piano nobile that signal the location of the meeting room that became a theater (Fig. 166). At the left corner of the medieval structure stands a design for an eighteenth-century clock and bell tower that, when constructed, intruded into Torelli's plan and eliminated boxes on every level.[45]

In February 1665, Torelli, along with sixteen other nobles of Fano, petitioned the General Council of the city for the free use of the Sala della Comedia, which they characterized as "almost useless because it cannot offer space or accommodation for those luxurious spectacles which at present and according to the custom of the century are presented in noble Cities."[46] Although an official positive answer to the petition was only finally given a

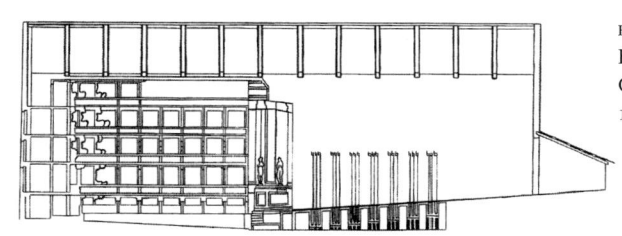

FIG. 168 Teatro della Fortuna, Fano, longitudinal section after Gabriel Pierre Martin Dumont, 1777 (Drawing: Troy Sipprelle)

decade later, in January 1676, in the intervening years a theater designed by Torelli was constructed ever so slowly. In 1676 only five of the seventeen nobles who had signed the original petition were still alive. On June 6, 1677 Torelli's theater was inaugurated under the title of Teatro della Fortuna, the ancient name of the Roman city having been Fanum Fortunae. Fortune being fickle, she gave Torelli only two years to enjoy his theater before he died.

We know the appearance of the theater thanks to a rare engraving by Fernando Galli Bibiena, probably made in 1719 when he was renewing the decorations of the auditorium and the original sets that Torelli had designed[47] (Fig. 167). As a youth, Bibiena had assisted with the original decorations of the theater, and so he knew it well. Bibiena framed a view of the auditorium from the stage inside a depiction of the proscenium, as if the *sipario* (stage curtain) of the theater were painted to be a mirror image of the auditorium. While the print instantly brings to mind instances of Baroque theatrical deceptions (one need only recall Gianlorenzo Bernini's famous example of raising a curtain to reveal a reproduction of the theater, so that the audience found itself looking at a mirror image of itself), it cannot be demonstrated that such a curtain ever existed at Fano.[48] On the other hand, the label on the engraving, "IACOMO TORELLI INVENT," can be interpreted to mean that Torelli invented everything one sees therein, including a curtain that mirrored the appearance of the auditorium.

The theater contained five ranks of boxes (Fig. 168). There were nineteen on the first level, to leave room for entrances to the platea on both sides of the auditorium, twenty-one on levels two to four, and eleven on the top level, with open seating between those boxes and the proscenium. This last was the least desirable area in the house. Seventeenth-century drawings of the plans of each level identify the families who originally subscribed to each box. The boxes became the permanent possession of the original owners and could be left to their heirs, a common pattern in theaters financed by sale of the boxes to wealthy locals.[49] Five boxes on the less desirable fifth level went begging; Torelli's plan was a bit ambitious for the modest population of Fano. An inscription in a later hand tells us that the five boxes originally claimed by the Torelli family passed at a later point to others. Alongside the noblesse of Fano, the fathers of S. Paterniano acquired a box in the third order.

FIG. 169 Cross section after Gabriel Pierre Martin Dumont of Teatro della Fortuna, Fano, inserted into cross section of Palazzo della Ragione, Fano, by Arcangelo Innocenzi (Drawing, after *Giacomo Torelli*, fig. 326, by Troy Sipprelle).

In his design of the auditorium Torelli made adjustments that improved sight lines for those in the boxes. He arranged those spaces so that their lines to either side diverged slightly toward the stage. At the same time, the fronts of the boxes receded slightly from the center of the auditorium as the levels rose (Fig. 169). For the same purpose he set the partitions between the boxes on diagonals. Most notably, he broke with the tradition of solid walls between boxes. Instead, he carved those walls away in the shape of large volutes, different on each level, that allowed much easier views of the stage, especially for those seated in the rear. The volutes retained a sense of separation for each box, but they did not retain the total privacy that might facilitate the arts of love (Fig. 169).

The magistrate of the city occupied the central box on the second level (Fig. 169). Fano, like Bologna and Ferrara, was part of the Papal States; thus the most desirable position in the theater was given to the person appointed by the

FIG. 170 Giacomo Torelli, *Cortile Regio*, set for *Il trionfo della continenza considerato in Scipione Africanus*, pen and watercolor, 1677 (Rome, Istituto Centrale per la Grafica, by kind concession of the Ministry for Cultural Resources and Activities and Tourism)

Vatican to govern the city. There seems to have been a decision in 1671 to construct "a more grandiose and more noble box as a gift to the Magistrate."[50] Was this a bribe to speed up the permit? The weight of the new projecting structure, with its columns and pediment, had to be supported on a thick podium that turned the box below it into something like a World War II bunker. The pediment, in turn, rose so high that it compromised the view of the stage from the central box of the third order. One cannot believe that Torelli, so concerned with his audience's ability to see the stage, designed this detail willingly. The image of the magistrate's box is so blurred in Bibiena's print (Fig. 167) that one wonders whether he may have made a deliberate effort to obscure its awkwardness.

One detail of Torelli's plan, the shape of the outline of the nine central boxes on each order, is hard to read in the engraving. The only drawings that survive from the time of the theater's construction, those with the names of the original box holders, show a trilobe arrangement to the front edge to the boxes, with the central five arranged on a continuous curve and the two toward the side walls organized on separate curves[51] (Fig. 169).

Torelli placed a remarkably fanciful curvilinear wall around his orchestra pit, giving the place of music an architectural fanfare (Fig. 167). The sober-sided

FIG. 171 Giacomo Torelli, *Galleria*, drawing, set for *Il trionfo della continenza considerato in Scipione Africanus*, pen and watercolor, 1677 (Rome, Istituto Centrale per la Grafica. By kind concession of the Ministry for Cultural Resources and Activities and Tourism)

proscenium walls, with closely packed Corinthian pilasters, carried a heavily carved, projecting entablature that featured the name of the theater in Latin, written in Roman caps (Bibiena failed to incise the *N* in Fortunae backward on the copper plate). Standing in front of the proscenium and framing the scenery were colossal statues of Painting (left) and Architecture, the arts Torelli practiced here. In the depth of the proscenium, above the orchestra pit, stood Juno holding a wreath (left) and Minerva holding a spear. Minerva, a goddess of Techne, belongs with architecture, but the reason for the pairing of Juno and Painting is not obvious, at least to this writer.[52]

A great scene designer, Torelli naturally designed an ample stage, much deeper than the depth of the auditorium, with an additional shed attached to the rear of the stage to make his deep perspectives even deeper. He designed all the sets for the new theater. Two perhaps will suffice to bring his brilliant career to a close in these pages: the *Cortile Regio* (Fig. 170) and the *Galleria* (Fig. 171). The *Galleria* opened the third act of the inaugural opera, *Il trionfo della continenza considerato in Scipione Africanus* (The Triumph of Continence Displayed by Scipio Africanus) (Fig. 171). The set consists of a claustrophobic, lowering, vaulted interior enclosed by pairs of giant, free-standing Ionic columns that support ominously crouching sphinxes, their bodies bent under the crushing weight of the low, segmental vaults. (The opera takes place in Carthage, thus the north African creatures.) No opportunity is missed to add disconcerting detail: the colossal statues peeking out from between the paired columns, the horizontal banding of the columns and the pilasters that stand close behind them, the richly carved arches, the projecting cornices above the heads of the sphinxes, the balcony squeezed up against the vaults. Through the central door the space continues into a brighter room that in turn leads to a seemingly infinite perspective.

In contrast, the *Cortile Regio* is open and airy (Fig. 170), its space flanked by noble classical architecture, Ionic below and Corinthian above, with an order of herms in the third level that rises above the rear of the courtyard. The openness is emphasized by the see-through spaces on the second and third levels in the rear, the central opening on the second level allowing a peekaboo view of the top of a dome with a lantern in the far distance. There are similarities, however: the perspectival view that goes into another space and seems to continue on forever; the narrowing of the foreground space by columns set parallel to the front of the stage and supporting an upper level; the horizontal banding of columns and pilasters that reinforces the foreshortening of the perspective.

If one imagines Torelli's *Galleria* inserted into Bibiena's engraving of the stage of the theater, one realizes what a complete work of art he created. Auditorium and set exhibit the same sensibility – the insistence on horizontal layering, the horizontals that guide the eye into depth and join the individual parts, the delight in seemingly endless varieties of inventive detail, the *horror vacui* in the architecture versus the infinite reach of the perspectival space. The aesthetic unity of auditorium and stage is compelling. Here one of the great masters of seventeenth-century stagecraft brought both parts of the visual spectacle of going to the theater into a marvelously unified visual experience.

11

TEATRO DI TORDINONA IN ROME, QUEEN CHRISTINA OF SWEDEN, AND CARLO FONTANA

In seventeenth-century Rome theatrical performances required papal permission. The rapid turnover of old men on the throne of Peter created an unpredictable discontinuity. One pope might allow free rein to theaters, at least for carnival, while his successor might forbid all such activity in the city at any time. Those who risked their luck in this game of papal roulette could pay a high price.[1]

The sad, scrambled story of the Teatro di Tordinona in Rome exemplifies the dicey history of theaters in the city in the seventeenth century, particularly that of opera houses for a paying public.[2] The Tordinona opened in January, 1671, under the high patronage of Queen Christina of Sweden, a fact that falsely suggested a promising future.

Christina, one of the most complex and interesting figures of seventeenth-century Europe, inherited the Swedish throne from her father, the great King Gustavus Adolphus, at age six.[3] After she came of age, she ran a brilliant court in Stockholm, but then she abdicated in favor of her cousin, Karl Gustav; left Sweden; and converted to Catholicism. In late 1655 she made her way to Rome, where she spent much of the rest of her life. The recently elected pope, Alexander VII Chigi, welcomed her with delight and even allowed her to lodge briefly in the Vatican, where women were never supposed to spend the night. The Barberini, the family of Urban VIII (two popes back), entertained her fabulously with a lavish outdoor performance outside their palace, and Ranuccio II Farnese, Duke of Parma and Piacenza, and descendant of Pope

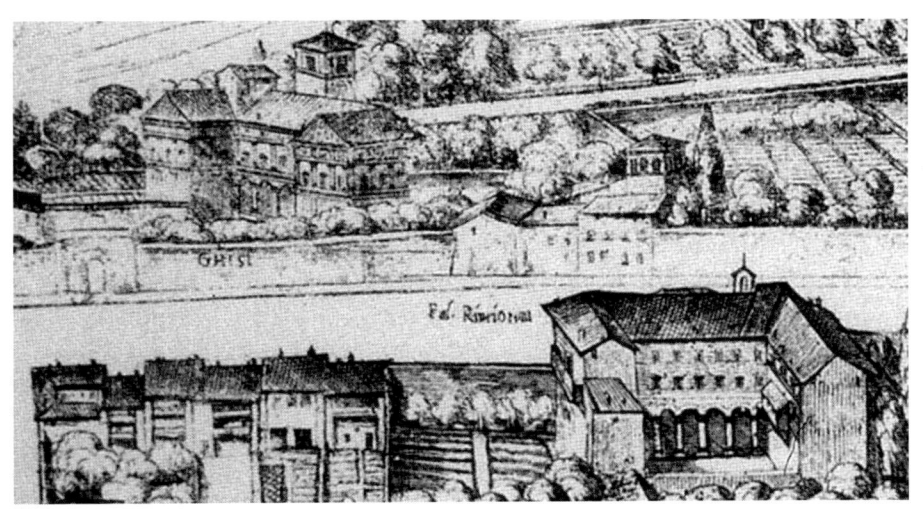

FIG. 172 Antonio Tempesta, detail of map of Rome, 1598, with Palazzo Riario at lower right. Note presence of Villa Farnesina, marked Ghisi, across the street (Photo: Author. Art in the public domain)

Paul III, invited her to live in the vast Palazzo Farnese until she found permanent lodging. Alexander VII appointed another theater enthusiast, Gian Carlo de' Medici, one of two cardinals to wait on Christina, but when the queen and the cardinal appeared to become too close, Alexander sent the cardinal home to Florence, where he became the patron of the Teatro della Pergola (see Chapter 10). For the popes, Christina was the catch of the century, a Protestant monarch who gave up her throne for the church. To the popes, she gave trouble.

Christina loved the performing arts. As queen, she imported French dancers and German and Italian musicians,[4] and she built a theater for ballet, designed by an Italian scene designer, Antonio Brunati, in her palace in Stockholm.[5] There she danced the role of the chaste Diana in a ballet designed to underscore her decision to remain unwed, even though the Swedish aristocracy was anxious for her to produce an heir to the throne. She was a superb horsewoman, an enthusiast of vigorous exercise, and, apparently, a remarkably good dancer.

Changing her religion did not suppress her enthusiasm for musical and theatrical arts. In Rome in July 1659, she finally settled into a rented palace in Via Lungara that had been built around 1511 by none other than Cardinal Raffaele Riario[6] (Fig. 172). Riario, one recalls, was the man who in the 1480s first revived public performances of ancient Roman plays in the city (see Chapter 2). In the Palazzo Riario Christina sponsored private musicales and learned literary discussions, and she built a modest private theater seating three hundred people.[7] But she had insufficient space or money to produce the large-scale entertainments that some Roman patricians offered in their far grander palaces.

Two drawings now in the National Museum, Stockholm, dated sometime after Christina moved into Palazzo Riario, show projects by an unknown architect to build a theater either on the grounds of her rented palace or across Via Lungara.[8] One of these plans (Fig. 173) tucked the theater behind stables that stood to the side of the palace, with an entrance off a *vicolo* that separated the two structures. The broad, U-shaped auditorium had twenty-five boxes, with the box on the central axis expanded to occupy the width of three regular boxes – clearly to create a special space for the queen. The wide auditorium allowed the queen's box to be closer to the stage than a longer, narrower shape would have permitted. There is no indication of the number of orders of boxes that were planned. The stage would have been as wide and deep as the auditorium, with an addition to the rear to accommodate elaborate perspectival effects. Two diagonal walls connected the stage to the addition to the rear. As a hidden private theater, this building would have made no impact on the urban environment, and so it would not have been a public affront to Alexander VII, a pope hardly keen on theatricals. Nonetheless, it would have given Christina the space to produce plays or ballets – or even opera, given the fact that a long, narrow orchestra pit was planned.

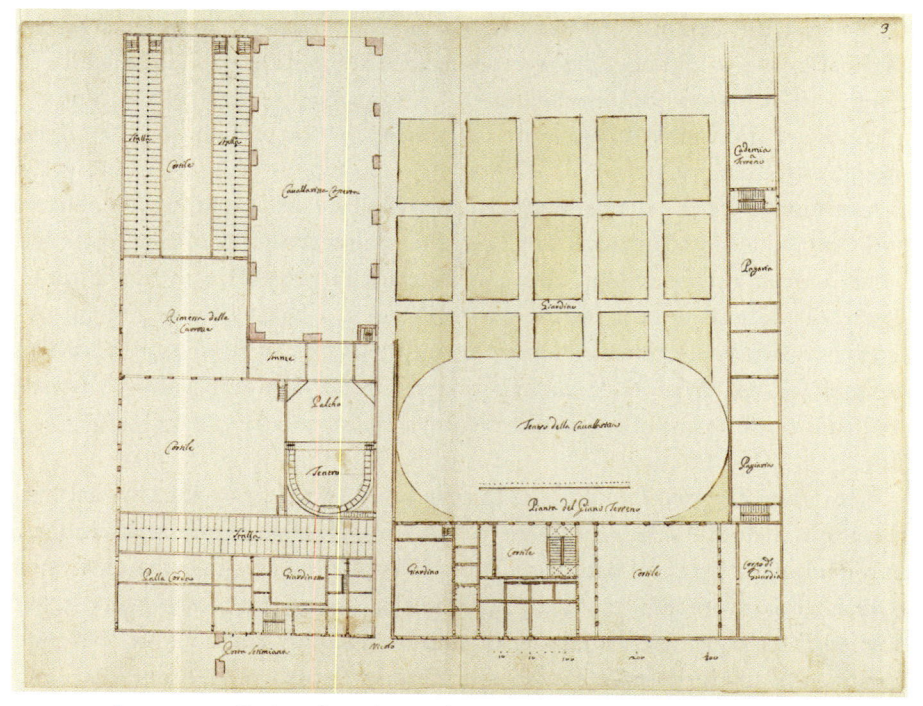

FIG. 173 Anonymous, Project for a theater for Queen Christina of Sweden in Via Lungara, Rome, alongside Palazzo Riario (Stockholm, National Museum, H1045/1960, 03r)

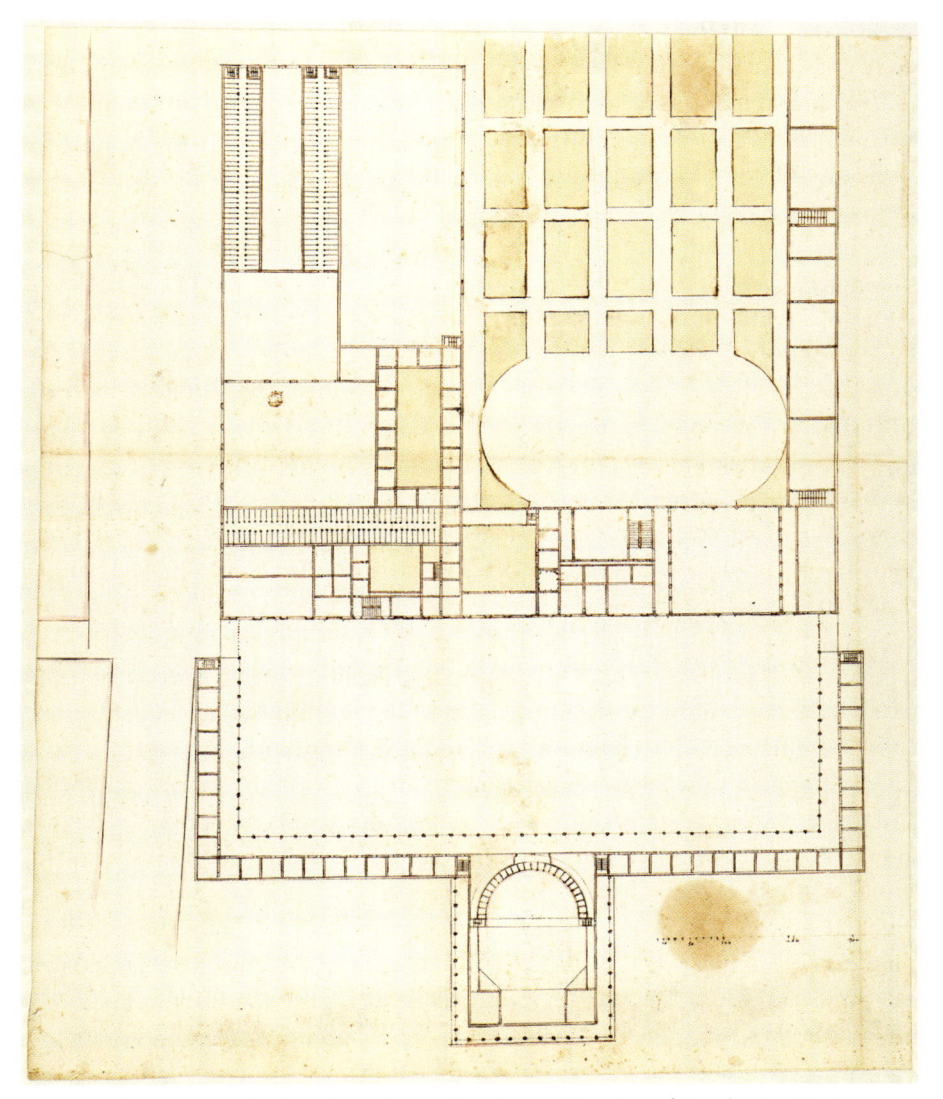

FIG. 174 Anonymous, Project for a theater for Queen Christina of Sweden in Via Lungara, Rome, across from Palazzo Riario (Stockholm, National Museum, H1045/1960, 02r)

The other drawing (Fig. 174) presents a bold scheme to create a piazza in front of the entire width of the rented Riario property, including the land occupied by the palace and the stables. The wide, rectangular space would have been bordered on three sides by porticoes, behind which would have opened forty-two square spaces presumably intended for shops whose rents would have supported the theater. A second level of similar spaces may have been planned, since at either end of the L-shaped wings there were stairs that presumably led up to something. The mass of the theater would have risen above the portico or porticoes, which continued across its front wall. A semicircular auditorium with twenty-five boxes faced a stage that reproduced the dimensions of the auditorium's width and depth, with an added space at the rear of the stage for perspectival effects, again connected to the side walls of the stage by diagonal walls. The similarity of the stages in the two drawings suggests that they were probably made by the same architect. Two lines behind the five central boxes indicate a wider space on the central axis for the queen, perhaps on a level above the boxes. Again, the number of orders of boxes is not indicated. The exterior of the sides and back of the theater would have been surrounded by porticoes turned away from the new piazza and the street. Stig Vänje has argued that these porticoes were a deliberate recollection of Roman theaters, as described by Vitruvius.[9]

This project would have been difficult, if not impossible to realize, because it required taking over property directly across the Via Lungara that belonged to the powerful Farnese. In the 1490s Cardinal Alessandro Farnese, the future Pope Paul III, had built a house on property next to the land on which Agostino Chigi in the early years of the sixteenth century erected the Villa Farnesina (Fig. 12). The project might even have required razing the Farnesina (!).

Christina's project represents, however, a significant and early scheme to make a theater building the central focus of an important regular urban space, something no one up to this time, as far as we know, had attempted. One can see in this project the seeds of what, for instance, Gottfried Semper achieved in the nineteenth century with his successive opera houses in Dresden that rose across the square from the ruler's palace.[10] Semper's theaters becames powerful visual symbols of the Elector's patronage of the arts. If Christina, who was given to improbable schemes, imagined that she could acquire the necessary permissions and property to carry out this plan, then she must have hoped that her project would attract the support of Alexander VII, who was committed to embellishing Rome with splendid urban spaces and buildings.[11] Alexander's approval would have been essential, as would that of Ranuccio II Farnese.

Unfortunately, Christina never had the money to build a private theater. If she wanted to be the patron of great entertainments in Rome, as she had been in Stockholm, her theater would have to support itself, either through associated rental properties (as in Fig. 174) or through box rentals and ticket sales. The latter type would have to be based on the economic model of the public theaters of Venice. As a site for such a new theater an unprepossessing, even ironic, locale offered itself: the former buildings of the notorious papal prison, the Tor di Nona, on the left bank of the Tiber just upstream from Ponte Sant' Angelo[12] (Fig. 175). The prison had been moved to a new site under Alexander's predecessor, Innocent X, and by 1657 the prison's former buildings were vacant. They had been permanently leased by the Vatican to the Archconfraternity of S. Girolamo della Carità, which used rents from the property to

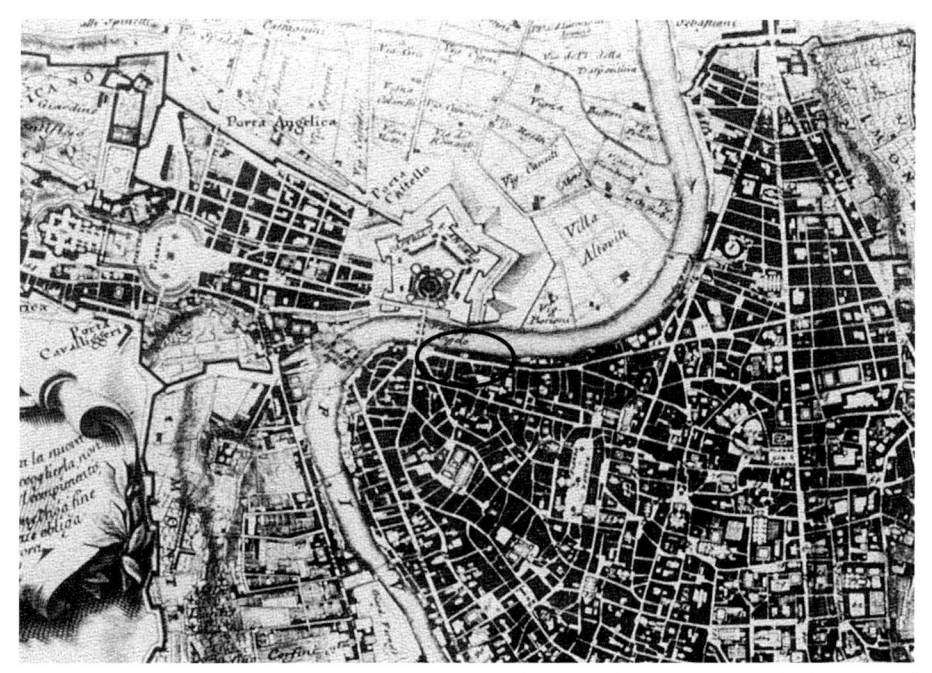

FIG. 175 Giovanni Battista Nolli, detail of the Piccola Pianta di Roma, 1748. The location of the Teatro Tordinona is marked by the oval (Visual Resources, Williams College)

fund pious works. Once the buildings were empty, the confraternity invested heavily in renovations to create a hostel for pilgrims, but that venture failed.

At this point, Christina's adviser, the French Count Jacques (or Giacomo in Italian) D'Alibert, stepped in to propose renting the buildings in order to construct inside them a commercial theater – surely at her instigation. The confraternity accepted the idea and petitioned Alexander VII in 1666 for permission to construct a new public theater for comedies in the former prison, as well as exclusive permission to present comedies in the city, so that there would be no competition. Alexander dodged the unwelcome request by sending it to a committee that thunderously said no. At that point, Christina's cousin the Swedish king died without an heir. She left Rome for her native land to try to reclaim her throne, or at least to straighten out her finances. By the time she returned to Rome in 1668, throneless and no richer, an old friend, Cardinal Giulio Rospigliosi, author of numerous opera libretti going back to the time of Urban VIII, had ascended the throne of Peter as Clement IX. Nothing could have been more favorable to her ends. In 1669 Clement gave the green light to the archconfraternity for the construction of a theater to perform comedies during carnival season only. In turn, the archconfraternity rented part of its property to D'Alibert, with the proviso that his theater be designed by the archconfraternity's architect,

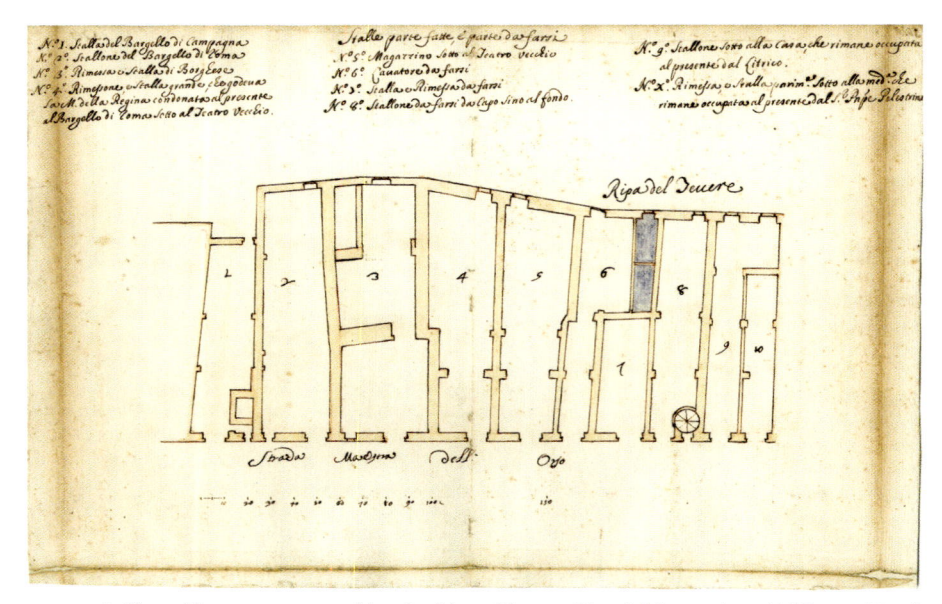

FIG. 176 Plan of houses on ground level of site of former Tor di Nona prison (ASR, 30, Notai Capitolini, uff. 25, vol. 340, c. 578. By concession of the Ministry for Cultural Resources and Activities and Tourism)

Carlo Fontana, prize architectural pupil of Rome's greatest artist of the day, Gianlorenzo Bernini.

The narrow, encumbered site, consisting of three contiguous houses squeezed between the street and the Tiber, was challenging. The ground floors of the buildings were rented as stalls, and the houses at either end of the property were also let. In the center on the first floor was the only available area, currently devoted to grain storage (Fig. 176). Because Fontana had to operate within a book-ended space too small to accommodate a theater designed with its long axis parallel to the street, he turned the theater 90 degrees, so that the auditorium was next to the street and the stage projected out over the Tiber[13] (Fig. 177). The auditorium was not large, measuring about 14 × 16 m, with an opening of roughly 8 m for the proscenium. The seating was arranged in a U shape with probably seven levels of twenty-one boxes each, to pile as many paying people as possible into the scanty space.[14] Bianca Tavassi La Greca believes that Fontana opened the back wall of the stage onto a view of the Tiber, but the nature of the evidence on which this idea is based suggests caution in accepting it.[15] Fontana left the exterior largely in its original condition, so that only the new shed roof over the auditorium was visible from the street, as we know from a remarkable drawing of the exterior, now in Berlin[16] (Fig. 178, upper).

Although Christina had invested little in the construction of the theater, inside it appeared to be hers. She took over the central five boxes in the second order – the choice location – and had a royal crown hung over the box on the

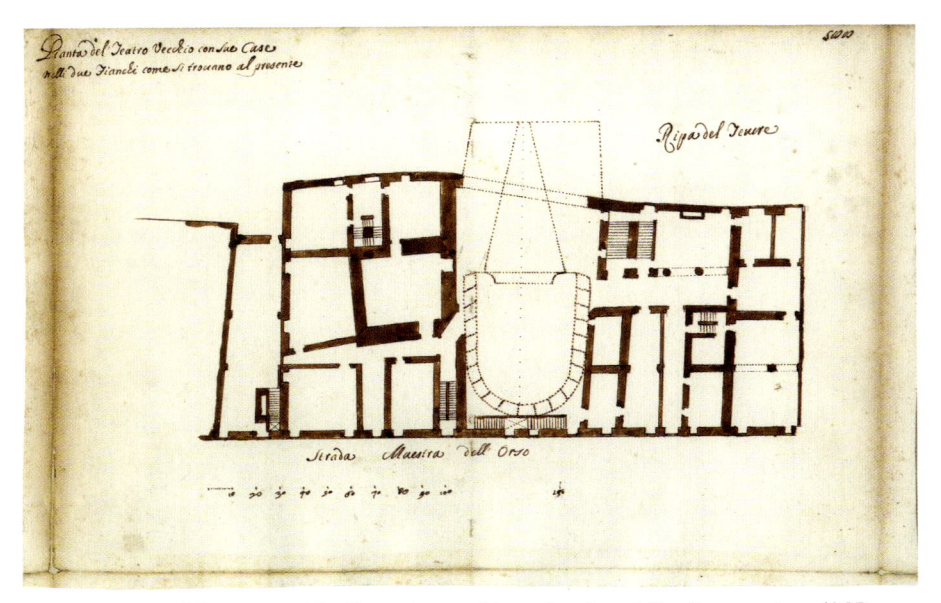

FIG. 177 Plan of first Teatro Tordinona inserted into abandoned Tordinona prison (ASR, 30, Notai Capitolini, uff. 25, vol. 340, c. 579 by concession of the Ministry for Cultural Resources and Tourism)

central axis and its front embellished with her Vasa family coat of arms. The interiors of all five boxes were covered in damask and gilded.[17] This is an early version of a royal box, but not necessarily the earliest, as is often claimed. Her five boxes were interconnected, so that she could entertain at least a dozen cardinals, who served as her court, at every performance. An experience she had in Ferrara in 1655, when she was entertained on her way to Rome, may have led her to choose this elevated position in the theater. An opera was performed in the Sala Grande of the Ferrarese ducal palace, refitted at the expense of the noble Bentivoglio family, who hoped for favors from the queen. A baldacchino, under which she was to sit, was placed in the center of the room. When she learned that the baldacchino blocked the view of many in the audience, she ordered it removed.[18]

In Rome the new theater was ready for the carnival of 1670, but Clement unfortunately died in December of 1669. No performances could take place during an interregnum, and so the first year of activity was lost. The contentious conclave that elevated the aging Cardinal Altieri to the papacy as Clement X lasted almost five months. If the loss of the first year was the first hiccup in the performance history of the Tordinona, many others were to follow. Clement X, annoyed by Christina's demand on the day of his election that he permit performances in her theater all year round, gave permission to a rich Florentine devotee of the theater, Filippo Acciaioli, to open a new house for the presentation of operas; this theater would have competed dangerously, perhaps disastrously,

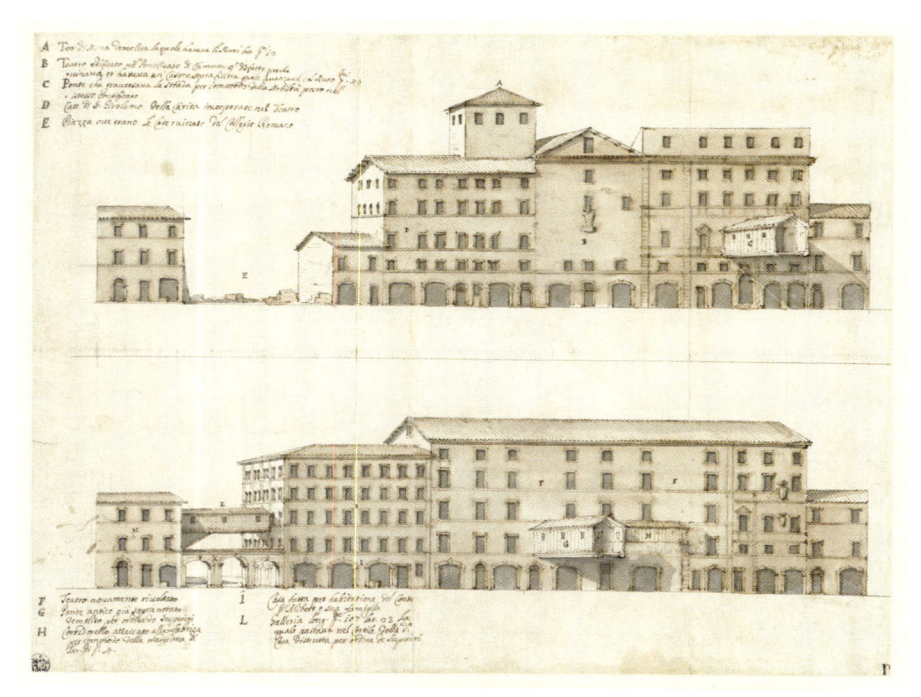

FIG. 178 Views of the exterior of Teatro Tordinona c. 1670–71 (upper) and c. 1695 (lower), drawing, c. 1695 (Berlin, Kunstbibliothek Staatliche Museum, Hdz01172)

with Christina's endeavor. Famous for unminced words, the enraged queen vowed to burn down Acciaioli's theater, should he dare to open it.

A compromise was reached. Acciaioli would rent the Tordinona theater from D'Alibert and take over its management. Fontana extended the depth of the stage to twelve meters to accommodate extensive sets for the *opere in musica* which Acciaioli planned to produce, and the architect also erected a bridge to the theater from nearby Piazza San Salvatore in Lauro, so that the audience could enter the theater even when the Tiber flooded, as it often did in winter (Fig. 178, upper). The theater opened to great acclaim for the carnival of 1671, and it ran uninterrupted for four years, with more or less continuous success, until the holy year of 1675, when all theatrical performances were banned.[19]

Christina, in her gilded box, attended almost all the performances in those years, accompanied by her favorite cardinals. She was indeed queen of the theater. But she had a rival as "queen" of Rome, the younger, more beautiful, and much richer Maria Mancini Colonna, who was a) niece of powerful Cardinal Jules Mazarin, b) former mistress of Louis XIV, and c) wife of Lorenzo Onofrio Colonna, head of one of the most ancient aristocratic families of Rome. If not a queen, Maria at least bore the title of princess of Paliano, thanks to her husband's many titles. She brought a vast fortune to her marriage, which for a time seems to have been successful.[20] The couple shared a love of music and theater; they visited Venice several times to attend operas during carnival. The Colonna rented four boxes in the Tordinona, three next to the proscenium on one side of the house and one next to the proscenium on the other, all on the second tier. They decorated the fronts of their boxes with Colonna arms, so that Christina could not look at the stage without seeing symbols of her rival.[21] Nor could anyone else in the theater. Christina, however, did not have to endure her rival's presence in her theater for long. In May 1672, Maria Mancini, disguised in men's clothes, ran away from Rome and Lorenzo Onofrio, finding in the inviolable sanctuary of a convent in Madrid safety from a husband she feared wanted her murdered. She returned to Rome only after both her husband and the Swedish queen had died in 1689, within a few days of each other.

The operas given during those four years, with one exception, had been produced previously in Venice.[22] Indeed, one of the operas the Colonna had seen there at the Teatro SS. Giovanni e Paolo in 1666 – *Tito*, with music by Marc'Antonio Cesti – they liked so much that Maria had it performed in Rome. The Venetian musical connection is important, because it underlines the Venetian architectural connection. When public opera was finally presented in Rome at the Tordinona, thirty and more years after the first such spectacle in Venice, both the musical and architectural forms were imports from the Serenissima. A contemporary noted that the design of the theater was "ad uso di Venezia."[23] In this sense, Rome in following Venice replicated the earlier experience of other Italian cities, such as Naples. The majority of the operas given at the Tordinona, with libretti adjusted for the new Roman setting, were dedicated to Christina.

In the fall of 1676 Clement X died, to be replaced by Cardinal Benedetto Odescalchi, who took the name of Innocent XI. As a cardinal, Innocent had frequently attended operas at the Tordinona as a guest in Christina's box. On ascending the throne of Peter, he abruptly and ungratefully banned all theatrical performances in the city. The one-year hiatus of 1675 (which inexplicably stretched into two) in the activity of the Tordinona turned into a closure that endured until the death of Innocent XI in August of 1689. Christina, who died in April of the same year, did not live long enough to occupy her royal box again.

During the pontificate of the despised Innocent XI, Christina found a way to defy his theatrical ban. She sponsored performances in the Collegio Clementino, a school run by the Padri Somaschi, which she used as a cover to circumvent Innocent's strictures. Theatrical works of high moral content had been produced at the Clementino since early in the century, and Christina had attended some performances long before the opening of the Tordinona. After that theater closed, she sought to introduce to the Clementino *dramma per musica*, sponsoring in 1679 and 1680 operas by the young Alessandro Scarlatti, for instance. The Collegio Clementino seems to have been a perfect screen, since the only theatrical works permitted during the holy year of 1675 had taken place there.[24]

The immediate success of the Tordinona in 1671 apparently encouraged Christina and company to plan a much larger theater on the same site. Evidence provided by two drawings shows that Christina and Acciaioli, and surely D'Alibert as well, plotted no later than the winter of 1672 to rebuild the Tordinona in a much more capacious form, turned 90 degrees to the first theater. The drawings (Figs. 179 and 180), at Windsor Castle and the National Museum, Stockholm, share the same shape for the auditorium, with rows of boxes that flare out from the stage and lead to a flat row of five central boxes, set parallel to the stage to optimize visibility.[25] The five central boxes in the second order would surely have been Christina's. She needed that number to accommodate her suite of cardinals. Both drawings must be dated no later than the winter of 1672, because they bear an inscription that tells us that the width of the opening of the proscenium had been approved by Filippo Acciaioli,[26] who resigned his role at the theater in February of that year. No documentation has come to light in the Roman archives that would aid in dating the Stockholm and Windsor drawings more precisely, but that lack might be explained by the fact that negotiations with the Archconfraternity of S. Gerolamo della Carità over renting the entire property had not been consummated, and so no official documents had been drawn up. The boxes in the proposed theater numbered thirty-three per tier, a greater than 50-percent increase over the number in the old house, that would have produced, in turn, a similar increase in revenue. The stage was far deeper than the one that projected out over the Tiber, and so the larger audience could be entertained with more elaborate scenery. The theater was essentially the same size as the theater as rebuilt in the 1690s (see later discussion).

The Acciaioli plan, as one may call the one represented in these two drawings, was superseded by a second, even more intriguing project recorded on a drawing now in the Konstakademi, Stockholm (Fig. 181) – an eighteenth-century copy of a plan by Carlo Fontana for the Tordinona made by the Swedish architect Carl Frederik Adelcrantz (1716–96), who was in Rome between 1741 and 1743 and again in 1750. The undated sheet bears an inscription: "Design for a theater to be built at Torre di Nona in Rome, by order of the Queen Christina of Sweden. Invention of Cav. Carlo Fontana."[27] In the lower left corner a man in armor holds a shield with Christina's Vasa family coat of arms. Like that shown in the Acciaioli plan, the long axis of the theater would have been parallel to the street. The regularity and symmetry of the exterior walls – something the theater never possessed – suggest that Fontana in his original drawing may have cleaned up the plan for publication. The detailed legend, the careful arrangement of forms on the page, and the visually arresting

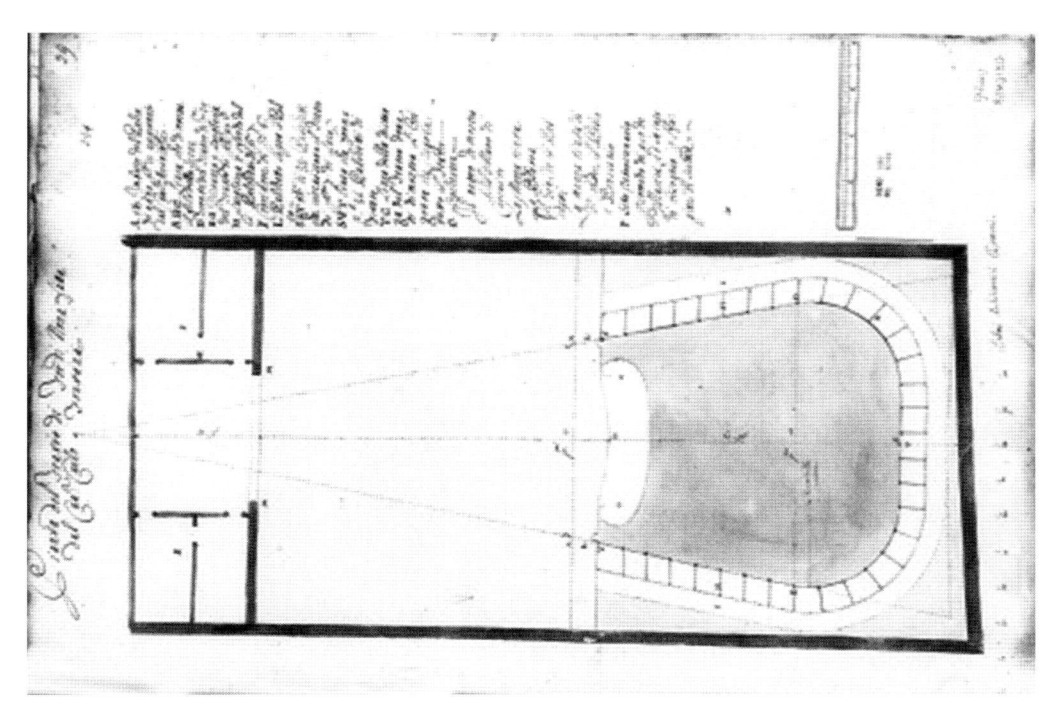

FIG. 179 Anonymous, project for Teatro Tordinona, c. 1671–72 (Royal Collection Trust / © Her Majesty Queen Elizabeth II 2016)

variety of line weights also point to the likelihood that Adelcrantz copied a drawing that Fontana intended to be the basis for an engraving.[28] The inscription "to be built" tells us that the plan was for the future.

There is no need to repeat Per Bjürstrom's fine analysis of the elaborate machinery on the deep stage,[29] but it is worth spending some time over the design of the auditorium, which has the relatively novel form of a truncated oval. While one often reads that Fontana invented the oval plan for theaters with boxes, that is not precisely the case.[30] One of the two Venetian comedy theaters with boxes of 1580 (the first theaters with boxes) had an oval plan, at least according to a contemporary account.[31] More to the point here, the Teatro della Pergola in Florence, designed in 1652 and opened in 1657, had an "ovate form," as the author of the contemporary description of that theater noted.[32] To be sure, Fontana's oval is pure, while that of the Pergola is extended into something of a horseshoe shape. Opposite the stage in the Adelcrantz drawing is a magnificent royal box, one that goes far beyond the five connected boxes Christina enjoyed in the first Tordinona theater. She was displeased that she had no private entrance to her box in that earlier theater. This design sets out not only to solve that problem, but also to make her presence in the theater even more commanding. The queen and twenty guests could enter her box through two diagonal corridors that were closed off by

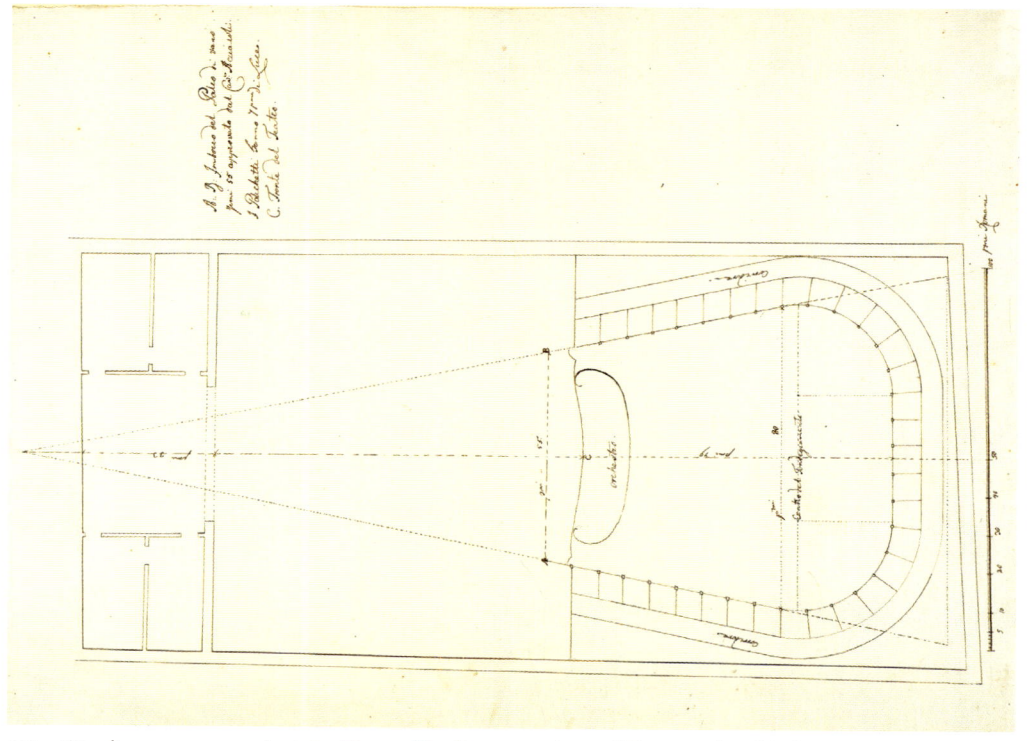

FIG. 180 Anonymous, project for Teatro Tordinona, variant of Fig. 179 (Stockholm, National Museum, THC 8509)

doors from other corridors that allowed access to the other boxes in the theater. She would sit in a wide seat on the central axis, at the top of a flight of five curving steps. At the new Tordinona, the rest of the audience would gain their seats by ascending four staircase towers that projected from the sides of the theater and rose up to the access corridors outside the boxes; two staircases served the central section, while one served each of the side sections.

Fontana often attached alternate schemes to his plans. With this drawing come two other proposals for the royal box (Fig. 182) One served up Christina and her cardinals on an oval platform set in front of the curve of the boxes.[33] If Christina wanted to make sure that she was seen by all, this solution would have been the one to choose (Fig. 182). It recalls vividly the elevated platforms for rulers, placed in the centers of court theaters, that we found, for instance, in Lyon and Florence in the previous century, while her position in the center of two rows of flanking cardinals brings to mind the seating arrangement for Leo X in 1519. This extravagant royal box, extending into the platea, may have its origins in the baldacchino for the Medici cardinal set into the auditorium at the Pergola (Fig. 161), or, even more likely, in her experience of the baldacchino she had ordered removed during her visit to Ferrara in 1655.

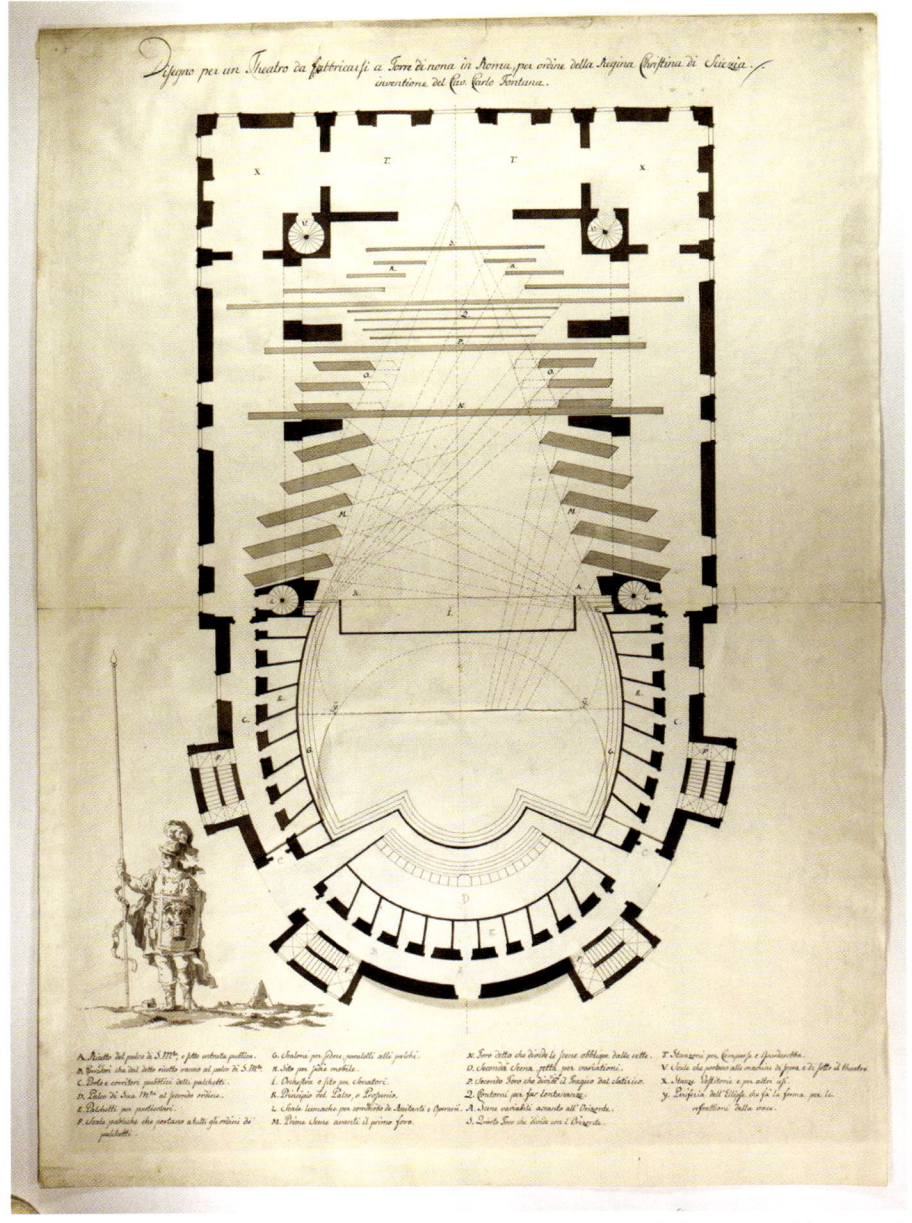

FIG. 181 Carl Fredrik Adelcrantz, "Design of a theater to be built for Queen Christina of Sweden, invention of Cav. Carlo Fontana," copy after a drawing of Carlo Fontana (Stockholm, Konstakademien, Ad 22)

This alternate plan seems also motivated by Fontana's desire to make a visually satisfactory design based on the interplay between a circle and an oval, just as he proposed in his project of c. 1675 to build a centrally planned

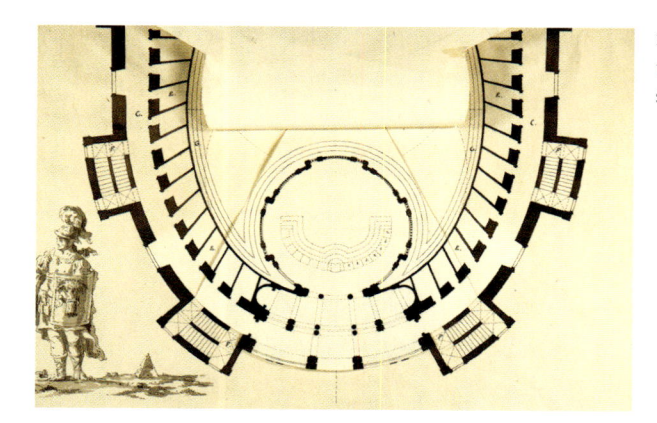

FIG. 182 Two variations of the box for Queen Christina shown in Fig. 181

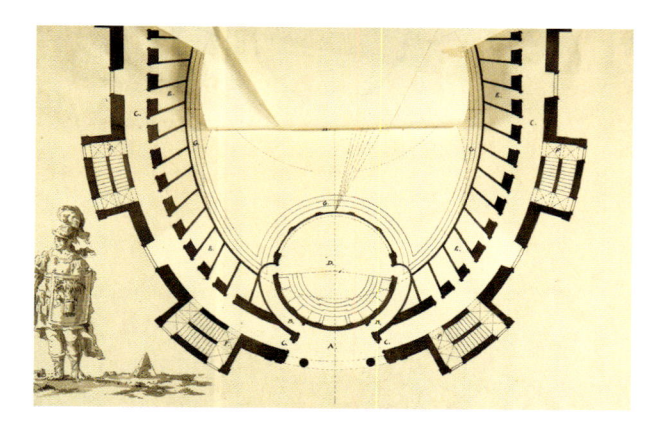

church in honor of early Christian martyrs inside the oval Colosseum (Fig. 183). Entrance to the circular platform would have been through two broad transverse halls that suggest church narthexes, or are reminiscent of the curved entrance to Baldassare Peruzzi's Palazzo Massimo alle Colonne in Rome.

The second alternate is more modest (Fig. 182). The circular platform retreats into the line of boxes, so that the seats for the queen and her guests are really no closer to the stage than those for the people seated in the boxes that flank the royal circle. Entrance to this more economical version would have been far less grand than in the previous one. In all cases, the four projecting staircases would have allowed access to the corridors outside the regular boxes, corridors closed off by doors from the queen's path to her seat.

Since the inscription on the Adelcrantz drawing mentions Christina, and Fontana designed three variations on a box for her, he must have made his original drawing before her death in 1689. Are we to date that original drawing

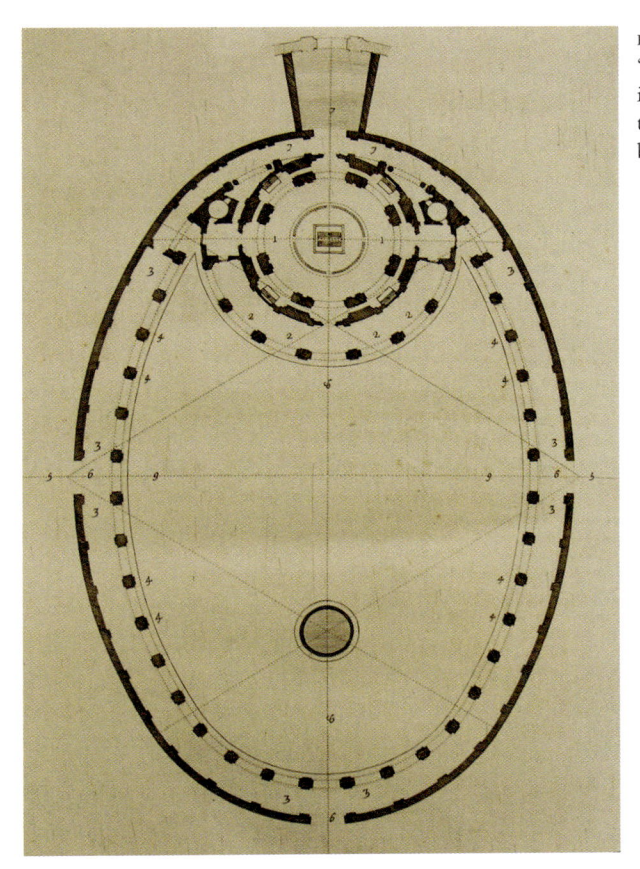

FIG. 183 Carlo Fontana, "Plan of the Amphitheater as it is at present with the temple that is proposed to be built" (from Fontana)

to the early years of the Tordinona, between 1671, the year of its successful opening, and 1676, the year in which Innocent XI's ban took effect? If so, it would have come along after Acciaioli left the theater in 1672. Or are we to think of it as a plan that Christina, D'Alibert, and Fontana conceived after 1676 in order to have a design ready to move forward as soon as Innocent XI might expire and a new pope prove favorable to theatrical activity?[34] The fact that the drawing seems never to have been engraved may accord better with the latter possibility. To publish the plan while Innocent still lived would have been unwise. The geometric play of oval and circle in Fontana's project of c. 1675 for the Colosseum and in the Adelcrantz drawing after his design for the Tordinona suggests that they may not have been far apart in time.

The death of Innocent XI in 1689 gave the Tordinona a new lease on life, even though its royal patron was no longer around to enjoy it. The new pope, the Venetian Alexander VIII Ottoboni, was not opposed to theaters, and the papal nephew, Cardinal Pietro Ottoboni, was another prince of the church who wrote libretti. Immediately in 1690 the twenty-two-year-old cardinal produced a theatrical work in his residence, the Cancelleria (shades of Cardinal Riario).[35] Count D'Alibert sprang into action, and in December 1689, he renewed the rent for the site of the Tordinona from the Archconfraternity of S. Gerolamo della Carità, which in the intervening years again had rented out the space for grain storage. For the carnival of 1690 D'Alibert reopened the old theater with an opera that had a shrewdly chosen libretto written by the papal nephew. In 1691 young Cardinal Ottoboni again provided the libretto for a new opera at the Tordinona to celebrate the first voyage of Christopher Columbus two hundred years earlier. Not a student of geography, Cardinal Ottoboni had Columbus set foot in the New World on the Pacific coast of Peru. The opera, particularly the libretto, was a failure, and the audience dwindled.[36] In February Alexander VIII Ottoboni died, to be replaced by Innocent XII Pignatelli, who at first gave no sign of prohibiting theatrical performances.

Although there seemed to be no ill wind blowing from the Vatican, D'Alibert suddenly found himself confronted with a rival opera house, the Teatro Capranica, whose noble owners had obtained permission for performances of opera from the new pope. D'Alibert was forced to compete with a grand gesture of his own. After some false starts, he convinced the Archconfraternity of S. Gerolamo della Carità to rent him the whole property in perpetuity. In June of 1695 he began the construction of a new and much

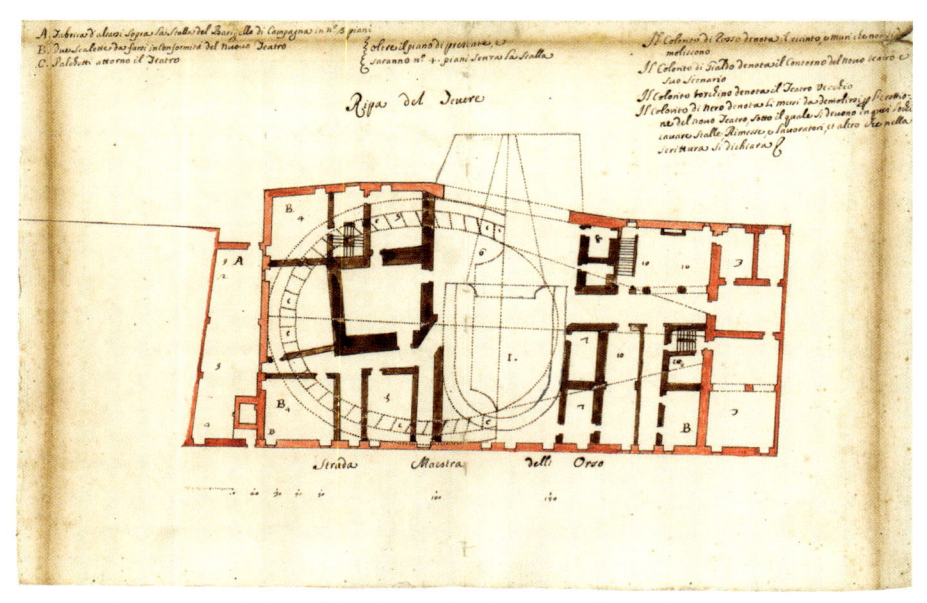

FIG. 184 Superimposed plans of first Teatro Tordinona (smaller) and second (ASR, 30, notari capitolini, Atti Perelli, uff. 25, prot. 440, c. 296. By concession of the Ministry for Cultural Resources and Activities and Tourism)

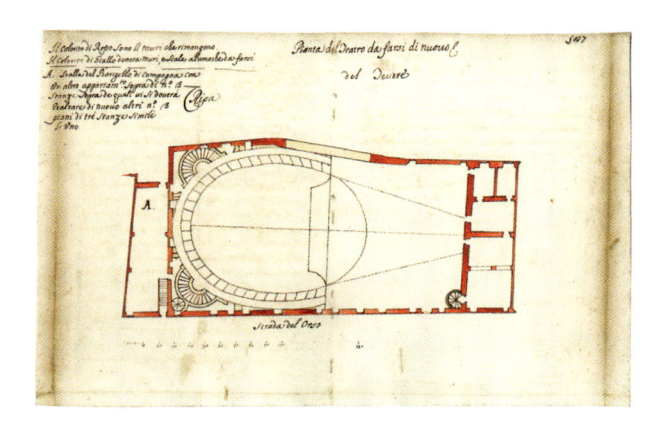

FIG. 185 Carlo Fontana, Project for second Teatro Tordinona, 1695 (ASR, 30 Notai Capitolini, uff. 25, vol. 340, c. 580. By concession of the Ministry for Cultural Resources and Activities and Tourism)

larger theater, again designed by Carlo Fontana, that opened for carnival in January, 1697 – built in the short period of seven and a half months.[37] Drawings by Fontana for both of his Tordinona theaters are preserved in the Archivio di Stato, Rome, attached to leases that D'Alibert signed with the archconfraternity in 1696.[38] One drawing that we have already encountered (Fig. 177) shows the first theater, turned toward the river and slipped into the narrow space between two houses. A second drawing superimposes the outline of the new theater on the outline of the old[39] (Fig. 184). In the outline of the new we recognize the truncated oval of the Adelcrantz plan, but minus the royal box and projecting staircases necessitated by Christina's desire for a private entrance. As Fontana in the Acciaioli and Adelcrantz plans had proposed years earlier, he rotated the theater 90 degrees to create a wider and longer auditorium and a deeper stage. The widest part of the oval cleverly occurs just where the walls of the old building splay toward the Tiber. At this point, in the summer of 1696, Fontana returned to his old idea described in the oval auditorim of the Adelcrantz plan. A separate drawing of this large, thirty-five-box theater alone (Fig. 185), inscribed "Theater to be built" (*Teatro da farsi*), adds a pair of semicircular staircases to reach the boxes. An inscription informs us that the house marked A will remain and be increased in height, presumably to increase income from rents.[40]

Our best source for the actual (and different) appearance of the second Tordinona theater, which no longer stands, is a group of drawings that Fontana bound into an album of drawings of this and other theaters, now in Sir John Soane's Museum, London.[41] Although the album has never been carefully analyzed in its entirety, it is clear that Fontana arranged the drawings for the Tordinona as built toward the album's beginning; in particular they are sheets numbered 4 through 8.[42] For convenience, the drawings in this album will be referred to by their Soane numbers. Three of these (Soane 5–7) are identified in Fontana's hand as the design that has been *stabilito,* or established.[43] Many of the other drawings in the album are preparatory sketches that experiment with geometric configurations for the auditorium, including both a number of variants on the truncated oval shape that appears in the drawings in the Archivio di Stato, Rome, as well as riffs on the form of a horseshoe.[44] Included in the album are three plans, all by other hands, of theaters in other cities: Teatro della Pergola, Florence (Fig. 163); Teatro degli Intronati, Siena (Fig. 165); and Teatro SS. Giovanni e Paolo, Venice (Fig. 152). We have encountered these precious drawings in earlier chapters. Presumably Fontana requested them to inform himself about important recent theaters in Italy.[45] All are large sheets that have been folded to fit into the album; only that of the Pergola has been removed and flattened (at least as of January, 2013).

As built, the new Tordinona abandoned the truncated oval of the Adelcrantz plan (Fig. 181) for a design with straight sides closer to the Acciaioli plan from 1671 to 1672 (Figs. 180 and 182), but with a segmentally curved section of boxes opposite the stage replacing the flat line of boxes designed for Christina.[46] Sergio Rotondi, in his splendid study of the Tordinona, calls the shape of this plan that of a "magnet,"[47] a just characterization that helps to distinguish it from oval and horseshoe plans, which have continuously curving

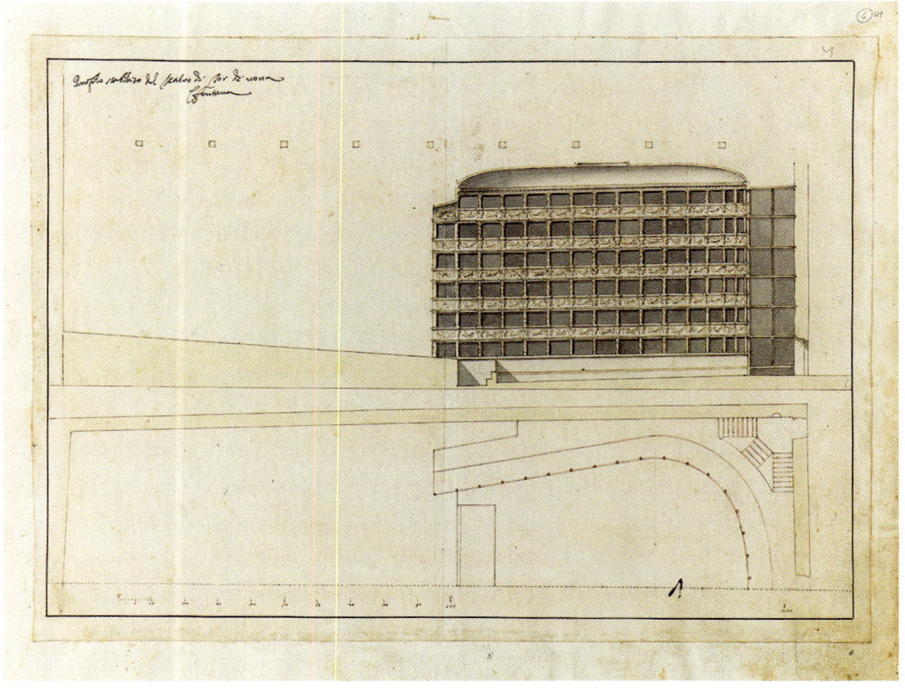

FIG. 186 Carlo Fontana, "Established profile of the Teatro di Tor di Nona," signed (© London, Sir John Soane's Museum, 117, 6)

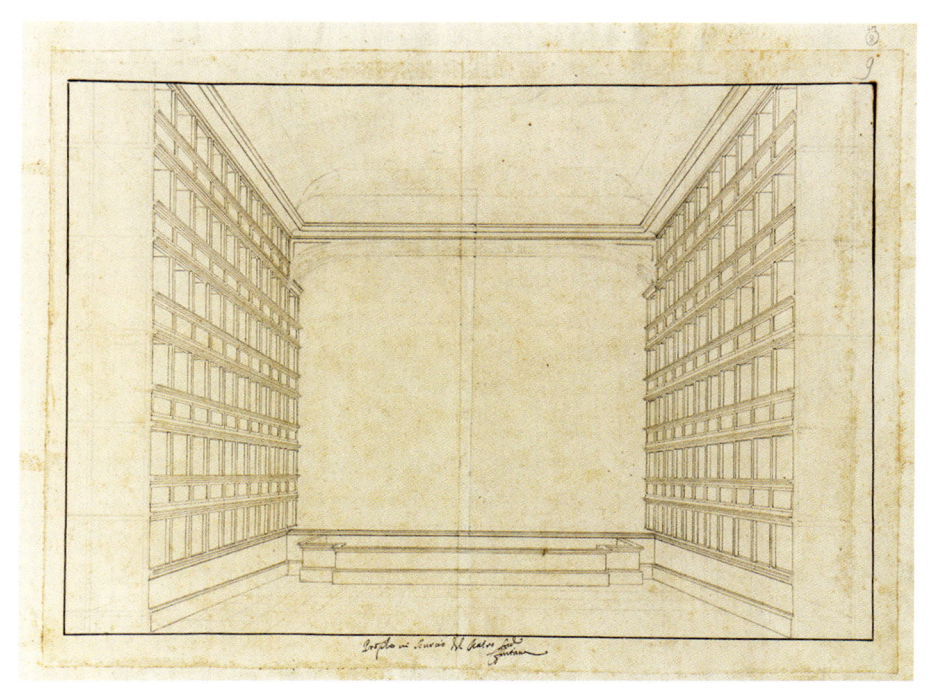

FIG. 187 Carlo Fontana, "Profile in perspective of the said theater" (© London, Sir John Soane's Museum, 117, 8)

sides. Why Fontana chose the magnet plan is not clear, but his decision may have had to do with budgetary concerns. Straight sides are easier and cheaper to construct than the continuous curves of an oval.

Soane 6 (Fig. 186), signed and identified by Fontana as "Established profile of the Teatro of Tordinona," presents a longitudinal section and a half-plan of the auditorium and stage.[48] There are five rows of thirty-five boxes and a sixth row of thirty-three, with no proscenium boxes at the top level. That range may have had open seating for the less well-to-do, who would not have appeared to merit the prominence of boxes in the proscenium. The floor of the auditorium slopes slightly toward the rectangular orchestra pit that encloses two steps facing the stage for the musicians. A coved ceiling with an oculus (surely for a chandelier) rises to a level below the beams that appear as squares at the top of the drawing.[49] Outside the boxes is a corridor. The magnet shape of the auditorium allows the curve of the boxes in the center to flow into the straight lines of the boxes on the sides. The stage is deeper than the auditorium and its floor more steeply raked. In the rear corner of the auditorium a three-part staircase provides access to the upper levels. The details of the boxes, sketched rapidly, indicate a uniform and relatively simple treatment of their fronts and of the vertical supports separating them. No extra money was wasted on the exteriors of the boxes, whose interiors were furnished by the

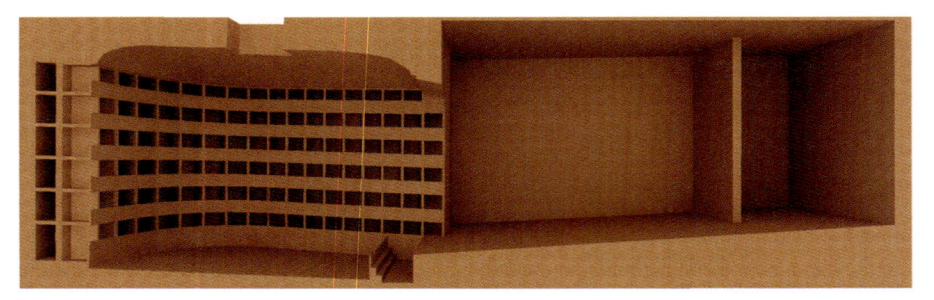

FIG. 188 Digital reconstruction of Teatro Tordinona as shown in Figs. 186 and 187, Soane 6 and 8 (Drawing by Benjamin Hoyle)

individual box holders. Soane 8 (Fig. 187) provides a perspective view of the interior, looking toward the stage, that underscores the simplicity and regularity of the décor. The low arch of the proscenium was sketched in later. On the basis of Soane 6 and 8 we have attempted digital reconstructions of this design for the Tordinona (Figs. 188 and 189).

Of particular importance is Soane 4 (Fig. 190), a plan of the area around the theater, apparently drawn to satisfy an order of the Governor of Rome.[50] At the top lies the edge of the river, with the bent wall of the theater next to the riverbank. To the left of the auditorium is a rectangular structure with a staircase leading to the central axis of the theater. Passageways flank the stairs and open through a triple arcade onto a small piazza crossed by a bridge that is supported on four columns. Along the street side of this building are three spaces that were probably shops that were rented out. To the left of the piazza a row of houses moves west toward Ponte Sant' Angelo. Spanning the street that passes the theater is a bridge that connects it to an opposite building through which the audience could pass to reach the bridge, and thus the theater, when the Tiber flooded. This probably reproduces, in a slightly different position, the bridge that was constructed to reach the earlier theater.

The newly built structure with the staircase to the left of the auditorium is of considerable importance in the history of theater architecture, in that it represents an attempt to give the theater a public façade as well as an embryonic monumental staircase with adjacent spaces that ultimately lead to such extravagant staircases in later opera houses, such as that in the Metropolitan Opera House in New York by Wallace K. Harrison, which opened in 1966. Fontana's appears to be the earliest such staircase deliberately built for an opera house that we know.

The exterior of the second Tordinona theater is recorded in the remarkable drawing in Berlin (Fig. 178, lower) that shows both the theater of 1670 and its replacement of 1695–97. Although the latter hardly has a prepossessing

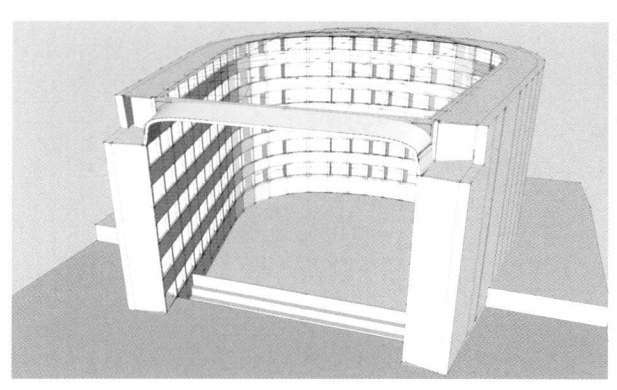

FIG. 189 Digital reconstruction of auditorium of Teatro Tordinona based on Figs. 186 and 187, Soane 6 and 8 (Drawing by Benjamin Hoyle)

appearance – in that way it is typical of theaters of the time – it does have a certain palatial scale and regularity, while the triple arcade supporting the bridge across the little piazza has a bit of grandeur, and the piazza gives the theater urban breathing room. The open space of the piazza was created by a lucky accident of which D'Alibert and Fontana took advantage. A flood of the Tiber destroyed houses belonging to the Collegio Romano that stood on the site, and D'Alibert rented the empty land.

The opening season of 1696 was a great success. The new Teatro di Tordinona was the largest and most beautiful theater in Rome. Instigated by the popularity of the new theater, a cry from righteous clerics against what they considered obscenities perpetrated in theaters reached full howl in August of 1697. At that point the Congregation of the Reform of Ecclesiastical Discipline, appointed by the pope, ordered the destruction of the Tordinona. Demolition began as soon as ordered. An eruption of protests from the whole city halted the work, but only for a day. Within another forty-eight hours the entire wooden structure of the theater had been removed; only the masonry walls remained. Innocent XII responded to an avalanche of lawsuits by absolving the church not only of financial responsibility to those who had suffered monetary losses, but also of the duty to pay for the demolition his committee had ordered. The ambassador from Turin reported that poor D'Alibert had "ended his scenes with this tearful tragedy."[51] Some lawsuits resulting from Innocent's act of destruction were not settled for almost eighty years.[52] Ironically, a later pope, Clement XII Corsini, rebuilt the Teatro di Tordinona in 1733.[53] That pope's family converted the Palazzo Riario in Via Lungara, in which lived two of the most important figures in the history of theater in Rome, Cardinal Riario and Queen Christina, into the vast Palazzo Corsini that stands on the site today. In the palace Christina's bedroom is preserved.

Carlo Fontana is in part rightly given credit for the invention of the oval or horseshoe plan for opera houses, but the story of that form's transmission to

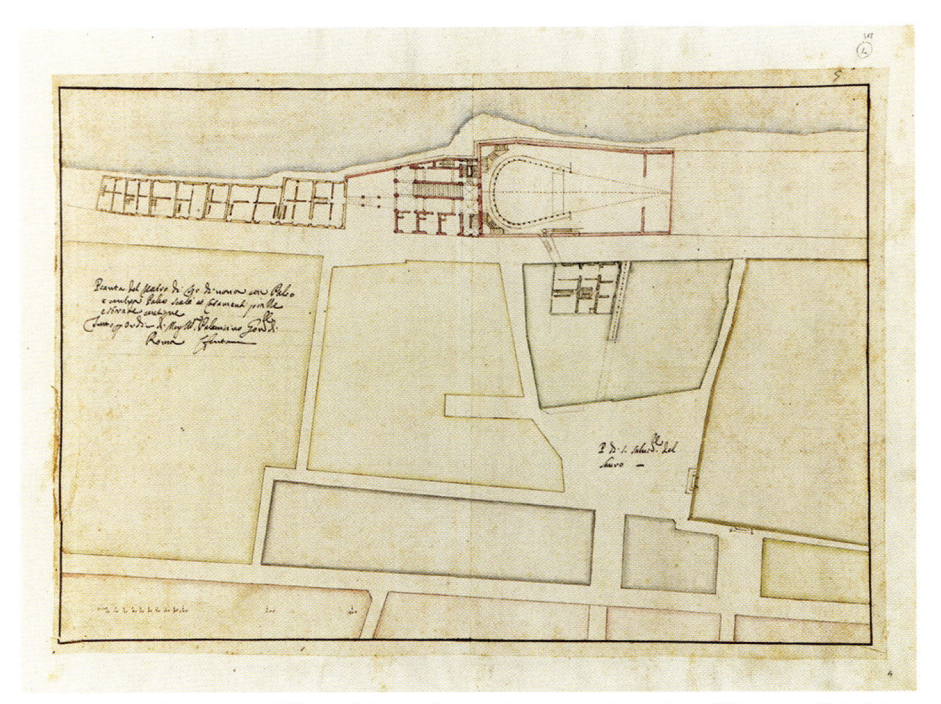

FIGS. 190 Carlo Fontana, "Plan of Teatro di Tor di Nona ... by order of Ill. str.mo Palavicino gov. of Rome," signed (© London, Sir John Soane's Museum, 117, 4)

later architects is complicated – in the first place, by the fact that the second Tordinona as built was not oval in plan. The only evidence of Fontana's parentage of the oval lies in the drawings that led up to its final design and in the Adelcrantz drawing, but not in the building as executed.[54] That building, which stood only a short while, disappeared without leaving a trace, except in the "established" plans preserved in the Soane album (Figs. 186, 187, and 190). With Fontana's second Tordinona the history of the architecture of Italian theaters before the eighteenth century comes to a grand, if calamitous, conclusion.

AFTERWORD

The territory and time we have covered, from Ferrara and the revival of the performance of Roman comedy in the courtyard of the Ducal Palace in the 1480s to the papal-ordered destruction of the Teatro Tordinona in Rome in the 1690s, give a consistent picture of how political the construction of theaters in postmedieval Italy often was. Theaters provided entertainment, presumably their primary function, but they also could underpin or threaten the political or religious order. Rulers lavished enormous funds on them, or rulers felt so threatened by them that they had them razed. Often they were among the most expensive artistic undertakings of a given prince, a sign of their enormous importance that should be more widely recognized than it often is. But the architecture of court theaters was not destined for long-term, worldwide success. That prize goes to the opera house, a commercial building type that originated in Venice in the 1630s and then followed the spread of the new art form of opera ever farther from the borders of Italy.

Italy in the Renaissance and Baroque eras was a hotbed of theatrical invention, not just in theater architecture, but also in scene design, comedic plays, dance, musical performances, and melodrama. The artists and architects who participated in the visual aspects of this lively world were often among the major figures of their day, as were the writers, composers, and performers who joined them in this grand collaborative endeavor.

In the English-speaking world, we are accustomed to think of the Elizabethan theater, and especially the plays of William Shakespeare, as the very foundation of the modern theater, and London's Globe Theater as the predecessor of the theaters we now frequent. The performance of the *Menaechmi* in Ferrara predates Shakespeare by something like a century. The architectural spaces invented first for commedia dell'arte in the mid- to late sixteenth century, and then the opera houses that arose to serve the new art form of opera in the 1630s and 1640s are the real predecessors of a new architectural form that has played an important role in cities around the globe. One can argue, without stretching the point, that it is one of the most successful inventions of a new building type in world history.

What this book demonstrates, one hopes, is the slow, incremental development of the form. It did not spring, gilded and draped in red velvet, from the head of some early impresario. There was a lot of trial and error. There were detours into blind alleys, eager acceptances of types of performances with relatively short-lived vogues, and offspring that offered credible new paths never followed. In short, it was a human invention. By the time the Teatro Tor di Nona came crashing down, the opera house as a codified, established architectural type was up and running on its seemingly unstoppable course. To paraphrase Louis Sullivan, it was an architectural form that followed the needs of a particular function. As such, it has endured down to the present. The Opera House in Guangzhou, China, opened in 2011, designed by the

FIG. 191 Zaha Hadid, Guangzhou Opera House, 2003–11, interior from stage (Photo: Virgile Simon Bertrand, courtesy of Zaha Hadid Associates)

late Iraq-born Zaha Hadid working out of London, boasts one of most glorious and inventive interiors of recent times (Fig. 191) Even so, one finds echoes of Italian theaters of the Renaissance and Baroque in its design. The starry, gilded heaven of its ceiling goes back at least to the Mantuan theater of 1501, and then to Alberti's statement that Roman theaters had cloth ceilings with heavenly attachments. Right in the middle of that ceiling is the magnet shape of the second version of the Teatro Tordinona, echoing the shapes of forms below it. Zaha Hadid may or may not consciously have recalled ideas from earlier theaters, but her design is surely a testament to their endurance.

APPENDIX

VITRUVIUS AND ALBERTI ON ANCIENT THEATERS

The primary source of knowledge about Greek and Roman theaters was Vitruvius, a Roman architect whose *De architectura* was written at the time of the Emperor Augustus, a bit before the year 1. It is the only ancient treatise on architecture to have come down to us. A manuscript of Vitruvius's treatise was "discovered" in the 1420s by an Italian scholar in the library of the monastery of St. Gall in Switzerland; copies of it spread with some rapidity in educated Italian circles. Vitruvius had much to say about the theaters he knew. Around 1450, a brilliant polymath, Leon Battista Alberti, composed the first architectural treatise of modern times, *De re aedificatoria*, in which he too discussed ancient theaters, partly basing his text on that of Vitruvius. The works of both men were printed – in Latin and without illustrations – in the 1480s, the same decade in which the first actual public performances of Roman plays since antiquity took place in Ferrara and Rome.[1] Although an illustrated Alberti did not appear until the middle of the sixteenth century, illustrated editions of Vitruvius, frequently with Italian translations of the text, appeared as early as 1511[2] and regularly throughout the sixteenth century. Those who designed theaters tended to know what both men had said about Greek and Roman theaters, and increasingly what the latter looked like, thanks to the rise of illustrated architectural books, which began to be printed in the early sixteenth century. Even though Renaissance architects possessed knowledge of the past, they almost never designed replicas of ancient theaters – the great exception being Andrea Palladio's theaters in Vicenza and Venice (see Chapter 6). From the beginning of the revival of the performance of Roman plays, the ancient architectural form did not work for the contemporary situation. As much as the Italians of the Renaissance admired and sought to emulate antiquity, they lived more than a millennium later in a wholly different society. They did, however, borrow details of theaters mentioned by Vitruvius and Alberti.

Vitruvius's descriptions of Greek and Roman theaters were difficult for Renaissance architects to interpret.[3] He sprinkled, for instance, his sometimes-inelegant prose with Greek words, when no Latin equivalents were available. Alberti, no fan of Vitruvius's literary style, remarked wryly that Romans would have thought Vitruvius wrote in Greek, and Greeks in Latin. Fortunately, Vitruvius has been well translated several times into English.[4] The theaters Vitruvius knew were built outdoors, with stepped, semicircular seating facing a rectangular stage. Between the front edge of the stage and the bottom row of seats was a half-moon-shaped area known as the orchestra, used in Greek theaters by the chorus and in Roman theaters for the seats of senators or other important audience members. At the top of the curved rows of seats, said Vitruvius, there should be a portico supported by columns on the side toward the stage and by a solid wall to the rear. This portico served two purposes: shelter from inclement weather and reinforcement to the theater's acoustics.

The most difficult section of Vitruvius for a Renaissance reader was his discussion of the *scenae frons*, or masonry wall at the rear of the stage. Whereas remains of semicircular seating areas were not uncommon in Italy, no complete example of a Roman *scenae frons* was preserved, and so there was no way to check Vitruvius's text against an actual structure. One could, however, try to ascertain whether what Vitruvius described accorded with the needs suggested by the texts of surviving plays. Vitruvius said that there should be a central or royal portal, decorated like the door of a palace, with two lesser doors to either side. The comedies of Plautus and Terence, which require two houses and perhaps the shrine of a god at center stage, contradict this idea. Tragedies, on the other hand, may require royal portals. The *scenae frons* could be two stories tall, wrote Vitruvius, or even three. Each story should be articulated by columns, and for acoustical reasons the height of the wall behind the stage should be level with the height of the top of the portico above the seating area.

While the architecture of the *scenae frons* was fixed, scenes could be changed by the use of *periaktoi*, rotating prisms with different scenes painted on each side. Where the *periaktoi* should be placed is left ambiguous in the Vitruvian text. In an instance of admirable clarity, he does state that there are three kinds of sets: the tragic, the comic, and the satiric. The first involves noble buildings, the second the houses of private citizens, and the third landscape features. By implication, it seems that these three types of sets would have to be restricted to the *periaktoi*, since the architecture of the back wall could not be modified. But Vitruvius does not say so directly.

Alberti was educated so well in Latin that he could, as a young man of twenty, pass off a play, *Philodoxus*,[5] as a Roman original.[6] (Faking antiquities was a favored pastime of precocious Renaissance youth.) If he knew Roman comedies well enough to forge one successfully, then he knew Roman drama well. Alberti made a living attached to the papal court, but his heart lay in studying and writing on many diverse subjects, including the visual arts. His books on sculpture, painting, and architecture, composed in that order, are fundamental documents for the art of the early Renaissance and the first treatises on these subjects of postmedieval times.[7]

The scholarly Alberti began by placing theaters in a general context of buildings used for public spectacles, introducing an overview of the history of these building types and making careful distinctions among the various purposes for which what he called "show buildings" were built. Theaters, he says, are buildings for poetry, comedy, and tragedy, while other types, such as circuses and amphitheaters, serve athletic purposes, such as chariot racing, fighting wild beasts, or even mock-naval battles. Some theaters we have encountered managed to fuse these types.

When Alberti came to the specifics of theaters, he synthesized much of what we have encountered in Vitruvius, adding to Vitruvius's comments his own knowledge of the remains of ancient structures. The Albertian theater is also semicircular with a semicircular *area* for the orchestra. The wall behind the stage has three doors, is articulated by at least two stories of columns or pilasters, and has provision (where, precisely, he doesn't say) for changing scenes as well. For acoustical reasons the front edges of the steps that climb the seating area should all be vertically aligned, as in Vitruvius, and to enhance the acoustics there should be a portico at the top of the seats, its columns facing the stage and its back wall solid. From this portico an awning studded with stars is to spread over the spectators – a detail Alberti did not find in Vitruvius.

Alberti said that the details of the orders of the exterior porticos of theaters should be drawn from the architecture of temples. For Alberti, temples were the noblest of all buildings, and so his admonition to use forms appropriate to temples on theaters bespeaks the importance he attached to theatrical structures. His models for theaters were Roman buildings he knew well, the Colosseum and the Theater of Marcellus. For Alberti the proper articulation for the exterior of a theater was a structure of piers and arches to which trabeated orders of columns and entablatures are engaged – just like those of the Colosseum. The theaters discussed here almost never had exterior architecture of the sort Alberti advocated.

NOTES

Introduction

1. Cf. Piermarini. Other views of the interior are readily available online.
2. Pinelli, 1973, 29. "non sono più i soli ad essere contemporaneamente spettatori e oggetto di spettacolo; la cornice del palchetto inquadra come un minusculo arcoscenico la rappresentazione del rito borghese del vedere e dell'essere visti, spettacolo nello spettacolo che, col tempo, tende ... quasi a prevalere sull'azione centrale."
3. Illuminating discussions of Renaissance books on architecture are found, for example, in D'Evelyn 2012, Klein and Zerner 1964, *Paper Palaces* and Payne 1999.
4. Notable are the contributions of Elena Povoledo in Pirotta and Povoledo, 281–383, and Glixon, 2006, 227–276, to this subject.

1 Ferrara and Mantua, 1486–1519

1. Tuohy, 1996 258.
2. Vitruvius, 1521, 75r.
3. Rosenberg, 1980 analyzes the political situation in Ferrara in 1486.
4. Ibid., and Gundersheimer, 1973, 210.
5. Marotti, 1974, 53. The treatise is undated. It contains firsthand observations of buildings in Rome, to which Prisciani was Ferrarese ambassador in 1501, but he had also visited that city earlier. See Rotondò, 1960, 70 and 72, n. 1.
6. The layout of the courtyard for the performance has been reconstructed by Povoledo, 1974, fig. xxv. As always, it is difficult to calculate how many spectators could have been accommodated, perhaps several hundred, or maybe even a thousand, but not the ten thousand contemporaries claimed.
7. Rosenberg, 1980, 533, believes that the audience was largely restricted to the upper classes, but the accessibility of the courtyard to the piazza suggests that some townsfolk, at least men, must have been able to enter.
8. Tuohy, 1996, 263, n. 164.
9. Povoledo, 1974, 110–11, fig. xxvi.
10. Tuohy, 1996, 258.
11. Luzio and Renier, 1900, 254: "ho principiato ad imparare architettura per forma che quando la S.V. me parlerà di suoi edifici, la intenderò meglio."
12. The courts were very competitive. For instance, Isabella d'Este, who was in Milan for the carnival of 1513, wrote to her husband that the comedies she has seen there had not been as well produced as the ones Francesco had staged in Mantua. Bourne, 2008, 216, n. 138.
13. Povoledo, 1974, 111–12, fig. xxvii.
14. Luzio and Renier, 1888, 182. I have translated the following somewhat freely: "et per pingere a V.S. come sta, bisogna che quella alquanto ponga in exercicio la imaginativa, e considri la sala grande di corte come stava per l'altre Comoedie. La sena de comici è, come suole, longo le fenestre, dal capo di sopre della sala è il tribunale, non come suole imperò che el primo grado è alto quatro pedi da terra dove era uno solo pede, poi camina per nove gradi alto. El tribunale, quale camina per longo della sala facto sopra modioni come scià V.S. e tanto magiore del solito, quanto che li modioni erano quatro pedi necti fuora del muro et adesso sono octo, poi camina per nove gradi alto quasi fino al solaro con le sue sbarre e colonelli, tucti coperte a bussi et verdure cum le arme et divise ducale, che è bellissimo a vedere. Tucti li tribunali sono coperti de panni rossi, bianchi et verdi, il resto de la sala parata a modo vecchio: da l'altro capo verso la credenza è formata el tribunale come da l'altro capo con simile ordine et parato."
15. See note 5.
16. Luzio and Renier, 1888, 186: "el popullo tanto strecto che apena si puoteva uno mettersi la

17 Luzio and Renier, 1888, 184–85: "in uno tracto furono accese torze assaissime e tirati cierti razi nanti alle finestre et quelle facte obscure, tal che vera nocte dimostrava."

18 I thank Molly Bourne for sending me the text of this letter of February 2, 1501 (ASM, b. 2112, c. 315).

19 Archivio did Stato di Mantova, Cancelleria Ducale, Ambasciatori, Mantova, b. 1, fasc. 48. Recently retranscribed by Bourne, 2008, 407, doc. 158, who corrects date wrongly given as 13 February by D'Ancona, 1885, 5, 29–31. The theater has been discussed by Pirotta and Povoledo, 1982, esp. 40–42 and 313, n. 6, among others.

20 Povoledo, ibid., 314, suggests that the architecture surrounding the Mantegna paintings was detached from the walls of the room, but this seems unlikely, given the complexity and expense of making the temporary architecture capable of standing alone.

21 This measurement almost exactly equals 6 Mantuan *braccia*, at 0.465 m to the *braccia* (2.78 m divided by 0.465 equals 5.978 *braccia*).

22 Povoledo in Pirotta and Povoledo, 1982, 313, n. 6, reconstructs the dimensions of the room and the architectural forms somewhat differently.

23 Part of this large room could have been walled off to create a space with the proportions of 3 to 4 mentioned by the ambassador.

24 Bourne, 2010, 151.

25 Again thanks to Molly Bourne, who provided the transcription of a letter to Francesco Gonzaga of February 4, 1501 (ASM, b. 2457, cc. 42–43) that discusses the making of the sky in the house of a local nobleman. The Ferrarese ambassador's letter does not mention the zodiac figures, but the letter of February 4 states that there were both stars and figures.

26 This passage is particularly difficult to visualize. Cf. Povoledo in Pirotta and Povoledo, 1982, 314, for one attempt.

27 The plays were *Poenulus* of Plautus, *Hippolytus* of Seneca, *Adelpoe* of Terence, and *Philonico* (*Phormio* of Terence?).

28 Archivio di Stato di Mantova, Copialettere, b. 2910, libro 169, 60v–61. Molly Bourne graciously provided the text of this letter.

29 D'Ancona, 1891, II, 385, n. 3.

30 The Ferrarese foot measured 0.403854 m, or 0.41 m, depending on which source one uses, and so that the room would have been roughly 59 × 18.6 m (190 × 61 ft).

31 Povoledo, 1974, 119, fig. xxviii.

32 D'Ancona, 1891, II, 383: "gli sono le case de le Comedie, che sono sei, non avantagiate del consueto."

33 D'Ancona, 1891, II, 383:" nè altro gli ho visto degno di noticia. Li travi del sollaro sono anchora de ligname, cossì nudi: ne sciò mò se li copriranno altramente."

34 The were the *Epidicus, Bacchidi, Miles Gloriosus, Asinaria,* and *Casina*.

35 Tuohy, 1996, 117–19 and 257–64, discusses this theater, whose existence he discovered in Ferrarese documents.

36 Tuohy, 1996, 118 and 259, who variously renders the measurements as 25.2 × 48.8 m or 25.5 × 49.3 m.

37 D'Ancona, 1891, II, 394, n. 2

38 Also known as Martino da Udine.

39 Bourne, 2008, 183–222, reconstructs the history of the palace, its layout and decorations.

40 Bussadori, 1986, 11, notes performances at carnival in 1512 and 1513. D'Ancona, 1891, II, 109, cites the comedy performed in the loggia on February 25, 1512.

41 Bourne, 2008, doc. 303.

42 Ibid., 216, doc. 321.

2 Rome, 1480s–1520

1 "Atque in hoc ipso speciosissimo paradisi spatio tria pulcherrima, atque optima aedificia exstabant. Primo namque a parte inferiori nobile quoddam egregiumque theatrum super columnis marmoreis fornicatum in altum elevabatur." Quoted in Magnuson, 355. (For a vastly different interpretation of Manetti's use of the word "theatrum," see Westfall, 152–54.) Alberti used architectural terms knowingly; Manetti presumably would have heard the word directly from Alberti in relation to the building planned by Nicholas. See also Danesi and Squarzina, 1980, 160.

2 Westfall, 1974, 184, doubts that the three buildings in the garden were worked out in detail, but he argues convincingly, 168–84, that Alberti was the brains behind Nicholas's ambitious plans for rebuilding the area of the Vatican and its approaches.

3 Vitruvius, 1488(?), *De architectura liber primus[decimus]*, Joannes Sulpitius Verulanus, ed., Rome, Eucharius Silber. The publication date

is not given; Ciapponi, 1984, 72, n. 2, lays out the attempts to date the issuance of the book, settling on a time between 1486 and 1492. A narrower date of 1487–88 has been convincingly suggested by E. Bentivoglio, 1984. See Frommel, 2005, 411, n. 37.

4   Neiiendam, 1969, 114, citing Fortunato Pintor, *Rappresentazioni romane di Seneca e Plauto nel rinascimento*, Perugia, Unione tipografica cooperativa, 1906, 9. The specific date of the letter is not given. The letter states: "Velim adfuissetis cum Epidicus Plauti agebant mimi Romani in capitolio utinam et hodies adessetis, cum spectaturi Hyppolitus Senecae simus. Singuinarium tamen spectaculum et in publico fit, probe Florae forum, ante aedes Rv.mi Camerarii." In 1486 the cardinal's house could not have been the immense palace, the Cancelleria, which he probably began only in 1489 (cf. n. 8), but the Cancelleria is near Campo de' Fiori.

5   Sulpizio's text reads: "Tu enim primus Tragoediae quam nos iuuentutem extitandi gratia et agere et cantare primi hoc aevo docuimus (Nam eius actionibus iam multis saeculis Roma non viderat) in medio foro pulpitum ad quinque pedum altitudinem erectum pulcerrime exornasti: Eandemque postquam in Hadriani mole Diuo Innocentio spectante est acta: rursus intra tuos penates tamquam in media circi cavea toto concessa umbraculis tecto: admisso populo et pluribus tui ordinis spectatoribus honorifice excepisti. Tu etiamque primus picturatae scaenae faciem quom Pomponiani comoediam agerent nostro saeculo ostendisti. Quare a te quoque theatrum nouum tota urba magnis votis expectat: Videt enim liberalitatem ingenii tui: qua ut uti possis deus et fortuna cocessit. Cum igitur nec desint tibi facultates, quid glorioius ist tua aetate facer possis?"

6   What Riario's stage may have looked like is suggested by one erected in Velletri between 1509 and 1513. Over a basement with four arched openings rose a platform with a backdrop composed of five arches. The arch in the center was tallest, while those at the sides were architecturally elaborate, with pediments supported by free-standing Corinthian columns set against pilasters. For the theater in Velletri, see Nocca, 1989.

7   An important forerunner of Riario's theatricals, as well as those in Ferrara, was the celebration staged in the spring of 1473 for the visit of Eleanora of Aragon, daughter of the King of Naples and new bride of the Duke of Ferrara, who was being escorted to Ferrara after her proxy marriage to the duke in Naples. The elaborate festivities took place over several days in front of the church of SS. Apostoli, on both sides of which two more of the cardinal nephews of Sixtus IV, Giuliano della Rovere and Pietro Riario, had palaces. Raffaele Riario must have been present. For the events in Rome, see Licht, 1996.

8   Frommel, 2005. Riario's activities are also discussed by Daly Davis.

9   Neiiendam, 1969, 121, and n. 61, where he quotes Verardus: "in tuis magnificentissimis aedibus eccitoto theatro, recenseri agi'q. curasti."

10   As pointed out by Lieberman, 2000.

11   For Chigi as patron, see Rowland, 1986, 2005.

12   Quinlan-McGrath, 1986, passim, makes a compelling case that the planets, sun and moon would particularly have smiled at noon of that day on the founding of the villa.

13   Frommel, 1973, 166–67.

14   Luzio, 1886, 525, quotes a letter of July 25, 1511 that says that the house "non è anchor finito."

15   In his Latin poem celebrating Chigi's villa, Blosio notes: "From here ... you will see the offering of Marcellus, and almost opposite this the Pompeian theater" (Quinlan-McGrath, 1990, 134). Quinlan-McGrath observes, ibid., 102, that like the ancient villa of Volpiscus described by Statius, Chigi's villa had two arms and a central court.

16   Anonymous, first half of sixteenth century, elevation of Villa Farnesina, Florence, Uffizi UA 365; also a second, New York, Metropolitan Museum of Art. The Uffizi drawing was pointed out by Frommel, 1961, Tafel VIb. For the theatrical nature of the north side of the villa, see ibid., 34–37.

17   Quinlan-McGrath, 1989. Gallo's Latin text, ibid., 93, reads: "Hic equites etiam sedeant, spectentque reposti / Bis septen gradibus, hic Pulvinaria dentur / Principibus. Magnisque Duces, et rebus honestis / Pontificum (dum animo indulgent) praesentia praesit." Quinlan-McGrath, ibid., 92, translates the passage: "Here also let the knights take up seats and watch reclining in their fourteen rows. Here let the Seats of Honor be given to the Princes. And let the great Dukes and / the presence of the Pontiffs preside over honorable

18 things (while they indulge their spirits)." The phrase "Bis septem gradibus" can be translated as "fourteen rows," or as "twice seven rows of steps." I prefer the latter, for reasons explained earlier.

18 Chigi and Francesco Gonzaga were certainly known to each other. In the fall of 1511 Chigi made an eventually failed attempt to arrange a marriage between himself and Francesco's natural daughter, Margherita (Luzio, 1886, 529–32). In 1506 or so both men began to build buildings with garden loggias that would be put to theatrical use, and both buildings were completed by 1512. Although we have no evidence that Gonzaga and Chigi corresponded about their loggias, it seems possible that each knew what the other was doing.

19 Bourne, 2008, 208, doc. 303.

20 Julius held the young Gonzaga in luxurious captivity in order to guarantee that his father, Francesco, would not take up arms against the pope's territories.

21 Luzio, 1886, 524–25.

22 Luzio, 1886, 542. Another Gonzaga correspondent reported the event somewhat differently (ibid., n. 1): "M. Agustino Gisso fece recitar una bella comedia inanti al S. Federico, che fu assai ridiculla per vulgar, ma li recitanti non era possibile a dir meglio et la lingua loro perfectissima."

23 The theatrical nature of the uses of the Colosseum motif on the façade of S. Marco and also inside the courtyard of the Palazzo Venezia, both built by Paul II, is discussed by Danesi and Squarzina, 1980, 163–66.

24 Ovid, 18: "so hasten the smartest women to the crowded games.... They come to see, they come that they may be seen." ["Sic ruit in celebres cultissima femina ludos.... Spectatum veniunt, veniunt spectentur ut ipsae."]

25 Padoan, 1970, provides a critical edition of the play.

26 Two other plays, one written by a fourteen-year-old and performed by a cast of the same age, were presented on the same stage in the days preceding the presentation of *La Calandra*.

27 Eleonora is perhaps best remembered in art history for having commissioned Titian's *Venus of Urbino* (Florence, Galleria degli Uffizi) as a gift for her husband.

28 Neiiendam, 1969, 136.

29 Francesco Maria's ascent to the Duchy of Urbino was complex. His predecessor as duke, Guidobaldo da Montefeltro, was the son of the famous Federico da Montefeltro, whose daughter married a Della Rovere and the lord of nearby Senigallia. Guidobaldo, husband of Elizabetta Gonzaga (sister of Francesco and sister-in-law of Isabella d'Este), was impotent and thus childless. He adopted his nephew, Francesco Maria, as his heir; thus a Della Rovere became Duke of Urbino, a papal fief in which Julius II confirmed Francesco Maria. Julius was also able to award the Duchy of Pesaro to Francesco Maria when that papal fief became vacant at the extinction of the branch of the Sforza family that previously held the title. Francesco took over Pesaro just before the performance of *La Calandra*, although the official bull was not signed by Julius until 20 February, the day before he died.

30 D'Ancona, 1891, II, 102–04. Letter published by Serrasi, vol. 1, 157, reproduced by Ruffini, 1976, 134–35, and Ruffini, 1986, 307–10. Discussed by Molinari, 1974, 64.

31 Ms. Vat. Urb. Lat. 490, 193v–96v. See Ruffini, 1976, 135–38, and Ruffini, 1986, 311–15, with discussion 353–63.

32 For the political situation, see the analysis of Fontes-Baratto, 1974.

33 Serlio, 1996, 37: "The knowledgable Girolamo Genga, was not he also an excellent painter and very skilful in perspective? The beautiful scenery painted by him to delight his patron Francesco Maria, Duke of Urbino, under whose aegis he became a fine architect, bears witness to that fact." Serlio worked in nearby Pesaro between 1511 and 1515, and so he was an eyewitness to Genga's sets.

34 First identified with certainty as the site of the production by Rotondi, 1987, 95.

35 Povoledo, 1964b, puts the towers on the opposite side of the room from the stage, probably erroneously.

36 Ruffini, 1976, 86.

37 The Vatican ms. (Ruffini, 1976, 136) gives the inscription differently: "Bella Foris, ludosque domi exercebat et ipse / Caesar, et haec nostri est utraque cura ducis." It is not clear which version is more accurate, but Meredith Hoppin finds the version in the Castiglione letter to possess a more elegant sense of Latin – to be a passable elegiac couplet – and thus to be preferred. Serassi, 1769 does not cite the location of Castiglione's letter, and I know of no recent scholar who has seen it.

38 I am enormously grateful to Meredith Hoppin for her translation and analysis of this inscription. She points out that the word "etenium" appears to be a misprint in the eighteenth-century publication; it should be rendered as "etenim."

39 Ruffini, 1976, 82. Castiglione wrote: "Dalla banda dove erano li gradi da sedere, era ornato delli panni di Troia: sopra li quali era un cornigione grande di relievo, et in esso lettere grandi gianche nel campo azzuro, che fornivano tutta quella mità della sala."

40 Povoledo, 1964b.

41 Ruffini, 1976, contains his reconstruction of the theater; Ruffini, 1986, is an amplified version of the first. Ruffini's argument contains reasonable points; here I offer an alternative reading of the evidence. Neither of us probably has the final answer.

42 See the letter in the previous chapter of Iano Pencaro to Isabella d'Este of February 9, 1499, in which he described the stage built in the *sala grande*: "the stage ... is, as usual, along the wall with windows," that is, on a long wall.

43 Conceivably, the open spaces in front of the windows could have been adapted, with a few steps or with short ladders, so that actors could make entrances and exits toward the center of the stage as well. The play requires the presence of two houses on stage; the two windows set toward the center of the long wall would easily have provided hidden access to those houses, set to either side of the centrally placed temple.

44 Even though this suggestion may seem far-fetched, the Vatican ms. notes that people at the performance related the central I of DELICIAE to the pope, since I was the first letter of his name: "che lo I era prima lettera dil nome suo." Ruffini, 1976, 74.

45 There is some dispute as to the authorship of the short prologue. The traditional attribution has been to Castiglione, but, following Giorgio Padoan, Fontes-Baratto, 1974, 58, n. 52, and 67, thinks it was written by Dovizi.

46 Molinari, 1964, 64. This point is taken up by Pallen, 1996, 92–94, who seems to accept Ruffini's idea that the seating was arranged in a U facing the stage, placed against the short west wall.

47 Ruffini, 1986, 311: "un aere alquanto nubiloso."

48 The descriptions of the set suggest that Genga may well have been influenced in his design by the famous Baltimore and Urbino panels that appear to represent the centers of ideal cities. For the latest thoughts on these mysterious paintings, cf. Alessandro Marchi and Maria Rosaria Valazzi, *La città ideale: l'utopia del Rinascimento a Urbino tra Piero della Francesca e Raffaelo*, Milan, Electa, 2012.

49 Serlio, 1996, 1545, II, 3, 26.

50 Ruffini, 1986, 314: "dilli quali sotto il palcho, primo sino a mezza testa, poi sino al collo, al mezzo dilla persona, poi sino sotto la coscia, et ultimamente armati tutti, si viddeno in piedi cum spade ignude in mano."

51 Povoledo, in Pirotta and Povoledo, 1982, 339–40, notes the relation of the speech of Amor to the current political situation, but she does not include an analysis of the inscription on the wall above the audience's seats.

52 Again thanks to Meredith Hoppin for her careful analysis of the Latin couplet.

53 St. Julius I, who reigned from 337 to 352, battled the Arian heresy, but one doubts that that struggle was in the mind of the newly elected Cardinal Della Rovere when he chose his papal name.

54 See n. 44.

55 Fontes-Baratto, 1974, 79, suggests that the Tuscan language used by Dovizi in *La calandra* inserted a theme of Medici hegemony into the Della Rovere celebrations, even though the play was meant to celebrate Francesco Maria's successes.

56 For Borgia and theater, cf. Neiiendam, 1969, 125–29.

57 Isabella's response to the production is not known (Luzio, 1906, 149). Bibbiena, the author of *La Calandra*, and Isabella were frequent, friendly correspondents.

58 For the theater see Cruciani, 1968, Bruschi, 1974, and Stinger, 1990. Ercole d'Este's unfinished theater in Ferrara was the first free-standing theater to be constructed, but presumably there was no performance in it.

59 Luzio, 1906, 127, n. 1. Another of Isabella's correspondents assured her that the theater, scenery, and costumes were not comparable in any way to hers (ibid., 127).

60 Neiiendam, 1969, 138, 142. Luzio, 1886, 524.

61 Bruschi, 1974, 199.

62 The contemporary sources do not agree on measurements. Cruciani, 1968, lxi.

63 The plan was first published by Thomas Ashby, *Papers of the British School in Rome* 1904. Cf.

Neiiendam, 1969, 118, who analyzed it before Bruschi reconstructed the theater as built.
64. Lieberman, 2005, 151.
65. Bruschi, 1974, 204ff.
66. Cruciani, 1968, 51 and 59.
67. Neiiendam, 1969, 151.
68. Bruschi's birds-eye reconstruction of the theater, fig. xxxv, does not show arches between the columns of the exterior entrance wall, but his reconstruction of the elevation of the façade, fig. xxxii, does.
69. In 1536 the villa became the property of Margaret, natural daughter of Emperor Charles V, after whom it became known as Villa Madama.
70. Heydenreich and Lotz, 1974, 173.
71. At that moment, Cibo was assigned apartments in Castel Sant'Angelo, and so the play likely was produced there. But his family also had a palace in the Vatican neighborhood that was razed to clear the area occupied by Bernini's Piazza San Pietro. The performance could have taken place there. Cibo was the son of Leo's sister.
72. Neiiendam, 1969, 172.

3 Early Theaters in Venice and the Veneto

1. Sanudo, 1879, passim.
2. Sanudo, 1879, vol. 7, 243.
3. Neiiendam, 1969, 131.
4. Sanudo, 1879, vol. 7, 311.
5. Ibid.
6. Neiiendam discusses his career at length.
7. The site is now occupied by the Palazzo dei Camerlenghi.
8. Sanudo, 1879, vol. 7, 701. ASV, Consiglio dei Dieci, Misti, R.o 32, 55v.
9. The records of the Council of Ten do not record individual votes. The vote was twelve for the ban, two against, and one abstention. The confusingly named Council of Ten had seventeen members: ten who were elected annually, plus the doge and his six councillors. Two of the ten elected members seem to have been absent.
10. D'Ancona. 1891, 2, 114–21, culled from Sanudo a long list of performances of plays btween 1508 and 1520.
11. The classic work on the compagnie is Venturi, 1908.
12. Sanudo, 1879, vol. 28, 248.
13. Ibid., 255.
14. Ibid., 256.
15. Ibid., 264.
16. Cf. n. 13.
17. Sanudo, 1879, vol. 53, 355.
18. Ibid., 361.
19. Petrarca, 1966, 237–38.
20. Norwich, 1983, 158.
21. Brown, 1988, passim.
22. Povoledo, 1964, 97, n. 3.
23. Sanudo, 1879, vol. 28, 533.
24. Ibid., 542.
25. Ibid., 552.
26. Ibid., 561.
27. Ibid., 239.
28. Muir, 1984, 59–77, gives an account of the festival.
29. Sanudo, 1879, vol. 44, 171–73.
30. The drawing is undated. One assumes that it was made for the production of a play with action placed in Venice.
31. Cited here is the excellent English translation of Serlio's work: Serlio, 1996.
32. Ibid., for a discussion of the importance of Serlio's publications and an exhaustive bibliography thereon.
33. Ibid., 90, specifically recalls a landscape set by Genga for the Duke of Urbino.
34. The saying goes back at least to Hildebert, Archbishop of Tours, in 1100. It was taken up in Francesco Albertini's popular guide to Rome of 1510, *Opusculum de mirabilis novae et veteris urbis Romae* – whence its appearance in Serlio, and later on the facade of the Odeon in Sabbioneta (see Chapter 7).
35. Ibid., 136–45.
36. Ibid., 82–85.
37. Ibid., 86–91.
38. Holberton's assertion, 1990, 83–85, that no plays took place in front of the loggia is not tenable in the face of visual and architectural evidence that he does not take into account. Perhaps he is correct, however, in arguing that no plays by Ruzzante were performed in front of the loggia.

4 Sixteenth-Century Florence, with Excursions to Venice, Lyon, and Siena

1. The standard account in English of Florentine theater under the Medici is Nagler, 1964, to which one can add the more specialized Saslow, 1996. The account given here is greatly indebted to both these works. See also Fara, 1996, 156–61.

2   Nagler, 1964, 5–12.
3   The most comprehensive account of this is in Mancini et al., 1995, 1, 41–66. See also Schulz, 1961 and Cairns, 1992.
4   Foscari, 1980.
5   Vasari, Milanesi, 1878 VI, 223–25.
6   Mancini et al., 1995, 1, 46–54, offer various possible reconstructions.
7   Schulz, 1961, 505
8   Mancini et al., 1995, 1, 46, interpret Vasari's measurments to mean 40.8 × 9.35.
9   For a discussion of herms, see Johnson, 2004, 439–44.
10 Although the drawing is autograph, the actual paintings were probably at least in part by assistants.
11 Schulz, 1961, n. 17, believes that the stage was not included in the 70 braccia length specified by Vasari for the room.
12 Catherine was the daughter of the Lorenzo de' Medici, who had been made Duke of Urbino by Leo X and who died young in 1519. Her mother, Madeleine de la Tour d'Auvergne, was related to the French royal family.
13 The festivities surrounding the entry, which lasted for a week, are chronicled in Scève, 1997. Richard Cooper's detailed analysis therein of the week-long entrance celebration is the basis for my discussion of the architecture of the theater. On the reconstruction of the theater we do not always agree. My reconstruction of the theater appears in Johnson, 2014.
14 Scève, 1997, 104. The players were the Compagnia della Cazzuola, headed by Domenicho Barlacchi. Apparently they had performed *La Calandra* previously. A life of Barlacchi states that he was called to France by the queen to perform. (Ibid., 114, n. 11)
15 The statues were the work of a Maestro Zanobio from Florence. Cooper (Scève, 104) believes he was Zanobio Lastricati (1508–90). Zanobio was also responsible for the statues inside the theater. Since all the sculpture was created very quickly, Zanobio must have had a number of assistants.
16 From the dimensions recorded by F.M., it is possible to calculate the approximate size of the room in which the performance took place as roughly 21 × 12 m, but the 21 m length probably does not include the depth of the stage, which F.M. does not record. Cooper (Scève, 1997, 105) calculates the room to have been about 16.25 × 9.75. Because the archibishop's palace has been remodelled several times since 1548, it is impossible to know the size of the room from the present disposition.
17 Johnson, 2014, 176–86.
18 The full list includes Lorenzo II de' Medici (Catherine's father), Giovanni delle Bande Nere, Pippo Spano, Farinata degli Uberti and Federico Folchi on the right and Claudian, Dante, Petrarch, Boccacio, Marsilio Ficino and Accorsio on the left. Notable by his absence was Cosimo de' Medici, current Duke of Tuscany, who was a supporter of Charles V, Henry's arch rival. Catherine loathed her cousin Cosimo, and his presence would have been an affront to Henry.
19 The towns were Pisa, Volterra, Cortona, Borgo San Sepolcro and Castrocaro on the right, and on the left Fiesole, Arezzo, Pistoia, Prato and Montelpulciano.
20 "Et estoient les dictes grandz figures douze en nombre, six toguez à l'antique & coronnez de Laurier, representanz six Poëtes Florentins: les six autres armez à l'antique pour les six Ancestres de la maason de Medicis, qui furent premiers restaurateurs des lettres Grecques, & Latines, Architecture, Sculpture, Paincture, & tous autres bons artz par eulx resuscitez, & introduictz en l'Europe Chrestiente, desquelz la rudesse des Gotz l'en avoient longtemps devestue." See Johnson, 2014, Appendix I, 197.
21 Illustrated in Serlio, 1996, Book III, Chapter 4, Fol. 66v.
22 Serlio, 1996, III, Chapter 4, Fol. 63r.
23 I thank Zirka Filipczak for advice on this point. She pointed out that putti bearing torches also appear in Peter Paul Rubens cycle of paintings for Marie de' Medici, wife of Henry IV of France, particularly in The Marriage at Lyon, where two putti holding torches ride a pair of lions, and in the Presentation of the Portrait of Marie to Henry, where the youthful winged god of marriage, Hymen, holds the portrait in his left hand and a torch in his right.
24 What sorts of back stage spaces may have been provided we do not know. Some portion of the Salle Saint-Jean in front of the fireplace must have been retained for the use of the performers.
25 For a more extensive discussion of the attribution to Serlio and the architecture of the theater, cf. Johnson 2014.

26 Frommel, 2003, S., 29, 95.
27 See n. 12 above.
28 Scève, 1997, 101. The Florentines had already put on Italian comedies for their own amusement and to amuse the locals at carnival.
29 Scève, 1997, 103.
30 Nagler, 1964, 13–35. Zorzi, 1975, 93–98.
31 Lenzi, 1985, 181.
32 I have not found the drawing published in the literature on the theater that I have been able to consult, and it is not included in Peter Ward Jackson, *Victoria and Albert Museum Catalogues. Italian Drawings. I 14th–16th Century*, London, 1979. Cordaro, 1983, 121 and 346, fig. 447, and Galli, 2010, 158, fig. 1, reproduce a chiaroscuro woodcut made in 1589 by G. Balsi after Riccio. There are differences between the drawing in London and the Balsi print. Galli, 2010, 161, tells us that Riccio's proscenium and set persisted for almost seventy years. Probably the proscenium was repainted before Balsi made his rendering of it. Cordaro, 1983 claims that the theater had "palchi di legno," but no documentation supports this claim. Galli, 2010, 160, cites a nineteenth century source that speaks of "loggie per le persone distinte."
33 De Marchi, 1990, 366.
34 The figures are identified by inscriptions: Poesis, with motto below, "Miscet Utile Dulci"; Augustus, "Poetae Praesidium"; Commedia, "Vitae Speculum"; Scipio Africanus, "Comicor Fautor". From the entablature, under the Medici coat of arms, hangs an inscription set over a squash, the symbol of the Accademia degli Intronati: "Generoso Intronato Thuscor Principi Intronatorum ilaritas." The prints bear the names of Riccio and Bolsi, set respectively below the left and right pilasters. Fargnoli, 1980, 233.
35 Benini, 1982, 143, suggests that the seats for the women may have been curved, in the manner of an ancient theater, but the evidence is not clear.
36 Benini, 1982, 140. She suggests, 144f., that the entrance of the Olympian gods from on high during the prologue should be understood as something like a mirror image of the paradisiacal arrangement of audience and rulers, who faced the stage and the descending gods.
37 Ibid., 140.
38 A reconstruction model of the room transformed into a theater was proposed in 1975 by Ludovico Zorzi and Cesare Lisi. *Teatro e spettacolo*, Tav. VIII.
39 Cooper (Scève, 1997, 101) believes that the stage in Lyon probably had a proscenium arch.
40 Mariotti, 1976, 592.
41 Zorzi, 1975, 32.
42 Benini, 141f.
43 The sets for the plays of 1565 and 1569 both focused on parts of Florence that were being transformed under Cosimo. Mariotti, 1976, 593, has pointed out the uniqueness of the contribution of Cosimo and Vasari to the history of city planning: "[Their] transformation of an urban structure from polar to linear represents an absolute novelty on an international level, because it is the first time that piazze, streets and bridges were tied together to create a true urban continuum." Via Maggio and the Uffizi were two of the most important parts of that new understanding of urban space.
44 A model of the stage with Lanci's set was made in 1980 by Ferdinando Ghelli, *Teatro e spettacolo*, Tav. IX.
45 Lessmann, 1975, provides an exhaustive study of the Uffizi. Lessmann, 1976, is an article in Italian drawn from her dissertation. Also see Satkowski, 1993.
46 Fleming, 2006, 703–08, discusses the ambiguity of the space and the difficulty, perhaps even impossibility, of finding an appropriate term for it. She cites earlier authors, but not Lessmann.
47 Lessmann, 1976, 246.
48 Ibid., who follows Berti, 1967. Also Mariotti, 1976, 595–96.
49 Lessmann, 1975, 219–20.
50 Ibid., 1975, 221, cites a commemorative oration given after the death of Cosimo I by Baccio Baldini. Forster, 1971, 86, n. 72, had already cited an oration given at the funeral of Cosimo I by Bernardo Davanzati, "Orazione Terza in morte del Gran Duca Cosimo Primo," *Prose Fiorentine raccolte dallo smarrito Accademico della Crusca*, Venice, 1735, 25.
51 Vasari, 1878, Milanesi, 3, 169, "ponevano gli antichi le imagini de gli huomini grandi ne' luoghi publici con onorate iscrizioni, che per accender l'animo di coloro che venivano, alla virtù et alla gloria." Quoted by Hermans, 2011, 102, n. 14.
52 Fleming, 2006, passim, esp. 717ff.
53 For the theatrical nature of the Piazzetta, see Johnson 2000.
54 Ferrari, 1902, 85.
55 For an outline of the building history of the Libreria, see Johnson, 2004, 432–33, with reference to earlier literature.

56 Mariotti, 1976, 593.
57 The theater in the Uffizi occupied the area given over since World War II to the first rooms of the Galleria degli Uffizi, which begin with the extraordinary space that displays three large altarpieces by Cimabue, Duccio and Giotto.
58 Heikamp, 1974, 326.
59 Ibid., 324. Heikamp argues that the space that became the theater was originally intended as a meeting hall for the magistracies housed in the Uffizi, but one doubts that such a hall would have required the sloped floor that the vaults beneath the room created.
60 For Buontalenti's interior see Nagler, 1964 58 ff., and *Teatro e spettacolo*, 167.
61 Anyone with the price of admission, however, could attend *commedia dell'arte* performances in the Baldracca theater, built just behind and adjacent to the Uffizi in these very years. That theater is discussed in the next chapter.
62 Heikamp, 1974, 325, discusses the apparent contradiction between the two portals.
63 Ferdinando succeeded his childless brother, Francesco I, when the latter died. He had to give up his cardinal's hat to do so, as well as his vow of celibacy. The celebration of his marriage to Christine of Lorraine was also a celebration of the hoped-for continuation of the Medici dynasty.
64 For the architecdture of the theater, see Nagler, 1964, 70 ff., *Teatro e spettacolo*, 169–71, Saslow, 1996, 78–81. The discussion of this theater is largely based on these works.
65 Saslow, 1996, 81.
66 Fara, 1995, fig. 350, cat. 145, reproduces a sketch by Buontalenti for the ducal platform.
67 Fara, 1995, 159
68 Ibid., 158
69 Ibid., 160.
70 Nagler, 1964, 133. Also Fara, 1995, 160.

5 Early Permanent Theaters and the Commedia dell'Arte

1 D'Ancona, 1891, 2, 137.
2 The set is described in a contemporary account: "si bruciò una scena del teatro sopra a detta sala grande il che era una cosa assai mirabile, e grande che pareva una cittadella con camere terrene, ed a solaro finestre poggioli botteghe, et chiese dove sopra detta sala si recitvano spese volte delle comedie." Monaldini, 1999, 28, n. 92, with additional citations.
3 Molinari, 1964, 66.
4 For this theater, see D'Ancona, 1891, 2, 441; Magagnato, 1980, 47; Ferrone, 1993, 128, n. 21; *Mantova: Le Arti*, 15; and Carpeggiani, 1975, 101–03.
5 Buratelli, 1999, 131, n. 104, points out that Antonio Maria Viani, to whom Carpeggiani, 1975, 106, attributed the theater, was not in Mantua in 1591–92, when the theater was rebuilt.
6 Luzio, 1913, 34. "Ricca è la scena: ù gl'istrioni intenti / A le bell'opre concorrono spesso, / I cui superbi e nobili ornamenti / Mostran quant'arte l'Arte ivi abbia messo. / Di travi fabricata e d'assamenti / A pittura, a rilievo, e segue appresso / Una città, qual par che sia ripiena / Di quant'arti e virtudi unqua ebbe Athena.
Contra il gran Palco che con grazia pende / Mille gradi il Bertan pose architetto, / Ch'un mezzo circol fanno, e vi s'ascende / Con gran facilità su fin al tetto; / Giù resta un campo, ove sovente accende / Il fiero Marte a' suoi seguaci il petto: / Templi, Torri, Palazzi e Prospettive, / E figure vi son che paion vive."
7 Buratelli, 1999, 131, n. 100.
8 D'Ancona, 1891, 2, 473, decree of February 17, 1580: "si permette, eccetto ai Religiosi, ai sudditi nostri di mascherarsi et di godere il trattenimento della comedia, che si fa questa sera nelle scene di questo castello, e perciò concediamo a ciascuno che dalle 23 ore fino ad una ora dopo finita la comedia, possano entrarvi mascherati, avvegnachè nella grida delle maschere abbiamo vietato alle maschere l'entrata delle porte che conducono in questa nostra Corte e Castello."
9 Vasari, 1885, 6, 583, is the source for most of the information on this theater.
10 *Dizionario biografico degli Italiani*, 2, 1960, 798.
11 Pastor, 1924, 64, notes that Julius had comedies performed in the Vatican in 1550 and 1551.
12 *Dizionario biografico degli Italiani*, 3, 1961, 307.
13 Sanudo, 1879, 46, 632, March 25, 1528, "una egloga pastoral molto bella, fatta per alcuni romani."
14 Sanudo, 1879, 57, 459: " A dì 24 gennaio.... In questa sera a Muran in chà di Prioli a San Stefano fo recità una comedia per alcuni forestieri, di Ruigo, et per veder si pagava soldi 12, fo assà persone, fo ben recitata, et intermedi di soni, et buffoni assai."

15 Ibid., 548, "et fo assà mascare per la terra, perchè questa terra al presente si è in paxe, è dato molto a Venere et Baco."
16 Henke, 2002, 59, offers a recent account of the beginning of the art form.
17 It is not clear when women first began to perform with traveling troupes. One observer of the play given in Lyon in 1548 noted charming women on stage, but his remarks are not corroborated. See Henke, 2002, 85–105, for the transformative effect created by the presence of women in the *commedia* companies.
18 For the *Corsini Scenarii* see Nagler, 1969; Katritzky, 2006, 182–87.
19 Coryat, 1905, 386–87. "I was at one of their Play-houses where I saw a Comedie acted. The house is very beggarly and base in comparison of our stately Play-houses in England.... Also their noble & famous Cortezans came to this Comedy.... They were so graced that they sate on high alone by themselves in the best roome of all the Play-house.... I saw some men also in the Play-house ... they sit not here in galleries as we doe in London. For there is but one or two little galleries in the house, wherein the Cortezans only sit. But all the men doe sit beneath in the yard or court, every man upon his severall stoole, for the which hee payeth a gazet."
20 Mangini, 1974, 34.
21 D'Ancona, 1891, 2, 405, letter of April 15, 1567: "chiederle ... un decreto di poter egli (Leone) solo per anni X dare stanza in Mant.a da rappresentare comedie, a coloro che per preo ne vanno recitando, offerendosi egli dare ogni anno a'poveri della Misericordia, sacchi due di formento per mostrarsi in parte grato de l'havuta gratia, over il prezzo di quello."
22 D'Ancona, 1891, 2, 404, letter of April 17, 1567: "è di qualche utilità a' poveri et di piacere alla città perchè intende di accomodare una stanza, nella quale comodam.te et honestam.te potranno stare e gentilhomini e gentildonne a vedere recitare Comedie."
23 Buratelli, 1999, 141–80, discusses this remarkable situation. Her remarks reflect the work of Simonsohn in the Archivio della Comunità Isrealitica di Mantova. The fundamental study of the theatrical activity of the Jews of Mantua is D'Ancona, 1891, 2, 398–429.
24 Buratelli, 1999, 150.
25 D'Ancona, 1891 2, 447–54.

26 Ibid., 452, Letter of Don Antonio Ceruto: "Non si attende ad altro che alle comedie, nè fra il popolo si siente dire altro che queste parole: *Io sono della parte di Flaminia:* et *io della Vicenza.*" Neither actress has been identified securely. Vincenza was murdered in Cremona in 1568 (Ibid., 461).
27 Ibid., 454.
28 Amadei, 1973, 1977, 15, gives the account of the performances interrupted by the young man from Verona.
29 D'Ancona, 1891, 2, 449, "nel luogo solito." Vincenza played "in casa del Lanzino."
30 Ferrucio Marotti, ed. of Sommi, 1968, 78, believes it likely that Sommi opened his theater.
31 Sommi, 1968, passim.
32 Ibid., 65, "il fumo, a poco a poco crescendo et condensandosi, avela sí fattamente (se non ha dove esalare), che pria che sia finito il secondo atto, non più uomeni, ma ombre ci paiono i recitanti."
33 Ibid., 63–64. For a summary of the bibliography on Sommi, cf. Buratelli, 1991, 171–172, n. 52.
34 Lenzi, 1985, 181.
35 Ibid.
36 The diligent research of Evangelista, who brought the existence of this theater to light, is the source for the account here. See entries under her name in the Bibliography.
37 The theater was attributed, probably erroneously, to Bernardo Buontalenti in the nineteenth century,
38 Evangelista, 1984, 52: "'nuovo salone sverginato stato è da' Zanni."
39 The last documented performance was in 1653. The plan was made before the space was converted to accommodate the Biblioteca Maggliabechiano. At present the room is used as storage by the Archivio di Stato.
40 Evangelista, 1984, 69.
41 "Il Cicognini haveva fatto stampare in lode di essa S.ra una Canzone et al fine della Commedia, da alcuni ragazzi che erano su ne gli ultimi stanzini, ne fece gettare al popolo m[ol]ta quantità e furno raccolti con m[ol]to applauso. Il sig. Cardinale hebbe fino l'anno passato la chiave dello stanzino dell'E.V. e mai l'ha resa et havendola chiesta quest'anno per accomodarla al Sign. residente me la fece rimandare e la tenni tre sere e poi ..., et al Sign. residente fece accomodare uno stanzino di quelli che

sono al secondo piano sopra quello del Ser.mo Gran Duca. Si servì dello stanzino ne primi giorni Monsig. Corcini che era qua e di poi l'ha hauta // il Sig. Tommaso Medici quasi sempre, eccetto che ne gl'ultimi otto o dieci giorni l'ebbe il Sig. Lione Nerli per la sua moglie con la quale è andata alcune volte la mia a udire le commedie; e con questa occasione ho vedute che molte donne che sono andate nello stanzino del Sig. Antella sono passate per quello di V.E. con tutta la libertà: cioè sono passate per la medesima strada e scala di V.E. Ill.ma."

42 Evangelista, 1984, 51. In ibid., 1979, 78–80, she discusses the vexed question of the *stanzini* with less certitude.

43 On the other hand, the *ragazzi* who threw down the leaflets from a *stanzino* on the top level may not have come into the theater with the great folks who are specified in Baroncelli's letter. They may have been a hired claque. Or they may have been young nobles, enthusiastic about a particular actress, who came through the restricted access.

44 Fantappiè, 2009, 235f.

45 Ibid., 236.

46 Johnson, 2002, analyzes the documentation for these theaters. The account here is a condensation of that article.

47 D'Ancona, 1891, 2, 452, cites a letter of July 8, 1567 in which Don Antonio Ceruto says, "Si è detto che in Consiglio grande fu proposto da molti gentiluomini veneziani che per ogni modo si doveva levar via questi comedianti." The proposal failed.

48 Pirotta, 1969, 58, makes this important point.

6 Theaters in the Ancient Manner and Andrea Palladio

1 For the history of Palazzo Farnese, Piacenza, see Adorni, 1982, 177–348, also Thoenes, 1974.

2 Margherita retired to her lands in the Abruzzi in 1569, rather than return to live in Piacenza. She subsequently built a palace in Ortona as a winter escape from the cold of L'Aquila.

3 On May 28, 1561 Vignola wrote to Margherita to explain that he was sending her eight drawings so that she could understand what she would have learned from a single model (Adorni, 1982, 261). She continued to be informed about the slow progress on what she referred to as "my palace" well into the 1560s.

4 Adorni, 1982, 202.

5 Ibid., 201.

6 Cornaro's description of his proposed theater (ASV, Savi alle Acque, B. 986, n. 4, cc. 23–25) was published by Mangini, 1974, 26–28.

7 Cornaro is also said to have built a theater in the ancient manner on a country estate.

8 Gros, 2006, 83. For a recent discussion of Palladio's relation to ancient theaters, see Gros, 2006, 82–95.

9 Barbaro's gloss on the Roman architect's complex explanation of musical harmonies, chapter 4 of Book V (Vitruvius, 1997), is masterful but outside the scope of this book. No difficulty with Vitruvius's text was too great for Barbaro to attempt to overcome, although he confessed that understanding the Roman author could be difficult.

10 Vitruvius, 1567. We hereafter cite this facsimile of the 1567 edition.

11 "perche quando il Theatro fusse di forme angulari, non pervenirebbe la voce egualmente alle orecchie, & alcuni udirebbono bene come piu vicini, alcuni male come piu lontani." Vitruvius, 1567, 216.

12 "i nobili haveranno i loro seggi da basso, accioche il fetore, che sale con lo aere causato dalla moltitudine, non gli offenda." Ibid., 224.

13 "si comprenderanno molte cose da noi dichiarite secondo la intentione di Vitr." Ibid., 255.

14 Ibid., Bk. 5, 6.

15 "havemo congiunto a diverso modo la scena del Theatro latino; come che questa si possa fare in piu modi. Ilche ci ha piaciuto come convenientissima forma, essendo stati avvertiti dalle ruine d'uno antico Theatro, che si trova in Vicenza tra gli horti, & le case d'alcuni cittadini, dove si scorgeno tre gran nicchi della scena, la ove noi havemo posto le tre porte, & il nicchio di mezo è bello, & grande." Ibid., 259.

16 Ibid., 224–225.

17 Puppi, 1974, 296. The theater "fu augmentato, e molto più adobbato et ampliato il medesimo apparato." Puppi believes that only the central arch of the *scenae frons* may have been enlarged to allow a more ample view of the city scene in perspective behind that arch. The tone of the document, however, suggests a more ample aggrandizement of the theater of the previous year.

18 Ibid., 303, n. 30.

19 Ibid., 303, n. 31, quotes a document of 1562 that gives the dimensions as "la facciata

20. Puppi, 1974, 296 and 306–307.
21. It is possible to arrange the twenty-four columns and sixteen niches in other ways, but the one proposed here seems most in keeping with Palladio's practices.
22. Cf. Figs. 76–78.
23. Puppi, 1974, 307, "Il piano della prospettiva era pinto in un partimento di quadri vaghissimo con certe fascie, i quali andavano riunnendosi verso lo stringersi di essa prospettiva, onde portavano gl'occhi de' riguardanti in oltre assaissimo, et tutto che brevissimo spacio fosse."
24. Mancini et al., 1995, 1, 67–85, contains the most extensive discussion of this theater, with references to earlier literature, documentation, and even the text of the play that was performed.
25. Temanza, 1778, XX. Repr. in Mancini et al., 1995, 1, 81. "ho fornito di far questo benedetto Theatro, nel quale ho fatto la penitentia de quanti peccati ho fatti e son per fare. Marti prossimo si reciterà la Tragedia, quando V.S. potesse vederla io la esortarei a venir, perché se spiera che debbia essere cosa rara."
26. Mancini et al., 1995, 1, 81. Letter of February 28, 1565 of Cosimo Bartoli. "non ha satisfatto molto."
27. The scholarly debate on the location of Palladio's theater is outlined in Mancini et al., 1995, I, 70–78. The authors opt for the courtyard of Ca' Foscari, now the seat of the University of Venice. The other location that still seems possible is in the vicinity of the Palazzo Foscari near San Simeon Piccola. See Olivato, 1982. A young Foscari was the leader of the Accesi.
28. Vasari-Milanesi, 1878, VII, 100, "un mezzo teatro di legname a uso di colosseo." Mancini et al., 1995, 81.
29. Mangini, 1974, 16.
30. Sansovino, "il teatro fu capacissimo di molte migliaia di persone. All'incontro del quale era posta la ricchissima scena, rassomigliante una città, con tanto bell'ordine di colonne et di altre prospetive che fu mirabil cosa a vedere."
31. Mancini et al., 1995, 76, surmise that the theater held fewer than 600 people.

32. Ibid., 81. First published by Loredana Olivato in *Architettura e Utopia*, 276. "Egli è ben vero che avevano fatto un teatro con una scena di legnami molto ricca di colonne, di gradi e di statue."
33. Vasari-Milanesi, 1878, VII, 100. "fece fare a Federigo dodici storie grandi, di sette piedi e mezzo l'una per ogni verso, con altre infinite cose de' fatti d'Ircano re di Ierusalem, secondo il soggetto della tragedia."
34. Mancini et al., 1995, 76.
35. Ibid., 68 (following Foscari, 1979a) demonstrate that many members of the Accesi belonged to the close-knit group of patrician Venetian families that patronized Palladio. No Barbaro was a member of the Accesi, but the Barbaro family belonged to this same group of patricians. Yet another sign of the connection of this performance to this group is the dedication of the published text of *Antigono* to Francesco Pisani, who had built a villa by Palladio just outside the walls of Montagnana. Ibid., 80, 82.
36. How long the theater stood is as mysterious as its location.
37. Barbieri, in *Vincenzo Scamozzi*, 2004, 167f., provides a synopsis of its use over time.
38. For the complex history leading up to the completion of the theater and the choice of the play, cf. Gordon, 1966.
39. Johnson, 2002, 951.
40. Mazzoni, 1998, 87–207, provides a copiously annotated account (727 notes) of the theater and its first performance. The account rendered here is deeply indebted to Mazzoni's splendid work.
41. The brackets supporting the balcony in the longitudinal section of Bertotti Scamozzi (Fig. 92) appear to have the same shape as the ones now on the building. Since the appearance of the present wall may go back to the original building of the theater, it is also possible that the balcony in its present form may date from that time. The balcony must have been needed from the beginning, but it need not have had its current appearance.
42. *Andrea Palladio, 1508–1580*, 1975, 43.
43. A drawing by Marcantonio Palladio of 1580 of two projects for the elevation of the stage wall (London, RIBA, SA77/XIII/5r. *Palladio, 128*) shows a much taller attic than the one actually built on its left side. Unfortunately, the drawing does not include a suggestion for the ceiling of the stage.

44 McReynolds, 2011, 71–101.
45 Ibid., 101. McReynolds, 2011, n. 108, cites the description by Tacitus of a star-studded purple canopy that Nero had installed in the Theater of Pompey as the probable ancient source for Temanza's point of view. The view of the theater from 1650 shows a painted sky with flights of birds, clouds, and a rainbow (Fig. 95). If Temanza was right, then this sky is a later addition. Mazzoni, 1998, 108, takes the view that the original ceiling over the stage was coffered.
46 As demonstrated in Nagel and Wood, 2010.
47 Mazoni, in *Vincenzo Scamozzi 1548–1616*, 2004, 73, refers to this door as the "portale scamozziano d'ingresso al vestibolo, all'odeo e alla sala." Scamozzi is surely the likely designer.
48 For a discussion of Scamozzi's scenery, see the essay by Valeria Cafà in *Vincenzo Scamozzi 1548–1616*, 2004, 251–260.
49 Mazzoni, 1998, convincingly compares the portrait of Valmarana in the theater (fig. 50) with a portrait of Charles V by Leone Leoni (fig. 51)
50 The statue is also visible in the drawing of c. 1600 of the *scenae frons* by Giambattista Albanese (London, RIBA, XIII, 4). Mazzoni, 1998, fig. 14.
51 Ibid., fig. 41. Milan, Biblioteca Ambrosiana, codex R 232 sup., 308r.
52 Mazzoni, 1998, 139.

7 Drama-Tourney Theaters

1 For a general discussion of Renaissance theatrical activity in Ferrara, see Mitchell, 1990, 11–18.
2 The history of tourneys in Italy is summarized by Povoledo, 1964, 95–100, and by Jarrard, 2003, 17–52.
3 Cesare Molinari called them "opera-tourneys," but these entertainments originated several decades before the invention of opera.
4 Povoledo, 1964, 104.
5 See ibid., 101–04, for a detailed description.
6 Forster, 1977, discusses the theater, as does Mazzoni, 1985, and also in *Vincenzo Scamozzi 1548–1616*, 71–88. The catalogue entry in *Vincenzo Scamozzi 1548–1616*, 2004, 276–82, by Valeria Cafà and Sandra Vendramin, contains a particularly useful summary.
7 What few precedents Scamozzi may have had to turn to have been lost. The exterior of the Bertani theater in Mantua, if it had some architectural distinction, may have served Scamozzi in some way.
8 Curran, 2012, 38, believes the earliest use of the phrase in postmedieval times occurs in Franceso Albertini, *Opusculum de mirabilibus novae et veteris Urbis Romae*, Rome, 1510, a popular guidebook. He cites its appearance on a drawing of the ruins of the Septizodium in Rome by Marten van Heemskerk, in Rome in the 1530s, and as the frontispiece of Serlio's Book III of 1544. The last would easily have been known to Scamozzi and Vespasiano Gonzaga. Thoenes, 1989, 14 and n. 39, on the other hand, believes the phrase is based on a statement made by Rome itself on the fifteenth century map of Mantua: "Quant'ego fuerim sola ruina docet." He notes the important change from "sola" to "ipsa" in Serlio's version, which he relates to the fact that the phrase in the frontispiece introduces Serlio's readers to the illustrations of ancient buildings that follow in Book III. Although the phrase clearly accords with the "Roman" themes taken up by the frescoes on the interior, why it plays such an important role on the exterior of the theater is not clear.
9 Hermans, 2011, 100, offers the interesting hypothesis that the exterior may refer to the Roman *curia*, where the leader would have met with his advisers.
10 Burroughs, 1993, 16–17. I am grateful to an anonymous reader of my MS for suggesting this reference.
11 Forster, 1977, 71.
12 Pointed out by Valeria Cafà and Sandra Vendramin, *Vincenzo Scamozzi 1548–1616*, 2004, 277.
13 The painter of the frescoes is named as Bernardo Vicenzino. cf. *The Mint*, 1923, 24.
14 Cited by Mazzoni, in *Vicenzo Scamozzi 1548–1616*, 2004, 81.
15 Buratelli, 1999, 131, n. 100, notes a description of the successor theater to Bertani's that says the new theater repeated the space between seats and stage of the original.
16 Mazzoni, in Vicenzo Scamozzi 1548–1616, 2004, 84.
17 Forster, 1977, 81.
18 Hermans, 2011, 99.
19 Bologna, Galleria Nazionale. The inscription reads: "Teatro del Torneo Per la liberatione d'Amore tentata da Venere – Rappresentato

19. (cont.) in Bologna li 20 di Marzo 1628 dall'Ill.ma Academia de Torbidi con l'accompagnamento del liberato Amore, che fu eseguito nel fine dalla Pace. Dedicate insieme con l'altre machine alla med.ma Ill.ma Acad.a da Gio. Batt.a Coriolani." I thank the staff of the print room of the Galleria Nazionale, Bologna, for their assistance.
20. I thank Zirka Filipczak and Sara Piccolo for their expertise in identifying seventeenth century male and female costumes.
21. It may have been customary to give women of a certain status ample space to sit. That is precisely the way the female spectators at a tourney are shown in a fifteenth century painting in the National Gallery, London, attributed to Domenico Morone. See Povoledo, 1964, pl. i, fig. 1.
22. "Giardino di Delo ov'era catenato Amore."
23. *L'ERMIONA* del S.r Marchese Pio Enea Obizzi. Per introduzione d'un Torneo à piedi, & à Cavallo E d'un Balletto rappresentato in Musica nella Citta di Padova l'Anno M.DC.-XXXVI. dedicata Al Sereniss.o Prencipe di Venetia Francesco Erizo descritta dal S. Nicolò Enea Bartolini Gentilhuomo, & Academ.o Senese, Padua, 1638.
24. ASV, Consiglio dei Dieci, Parti Criminali, Reg. 53, 1636, 108v.
25. Petrobelli's 1965 study of *Ermiona* is the basis for this discussion.
26. "Alfonso Chenda detto il Rivarola ferrarese Ingegniero di tutte le Scene e machine, huomo degno d'ogni venerazione per la sua somma virtù, e modestia."
27. Petrobelli, 1965, 128. "Giravano d'intorno intorno cinque file di loggie l'una soprapposta al altra con parapetti avanti à balaustri di marmo, distinguevano li Spazi commodi à sedici spettatori alcuni tramezi, che terminavano nelle parte esteriore à forgia di colonne, dove si sporgevano infuore braccia di legno in argentate, che sostenevano i doppieri, ch'illuminavano il Teatro. Le due piú alte, e piú lontane file erano ripiene di cittadinanza, nella terza sedevano i signori Scolari, e i nobili stranieri, il secondo come luogo piú degno era dei Sig. Rettori e de' Nobili veneti, e nel primo se ne stavano le gentildonne, e i principali gentilhuomini della città."
28. Lenzi's 1985 exemplary study forms the basis of this discussion.
29. The legend reads: "A. Una delle scene rappresentante Sicilia; B. Ultima Machina con un Deità [?]; C. Ponte per il quale scesero i Cavallieri nel piano della sala d.a del Podestà; D. Proscenio alla parte verso Levante; E. Iride che scese dal Cielo nel mezo del la Sala che da Ponente haveva un altro simile Proscenio; F. Piano nel quale si ormeggiò a piedi et à cavallo.; G. Luogo per I Sig.ri Cardinali Ducchi et Principi; H. Luogo dei Sig.ri Anziani e Confalon; I. Ponti 160 in tuto per i spettatori et quali [?] continuando si alungano sino all'altra scena figurando la citta di Laurento." Above the stage are inscribed the words "Prospettiva Della metà del Teatro che servì al Torneo Festeggiando in Bologna l'Anno MDCXXXIX." The miniature is signed by Lodi at the bottom of the scene toward the right.

8 Ferrara, Parma, Pesaro and Theaters of Giovanni Battista Aleotti

1. There is no scholarly consensus on the autograph nature of this plan, but there is agreement that it represents Aleotti's theater.
2. Fabbri, 1998.
3. The inscription reads: "Even if it is the case that the Theater of Ferrara erected many years ago by this most illustrious Academy of the Intrepidi by means of my designs has still not reached that level of perfection that it ought to have, both in terms of the variety of Sets and of its many types of Machines, it still has in itself so much nobility and beauty in that part that is finished, that it offers the visitor no mean delight and pleasure." [Se bene il Teatro di Ferrara eretto, molt'anni sono, da quest'illustrissima Accademia degl'Intrepidi col mezo de'miei disegni non è per anco ridotto a quella perfezione che se gli deve, e per la varietà delle Scene, e per la multiplicità delle Macchine, ha tuttavia in sé tanto di nobilità e di vaghezza, per quella parte in ch'egli è compiuto, che non mediocre diletto e piacere porge a'riguardanti.]
4. Ziosi, 2002, 225, doubts that the theater was ever completed before it was taken over by Roberto degli Obizzi in 1640.
5. Mazzoni, 1998, 62–63.
6. Contemporary documents often refer to the theater as the *Salone*, or big room. For clarity we will not use that term in these pages.
7. The essential bibliography is cited and analyzed by Adorni, 2003, 223, who gives an excellent

synthesis of what we now know about the theater. Ciancarelli, 1974 and 1987, both contain additional citations of numerous other sources. For English-speaking readers, three major essays by Italian scholars published in 1992 in a luxuriously illustrated book, *Lo Spettacolo e la Meraviglia. Il Teatro Farnese di Parma*, are translated at the end of the volume. The essays are by Marzio Dall'Acqua, 1992, on the architecture, Pompeo De Angelis on *Mercurio e Marte*, the tourney with music of 1628, and Claudio Gallico on the music by Claudio Monteverdi. See bibliography under authors' names. Adorni, 2003, 223, notes the confusion caused by publishing in this volume numerous drawings of seventeenth century stage machinery that have nothing to do with the Farnese theater.

8 An irony noted by Ciancarelli, 1987, 24f., who believes that Ranuccio may have built the theater in an effort to attract Cosimo to Parma.

9 See Chapter 6.

10 Ranuccio's eldest son, born deaf and mute, was not considered fit to inherit power, and his only other son was illegitimate – thus the infant heir.

11 Dall'Acqua, 1992, 33.

12 Ciancarelli, 1974, convincingly proposed this interpretation of Ranuccio's motives.

13 Ibid., 37–48, gives an extensive account of this tourney and of the documentation that links Aleotti to it.

14 The stairs and dome are usually attributed to Simone Moschino.

15 "The theater of Bellona and the Muses Ranuccio Farnese Fourth Duke of Parma and Piacenza and of Castro the Fifth with Regal Magnificence Opened in the Year 1618."

16 The door at stage left, set against the exterior wall, is false.

17 I am grateful to Mattea Gazzola of the Biblioteca comunale Bertoliana, Vicenza, for identifying the source of this print. It was published in *Andrea Palladio 1508–1580, the portico and the farmyard*, 1975, #28, p. 27, as a photograph of an item in the Museo Civico, Vicenza without an inventory number.

18 Dall'Acqua, 1992, 80ff.

19 The importance of this point is stressed by Gandolfi, 1980, 58–59, and fig. 77. Gandolfi's measured drawings provide a splendid means to understand the architecture of the theater in detail.

20 The scholarly debate over Aleotti's role in the design of the theater and the possible intervention of Bentivoglio in the planning are laid out by Ciancarelli, 1987, 43, n. 7. The problem cannot entirely be resolved at this point; for the purposes of the discussion here, Aleotti will be considered the sole architect. He did tell the duke, in a letter of February 17, 1618, that he did not think it necessary to change the plan: "non m'occore muttare la pianta (quando Vostra Altezza non comandi in contrario)" (ibid., 164, quoting Lombardi, 31). Gandolfi, 1980, 59–61, shrewdly notes several anomalies in the architectural details of the auditorium that may well indicate interventions by others.

21 Dall'Acqua, 1992, 61, calls this part of the plan "il luogo per l'orchestra."

22 This arrangement may reflect the influence of the seating in a tourney theater in Bologna of 1615; cf. Lavin, 1964, 112.

23 Ciancarelli, 1987, 160, quoting Lombardi, 1909, 28. Ibid., 53, n. 24, concludes that by the time Aleotti quit Parma, the theater was largely constructed: "Nel marzo 1618 l'Aleotti dunque mostra di aver quasi definitivamente concluso il progetto di risrutturazione della sala d'armi in Teatro." One might add that in the letter of March 18, 1618 Aleotti addressed to the duke, he said that he was no longer needed in Parma: "ella (the Duke) . . . di presente non ha bisogno di me" (ibid., 166). We do not know how the audience would have been arranged.

24 Ciancarelli, 1987, 264: "il Salone li è piacciuto in estremo, e dice che non ha visto il più magnifico né più superbo teatro, maggio assai del loro di Firenze. La scena gli è parsa più piccola della loro: lo spazio che abbiamo dentro, dice che è tale, che essi non ne hanno la sesta parte."

25 Ciancarelli, 1987, 87–141, published the text of the libretto and Ciancarelli, 1974, 132, analyzed its message of peace.

26 Ciancarelli, 1984, 177. Letter from Parma of Enzo Bentivoglio to Ippolito Bentivoglio, April 30, 1618: "io spero di far fare a Sua Altezza la più bella festa che mai sia stata fatta in Europa."

27 The marriage was finally contracted in 1620, with Maria Cristina de' Medici as the bride. But the Medici reserved the right to supply a different bride during a six-year period. Margherita, a younger sister, became the final

choice only in 1627. See Dall'Acqua, 1992, 129.
28. See Chapter 4.
29. Bibioteca Oliveriana, Pesaro, Ms. 387, XXXIII, 173. The drawing bears the inscription "Disegno del Teatro fatto alzare per il Ser.mo Sig.e Duca d'Urbino nella sala della corte di Pesaro per le nozze del Ser.mo Principe Federico Ubaldo." The legend reads: "1 Porticco che gira sopra la scalinata; 2 Scalinate dove stà a sedere il popolo; 3 Piano della sala; 4 orchestra per musici; 5 scena; 6 Proscenio; A Pianta del teatro." The writing that appears above the arcade on some reproductions of the drawing belongs to the next sheet bound into the album, not to the drawing of the theater. I am grateful for the generous reception I received from the staff of the library.
30. Cavicchi, 1969, 233, says that the drawing is clearly by Aleotti's hand.
31. Ibid., 235.
32. The plan gives no indication of a means for horses to enter, and it probably was not possible for horses to reach the floor of the building in which the theater was erected.
33. Cavicchi, 1969, 234. See Lavin, 1964, 115f., for the discussion of the Guiti drawing of 1628. Lavin, 1964, 116, notes that in 1622 in Florence, for a performance of *Il Martirio di Sant'Agata* of Jacopo Cicognini, musicians were placed in front of the stage behind a parapet. Aleotti's innovation moved quickly, then, to Florence, home of many guests at the wedding in Pesaro.
34. In a letter of October 24, 1627 (Lavin, 1964, 125) Guitti notes that the Bolognese painters of a set of the city of Carthage object to the fact that musicians are to sit on top of palaces.
35. For the second theater, designed by Francesco Guitti, see ibid., 109ff.
36. De Angelis, 1992, 162.
37. See ibid., 169–209 (Eng. trans. 350–56) for a detailed account of the performance.
38. Ibid., 208, "Faccian amica parte / de le lor proprie glorie / e le carte a la spada / e la spada a le carte." Ibid., 356, trans. Richard Kamm.
39. By 1628 the use of the term "orchestra" as the place for musicians seems to have become common. We encounter it in Aleotti's drawing for the theater of 1621 in Pesaro. In his description of the festivities in Parma of December 1628, Marcello Buttigli says of Guitti's space for musicians at the front of the stage, "this place is called Orchestra by Vitruvius" ("questo luogo da Vitruvio dicesi Orchestra." Buttigli, 263, quoted in Gallico, 1992, 241). Gallico, 1992, 241, unaware of the infrequently mentioned Pesaro drawing, called Buttigli's use of the word an "authentic first." What seems at this point to be the case is that the earliest known instance of the use of the word as nomenclature for the location of musicians in a theater is by Aleotti on the Pesaro drawing of 1621. But it is entirely possible that the word had been used earlier, especially in Ferrara, with its long history of Vitruvian studies going back to Pellegrino Prisciani in the fifteenth century. See also Pirotta, 1975, 141–43.
40. Ibid., 127–28 and pl. II, fig. 3. Guitti's letter reads, in part: "Il s.re Monteverde hà finalm.te trovata l'Armonia, perche io gli hò accomodato un loco per suo beneficio, che molto gli giova; il quale è sul piano della scala inferiore in q.ta maniera. Il Campo A è forato, e và su'l piano del Salone, e serà coperto da una Ballaustra che lo circonda, e non seranno veduti gl'Instrum.ti anzi accompagna mirabilm.te la Scena, e da commmodità d'illuminare pur le Balaustrate C. et avanza tanto piano B., che resta spazio grandiss.o per S. A. S.ma per scendere. Le Scale possono essere dentro, e quando si vorrà, si possono spingere fuori con bella maniera, e 'l semicircolo C serà vestito d'une muraglia, che difenderà i Musici dall'acqua, Ma lo schizzo è senza misura, basta, che V. S. Ill.ma l'intenda, e che veram.te serve bene alla veduta, et alla Musica, e la prova hà dichiarato buona q.ta risoluzione."
41. See n. 38 above.
42. Gallico, 1992, 233. Letter from Claudio Monteverdi to Enzo Bentivoglio from Venice, September 25, 1627: "et sarà cosa cauta, l'andar a vedere il Theatro in Parma per poterli applicare più possibile le proprie armonie decenti al gran sito." Also Stevens, 375.
43. Lavin, 1964, 129. Letter of November 16, 1627 from Francesco Mazzi to Bentivoglio. Noted in Gallico, 1992, 237. "il sig.r Monteverde è stato à veder i luoghi per la Musica è vi è una buona dificultà a darli sadisfatione conforme il suo pensiero, et alla prima à cominciato a dire, che non può capirvi, però non mancheremo in ogni maniera di procurar di sodisfarlo."
44. Lavin, 1964, 148, noted in Gallico, 1992, 245. There may have been an earlier arrangement of

an orchestra pit for Enzo Bentivoglio, because the Ferrarese composer Antonio Goretti, in a letter of February 18, 1628 to Bentivoglio (Lavin, 1964, 146), states that Guitti's design is just like something they have already done for him: "questo per le musiche, onde serà nella medesima maniera che facessimo per V.S. Ill.ma."

45 Ibid., 146. trans. Richard Kamm, in Gallico, 1992, 362.
46 For the history of the theater from 1640 to 1660, see Ziosi, 2002, 226–37.
47 The description by Florio Tosi, quoted in ibid., 238, was included in the libretto of a tourney, *Amore riformato, con le gare marine sedate*, presented May 22, 1671.

9 Seventeenth-Century Theaters in Venice, The Invention of the Opera House

1 Specialized studies on the history of Venetian theaters in the seventeenth century, which often include detailed accounts of each theater built during that period, include Worsthorne [1954]; *Teatri pubblici* [1971]; Mangini, 1974; Leclerc, 1987; Mancini et al., 1995.
2 Mangini, 1974, 33–42.
3 Ferrone, 1993, 125–26, n. 10
4 Ibid., 90. The correspondent writes that Giustiniani will give them "il loco libero [affitto gratuito], li [darà] l'utile delle sedie et scagni, et delli palchi ... quella porzione che sarà giudicata ragguardevole."
5 Johnson, 2000, n. 6, cites earlier sources.
6 Ibid., 953–54.
7 Mancini et al., 1995, I, 127–30.
8 Ibid., 128, "Sogliano li signori Troni dare alli comici che recitano nella lor stanza il quarto di quello si cava delli palchetti.... hora à scritto il signor Ettore alla compagnia che non intende darli nulla de' palchetti, cosa che non si è usata mai."
9 Mangini, 1974, 43–47.
10 *Comici dell'Arte*, 1993, I, 261.
11 Mangini, 1974, 49–50.
12 *Teatri pubblici*, 1971, 90, n. 75. "Ch.mo Sig.r Alvise (Vendramin) ... sia obbligato far un ... Teatro per recitar Commedie nel qual promette spender ducati tre mille in circa.... s'obliga darla fatta in tutto ... per il Natal 1622."
13 Mancini et al., 1995, I, 222.
14 Ibid., 261. "si obligano essi sig.ri [Vendramin] di dare alla Compagnia *Palco uno per loro uso*."
15 ASV, Consiglio de' X, Parti Criminali, R. 38, 82v–83r.
16 ASV, Consiglio de' X, Parti Criminali, R. 49, 1632, 151r and v.
17 ASV, Consiglio de' X, Parti Criminali, R. 50, 1633, 4r.
18 ASV, Consiglio de' X, Parti Criminali, R. 50, 1633, 163v, 175r. Unfortunately, I could find no trace of the letter from the mother and widow in the archives. Gritti's sons were young, having been born in 1623, 1624, and 1626. See Barbaro, IV, 17, 187.
19 Museo Civico Correr, Mss. Cicogna 2991/II, 27.
20 Molmenti, 1927–29, III, 365, n. 1.
21 Giazotto, 1967–71, I, 2, 1967, 250, quotes Museo Correr, codice Cicogna 3234: "Teatro Tron ridotto in cenere."
22 ASV, Inquisitori di Stato, B. 628, Rossi, Agostino, 1630–34, under date December 16, 1633.
23 The imperial ambassador, it was suggested, might request a box at San Luca. Ibid., December 22, 1633.
24 Giazotto, 1967–71, I, 2, 1967, 253. He gives the location of the document as ASV, Consiglio de' X, Parti Comuni, R. 150, c. 198 r., 1636, 2 maggio, but it is not there. I was not able to locate it elsewhere in the archives. The text, as published by Giazotto, reads, "Per l'indizio sopravenuto a' questi M.ci M.ti da li NN.HH. Tron di S. Benetto circa l'intention de aprir Theatro de musica qual se prattica in più parte per lo diletto de l'insigni pubblici ... se da parte *pro cognitis et incognitis causis* se possa aprirsene uno doppo che li fiscali averanno reconsosciuti con li patroni et proprietarij tutte le obligattioni afinchè procedono ad agravarsene secondo che prescrive giustitia nelle presenti circonstantie."
25 Mancini et al., 1995, I, 118–20, 141–42.
26 Ibid., 141. "operationi simili à Prencipe costano infinito danaro."
27 ASV, Consiglio de' X, Parti Criminali, R. 31, 1614, 48 and 56.
28 ASV, Consiglio de' X, Parti Criminali, R. 40, 1623, 29v and 49v.
29 ASV, Consiglio de' X, Parti Criminali, R. 47, 1630, 31v, 32r, 53v, 72v, 74v, 78r, 78v, 79v.
30 ASV, Consiglio de' X, Parti Criminali, R. 49, 1632, 166v, 167v.
31 Quoted in Mancini et al., 1995, I, 312: "quel nobilissimo teatro ch'egli, in questa città di Venezia, nello spazio di pochi giorni ha con tanta grandezza d'animo fatto nascere, per così

32 Mangini, 1974, 56–66, and Mancini et al., 1995, 1, 294–322.
  dire per dover durar molti anni a solo beneficio della musica. E in vero mi son parse le pietre unirsi da se stesse, quasi invitate dall'armonia di novelli Anfioni, con si poca fatica è sorto da fondamenti quell'ampio e sicuro theatro."
33 Quoted in ibid., 300.
34 See n. 28.
35 Mancini et al., 1995, 1, 300, suggest that Chenda may have been consulted but do not insist on naming him as architect.
36 Mangini, 1974, 59, plausibly suggests this date because the libretto for the first opera given in the theater the following year characterizes it as "novissimo." On the other hand, in a tax declaration that Mangini, 57, found in the Archivio di Stato, Venice, Grimani states: "In contrà S. Marina. In calle della Testa un Theatro fabricato da me questi ultimi anni per fari recita Opere in musica." That could mean that the theater was refurbished around 1660 and was still considered *novissimo* a few years later.
37 Skipon, 1745, 520. For Skipon's lengthy discussion of the stage machinery, see Larson, 1980. Glixon, 2006, devotes a remarkable chapter to the machinery of Baroque opera (cf. Introduction, n. 4).
38 Mangini, 1974, 62–66. The account of the theater's history in Mancini et al., 1995, I, 323–60, is the basis for the discussion here.
39 Ibid., 342, contract of October 2, 1640, ASV, SS. Giovanni e Paolo, Busta Y-V, fasc. 54, 1–36. "hanno tagliato il coverto in parte, per far palchetti."
40 Ibid., "hanno principiato a far l'armatura per detti palchetti."
41 Quoted in Ibid., 353. "l'angustia di esse toglierebbe il poter perfettamente operare anco à singolar architetto."
42 Ibid., 343. "che possa oltre la tezza servirsi del terreno per la scena e sfondri per quella quantità solamente che è descritta nel disegno, et nel modo contiene esso disegno, che è appresso detti padri, fatto con le sue misure."
43 Ibid., 342, "un Teatro per recitar opere in musica."
44 Ibid., 343, "che non si possa in detto luogo, et teatro recitar altre opere che in musica ma non intendendo, che per niun modo si rapresentino comedie boffonesche, o di altra natura ma solo delle sopradette eroiche opere in canto."
45 For accounts of Torelli's career, see Bjurström, 1962, and *Giacomo Torelli*.
46 Giulio del Colle, "Descrizione de gli Apparati del Bellerofonte," in Vincenzo Nolfi, *Il Bellero Fonte. Drama Musicale del Sig.r Vincenzo Nolfi da F. Rappresentato nel Teatro Novissimo in Venetia da Giacomo Torelli da Fano Inventore delli Apparati. Dedicato al Ser.mo Ferdinando II Gran Duca di Toscana*. In Venetia, Presso Gio. Vecellio, e Matteo Lini, 1644, 8. "viddesi sorger dal mare in modello la Città di Venetia così esquisita, e vivamente formata, che la confessò ogn'uno un sforzo dell'arte: Ingannava l'occhio la Piazza con le fabriche publiche al naturale immitate, e dell'inganno ogn'hor più godeva scordandosi quasi per quella finta della vera dove realmente si tratteneva." The illustration is Pl. 2 of this volume, BNM-215.C.32.1.
47 *Apparati scenici per lo teatro nouissimo di Venetia. Nell'anno 1644 d'inuentione e cura di Iacomo Torelli da Fano*, In Venetia : presso Gio. Vecellio, e Matteo Leni, 1644, Pl. 1. BNM-215.C.32.2.
48 Johnson, 2013, 192.
49 Rosand, E., 1991, esp. 112–24.
50 Ibid., 112.
51 The drawing is number 34 in an album, number 117, in Sir John Soane's Museum, London, with the inscription "Disegni n.o 36 per il teatro di tordinon fatti da me Carlo Cav. Fontana l'anno –" The drawing, first published in 1927 (see The Mask) has been much discussed. Mancini et al., 1995, 1, 302, note, n. 60, that there are some imprecisions in the measurements on the drawing. My thanks to Stephen Astley, Curator of Drawings at the Soane Museum, for generous assistance over two days.
52 Mancini et al., 1995, I, 302, date the drawing 1691–93, because that was the time that Bezzi worked at the Teatro S. Giovanni Grisogono for the Grimani, but they do not link that date to the fact that in 1690–91 the Tordinona theater in Rome was beginning a second life that would lead to a new design by Fontana for that theater, rebuilt in 1695. See Chapter 11. It seems completely reasonable to assign a date of 1691–95 to the Soane drawing.
53 Giazotto, 1967–71. 1,2, 1967, 277. "un tale signor Zuane Cardon mentre se faceva l'oppera al S. Moisè in tempo de musica con concorso de strepito con le mani et con la bocca e co' piedi habia fatti li sconci che da tempo se praticano ne li theatri de la città et che fue veduto con altri in quantità gitare su la scena e contro li palchi le

careghe et la robba che se vende al boteghin de fora del theatro de mangiare e de bever."

54 See n. 52. "lo strepitio fu tanto che li zentilomeni col protestare sortirono de li palchi e vi fu chi se diede ne le mani e fu sparato anco con la pistolla e vi fu fuggi fuggi da per tutto."

55 Molmenti, 1920, 317, quoted in Mangini, 1974, 30. "La spesa, chi si recerca a chi li vuol vedere, non passa in tutto che la metà di un scudo, et quasi ogn'uno in Venetia, senza suo grande incommodo, lo può spendere, perché il denaro vi abonda." The writer, Francesco de' Pannocchieschi, was nephew of the papal nunzio.

56 Worsthorne, 1954, 4.

57 Molmenti, 1927–29, 3, 408.

58 Chassebras de Cremailles, 1683, 202–03. "Le Theatre de S. Jean & Paul est encor un des plus beaux de cette Ville. Il est extrémement profond, & contient cinq rangs de Pales, trente & un à chaque rang. Il est peint & doré comme les autres, & appartient encore à Messieurs Grimani Freres."

59 Mangini, 1974, 77–83, Mancini et al., 1985, 2, 63–126, Muraro, 1987. The architect is not known. Mangini, 1974, 78, suggests either Tommaso Bezzi or, more likely, Gaspare Mauro. Muraro, 1987, leans toward Bezzi, as do Mancini et al., 1995, 2, 72.

60 It continued to be active until 1714. In 1718 the roof collapsed and the structure became a ruin.

61 Mancini et al., 1995, 2, 99, give the contract of the sale and plot plan attached thereto.

62 Ibid., 115–21.

63 Ibid., 117, "L'*udienza* dove sono seduti gli spettatori presenta sul fondo una linea retta . . .; il che torna a vantaggio dei palchi di fondo dai quali si gode perciò una visuale migliore che se la parete fosse concava; e questo anche se la parete curva . . . è ritenuta più vantaggiosa per l'ascolto delle voci."

64 Chassebras de Cremailles, 1683, 175–81.

65 The print of 1709 omits the figures at ground level. Had they been removed by that time?

66 Chassebras de Cremailles does not give the dimensions of the orchestra pit, but a description of the theater in the *Mercure Galant* of 1679 says that the pit held forty musicians. Mancini et al., 1995, 2, 113.

10 Seventeenth-Century Theaters for Comedy and Opera

1 The precise location of the performance of *Orfeo* in the Gonzaga palace is disputed. See the exchange between Nino Pirotta and Claudio Gallico in Pirotta, 1969, 65–66. Pirotta, ibid., 49–53, citing earlier sources, offers a possible reconstruction of the general disposition of the room in which the opera was produced. His reconstruction of events is followed here.

2 Ibid., 45–48.

3 What hid the curtain, once raised, is not clear. That in Mantua of 1608 appears to be an early instance of a curtain that rose and disappeared. Other curtains descended into the stage floor. Adami, 2003, 258–61, gives a recent synopsis of the history of curtains.

4 Nagler, 1964, 179–85, gives a detailed account of *L'Idropica*.

5 Bianconi and Walker, 1975, 406, note that the Jesuit author Giovan Domenico Ottonelli, *Della Christiana Moderatione del Theatro*, Florence, 1652, wrote that there are three types of theaters: princely, academic, and commercial.

6 C. Ricci, 1888, 78. "I palchetti, secondo che dalle scene camminano verso il mezzo del Teatro vadano sempre salendo di qualche once l'uno sopra l'altro, e similmente vadano di qualche once sempre più sporgendo all'infuori. Per tal via meglio si affaccia in certo modo ogni palchetto alla scena, e l'uno non impedisce punto la vista dell'altro."

7 A different plan was published by Lenzi, 1985, fig. 11.

8 Battistelli, 2000, 312, lists, in addition to theaters with similar plans mentioned here, the Teatro Falcone, Genoa, as reconstructed by Carlo Fontana in 1705; Teatro di Corte, Mantua, 1732, by Ferdinando Bibbiena and Andrea Galuzzi; and Teatro della Cittadella, Reggio Emilia, 1741, by Antonio Cugini.

9 Bianconi and Walker, 1975, 379.

10 Ibid.

11 Ibid., 380.

12 For earlier theaters in Naples, see Croce, 1992 and Proto-Giuleo.

13 Croce, 1992, 90: a "sollevato palco, d'ogni intorno da gelosie guardato, per gelosia di chi aborrische l'esservi veduto, costrutto ad uso del Cardinale." The cardinal viewed a "spaziosa e nobile sala, per serici broccati rilucente, per accessi doppierir luminosa, e molto più per gli adunati lumi delle bellissime dame fiammeggiante, teatro non meno alle vere battaglie degli spettatori che alle finte rappresentazioni degli spettacoli."

14 Ibid., 87.

15 Bianconi and Walker, 1975, 379.
16 Ibid., 381.
17 Ibid., 383: "conspiraranno all'otio erudito di V. E. la Poesia, la Musica, e la'rchitettura; segnalandomi però quest'ultima nella divotione, verso la Sua Eccellentissima Persona."
18 Ibid., 387ff., is the source for this discussion of the viceroy's politics.
19 The discussion of the theater in Modena is based on Jarrard, 2003, 70–89. For reasons of space the magnificent amphitheater built by Francesco in 1652 is not discussed here. See ibid., 37–48.
20 Vigarani played an important role in the importation of Italian architecture into the court of Louis XIV. For that king he designed the Salle des Machines, the royal opera house in the Tuileries palace in Paris. See ibid., 192–208, illustrated Fig. 117, p. 201. The superimposed two rows of columns Vigarani used in Paris may well give us an idea of the rows of Corinthian columns in the theater in Modena.
21 In Paris Vigarani also repeated the coffered ceiling and the royal box in the center of the auditorium, so that the audience could enjoy the performance of Louis watching the performance.
22 *Principum* is a corrupt or mistaken form of *principium*, the genitive plural of the noun *princeps*. I am grateful to my colleagues Elizabeth McGowan and Amanda Wilcox for their help with the translation of the Latin inscription.
23 Decroisette, 1987, 31, cites a search ordered by the court in 1651 for an appropriate space to entertain the duke of Modena and the archduke of Austria, both of whom were expected to visit Florence. The search was without success; no space was sufficiently large or sufficiently well equipped.
24 See Mamone, 2003, 379, a letter of January 3, 1653, informing the cardinal of Ferdinando Tacca's involvement in designing sets for the theater.
25 Decroisette, 1987, 30–31.
26 *Descrizione della Presa d'Argo e de gli Amori di Linceo con Hipermestra; Festa Teatrale rappresentata dal Signor Principe Cardinal Gio. Carlo di Toscana Generaliss. del Mare, e Comprotettore de Negozi di Sua Maestà Cattolica in Roma, per celebrare il natale del Sereniss. Principe di Spagna*, Florence, Nella Stamperia di S.A.S., 1658. Most of the description was republished, with some errors, by Morini, 1926, 4–7.

27 Decroisette, 1987, 27, verified the measurements on the plan on site. See her figures on 24, 28.
28 The contemporary text, 7, reads "figura ovata." Decroisette, 1987, 25, quotes a passage from that description that mentions the shape of a hyperbola, but this passage does not appear in the copy of the text at my disposal: "Molte colonne con lor recinto una loggia formavano di figura a quella che i geometri iperbola vien nomata somiglievole … per lo miglior repercuotimento della voce."
29 Ibid., 31, n. 31.
30 Mamone, 2003, 443, "li teatri di questa città." Since the cardinal had no agent or relative in Bologna, he had written ahead to Malvezzi to introduce Tacca. In all the other cities, Tacca presented letters of introduction that Gian Carlo had given him.
31 Ibid., 436.
32 Ibid., 446, "fu subito data comodita did veder questo teatro e di considerar in esso tutto ciò che egli ha mostrato di desiderare."
33 What those may have looked like is not easy to say, because, as Buratelli, 1999, 101–03, has pointed out, we know little about the architecture of the theaters of Mantua at that date. There was a theater in the ducal palace, in a wing across the piazza from the flank of the cathedral, and a smaller theater for comedies located on the opposite side of the palace, in a less conspicuous position. Both were connected by corridors to the palace, so that the duke could go unobserved to either. A fire in 1591 badly damaged the palace theater by Bertani; it was rebuilt the following year. A description from 1606 (ibid., 131, n. 100) says that in the rebuilt theater there was semicircular seating on steps, like that of Bertani's building. The steps were separated from the stage to leave an open area, again like Bertani's. Between steps and stage were two large *palchi*, the one to the right holding "i gentilhuomini degli ambasciatori" and the other "un gran numero di musici con instromenti diversi da corda e da fiato." No orchestra pit yet. The men and women of the court, including the duke and duchess, sat on the steps.
34 Mamone, 2003, 448. "i miei teatri …" "l'ho trovato un ingegno di garbo."
35 Ibid., 449. "egli fosse condotto a vedere li due teatri che vi sono … potessi coll'inspezione di quello pienamente sodisfarsi,

conforme l'E.V. si degnera di sentire al di lui ritorno constà."
36 Ibid., 450–51. "(la) forma de' it teatri di questa città."
37 Decroisette, 1997, 31. She notes that the no-longer-in-use warehouse for wool cloth, once a principal product of the city, was symptomatic of the shift in the Florentine economy from mercantilism with many participants to one dependent on the ruling prince. "La puissance médicéenne n'est plu fondée, dans les dernières décennies du XVIIe siècle, sur le commerce et la banque, mais sure l'illusion produites par la perpétuelle mise en scène du pouvoir dans ses fêtes et ses spectacles."
38 Ibid., fig. 9.
39 Since the Intronati figure in the drawing by Riccio of the original organization of the stage in 1560 (see Chapter 6), the theater must have been under their purview from the beginning.
40 Bianconi and Walker, 1975, 435: "nel 1646 d'ordine del. Ser.mo Sig.r Pr.pe Mattias Governatore fabbricò di legname, e riordinò in miglior forma l'Antico Teatro."
41 Ibid., 436.
42 Cordaro, 1983, 122. Traditionally the theater has been credited to Giovanni Battista Piccolomini (Galli, 164, gives the source of the attribution), about whose architectural activity little is known. Galli, 2010, 162f., cautiously accepts Cordaro's attribution, but notes the lack of documentation. Galli, 164, also points to Fontana's connection with the Chigi family of Siena, and to the fact that Piccolomini was married to a Chigi. None of the hundreds of drawings by Fontana illustrated in Braham and Hager contain similarly fancifully curved shapes.
43 Not "Teatro di Siena di muro," as Cordaro, 1983, and Galli, 2010, 164, would have it.
44 Odoardo must have seen Torelli's work in Venice. The dukes of Parma and Mantua kept boxes in Venetian theaters.
45 The drawing shows a proposed design by Luigi Vanvitelli; the actual tower was erected after 1740 on a design by Gianfrancesco Buonamici. When built, the tower broke into a corner of Torelli's design.
46 "quasi inutile per non essere né capace né accomodato a quei spettacoli in ordine al lusso, che al presente e costumanza del secolo si praticano nelle Città nobili." Battistelli, 2000a, 315.

47 Battistelli, 2000b, 387, records only two copies of the print, which was first published in the *Enciclopedia dello Spettacolo*, V, Tav. IV, 1958. In the lower left the etching is signed "*Ferdinando Galli Bibbiena intalio*" (not *ideavit*, as Battistelli read it). At bottom center Bibiena labeled the print "IACOMO TORELLI INVENT" to give credit where credit was due.
48 Warwick, 2012, 23–36, gives a particularly detailed account of Bernini's spectacular theatrical illusions.
49 Battistelli, 2000a, 316. "[I palchetti] come propri vendere, et alienare a chi li vorrà comprare talmente che il Comune non possa mai pretendere né dagli Oratori, né da essi parte alcuna del prezzo, ma li detti Palchetti si trasmettino liberi negli Heredi e successori de medesimi Compratori, sì come si è ultimamente praticato in Ancona e si pratica in altre Città dello stato ecclesiastico."
50 Ibid., "si dispose per la costruzione di un palco più grandioso e più nobile da far dono al Magistrato."
51 Subsequent plans, made in the following century, diverge in this detail. The boxes on the fifth order have the scalloped edges, but those at the other levels do not. Instead, their fronts show a polygonal outline, with the fronts of the third boxes from the center running parallel to the stage to improve visibility.
52 I thank Elizabeth McGowan for her help with this question.

11 Teatro di Tordinona in Rome, Queen Christina of Sweden, and Carlo Fontana

1 An exception to this statement is the highly successful theater operated by the Barberini, the family of Urban VIII. Since we have almost no information about this theater's conformation, it is not discussed in these pages, despite its high patronage and its association with Gianlorenzo Bernini.
2 The complex history of this theater and its musical presentations is laid out in remarkable detail by Cametti, 1938. More recently S. Rotondi, 1969 has updated Cametti's work. Rotondi's notes add rich new documentation to the theater's history. The account contained here is largely drawn from these two sources. Tavassi La Greca, 1989, 1–20, provides a concise history of the theater and the literature

thereon, and the theater is also discussed by Bilardello, 1989.
3 See Masson, 1968 for a lively, thoughtful account of Christina's life.
4 Fogelberg Rota, 2005, 209–25.
5 Ibid., 216–17.
6 Borsellino, 1988, 24. C. Frommel, 1973, I, 99–100, II, 281–91, III, 118–20.
7 S. Rotondi, 1969, fig. 19; Vänje, 1966, 378.
8 Stockholm, National Museum, attributed to Camillo Arcucci and dated c. 1660. First drawing C. Frommel, 1973, III, 120d. According to Borsellino, 1988, 31, n. 37, Camillo Arcucci appeared in Christina's account books in 1664 and 1666. The drawings must date from after Christina moved into Palazzo Riario in July 1659 and before the proposal of 1666 to construct a theater at the site of the former Tor di Nona prison. Braham and Hager, 1977, 183, think it possible that the drawings may be by Carlo Fontana. The plan that places the theater in the center of a piazza surrounded by shops and across from Christina's palace bears a striking similarity to the combination of church, S. Maria dell'Assunzione, and flanking symmetrical porticos across from the Palazzo Chigi at Ariccia, designed by Gianlorenzo Bernini and built between 1662 and its dedication in 1665. This parallelism may suggest a date of c. 1664–65 for Christina's drawings, while leaving open possible authorship by either Arcucci or Fontana.
9 Vänje, 1966, 386–87.
10 Semper designed two opera houses for Dresden, built successively on the same site. The first opened in 1841 and burned in 1869; the second opened in 1878.
11 Krautheimer, 1985, *passim*. After Christina's trip to France in 1656–58, she lost the support of the pope, who was appalled by the brutal execution she ordered in that country of an Italian nobleman in her suite whom she deemed a traitor. Perhaps she hoped to win back his favor with this proposal?
12 A contemporary wrote that on the site of a former: "seraglio dei malveventi e tormentosa macerazione de' corpi, hora di nuovo con bizzarre metamorfosi si sta costruendo un magnifico teatro per dar sollievo e d'allegrezza alla città." S. Rotondi, 1969, n. 19.
13 The drawing is inscribed in the upper left corner "Pianta del Teatro Vecchio con sue Case nelli due Fianchi come si trovano al presente."
14 Ibid., n. 15 and 27.

15 Tavassi La Greca, 1989, 20–24. Giorgi, 1795, 49, whose history of the Tordinona is riddled with inaccuracies, expanded a late-eighteenth-century mention of a view of the water from the theater into something far grander that no existing evidence supports. S. Rotondi, 1969, n. 28, is also not inclined to accept the interpretation of Tavassi La Greca.
16 Bjürström, 1966, 107.
17 Cametti, 1938, I, 61 and 67–68, S. Rotondi, 1969, n. 20.
18 Monaldini, 1999, 79. "Sua Maestà stava a sedere sotto il Baldacchino in mezzo della sala, et perché fù avvisata che per causa d'esso baldacchino molti non poteano vedere, né goder l'opera, commandò, che fusse levato."
19 The Tordinona is generally cited as the earliest public theater in Rome (cf. Tavassi La Greca, 1989, 24), but Antonella Pempolone has demonstrated that the Teatro alle Stufe dei Mellini, the predecessor of the Teatro Pace, opened a few years earlier. I thank her for making me aware of her work. The Tor di Nona was indeed the first public theater for opera, however.
20 See Tamburini, 1997, 11–77, for a history of their lives and interest in the theater. In 1682 Lorenzo Onofrio opened a private theater, also designed by Carlo Fontana, in his palace on Piazza Santi Apostoli in Rome. Tamburini deals extensively with this theater and includes a schematic reconstruction by Sergio Rotondi.
21 Ibid., 120.
22 Cametti, 1938, 2, 323–42, gives an account of these operas. The Venetian musical connection has been pointed out by Staffieri, 1998, 21.
23 S. Rotondi, 1969, n. 32.
24 Povoledo, 1998, 204–05.
25 Bjürström, 1966, 108, 149.
26 "Imbocco del Palco di vano P(al)mi 55 approvato dal cav. Acciaioli." See ibid., 149, cat. 108, for full text of inscription on Windsor drawing.
27 "Disegno per un Theatro da fabbricarsi a Torre de nona in Roma, per ordine della Regina Christina di Svezia. inventione del Ca. Carlo Fontana." Ibid., 150.
28 Cametti, 1938, I, 86f., quotes a letter of February 7, 1696, written by the director of the French Academy, La Tuelière, who says that Fontana told him that he intended to have the plan engraved, but no engraving is known. This plan, of course, would be the "magnet" plan that was built, not the oval plan of the Adelcrantz drawing. Even if the letter does not refer to the

Adelcrantz plan, it makes clear that Fontana considered having a plan for the theater engraved.
29 Bjurström, 1966, 110–12.
30 For instance, Tavassi La Greca, 1989, 24, points to Fontana's invention of both the truncated oval and horseshoe plan for theaters.
31 See Chapter 4.
32 See Chapter 10.
33 S. Rotondi, 1969, fig. 24, rightly compares this design to Fontana's project for a centrally planned church to be built in the oval Colosseum.
34 D'Alibert went to Turin in the spring of 1677 and only returned to Rome a year later. Cametti, 1938, I, 70.
35 Volpicelli, 1989, 689ff.
36 See Cametti, 1938, II, 345–47, for the severe local criticism of the opera. One he quotes, I, 77, is worth repeating: "Italia mia, l'onnipotente mano / Con più giusti flagelli oggi ti doma: / L'armi estranie a Torino ed a Milano, / La peste in Regno, ed il *Colombo* a Roma."
37 See Cametti, I, 78–89, for details of the negotiations for and construction of this theater.
38 S. Rotondi, 1969, figs. 4, 9, 11, 27, 28, 30.
39 The inscriptions on the drawing read, from upper left: "A. Fabrica d'alzarsi sopra la stalla del Bargello di Campagna in n.o 3 piani oltre il piano di presente, e saranno n.o 4. piani senza la stalla. B. Due scalette da farsi in conformita del nuovo Teatro C. Palchetti attorno il Teatro." At upper right: "Il colorito di Rosso denota il ricinto, e muri che non si demoliscono Il colorito di Giallo denota il contorno del novo teatro e suo scenario Il colorito torchino denota il Teatro Vecchio Il colorito di nero denota li muri da demolirsi per l'erettione del novo Teatro, sotto il quale si devono in quei lochi cavare stalle, Rimesse, e lavoratori, et altro che nella scrittura si dichiara." The yellow and blue colors have faded over time.
40 "Pianta del Teatro da farsi di nuovo." The inscription in the upper left corner reads: "Il colorito di Rosso sono li muri che rimangono. Il colorito di Giallo denota muri e scale alumache da farsi. A. Stalla del Bargello di campagna con un altro appartam.to sopra di n.o 3 Stanze sopra de quali ivi si doverá realzare di nuovo altri n.o 3 piani di tré stanze simili di uno."
41 Sir John Soane's Museum 117. Inscribed "Disegni n.o 36 per il teatro di tordinon fatti da me Carlo Cav. Fontana lanno –" A date is lacking. The album was purchased by Soane in 1818 at the sale of books belonging to Robert Adam, who had acquired the album in Rome. Fontana created at least twenty-six such albums, of which nineteen are known. See Braham and Hager, 1977, 1–6.
42 This is not the place to attempt an analysis of the entire album, which will be much more readily accomplished once the Soane Museum has been able to carry out its plans to post images of all of its drawings on the Internet. Many of the drawings are published by S. Rotondi, 1969, whose purpose, however, was to write a history of the architecture of the theater, not an analysis of the album.
43 S. Rotondi, 1969, fig. 41–43, appears to be the first to have taken the inscriptions on these drawings seriously to mean that they represent the theater as built. Bilardello, 1989, 49ff, in his discussion of drawings in the Soane album, believes the truncated oval plans to have come after the horseshoe plan that Fontana labeled "established." Neither Tavassi La Greca, 1989, nor Bilardello seems to have been aware of Stefano Rontondi's work.
44 Truncated oval and horseshoe plans are close in shape. The difference largely depends on the geometry employed to arrive at the form. Both have side walls with continuous curves. Following a misstatement by Carini Motta, 1972, 37, both Tavassi La Greca, 1989, 24–26, and S. Rotondi, 1969, n. 35, state that Alberti wrote that ancient theaters followed the shape of a horseshoe. Both cite Alberti, 1966, II, 742, as the source, but Alberti, 1966, II, 728, has the correct text: "forma senescenti lunae simile est," that is: a shape similar to a waning moon. We do not know whether Fontana accepted Carini Motta's misstatement.
45 Respectively numbered 34, 32, and 36 and identified in Fontana's hand as "Teatro di S. Gio: Pauolo di Venetia," "Teatro di Firenze," and "Teatro di Siena di nuovo."
46 Cametti, 1938, I, 87, who did not know the Soane drawings, believed the building as built followed the truncated oval of the plan in the Roman Archivio di Stato.
47 S. Rotondi, 1969, fig. 42 and n. 50.
48 "Profilo stabilito del teatro di tor di nona."
49 Soane 12, a variant on the longitudinal section, contains in the center of the vault a space marked "G Posto del candelabro."
50 The drawing is inscribed: "Pianta del teatro di tor di nona con Palco e contra Palco Scale et casamenti piatte a strade contigue. Tutto p ordine di Illmo Palavicino Gov.re di Roma C fontana." S. Rotondi, 1969, n. 51, reports that Rainuzo Pallavicini became governor of Rome on March 16, 1696,

51 Cametti, 1938, I, 96: "Il povero conte D'Alimbert, *dux theatralium operum*, finisce tutte le sue scene con questa per lui lacrimevole tragedia."
52 Ibid., 105–18.
53 Ibid., 119–34. According to Cametti, Clement hoped that the new theater would relieve him of the nuisance of the constant jockeying for prestigious boxes among the foreign ambassadors at his court. He decreed that the boxes would be awarded annually to the ambassadors by lot, and no ambassador would be allowed to furnish a box or to put up emblems of his country. Of course those orders were ignored.
54 S. Rotondi, 1969, n. 38, posits a plausible connection between Fontana and Benedetto Alfieri, architect of the oval plan of the Teatro Regio in Turin of 1737–40, via Filippo Juvarra, pupil of the former and teacher of the latter.

Appendix

1 Vitruvius, 1488(?); Alberti, 1486.
2 Vitruvius, 1511. See also Rowland, 2011.
3 See Gros, 83–95, for an extensive discussion of the ambiguities of the Vitruvian text.
4 Richard Schofield's (Vitruvius, 2009) is particularly engaging, because Schofield has rendered the book readable for a contemporary audience without sacrificing accuracy.
5 Now available in English translation by Joseph R. Jones and Lucia Guzzi: http://parnaseo.uv.es/Celestinesca/Numeros/1993/VOL%2017/NUM%201/1_documento.pdf.
6 In the fifteenth century Alberti was not alone in composing a play in the Roman manner. For example, Aeneas Silvius Piccolomini, later Pope Pius II, in 1444 wrote a comedy, *Chrysis*, notable for its raunchy subject matter but recently held to be a critique of moral philosophy. See Emily O'Brien, "Aeneas Silvius Piccolomini's Chrysis: Prurient Pastime – or Something More?" *MLN*, 124, 1, January, 2009, 111–36.
7 For Alberti there is a good recent English translation: Alberti, 1988.

BIBLIOGRAPHY

Aasted, Elsbeth, "What the Corsini Scenari Tell Us about the Commedia dell'Arte," *Analecta Romana Istituti Danici*, XX, 1992, 159–181.

Acidini Luchinat, Cristina et al., *Medici, Michelangelo, and the Art of Late Renaissance Florence*, New Haven, CT, Yale University Press, 2002.

Adami, Giuseppe, "Nel segno di Aleotti. Materiali per lo sviluppo della tradizione teatrale ferrarese del Seicento," *Giovanni Battista Aleotti e L'Architettura*, Costanza Cavicchi et al., eds., Reggio Emilia, Diabasis, 2003, 253–266.

Adami, Giuseppe, *Scenografia e Scenatecnica Barocca tra Ferrara e Parma (1625–1631)*, Rome, "L'Erma" di Bretschneider, 2003.

Ademollo, Alessandro, *I Teatri di Roma nel secolo decimosettimo*, Rome, Pasqualucci, 1888.

Adorni, Bruno, *L'Architettura Farnesiana a Parma 1545–1630*, Parma, Luigi Battei, 1974.

Adorni, Bruno, *L'Architettura Farnesiana a Piacenza 1545–1600*, Parma, Luigi Battei, 1982.

Adorni, Bruno, "La chiesa come il teatro: due architetture di Gaspare Vigarani," *Barocco romano e barocco italiano: Il teatro, l'effimero, l'allegoria*, Marcello Fagiolo and Maria Luisa Madonna, eds., Rome, Gangemi Editore, 1985, 234–250.

Adorni, Bruno, "Il Teatro Farnese a Parma," *Giovanni Battista Aleotti e L'Architettura*, Costanza Cavicchi et al., eds., Reggio Emilia, Diabasis, 2003, 205–226.

Albach, B., "De schouwburg van Jacob van Campen," *Oud Holland*, LXXXV, 1970, 85–109.

Alberti, Leon Battista, *de re aedificatoria*, Florence, Nicolai Laurentii Alamani, 1486.

Alberti, Leon Battista, *L'Architettura [de re aedificatoria]*, trans. Giovanni Orlandi, intro. Paolo Portoghesi, 2 vols., Milan, Il Polifilo, 1966.

Alberti, Leon Battista, *On the Art of Building in Ten Books*, tr. Joseph Rykwert, Neil Leach, Robert Tavernor, Cambridge, MA, and London, MIT Press, 1988.

Alm, Irene, "Giovanni Battista Balbi 'Veneziano Ballarino celebre,'" in *Giacomo Torelli*, 214–226.

Amadei, Giuseppe, *I 150 anni del Sociale nella storia dei Teatri di Mantova*, Mantova, 1973.

Amadei, Giuseppe, "Note sul teatro a Mantova nel Rinascimento," *Mantova e i Gonzaga nella civiltà del rinascimento*, Mantua, Città di Mantova in collaboration with A. Mondadori, 1977, 155–162.

Andrea Palladio 1508–1580, the Portico and the Farmyard, Howard Burns, Lynda Fairbairn and Bruce Boucher, eds., ex. cat., Arts Council of Great Britain and Centro Internazionale di Studi di Architettura Andrea Palladido, 1975.

Apparati scenici per lo teatro nouissimo di Venetia. Nell'anno 1644 d'inuentione e cura di Iacomo Torelli da Fano, In Venetia: presso Gio. Vecellio, e Matteo Leni, 1644.

Architettura e Utopia nella Venezia del Cinquecento, Lionello Puppi, ed., ex. cat., Milan, 1980.

Aubrun, Charles V., "Les débuts du drame lyrique en Espagne," *Le lieu théâtral a la renaissance*, Jean Jacquot, ed., Paris, Éditions du Centre National de la Recherche Scientifique, 1964, 423–444.

Baldassare Peruzzi pittura, scena e architettura nel Cinquecento, Marcello Fagiolo and Maria Luisa Madonna, eds., Rome, Istituto della Enciclopedia Italiana, 1987.

Balestrieri, Lina, *Feste e spettacoli alla corte dei Farnese*, Quaderni Parmigiani 6, Parma, Palatina Editrice, 1981.

Barbaro, Marco, *Albori de' patrizi veneti*, ms., ASV, Misc. Cod. Serie I, Storia Veneta.

Barocco europeo e barocco veneziano, Vittore Branca, ed., Florence, Sansoni, 1963.

Barocco romano e barocco italiano: Il teatro, l'effimero, l'allegoria, Marcello Fagiolo and Maria Luisa Madonna, eds., Rome, Gangemi Editore, 1985.

Bartolini, Nicolò Enea, *L'Ermiona del sr. marchese Pio Enea Obizzi: per introduzione d'un torneo à piede, & à cavallo: e d'un balletto rappresentato in musica nella citta di Padoua l'anno MDCXXXVI: dedicata al sereniss.o principe di Venetia Francesco Erizo/ descritta dal s. Nicolò Enea Bartolini, gentilhuomo & academ. senese*, Padua, Paolo Frambotto, 1638.

Bassi, Elena, "I teatri veneziani dal Cinque al Settecento," *Ateneo Veneto*, CLII, 45, July–December 2, 1961, 19–30.

Battistelli, Franco, "Scenografia, scenotecnica e teatri: Sabbatini e Torelli," *Arte e Cultura nella Provincia di Pesaro e Urbino dalle origini a oggi*, F. Battistelli, ed., Venice, Marsilio Editore, 1986, 377–386.

Battistelli, Franco, *L'antico e il nuovo Teatro della Fortuna di Fano (1677–1944): storia dell'edificio e delle sue vicende artistiche*, Fano, Tipografia Editrice Sangallo, 1972.

Battistelli, Franco, "Le origini del teatro 'all'italiana' e il Teatro della Fortuna di Giacomo Torelli," in *Giacomo Torelli*, 311–350.

Battistelli, Franco, "Gli interventi di Ferdinando Galli Bibiena nel teatro torelliano," in *Giacomo Torelli*, 383–406.

Baur-Heinhold, Margarete, *The Baroque Theatre: A Cultural History of the 17th and 18th Centuries*, trans. Mary Whitall, New York and Toronto, McGraw-Hill Book Company, 1967.

Bellero Fonte (Il) drama musicale del sig.r Vicenzo Nolfi da F. rappresentato nel teatro nouissimo in Venetia da Giacomo Torelli da Fano inuentore delli apparati dedicato al ser.mo Ferdinando 2. Gran Duca di Toscana, 1642.

Bellina, Anna Laura, and Thomas Walker, "Il melodramma: poesia e musica nell'esperienza teatrale," *Storia della Cultura Veneta. Dalla Contrariforma alla fine della Repubblica*, 4/I, Girolamo Arnaldi and Manlio Pastore Stocchi, eds., Vicenza, Neri Pozza Editore, 1983, 409–432.

Benedetti, Silvano, "Il teatro musicale a Venezia nel '600: aspetti organizzativi," *Studi veneziani*, n. s. VIII, 1984, 185–220.

Benini, Enrica, "Il teatro del Vasari per le nozze di Francesco de' Medici con Giovanna d'Austria (1565). Un esempio del rapporto committente-artista nell'ambiente fiorentino," *Quaderni di teatro*, 4, 15, 1982, 136–150.

Berti, Luciano, "L'architettura manieristica a Firenze e in Toscana," *Bolletino del Centro Internazionale di Studi di Architettura Andrea Palladio*, 1967, 211–219.

Bianconi, Lorenzo, *Music in the Seventeenth Century*, trans. David Bryant, Cambridge, Cambridge University Press, 1987. Originally published in italian as *Il Seicento*, Edizioni di Torino, Turin, 1982.

Bianconi, Lorenzo, and Thomas Walker, "Dalla Finta Pazza alla Veremonda: Storie di Febiarmonici," *Rivista italiana di musicologia*, 10, 1975, 379–454.

Bianconi, Lorenzo, and Thomas Walker, "Production, Consumption and Political Function of Seventeenth Century Opera," *Early Music History*, 4, 1984, 211–299.

Biggi, Maria Ida, and Giorgio Mangini, *Teatro Malibran Venezia a San Giovanni Grisostomo*, Venice, Marsilio, 2001.

Bilardello, Enzo, "L'evoluzione del teatro barocco: pratica e trattati," *Il Teatro a Roma nel Settecento*, Rome, Istituto della Enciclopedia Italiana, 1989, vol. I, 35–70.

Bjurström, Per, *Giacomo Torelli and Baroque Stage Design, Figura, Uppsala Studies in the History of Art, New Series 2*, 2nd ed., Stockholm, Almqvist & Wiksell, 1962.

Bjurström, Per, *Feast and Theatre in Queen Christina's Rome*, Stockholm, Nationalmuseum, Nationalmusei Skriftserie 14, 1966.

BoCSAP. *Bolletino del Centro di Studi di Architettura Andrea Palladio*, XVI, 1974, "L'Architettura teatrale dall'epoca greca al Palladio."

Borsellino, Enzo, *Palazzo Corsini alla Lungara. Storia di un cantiere*, Fasano, Schena, 1988.

Bourne, Molly, *Francesco II Gonzaga. The Soldier-Prince as Patron*, Rome, Bulzoni Editore, 2008.

Bourne, Molly, "The Art of Diplomacy: Mantua and the Gonzaga, 1328–1630," in *Court Cities*, 2010, 138–195.

Braham, Alan, Helmut Hager, and Carlo Fontana, *The Drawings at Windsor Castle*, London, Zwemmer, 1977.

Brown, Patricia Fortini, *Venetian Painting in the Age of Carpaccio*, New Haven, CT, and London, Yale University Press, 1988.

Bruschi, Arnaldo, "Il Teatro Capitolino del 1513," *Bolletino del Centro di Studi di Architettura Andrea Palladio*, XVI, 1974, 189–218.

Buccheri, Alessandra, *The Spectacle of Clouds, 1439–1650: Italian Art and Theatre*, Burlington, VT, and Farnam, Surrey, Ashgate, 2014.

Buratelli, Claudia, *Spettacoli di corte a Mantova tra Cinque e Seicento*, Florence, Le Lettere, 1999.

Burke, Jill, *Rethinking the High Renaissance: The Visual Culture of the Visual Arts in Early Sixteenth-Century Rome*, Farnham, UK and Burlington, VT, Ashgate, 2012.

Burroughs, Charles, "The Building's Face and the Herculean Paradigm: Agendas and Agency in Roman Renaissance Architecture," *RES: Anthropology and Aesthetics*, 23, Spring, 1993, 7–30.

Bussadori, Paola, *Il giardino e la scena, Francesco Bagnara 1784–1866*, Castelfranco Veneto, mp/edizioni, 1986.

Buttigli, Marcello, *Descrizione dell'apparato fatto per onorare la prima e solenne entrata in Parma della serenissima principessa Margherita di Toscana*, Parma, Viotti, 1629.

Cairns, Christopher, "Theater as Festival: The Staging of Aretino's *Talanta* (1542) and the Influnece of Vasari," *Italian Renaissance Festivals and the European Influence*, ed. J. R. Mulryne and Margaret Shewring, Lewiston, ME, Edwin Mellen Press, 1992, 105–117.

Calore, Marina, *Spettacoli a Modena tra '500 e '600 dalla città alla capitale*, Modena, Aedes Muratoriana, 1983.

Cametti, Alberto, *Cristina di Svezia, l'arte musicale e gli spettacoli teatrali in Roma*, Rome, Nuova antologia, 1911.

Cametti, Alberto, *Il Teatro di Tordinona poi di Apollo*, 2 vols., Tivoli, Aldo Chicca, 1938.

Carini Motta, Fabrizio, *Trattato sopra la struttura de' teatri e scene*, Guastalla, 1676, reprinted a cura di E. A. Craig, Milan: Il Polifilo, 1972. Facsimile in Edward A. Craig, *Baroque Theater Construction*, Haddenham, Bucks, Bedlow Press, 1982.

Carini Motta, Fabricio, *The Theatrical Writings of Fabrizio Carini Motta*, Orville K. Larson, ed., Carbondale and Edwardsville, Southern Illinois University Press, 1987. (contains trans. of *Trattato sopra la struttura de' Theatri e scene* and *Costruzione de'teatri e machine teatrali*, an unpubl ms. of 1688, copy dated 1773 in the Campori Collection, Biblioteca estense, Modena).

Carpeggiani, Paolo, "Teatri e apparati scenici alla corte dei Gonzaga tra cinque e seicento," *Bollettino del Centro Internazionale di Studi di Architettura Andrea Palladio*, 17, 1975, 101–118.

Cavicchi, Adriano, "Teatro monteverdiano e tradizione teatrale Ferrarese," *Congresso internazionale sul tema Claudio Monteverdi e il suo tempo. Relazioni e comunicazioni*, Raffaello Monterosso, ed., Verona, Stamperia Valdonega, 1969, 139–156.

Cavicchi, Adriano, "Il Teatro Farnese di Parma," *Bolletino del Centro di Studi di Architettura Andrea Palladio*, XVI, 1974, 333–342.

Cavicchi, Adriano, "Appunti sulle tipologie teatrali dell'Aleotti," *Giovanni Battista Aleotti e L'Architettura*, Costanza Cavicchi et al., eds. Reggio Emilia, Diabasis, 2003, 227–242.

Cecchetti, B., "Carte relative ai teatri di San Cassiano e dei santi Giovanni e Paolo," *Archivio Veneto*, XXXIV, 1887, 246.

Chambers, David S., *The Imperial Age of Venice 1380–1580*, London: Thames and Hudson, 1970.

Chambers, David S., "Merit and Money: The Procurators of St. Mark and their *Commissioni*, 1443–1605," *Journal of the Warburg and Courtauld Institutes*, 60, 1997, 23–88.

Chassebras de Cremailles, Jacques de, "Relation des opera representez à Venise pendant le Carnaval de l'année 1683," *Mercure Gallant*, March, 1683, 164–229.

Chastel, André, "Cortile et Théatre," *Le lieu théâtral a la renaissance*, Jean Jacquot, ed., Paris, Éditions du Centre National de la Recherche Scientifique, 1964, 41–48.

Ciancarelli, Roberto, "Il Teatro Farnese e lo spettacolo del 1618: la committenza, l'organizzazione progettuale ed esecutiva, gli intenti programmatici e il testo," *Biblioteca teatrale*, 10, 11, 1974, 122–138.

Ciancarelli, Roberto, *Il progetto di una festa barocca. Alle origini del Teatro Farnese di Parma (1618–1629)*, Rome, Bulzoni, 1987.

Ciapponi, Lucia A., "Fra Giocondo da Verona and His Edition of Vitruvius," *Journal of the Warburg and Courtauld Institutes*, 47, 1984, 72–90.

Coffin, David R., *The Villa d'Este at Tivoli*, Princeton, NJ, Princeton University Press, 1960.

Comici dell'Arte. Corrispondenze (G. B. Andreini, N. Barbieri, P. M. Cecchini, S. Fiorillo, T. Martinelli, F. Scala), edizione diretta da S. Ferrone, a cura di C. Buratelli, D. Landolfi, A. Zinanni, Le Lettere (collana "Storia dello Spettacolo. Fonti"), Firenze, 1993, 2 vols.

Cordaro, Michele, "Le vicende costruttive," in *Palazzo Pubblico di Siena. Vicende costruttive e decorazione*, Cesare Brandi, ed., Siena, Monte dei Paschi di Siena, Milan, Silvana Editoriale, 1983, 29–143.

Coryat, Thomas, *Coryat's Crudities*, 2 vols., Glasgow, James MacLehose and Sons, 1905, reprint of 1611 edition.

Court Cities: The Court Cities of Northern Italy, Milan, Parma, Piacenza, Mantua, Ferrara, Bologna, Urbino, Pesaro and Rimini, Charles M. Rosenberg, ed., Cambridge and New York, Cambridge University Press, 1910.

Cozzi, Gaetano, "Appunti sul teatro e i teatri a Venezia agli inizi del Seicento," *Bollettino dell'Istituto di Storia della Società e dello Stato Veneziano*, I, 1959, 187–192.

Croce, Benedetto, *I teatri di Napoli dal rinascimento alla fine del secolo decimottavo*, a cura di Giuseppe Galasso, Milan, Adelphi Edizioni, 1992.

Cruciani, Fabrizio, *Il Teatro del Campidoglio e le feste romane del 1513, con la ricostruzione architettonica del teatro di Arnaldo Brushi*, Milan: Edizioni Il Polifilo, 1968.

Cruciani, Fabrizio, *Teatro nel Rinascimento: Roma 1450–1550*, Rome, Bulzoni Editore, 1983.

Curran, Brian A., "Teaching (and Thinking about) the High Renaissance: With Some Observations on Its Relationship to Classical Antiquity," in *Rethinking the High Renaissance. The Culture of the Visual Arts*, Jill Burke, ed., Farnam, UK and Burlington, VT, 2012, 27–56.

Dall'Acqua, Marzio, "Il Teatro Farnese di Parma," *Lo Spettacolo e la Meraviglia. Il Teatro Farnese di Parma e la Festa Barocco*, Turin, Nuova ERI, 1992, 17–150; Eng. trans., Richard Kamm, 321–347.

Daly Davis, Margaret, "'Opus isodomu' at the Palazzo della Cancelleria: Vitruvian Studies and Archaeological and Antiquarian Interests at the Court of Raffaele Riario," *Il teatro italiano del Rinascimento*, Maristella de Panizza Lorch, ed., Milan, Edizioni di Comunità, 1980, 442–457.

Damerini, Gino, "Il trapianto dello spettacolo teatrale veneziano del Seicento nell civiltà barocca europea," *Barocco europeo e barocco veneziano*, Vittore Branca, ed., Florence, Sansoni, 1963, 223–240.

D'Amia, Giovanna, "Giovan Battista Aleotti e la storiografia dell'architettura teatrale," *Giovanni Battista Aleotti e L'Architettura*, Costanza Cavicchi et al., eds., Reggio Emilia, Diabasis, 2003, 197–203.

D'Ancona, Alessandro, "Il teatro mantovano," *Giornale storico della letteratura italiana*, 5, 1885, 1–79; 6, 1885, 1–52, 313–351.

D'Ancona, Alessandro, *Origini del teatro italiano*, 2 vols., 2nd ed., Torino, Ermanno Loescher, 1891.

Danesi, Silvia and Luigi Squarzina, "Cultura 'antiquaria' e centralità dell'immagine di Roma nel modello di luogo teatrale dell'Umanesimo," *Il teatro italiano del Rinascimento*, Maristella de Panizza Lorch, ed., Milan, Edizioni di Comunità, 1980, 151–175.

Davis, Robert, "Selling Venice, 1600–1800," *Studi veneziani*, N.S. XLVI, 2003, 131–139.

De Angelis, Pompeo, "Macchine e Allegorie per le Feste Nuziali di Odoardo Farnese e Margherita de' Medici (1628)," *Lo Spettacolo e la Meraviglia. Il Teatro Farnese di Parma e la Festa Barocca*, Turin, Nuova ERI, 1992, 151–220; Eng. trans., Richard Kamm, 348–358.

Decroisette, Françoise, "Florence et ses théâtres (xvii–xviii s.)," *Le théâtre dans la ville: Espaces et lieux urbains theatralisées. Théâtres-monuments et urbanisme. Théâtres de banlieues et de villes nouvelles*, Paris, Éditions CNRS, 1987, 15–45.

De Marchi, Andrea, "Bartolomeo Neroni detto il 'Riccio,'" *Domenico Beccafuni e il suo Tempo*, Milan, Electa, 1990, 366.

D'Evelyn, Margaret Muther, *Venice & Vitruvius: Reading Venice with Daniele Barbaro and Andrea Palladio*, New Haven, CT, and London, Yale University Press, 2012.

Di Luca, Claudia, "Tra sperimentazione e professionismo teatrale; Pio Enea II Obizzi e lo spettacolo nel Seicento," *Teatro e storia, VI*, 2, 1991, 257–303.

Di Luca, Claudia, "Pio Enea II degli Obizzi promotore di spettacoli musicali fra Padova e Ferrara," *Seicento inesplorato: l'evento musicale tra prassi e stile: un modello di interdipendenza. Atti del III Convegno internazionale sulla musica in area lombardo-padana nel secolo XVII*, Alberto Colzani et al., eds., Como, A.M.I.S, 1993, 497–508.

Dizionario biografico degli Italiani, Rome, Istituto della Inciclopedia italiana, 1960–.

Dupuy, Christel, *Le cardinal de Tournon (1489–1562) mécène et humaniste. Un prélat et sa maisonnée dans la Rome du XVIe siècle*, 2 vols., dissertation, Université Lumière Lyon 2, 2008.

Eiche, Sabine, Massimo Frenquellucci, and Maristella Casciato, *La Corte di Pesaro, Storia di una residenza signorile*, Modena, Edizioni Panini, 1986.

Eisler, Colin, *The Genius of Jacopo Bellini, The Complete Paintings and Drawings*, New York, Abrams, 1989.

L'Ermiona del sr. marchese Pio Enea Obizzi: per introduzione d'un torneo à piede, & à cavallo: e d'un balletto rappresentato in musica nella città di Padoua l'anno MDCXXXVI: dedicata al sereniss. o principe di Venetia Francesco Erizo/ descritta dal s. Nicolò Enea Bartolini, gentilhuomo & academ. senese, Padua, Paolo Frambotto, 1638.

Evangelista, Annamaria, "Il teatro dei comici dell'Arte a Firenze ...," *Biblioteca teatrale*, 23–24, 1979, 70–86.

Evangelista, Annamaria, "Il teatro della Commedia dell'Arte a Firenze (1576–1653 circa) ... ," *Quaderni di teatro, II*, 7, 1980a, 169–176.

Evangelista, Annamaria, "Il teatro della Dogana detto di Baldracca," in *La scena del principe*, E. Garbero Zorzi et al., eds., Florence, 1980b, 370–374.

Evangelista, Annamaria, "Le compagnie dei Comici dell'Arte nel teatrino di Baldracca a Firenze ....," *Quaderni di teatro, VI*, 24, 1984, 50–72.

Evangelista, Annamaria, "Teatro di Baldracca," in *I teatri storici della Toscana*. Vol. VIII, *Firenze*, Elvira Garbero Zorzi and Luigi Zangheri, eds, Venice, Marsilio, 2000, 83–87.

Fabbri, Paolo et al., "Il teatro degli Intrepidi di Giovan Battista Aleotti rivive attraverso le nuove techniche dell'acustica virtuale," *Giambattista Aleotti e gli ingegneri del Rinascimento*, Alessandra Fiocca, ed., Florence, Olschki, 1998, 195–205.

Fabbri, Paolo, "Prefazione," *I Teatri di Ferrara. Commedia, Opera e Ballo nel Sei e Settecento*, Paolo Fabbri, ed., Lucca, Libreria Musicale Italiana, 2002, ix–xxxvi.

Fantappiè, Francesca, "Sale per lo spettacolo a Pitti (1600–1650)," *Vivere in Pitti: una reggia dai Medici ai Savoia*, Sergio Bertelli and Renato Pasta, eds., Florence, Olschki, 2003, 135–180.

Fantappiè, Francesca, "'Angelina senese' alias Angela Signorini Nelli. Vita artistica di un'attrice nel Seicento italiano: Dal Don Giovanni ai libertini," *Bolletino senese di storia patria*, CXVI, 2009, 212–267.

Fantappiè, Francesca, "Per teatri non è Bergamo sito." *La società bergamasca e l'organizzazione dei teatri pubblici tra '600 e '700*, Bergamo, Fondazione per la Storia Economica e Sociale di Bergamo, Castelli Bolis Poligrafiche, 2010.

Fara, Amelio, *Bernardo Buontalenti*, Milan, Electa, 1995.

Fargnoli, Narcisa, "Il 'Proscenio' di G. Bolsi (da B. Neroni), *L'arte a Siena sotto I Medici*, Rome, De Luca Editore, 1980, 234–235.

Felisatti, Massimo, *A teatro con gli Estensi*, Ferrara, Corbo, 1999.

Fenlon, Iain, "Monteverdi's Mantuan 'Orfeo': Some New Documentation," *Early Music*, 12, 2, 1984, 163–172.

Ferrari, G. *La scenografia*, Milan, 1902.

Ferrone, Siro, *Attori mercanti corsari La Commedia dell'Arte in Europa tra Cinque e Seicento*, Turin, Einaudi, 1993.

Fleming, Alison C., "Presenting the Spectators as the Show: The Piazza degli Uffizi as Theater and Stage," *Sixteenth Century Journal*, 37, 3, 2006, 701–720.

Fogelberg Rota, Stefano, "Il teatro in Svezia durante il regno di Cristina," in *Letteratura, arte e musica alla corte romana di Cristina di Svezia, Atti del Convegno di studi Lumsa, Roma, 4 novembre 2003*, eds. Rossana Maria Caira and Stefano Fogelberg Rota, Rome, Aracne, 2005, 209–225.

Fontes-Baratto, Ann, "Les fêtes à Urbin en 1513 et la 'Calandria' de Bernardo Dovizi da Bibbiena," *Les écrivains et le pouvoir en Italie à lépoque de la Renaissance*, Paris, Université de la Sorbonne Nouvelle, 3, 1974, 45–79.

Forster, Kurt W., "Metaphors of Rule: Political Ideology and History in the Portraits of Cosimo I de' Medici," *Mitteilungen des Kunsthistorischen Institutes in Florenz*, 15, 1971, 65–104.

Forster, Kurt W., "Stagecraft and Statecraft: The Architectural Integration of Public Life and Spectacle in Scamozzi's Theater in Sabbioneta," *Oppositions*, 9, 1977, 63–87.

Foscari, Antonio, "Ricerche sugli Accesi," *Notizie da Palazzo Albani*, I, 1979a, 6–8.

Foscari, Antonio, "Richerche sugli 'Accesi' e su 'questo benedetto theatro' costruito da Palladio in Venezia nel 1565," *Notizie da Palazzo Albani*, 8, 1979b, 68–83.

Foscari, Antonio, "l'allestimento teatrale del Vasari per i Sempiterni (1542)," in *Architettura e Utopia*, 273–274.

Frabetti Alessandra, "L'Aleotti e il Bentivoglio," *Il Carrobio*, IX, 1984, 198–208.

Frabetti, Alessandra, "Il teatro Farnese e il suo doppio," *Giovanni Battista Aleotti e L'Architettura*, Costanza Cavicchi et al., eds. Reggio Emilia, Diabasis, 2003, 243–252.

Frommel, Christoph Luitpold, *Die Farnesina und Peruzzis Architektonisches Frühwerk*, Berlin, Walter De Gruyter, 1961.

Frommel, Christof Luitpold, *Der Römische Palastbau der Hochrenaissance*, 3 vols., Tübingen, Wasmuth, 1973.

Frommel, Christoph Luitpold, "Raffaele Riario, Committente della Cancelleria," in *Architettura e commitenza da Alberti a Bramante*, Florence, Olschki, 2005, 395–426.

Frommel, Sabine, *Sebastiano Serlio Architect*, trans. Peter Spring, Milan, Electa, 2003 (orig. pub. in German, Milan, Electa, 1988).

Galli, Letizia, "Dal palazzo della Campana al Teatro degli Intronati (1560–1798)," *Storia e restauri del Teatro dei Rinnovati di Siena Dal consiglio della Campana al salone delle commedie*, eds. Laura Vigni and Ettore Vio, Siena, Comune di Siena, Pisa, Pacini Editore, 2010, 159–185.

Gallico, Claudio, "'Le proprie armonie decenti al gran sito': Monteverdi nel gran teatro dei Farnese a Parma," *Lo Spettacolo e la Meraviglia. Il Teatro Farnese di Parma e la Festa Barocco*, Turin, Nuova ERI, 1992, 221–247; Eng. trans., Richard Kamm, 359–364.

Gallo, Alberto, *La prima rappresentazione al Teatro Olimpico. Con I progetti e le relazioni dei contemporanei*, Milan, Il polifilo, 1973.

Gandolfi, Vittorio, *Il Teatro Farnese di Parma*, Parma, L. Battei, 1980.

Garbero Zorzi, Elvira, "Il passaggio a Reggio Emilia di Gaspare Vigarani," *Barocco romano e barocco italiano: Il teatro, l'effimero, l'allegoria*, ed. Marcello Fagiolo and Maria Luisa Madonna, Rome, Gangemi Editore, 1985, 228–233.

Gesuiti (I) e Venezia. Momenti e problemi di storia veneziana della Compagnia di Gesù, Atti del convegno di Studi, Venezia 2–5 ottobre 1990, a cura di Maria Zanardi, Padua, Gregoriana libreria editrice, 1994.

Giacomo Torelli: L'invenzione scenica nell'Europa barocca, Francesco Milesi, ed., Fano, Fondazione Cassa di Risparmio di Fano, 2000.

Giazotto, Remo, "I teatri d'opera veneziani dal 1637 alla Fenice," in *La Fenice*, Milan, Nuove Edizioni di G. de Florentiis, 1972, 14–52.

Giazotto, Remo, "La Guerra dei palchi," *Nuova Rivista Musicale Italiana*, 1, 2, 1967, 245–286; 1, 3, 1967, 465–508; 3, 5, 1969, 906–933; 5, 6, 1971, 1034–1052.

Giorgi, Felice, *Descrizione istorica del Teatro Tor di Nona*, Rome, Cannetti, 1795.

Giovanni Battista Aleotti e L'Architettura, Costanza Cavicchi et al., eds. Reggio Emilia, Diabasis, 2003.

Glixon, Jonathan E. and Beth Glixon, "Marco Faustini and Venetian Opera Production in the 1650s," *Journal of Musicology*, 10, 1992, 48–73.

Glixon, Jonathan E. and Beth Glixon, "Oil and Opera Don't Mix: The Biography of S. Aponal, a Seventeenth-Century Venetian Opera Theater," in *Music in the Theater, Church, and Villa: Essays in Honor of Robert Lamar Weaver and Norma Wright Weaver*, ed. Susan Parisi with collaboration of Ernest Harriss II and Calvin M. Bower, 131–144. Sterling Heights, MI Harmonie Park Press, 2000.

Glixon, Beth L., and Jonathan E. Glixon, *Inventing the Business of Opera. The Impresario and His World in Seventeenth-Century Venice*, Oxford and New York, Oxford University Press, 2006.

Glover, Jane, "The Peak Period of Venetian Public Opera," *Proceedings of the Royal Musical Association*, 102, 1975–76, 67–82.

Gordon, D. J., "Academicians build a theatre and give a play: the Accademia Olimpica, 1579–1585," *Friendship's Garland: esssays presented to Mario Praz on his seventieth birthday*, Vittorio Gabrieli, ed., Rome, Edizioni di storia e letteratura, 1966, 1, 105–138.

Gros, Pierre, *Palladio e l'antico*, Venice, Marsilio Editore, 2006.

Guarino, Raimondo, "Torelli a Venezia: L'ingegniere teatrale tra scena e apparato," *Teatro e storia*, 7, 1992, 35–72.

Gundersheimer, Werner L., *Ferrara: The Style of a Renaissance Despotism*, Princeton, NJ, Princeton University Press, 1973.

Gundersheimer, Werner L., "Popular Spectacle and the Theatre in Renaissance Ferrara," *Il teatro italiano del Rinascimento*, Maristella de Panizza Lorch, ed., Milan, Edizioni di Comunità, 1980, 25–33.

Hammond, Frederick, *Music & Spectacle in Baroque Rome. Barberini Patronage under Urban VIII*, New Haven, CT, and London, Yale University Press, 1994.

Heikamp, Detlef, "Il Teatro Mediceo degli Uffizi," *Bolletino del Centro Internazionale di Studi di Architettura Andrea Palladio*, XVI, 1974, 323–332.

Hellinga, Wytze. Gs., "La représentation de 'Gijsbrecht van Aemstel' de Vondel: Inauguration du Schouwburg d'Amsterdam (1638)," *Le lieu théâtral a la renaissance*, Jean Jacquot, ed., Paris, Éditions du Centre National de la Recherche Scientifique, 1964, 323–346.

Henke, Robert, *Performance and Literature in the Commedia dell'Arte*, Cambridge, Cambridge University Press, 2002.

Hermans, Les, "The Performing Venue: The Visual Play of Italian Courtly Theatres in the Sixteenth Century," in *Theatricality*, 93–103.

Heydenreich, Ludwig H., and Wolfgang Lotz, *Architecture in Italy 1400–1600*, Harmondsworth, Penguin, 1974.

Hipermestra festa teatrale rappresentata dal sereniss. principe cardinale Gio. Carlo di Toscana per celebrare il giorno natalizio del real principe di Spagna, Florence, nella stamperia di S.AS., 1658.

Holberton, Paul, *Palladio's Villas. Life in the Renaissance Countryside*, London, John Murray, 1990.

Howard, Deborah, *The Architectural History of Venice*, London: Batsford, 1980.

Howard, Deborah, and Laura Moretti, *Sound and Space in Renaissance Venice. Architecture, Music, Acoustics*, New Haven, CT, and London, Yale University Press, 2009.

Hunningher, Benjamin. "De Amsterdamse Schouwburg van 1637," *Nederlands Kunsthisorisch Jaarboek*, 9, 1958, 109–171.

Iovino, Roberto., I Mattioni, and G. Tanasini, *I Palcoscenici della lirica: Dal Falcone al Carlo Felice*, Genoa, Sagep Editrice, 1990.

Iovino, Roberto., I. Aliprandi, S. Licciardello, and K. Tocchi, *I Palcoscenici della lirica: cronologia dal Falcone al nuovo Carlo Felice (1645–1992)*, Genoa, Sagep Editrice, 1993.

Ivaldi, A. F., "Gli Adorno e l'Hostaria-Teatro del Falcone a Genova (1600–1680)," *Rivista italiana di musicologia*, 15, 1980, 87–152.

Ivanoff, Nicola, "La Libreria Marciana: Arte e Iconologia," *Saggi e memorie di storia dell'arte*, 6, 1968, 33–78.

Ivanovich, Cristoforo, *Minerva al tavolino*, Venice, 1681.

Ivanovich, Cristoforo, *Memorie teatrali di Venezia*, Norbert Dubowy, ed., Repr. Lucca, Libreria musicale italiana, 1993.

Jacob van Campen, Het klassieke ideaal in de Gouden Eeuw, ex. cat., Architectura & Natura Pers, Amsterdam, 1995, 169–172.

Jacquot, Jean, "Les types de lieu théâtral et leurs transforamtions de la fin du Moyen Age au milieu du XVIIe siècle," *Le lieu théâtral a la renaissance*, Jean Jacquot, ed., Paris, Éditions du Centre National de la Recherche Scientifique, 1964, 473–509.

Jarrard, Alice, *Architecture as Performance in Seventeenth-Century Europe. Court Ritual in Modena, Rome and Paris*, Cambridge, Cambridge University Press, 2003.

Johnson, Eugene J., "Jacopo Sansovino, Giacomo Torelli, and the Theatricality of the Piazzetta in Venice," *Journal of the Society of Architectural Historians*, 59, 4, December, 2000, 436–453.

Johnson, Eugene J., "The Short, Lascivious Lives of Two Venetian Theaters, 1580–1585," *Renaissance Quarterly*, LV, 3, 2002, 936–968.

Johnson, Eugene J., "Portal of Empire and Wealth: Jacopo Sansovino's Entrance to the Venetian Mint," *Art Bulletin*, LXXXVI, 3, September, 2004, 431–458.

Johnson, Eugene J., "The Architecture of Italian Theaters around the Time of William Shakespeare," *Shakespeare Studies*, XXXIII, 2005, 23–52.

Johnson, Eugene J., "Inventing the Opera House in Seventeenth Century Venice," *Art and Music in Venice: from the Renaissance to the Baroque*, ed. Hilliard T. Goldfarb, exh. cat., Montreal Museum of Fine Arts, Paris, Hazan, 2013, 189–194.

Johnson, Eugene J., "The Theater at Lyon of 1548: A Reconstruction and Attribution," *Artibus et Historiae*, 69 (XXX), 2014, 173–202.

Katritzky, M. A., *The Art of Commedia: A Study of the Commedia Dell'Arte 1560–1620*, Amsterdam, Rodopi, 2006.

Kernodle, George Riley, *From Art to Theatre: Form and Convention in the Renaissance*, Chicago, University of Chicago Press, 1944.

Klein, Robert, and Henri Zerner, "Vitruve et le théâtre de la renaissance italienne," *Le lieu théâtral a la renaissance*, Jean Jacquot, ed., Paris, Éditions du Centre National de la Recherche Scientifique, 1964, 49–60.

Knecht, Robert J., *Catherine de' Medici*, London and New York, Longman, 1998.

Krautheimer, Richard, *The Rome of Alesander VII, 1655–1667*, Princeton, NJ, Princeton University Press, 1985.

Kuyper, "Een Maniëristisch Theater van een Barock Architect," *Bulletin van de Koninklijke Nederlandse Oudheidkundige Bond*, 69, 1970, 99–117.

La Calandra, commedia elegantissima per Messer Bernardo Dovizi da Bibbiena, Giorgio Padoan, ed., Padua, Editrice Antenore, 1985.

Lane, Frederic C., *Venice: A Maritime Republic*, Baltmore, Johns Hopkins Univ. Press, 1973.

Larson, Orville K., "Giacomo Torelli, Sir Philip Skippon, and Stage Machinery for the Venetian Opera," *Theater Journal*, 32, 1980, 448–459.

Lavin, Irving, "Lettres de Parmes (1618, 1627–28) et débuts du théâtre Baroque," *Le lieu théâtral a la renaissance*, Jean Jacquot, ed., Paris, Éditions du Centre National de la Recherche Scientifique, 1964, 107–158.

Lavin, Irving, *Bernini and the Unity of the Visual Arts*, 2 vols., New York and London, Oxford University Press, 1980.

Lavin, Irving, "On the Unity of the Arts and the Early Baroque Opera House," *Perspecta*, 26, 1990, 1–20.

Lavin, Irving, "On the Unity of the Arts and the Early Baroque Opera House," *Art and Pageantry in the Renaissance and Baroque*, B. Wisch and S. Scott Munshower, eds., Part 2, State College, Pennsylvania State University Press, 1990, 519–579.

Lawrenson, Thomas E., *The French Stage and Playhouse in the XVIIth Century, A Study in the Advent of the Italian Order*, 2nd ed., New York, AMS Press, 1986.

L'idea di vn prencipe et eroe christiano in Francesco 1. d'Este di Modona, e Reggio duca 8. . . . Composto, e di poi descritto, per ordine della medesima altezza dal p. Domenico Gamberti della Compagnia di Gesù, In Modona: per Bartolomeo Soliani stampator ducale, 1659.

LeClerc, Hélène, *Les origines italiennes de l'architecture théâtrale moderne. L'évolution des formes en Italie de la renaissance a la fin du xvii.e siècle*, Paris, Librairie E. Droz, 1946.

Leclerc, Hélène, *Venise et l'avènement de l'opéra public a l'age baroque*, Paris, Armand Colin, 1987.

Le lieu théâtral a la renaissance, Jean Jacquot, ed., Paris, Éditions du Centre National de la Rechereche Scientifique, 1964.

Lenzi, Deanna, "Teatri e anfiteatri a Bologna nei secoli XVI e XVII," *Barocco romano e barocco italiano: Il teatro, l'effimero, l'allegoria*, ed. Marcello Fagiolo and Maria Luisa Madonna, Rome, Gangemi Editore, 1985, 174–191.

Lessmann, Johanna, *Studien zu einer Baumonographie der Uffizien Giorgio Vasaris in Florenz*, Bonn, Rheinischen Friedrich-Wilhelms-Universität, 1975.

Lessmann, Johanna, "Gli Uffizi: Aspetti di funzione, tipologia e segnificato urbanistico," *Il Vasari storiografo e artista. Atti del congresso internazionale nel iv centenario della morte*, Florence, Istituto nazionale di studi sul Rinascimento, 1976, 233–247.

Licht, Meg, "Elysium: A Prelude to Renaissance Theater," *Renaissance Quarterly*, 49, 1, 1996, 1–29.

Lieberman, Ralph, *Renaissance Architecture in Venice 1450–1540*, New York, Abbeville Press, 1982.

Lieberman, Ralph, "Regarding Michelangelo's Bacchus," *Artibus et Historiae* 43, XXII, 2000, 65–74.

Lieberman, Ralph, "A Scene from the Life of Peruzzi," in *Reading Vasari*, Anne B. Barrriault et al., eds., Athens, Philip Wilson Publishers and Georgia Museum of Art, 2005, 147–153.

Limojon de St. Didier, Alexandre-Toussaint *La ville et la république de Venise*, Amsterdam, Daniel Elsevier, 1680.

Logan, Oliver, *Culture and Society in Venice 1470–1790*, London, Batsford, 1972.

Lombardi, Glauco, "Il Teatro farnesiano di Parma," *Archivio storico per le province parmensi*, n.s. IX, 1909, 1–51.

Lucchesini, Paolo, *I teatri di Firenze*, Rome, Newton Compton editori, 1991.

Luzio, Alessandro, "Federico Gonzaga ostaggio alla corte di Giulio II," *Archivio della R. Società romana di storia patria*, 9, 1886, 509–582.

Luzio, Alessandro, "Isabella d'Este ne' primordi del papato di Leone X e il suo viaggio a Roma nel 1514–1515," *Archivio storico lombardo*, 6, 1906, 99–180, 454–489.

Luzio, Alessandro, *La Galleria dei Gonzaga venduta all'Inghilterra nel 1627–28*, Milan, Cogliati, 1913.

Luzio, Alessandro and R. Renier, "Commedie classiche in Ferrara nel 1499," *Giornale storico della letteratura italiana*, xi, 1888, 177–189.

Luzio, Alessandro and R. Renier, "La coltura e le relazioni letterarie di Isabella d'Este Gonzaga," *Giornale storico della letteratura italiana*, XXXV, 1900, 252–257.

Mabellini, Adolfo, "L'antico teatro della fortuna in Fano," *Stud. Picena*, vii, 1931, 161.

Magagnato, Licisco, *I teatri italiani del cinquecento*, ex. cat., Mantua, Palazzo Ducale, 1980.

Magnuson, Torgil, *Studies in Roman Quattrocento Architecture*, Stockholm, Almqvist & Wiksell, 1958.

Mamone, Sara, *Serenissimi fratelli principi impresari. Notizie di spettacolo nei carteggi medicei*, Florence, Le Lettere, 2003.

Mancini, Franco, Maria Teresa Muraro, and Elena Povoledo, ed., *Illusione e pratica teatrale. Proposte per una lettura dello spazio scenico dagli Intermedi fiorentini all'Opera comica veneziana*, Venice, Neri Pozza Editore, 1975.

Mancini, Franco, Maria Teresa Muraro, and Elena Povoledo, *I Teatri di Venezia*, 2 vols., Venice, Corbo e Fiore, 1995.

Mangini, Nicola, "Per una storia dei teatri veneziani, problemi e pospettive," *Archivio Veneto*, 135, 1973, 197–226.

Mangini, Nicola, *I Teatri di Venezia*, Milan, Mursia, 1974.

Mangini, Nicola, "Il teatro veneto al tempo della contrariforma," in *Luigi Groto e il suo tempo (1541–1585), Atti del convegno di studi, Adria, 27–29 aprile 1984*, Giorgio Brunello and Antonio Lodo, eds., Rovigo, Associazione Culturale Minelliana, 1987, 119–137.

Mangini, Nicola, "Alle origini del teatro moderno: lo spettacolo pubblico nel Veneto tra Cinquecento e Seicento," *Biblioteca Teatrale*, n.s., 5/6, 1987, 87–103. Reprinted in Nicola Mangini, *Alle origini del teatro moderno e altri saggi*, Modena, Mucchi Editore, 1989, 11–31.

Mangini, Nicola, "La situazione teatrale a Padova al tempo di Carlo de' Dottori," *Alle origini del teatro moderno e altri saggi*, Modena, Mucchi editori, 1989, 33–53. Reprinted from *Quaderni Veneti*, 8, 1988, 131–146.

Marani, Ercolano, and Chiara Perina, *Mantova: Le Arti*, Mantua, Istituto Carlo D'Arco, 1965, vol. 3, part 1.

Marchelli, Renzo, "Gli inizi del teatro pubblico italiano e Andrea Sighizzi," *Commentari*, VI, 1955, 117–126.

Mariotti, Andrea, "Il tema della città nell'attività architettonico del Vasari," *Il Vasari storiografo e artista: atti del Congresso internazionale nel IV centenario della morte, Arezzo-Firenze, 2–8 settembre 1974*, Florence, Istituto nazionale di studi sul Rinascimento, 1976, 587–605.

Marotti, Ferruccio, "Gli 'Spectacula' di Pellegrino Prisciano," in idem, *Storia documentario del teatro italiano: lo spettacolo dall'umanesimo al manierismo: teoria e tecnica*, Milan, Feltrinelli, 1974, 53–72.

Masson, Georgina, *Queen Christina*, New York, Farrar, Strauss & Giroux, 1968.

Mazzoni, Stefano, and Ovidio Guaita, *Il teatro di Sabbioneta*, Florence, Olschki, 1985.

Mazzoni, Stefano, *L'Olimpico di Vicenza: un teatro e la sua "perpetua memoria,"* Florence, Le Lettere, 1998.

McManaway, James G., "L'Héritage de la renaissance dans la mise en scène en Angleterre (1642–1700), *Le lieu théâtral a la renaissance*, Jean Jacquot, ed., Paris, Éditions du Centre National de la Recherche Scientifique, 1964, 459–472.

McReynolds, Daniel, *Palladio's Legacy. Architectural Polemics in Eighteenth-Century Venice*, Centro Internazionale di Studi di Architettura Andrea Palladio, Venice, Marsilio, 2011.

Milizia, Francesco, *Trattato completo, formale e materiale del teatro*, Venice, nella stamperia di Pietro Q. Gio. Batt. Pasquali, 1794. Reprint Bologna, Forni, 1969.

Miller, Naomi, *Renaissance Bologna: A Study in Architectural Form and Content*, University of Kansas Humanistic Studies, New York, Bern, Frankfurt am Main, Paris, Peter Lang, 1989, vol. 56.

Minieri Ricci, Camillo, *Memorie storiche degli scrittori nati nel Regno di Napoli*, Naples, Tipografia dell'Aquila di V. Puzziello, 1844.

Minor, Andrew C., and Bonner Mitchell, *A Renaissance Entertainment. Festivities for the Marriage of Cosimo I, Duke of Florence, in 1539*, Columbia, University of Missouri Press, 1968.

Mitchell, Bonner, "Les Intermèdes au service de l'État," *Les Fêtes de la Renaissance*, Paris, Éditions du Centre de la Recherche Scientifique, 1975, vol. III, 117–131.

Mitchell, Bonner, "Firenze Illustrissima: l'immagine della patria negli apparati delle nazioni fiorentine per le feste di Lione del 1548 e di Anversa del 1549," *Firenze e la Toscana dei Medici nell'Europa del '500, Relazioni artistiche; il linguaggio architettonico*, Florence, Olschki, 1983, vol. III, 995–1004.

Mitchell, Bonner, *1598. A Year of Pageantry in Late Renaissance Ferrara*, Medieval & Renaissance Texts and Studies, Binghamton, NY, 1990.

Molinari, Cesare, "Les rapports entre la scène et les spectateurs dan le théâtre italien du XVIe siècle," *Le lieu théâtral a la renaissance*, Jean Jacquot, ed., Paris, Éditions du Centre National de la Recherche Scientifique, 1964, 61–71.

Molinari, Cesare, "Gli spettatori e lo spazio scenico nel teatro del Cinquecento," *Bolletino del Centro Internazionale di Studi di Architettura Andrea Palladio*, XVI, 1974, 145–154.

Molinari, Cesare, *La Commedia dell'Arte*, Milan, Mondadori, 1985.

Molmenti, Pompeo, "Le prime rappresentazioni teatrali a Venezia," *La rassegna Nazionale*, Anno XXVIII, CL, August 1, 1906, 424–439.

Molmenti, Pompeo, *Curiosità di storia veneziana*, Bologna, Zanichelli, 1920.

Molmenti, Pompeo, *La Storia di Venezia nella vita privata dalle origini alla caduta della repubblica*, 3 vols., 7th ed., Bergamo, Istituto italiano d'arti grafiche, 1927–1929. Reprint Trieste, 1981.

Monaldini, Sergio, "La montagna fulminata: Giostre e tornei a Bologna nel Seicento," *Musica in torneo nell'Italia del Seicento*, Paolo Fabbri, ed., Lucca, Libreria Musicale Italiana, 1999, 103–133.

Monaldini, Sergio, "I teatri della commedia dell'arte. Le prime sale, il teatro della Sala Grande, l'ex Cappella Ducale," *I Teatri di Ferrara. Commedia, Opera e Ballo nel Sei e Settecento*, Paolo Fabbri, ed., Lucca, Libreria Musicale Italiana, 2002, 3–218.

Morelli, Giovanni, and Thomas Walker, "Tre controversie intorno al San Cassiano," *Venezia e il melodramma nel Seicento*, Maria Teresa Muraro, ed., Florence, Olschki, 1994, 97–120.

Morini, Ugo, *La R. Accdemia degli Immobili ed il suo Teatro "La Pergola" (1649–1925)*, Pisa, Tipografia Ferdinando Simoncini, 1926.

Moronato, Stefania, "La collezione di tessuti Michelangelo Guggenheim," in *Una Città e il suo Museo, un secolo e mezzo di collezioni civiche veneziane*, Museo Correr Venezia, in *Bolletino Civici Musei Veneziani d'Arte e di Storia*, XXX, 1–4, 1986, 205–212.

Muir, Edward, *Civic Ritual in Renaissance Venice*, Princeton, NJ, Princeton University Press, 1981.

Muir, Edward, "Manifestazioni e ceremonie nella Venezia di Andrea Gritti," *"Renovatio Urbis" Venezia nell'età di Andrea Gritti (1523–1538)*, Manfredo Tafuri, ed., Rome, Officina Edizioni, 1984, 59–77.

Mullin, Donald C., *The Development of the Playhouse: A Survey of Theater Architecture from the Renaissance to the Present*, Berkeley, University of California Press, 1970.

Muraro, Maria Teresa, "Le lieu des spectacles (publics ou privés) a Venise au XVe et au XVIe siècles," *Le lieu théâtral a la renaissance*, Jean Jacquot, ed., Paris, Éditions du Centre National de la Recherche Scientifique, 1964, 85–93.

Muraro, Maria Teresa, "Il teatro Grimani a San Giovanni Grisostomo," *Biblioteca teatrale*, 5–6, 1987, 105–113.

Nagel, Alexander, and Christopher S. Wood, *Anachhronic Renaissance*, Cambridge, MA, MIT Press, 2010.

Nagler, A. M., *Theatre Festicals of the Medici 1539–1637*, New Haven, CT, and London, Yale University Press, 1964.

Nagler, A. M., "The Commedia Drawings of the Corsini Scenari," *Maske und Kothurn*, 15, 1969, 6–10, Pl. I–IV.

Neiiendam, Klaus, "Le théâtre de la Renaissance à Rome," *Analecta Romana Instituti Danici*, V, 1969, 103–197.

Newbigin, Nerida, "Politics and Comedy in the Early Years of the Accademia degli Intronati of Siena," *Il teatro italiano del Rinascimento*, Maristella de Panizza Lorch, ed., Milan, Edizioni di Comunità, 1980, 123–133.

Norwich, John Julius, *A History of Venice*, London, 1983.

Nocca, Marco, "'Theatrum novum tota urbs magnis votis expectat': il teatro della Passione di Velletri, Antonio da Faenza architetto antiquario e Raffaele Riario," *Roma, centro ideale della cultura dell'Antico nei secoli XV e XVI, Da Martino V al Sacco di Roma 1417–1527*, Silvia Danesi Squarzina, ed., Milan, Electa, 1989, 291–302.

Olivato, Loredana, "Il luogo del teatro palladiano per gli 'Accesi,' *Palladio e Venezia*, 1982, 95–102.

Orgel, Stephen, *The Illusion of Power: Political Theater in the English Renaissance*, Berkeley, Los Angeles, and London, University of California Press, 1975.

Ovid, *The Art of Love and Other Poems*, with an English translation by J. H. Mozley, London, William Heinemann, Cambridge, MA, Harvard University Press, 1969.

Pacifici, Vincenzo, *Ippolito II d'Este Cardinale di Ferrara*, Tivoli, Società di Storia e d'Arte in Villa d'Este, 1920.

Padoan, Giorgio, *Bernardo Dovizi da Bibbiena, Calandria*, Bibbiena, Comitato per le onoranze al cardinal Bibbiena nel quinto centenario della nascita, 1970.

Padoan, Giorgio, *La commedia rinascimentale veneta (1433–1565)*, Vicenza, Neri Pozza, 1982.

Padoan Urban, Lina, "Teatri e 'teatri del mondo' nella Venezia del cinquecento," *Arte Veneta*, XX, 1966, 137–146.

Padoan Urban, Lina, "Feste ufficiali e trattenimenti privati," in *Storia della Cultura Veneta, Dalla Controriforma all fine della Repubblica*, 4/1, Vicenza, Neri Pozza Editore, 1983, 575–600.

Palladio, Guido Beltramini and Howard Burns, eds., London, Royal Academy of Arts, 2008.

Pallen, Thomas A., "Decking the Hall. Italian Renaissance Extension of Performance Motifs into Audience Space," *Theater Symposium*, 4, University of Alabama Press, Tuscaloosa, 1996, 91–100.

Paper Palaces: The Rise of the Renaissance Architectural Treatise, Vaughan Hart and Peter Hicks, eds., New Haven, CT, Yale University Press, 1998.

Pastor, Ludwig Freiherr von, *The History of the Popes*, Ralph Francis Kerr, trans. and ed., XIII, Julius III, London, Kegan, Paul, Trench Trubner, 1924.

Patin, Charles, *Le pompose feste di Vicenza fatte nel mese di giugno 1680*, Padua, Pasquati, 1680.

Payne, Alina, *The Architectural Treatise in the Italian Renaissance: Architectural Invention, Ornament, and Literary Culture*, Cambridge and New York, Cambridge University Press, 1999.

Petrarca, Francesco, *Letters from Petrarch, Selected and Translated by Morris Bishop*, Bloomington and London, Indiana University Press, 1966.

Petrobelli, Pierluigi, "L'ermiona di Pio Enea degli Obizzi ed i primi spettacoli d'opera veneziani," *Quaderni della Rassegna musicale*, 3, 1965, 125–141.

Pieri, Marzia, *La nascita del teatro moderno in Italia tra XV e XVI secolo*, Turin, Bollari Boringhieri, 1989.

Pigozzi, Marinella, "Il 'Cromuele' di Girolamo Graziani e Prospero Manzini," *Barocco romano e barocco italiano: Il teatro, l'effimero, l'allegoria*, Marcello Fagiolo and Maria Luisa Madonna, eds., Rome, Gangemi Editore, 1985, 192–203.

Pinelli, Antonio, *I teatri. lo spazio dello spettacolo dal teatro umanistico al teatro dell'opera*, Florence, Sansoni, 1973.

Pintor, Fortunato, *Rappresentazioni romane di Seneca e Plauto nel rinascimento*, Perugia, Unione tipografica cooperativa, 1906.

Pirrotta, Nino, "*Commedia dell' arte* and Opera," *Musical Quarterly*, vol. 41, part 3, 1955, 305–324.

Pirotta, Nino, "Teatro, scene e musica nelle opere di Monteverdi," *Congresso internazionale sul tema Claudio Monteverdi e il suo tempo. Relazioni e comunicazioni*, Raffaello Monterosso, ed., Verona, Stamperia Valdonega, 1969, 45–67.

Pirotta, Nino, "Il luogo dell'orchestra," in Mancini et al., 1975, 137–143.

Pirotta, Nino, and Elena Povoledo, *Music and Theater from Poliziano to Monteverdi*, Cambridge and New York, Cambridge University Press, 1982, translation of idem, *I due Orfei*.

Pochat, Götz, *Theater und bildende Kunst im Mittelalter und in der Renaissance in Italien*, Graz, Akademische Druck-und-Verlagsanstalt, 1990.

Povoledo, Elena, "Lo Schioppi Viniziano, pittor di teatro," *Prospettive*, 16, 1957, 45–50.

Povoledo, Elena, "Le théâtre de tournoi en Italie pendant la renaissance," *Le lieu théâtral a la renaissance*, Jean Jacquot, ed., Paris, Éditions du Centre National de la Recherche Scientifique, 1964a, 95–106.

Povoledo, Elena, "Scenografia," Encyclopedia dello spettacolo, Venice and Rome, Istituto per la collaborazione culturale, 1964b.

Povoledo, Elena, "La sala teatrale a Ferrara: da Pellegrino Prisciani a Ludovico Ariosto," *Bolletino del Centro Internazionale di Studi di Architettura Andrea Palladio*, XVI, 1974, 105–138.

Povoledo, Elena, "I comici professionisti e la commedia dell'arte: caratteri, techniche, fortuna," *Storia della Cultura Veneta. Dalla Contrariforma alla fine della Repubblica*, vol. 4, part 1, Girolamo Arnaldi and Manlio Pastore Stocchi, eds., Vicenza, Neri Pozza Editore, 1983, 381–408.

Povoledo, Elena, "Aspetti dell'allestimento scenico a Roma al tempo di Christina di Svezia," *Christina di Svezia e la Musica*, Rome, Accademia Nazionale dei Lincei, 1998, 169–215.

Prisciano, Pellegrino, *Spectacula*, in Marotti, *Storia documentario del teatro italiano: lo spettacolo dall'umanesimo al manierismo: teoria e tecnica*, Milan, Feltrinelli, 1974, 53–72.

Prota-Giurleo, Ulisse, *I Teatri di Napoli nel secolo XVII*, 3 vols., Naples, Il Quartiere, 2002. Reprint Naples, F. Fiorentino, 1962.

Puppi, Lionello, "La prima rappresentazione inaugurale dell'Olimpico," *Critica d'arte*, 1962, 51, 57–64.

Puppi, Lionello, "Le esperienze scenografiche palladiane prima dell'Olimpico," *Bolletino del Centro di Studi di Architettura Andrea Palladio*, XVI, 1974, 287–307.

Purkis, Helen, "La décoration de la salle et les rapports entre la scène et le public dans les mascarades et les intermèdes florentins, 1539–1608," *Les Fêtes de la Renaissance*, III, Jean Jacquot and Elie Konigson, eds., Paris,

Éditions du Centre National de la Recherche Scientifique, 1975, 239–251.

Quinlan-McGrath, Mary, "A Proposal for the Foundation Date of the Villa Farnesina," *Journal of the Warbug and Courtauld Institutes*, 49, 1986, 245–250.

Quinlan-McGrath, Mary, "Aegidius Gallus, *De Viridario Augustini Chigii Vera Libellus*. Introduction, Latin Text and English Translation," *Humanistica Lovaniensia*, 38, 1989, 1–99.

Quinlan-McGrath, Mary, "Blosius Palladius, *Suburbanum Augustini Chisii*. Introduction, Latin Text and English Translation," *Humanistia Lovaniensia*, 39, 1990, 93–156.

Rabb, Theodore K., "Politics and the Arts in the Age of Christina," *Politics and Culture in the Age of Christina. Acta from a conference held at the Wenner-Gren Center in Stockholm, May 4–6, 1995*, Marie-Louise Rodén, ed., Stockholm, Suecoromana IV, 1997, 9–22.

Radcliff-Umstead, Douglas, *The Birth of Modern Comedy in Renaissance Italy*, Chicago and London, University of Chicago Press, 1969.

Rava, Arnaldo, *I teatri di Roma*, Rome, Fratelli Palombi Editori, 1953.

Reggio Emilia. Teatro Municipale, *Teatri storici in Emilia Romagna*, Simonetta M. Bondoni, ed., Bologna, Istituto per i beni culturali della Regione Emilia-Romagna, 1982.

Reiner, Stuart, "Preparations in Parma 1618: 1627–1628," *The Music Review*, 25, 1964, 273–300.

Ricci, Corrado, *I Teatri di Bologna nei secoli XVII e XVIII. Storia anecdotica*, Bologna, Arnaldo Forni Editore, 1888.

Ricci, Giuliana, *Teatri d'Italia dalla Magna Grecia all'Ottocento*, Milan, Bramante Editrice, 1971.

Robinson, Michael F., *Naples and Neapolitan Opera*, Oxford, Clarendon Press, 1972.

Roma, centro ideale della cultura dell'Antico nei secoli XV e XVI. Da Martino V al Sacco di Roma 1417–1527, Silvia Danesi Squarzina, ed., Milan, Electa, 1989.

Roma Splendidissima e Magnifica. Luoghi di spettacolo a Roma dall'umanesimo ad oggi, ex. cat., Milan, Electa, 1997.

Romanelli, Giandomenico, "La Libreria Marciana: Il progetto di Sansovino e lo scalone," *Da Tiziano a el Greco: Per la storia del Maniereismo a Venezia, 1540–1590*, Milan, Electa, 1981, 277–284.

Ronconi, Luca, *Lo spettacolo e la meravigali: Il Teatro Farnese di Parma e la festa barocca*, Turin, Nuova Eri, 1992.

Rosand, David, "Venezia e gli dei," *"Renovatio Urbis": Venezia nell'età di Andrea Gritti (1523–1538)*, Manfredo Tafuri, ed., Rome, Rome Officina Edizioni, 1984, 201–215.

Rosand, Ellen, *Opera in Seventeeth-Century Venice: The Creation of a Genre*, Berkeley, University of California Press, 1991.

Rosenberg, Charles M., "The Use of Celebrations in Public and Semi-Public Affairs in Fifteenth Century Ferrara," *Il teatro italiano del Rinascimento*, Maristella de Panizza Lorch, ed., Milan, Edizioni di Comunità, 1980, 521–535.

Rossi di Gerardo, Giovanni, *Storia delle leggi e de' costumi de Veneziani*, ms. Biblioteca Marciana, cl. 7, no. 1396.

Rotondi, Pasquale, *The Ducal Palace of Urbino: Its Architecture and Decoration*, New York, Translatlantic Arts, 1969.

Rotondi, Sergio, *Il Teatro Tordinona. Storia, progetti, archittetura*, Rome, Edizioni Kappa, 1987.

Rotondò, Antonio, "Pellegrino Prisciani," *Rinascimento*, xi, 1960, 69–110.

Rowland, Ingrid D., "Render unto Caesar the Things Which Are Caesar's: Humanism and the Arts in the Patronage of Agostino Chigi," *Renaissance Quarterly* 39, 1986, 673–730.

Rowland, Ingrid D., *The Roman Garden of Agostino Chigi*, Groningen, The Gerson Lectures Foundation, 2005.

Rowland, Ingrid D., "The Fra Giocondo Vitruvius at 500 (1511–2011)," *Journal of the Society of Architectural Historians*, 70, 3, 2011, 285–289.

Ruffini, Franco, "Analisi contestuale della 'Calandria' nella rappresentazione urbinate del 1513: 1. Il luogo teatrale," *Biblioteca teatrale*, 15/16, 1976, 70–139.

Ruffini, Franco, *Commedia e festa nel Rinascimento: la "Calandria" alla corte di Urbino*, Bologna, Il Mulino, 1986.

Sabbadini, Remigio, *Le scoperte dei codici latini e greci ne' secoli XIV e XV*, 2 vols., Florence, Sansoni, 1905 and 1914.

Sabbattini, Nicola, *Pratica de Fabricar scene e machine ne'teatri*, 2nd ed., Ravenna, 1638, Willi Flemming, ed. and trans., Weimar, Gesellschaft der Bibliophilen, 1926.

Salvioli, Livio Niso, *I teatri musicali di Venezia nel secolo XVI (1637–1700): memorie storiche e bibliografche*, Milan, Ricordi, 1878. I .

Sansovino, Francesco, *Venetia città nobilissima et singolare*, Venice, 1581. With additions by Giovanni Stringa, Venice, 1604. With additions by Giustiniano Martinioni, Venice, 1663. Reprint with an analytical index by Lino Moretti, Venice, Fillipi Editore, 1968.

Sanudo, Marino, *I diarii* (1496–1533), vols. 1–59, ed. R. Fulin, F. Stefani, N. Barozzi, and M. Allegri. Venice, Visentini, 1879–1903.

Sartori, Claudio, "Ancora della 'Finta Pazza' di Strozzi e Sacrati," *Nuova Rivista Musicale Italiana*, 11, 1977, 335–338.

Saslow, James M., *The Medici Wedding of 1589: Florentine Festival as Theatrum Mundi*, New Haven, CT, and London, Yale University Press, 1996.

Satkowski, Leon, *Giorgio Vasari, Architect and Courtier*, Princeton, NJ, Princeton University Press, 1993.

Savoy, Daniel, *Venice from the Water*, New Haven, CT, and London, Yale University Press, 2012.

Scève. *Maurice Scève, The Entry of Henri II into Lyon: September 1548*, facsimile with an intro. by Richard Cooper, Tempe, Arizona, Medieval and Renaissance Texts and Studies, 1997.

Schöne, Günter, "Les fêtes de la renaissance a la cour de Bavière," *Le lieu théâtral a la renaissance*, Jean Jacquot, ed., Paris, Éditions du Centre National de la Recherche Scientifique, 1964, 171–183.

Schrade, Leo, *La représentation d'Edipo Tiranno au Teatro Olimpico, Vicence 1585*, Paris, Centre National de la Recerche Scientifique, 1960.

Schulz, Juergen, "Vasari at Venice," *Burllngton Magazine*, CIII, 705, December, 1961, 500–511.

Scoglio, Egidio, *Il teatro alla corte Estense*, Lodi, Biancardi, 1965.

Scritti in onore di Nicola Mangini, Carmelo Alberti and Giovanni Morelli, eds., Rome, Viella, 1994.

Serassi, Pierantonio, *Lettere del Conte Baldessar Castiglione ora per la prima volta date in luce e con Annotazioni Storiche illustrate*, 2 vols., Padua, presso Giuseppe Comino, 1769.

Serlio, *Sebastiano Serlio on Architecture*, trans. with intro. and commentary by Vaughan Hart and Peter Hicks, New Haven, CT, and London, Yale University Press, 1996.

Sforza, Giovanni, *F. M. Fiorentini ed i suoi contemporanei lucchesi. Saggio di storia letteraria del secolo XVII*, Florence, F. Menozzi e comp., 1879.

Simonsohn, Shlomo, *History of the jews in the duchy of Mantua*, Jerusalem, Kiriath-Sefer, 1977 (trans. of Hebrew edition of 1962–64).

Sinisgalli, Rocco, *Storia Della Scena Prospettica Dal Rinascimento Al Barocco*, Florence, Cadmo, 2000. (English version: *A History of the Perspective Scene from the Renaissance to the Baroque: Borromini in Four Dimensions*, postscript by Paolo Portoghesi, Florence, Cadmo, 2000)

Skipon, Philip, *An account of a journey made through the Low Countries, Germany, Italy, France*, London, 1745.

Solerti, Angelo, "Le rappresentazioni musicali di Venezia dal 1571 al 1605, per la prima volta descritta," *Rivista musicale italiana*, 9, 1902, 503–558.

Solerti, Angelo, and Domenico Lanza, "Il teatro Ferrarese nella seconda metà del secolo XVI," *Giornale storico della letteratura italiana*, XVIII, 1891, 148–185.

Sommi, Leone de', *Quattro dialoghi in materia di rappresentazioni sceniche*, Ferruccio Marotti, ed., Milan, Il Polifilo, 1968.

Staffieri, Gloria, "'La reine s'amuse': L'*Alcasta* di Apolloni e pasquini al Tordinona (1673)," *Cristina di Svezia e la musica*, Rome, Accademia Nazionale dei Lincei, 1998, 21–43.

Stevens, Denis, *The letters of Claudio Monteverdi*, Oxford, Clarendon Press, New York, Oxford University Press, 1995.

Stinger, Charles L., "The Campidoglio as the Locus of *Renovatio Imperii* in Renaissance Rome," *Art and Politics in Medieval and Early Renaissance Italy: 1250–1500*, Charles M. Rosenberg, ed., Notre Dame and London, University of Notre Dame Press,1990, 135–156.

Storia dell'opera italiana, Lorenzo Bianconi and Giorgio Pestelli, ed., Part II, vol. 4, *I sistemi*, Turin, E. D. T. Edizioni, 1987, part II, vol. 5, *la spettacolarità*, Turin, E. D. T. Edizioni, 1988.

Storia di Venezia, dalle origini alla caduta della Serenissima, VI, Dal Rinascimento al Barocco, ed. Gaetano Cozzi e Paolo Prodi, Rome, Isituto della Enciclopedia Italiana, 1994.

Tamassia Mazzarotto, Bianca, *Le feste Veneziane*, Florence, Sansoni, 1961.

Tamburini, Elena, *Due Teatri per il Principe. Studi sulla committenza teatrale di Lorenzo Onofrio Colonna (1659–1689)*, Rome, Bulzoni, 1997.

Tavassi La Greca, Bianca, "Alcuni problemi inerenti l'attività teorica di Carlo Fontana," Storia dell'arte, 29, 1977, 39–59.

Tavassi La Greca, Bianca, "Carlo Fontana e il Teatro di Tor di Nona," *Il Teatro a Roma nel Settecento*, Rome, Istituto della Enciclopedia Italiana, 1989, vol. I, 19–34.

Taviani, Ferdinando, *La Commedia dell'arte e la società barocca. La fascinazione del teatro*, Rome, Mario Bulzoni Editore, 1969.

Teatri e scenografie, intro. di Luigi Squarzina, saggio storico-critico di Manfredo Tafuri, Milan, Touring Club Italiano, 1976.

Teatri (I) di Parma 'dal Farnese al Regio', Ivo Allodi, ed., Milan, Nuove Edizioni, 1969.

Il teatro italiano del Rinascimento, Maristella de Panizza Lorch, ed., Milan, Edizioni di Comunità, 1980.

Teatri pubblici. I teatri pubblici di Venezia (secoli XVII-XVIII), Ludovico Zorzi, Maria Teresa Muraro, Gianfranco Prato, and Elvi Zorzi, eds., ex. cat., Venice, La Benennale di Venezia, 1971.

Teatro della Scala in Milano, Architettura del regio professore Giuseppe Piermarini, unpaginated, Rome, Calcografia camerale, 1836 (reprint, Perugia, Volumnia Editrice, 1970).

Teatro e spettacolo nella Firenze dei Medici. Modelli dei luoghi teatrali, ex. cat., Elvira Garbero Zorzi and Mario Sperenzi, eds., Florence, Olschki, 2001.

Teatro (Il) italiano del Rinascimento, Maristella de Panizza Lorch, ed., Milan, Edizioni di Comunità, 1980.

Temanza, Tommaso, *Vita di Andrea Palladio Vicentino*, Venice, Pasquali, 1772.

Temanza, Tommaso, *Vite dei più celebri architetti, e scultori veneziani che fiorirono nel Secolo Decimosesto*, Venice, C. Palese, 1778.

Tenenti, Alberto., "L'uso scenografico degli spazi pubblici: 1490–1580," *Tiziano e Venezia: convegno internazionale di studi, Venezia, 1976*, Vicenza, Neri Pozza, 1980, 21–26.

Testaverde Matteini, Annamaria, *L'officina delle nuvole: il Teatro mediceo nel 1589 e gli 'Intermedi' del Buontalenti nel 'Memoriale' di Girolamo Seriacopi*, Milan, Amici della Scala, 1991.

Terzaghi, Antonio, "Piani originali del Vignola per il palazzo Farnese di Piacenza," *Arte antica e moderna*, 1958, 4, 375–387, figs. 145–150.

The Mask, 1923. "The Theatre of Sabbbioneta. Some notes translated from old Italian writers," The Mask, 9, 1923, 24–25.

The Mask, 1927. "An Astounding Discovery made by a Subscriber to the "The Mask," Mask, 12 bis, No. 3, July-August-September, 1927, p. 87–88, pl. 12; 12 bis. no. 4, October-November-December, 1927, 133–147, "Some Freshly Discovered Theatre Plans. Now Brought for the First Time to the Service of the Student and the Historian."

The Mask, 1927. *Theatricality in Early Modern Art and Architecture*, Caroline van Eck and Stijn Bussels, eds., Malden, MA, and Oxford, UK, Wiley-Blackwell, 2011, 93–103.

Thoenes, Christof, "Vignola e il Teatro Farnese a Piacenza," *Bolletino del Centro di Studi di Architettura Andrea Palladio*, XVI, 1974, 243–256.

Thoenes, Christof, "Serlio e la trattatistica," *Sebastiano Serlio: Sesto Seminario internazionale di storia dell'architettura, Vicenza, 31 agosto-4 settembre 1987*, Christof Thoenes, ed., Milan, Electa, 1989, 9–18.

Thompson, David, ed., *Les Plus Excellents Bastiments de France par J.-A. du Cerceau*, Paris, Sand & Conti, 1988.

Tieri, Guglielmina Verardo, "Il Teatro Novissimo. Storia di 'mutazioni, macchine e musiche,'" *Nuova Rivista Musicale Italiana*, 10, 4, ott./dic, 1976, 555–595; 11, 1, gen/mar, 1977, 3–25.

Tintelnot, Hans, *Barocktheater und Barocke Kunst, Die Entwicklungsgeschichte der Fest-und- Theater-Dekoration in Ihrem Verhältnis zur Barocken Kunst*, Berlin, Gebrüder Mann, 1939.

Tomani-Amiani, Stefano. *Del teatro antico della fortuna in Fano*, Sanseverino-Marche, tipografia sociale C. Corradetti, 1867.

Toschi, Paolo, *Le origini del teatro italiano*, Turin, Einaudi, 1955.

Tuohy, Thomas, *Herculean Ferrara. Ercole D'Este, 1471–1505, and the Invention of a Ducal Capital*, Cambridge, Cambridge University Press, 1996.

Vänje, Stig, "Queen Christina and the Vitruvian Theatre," *Queen Christina of Sweden: Documents and Studies*, Magnus von Platen, ed., Stockholm, Kungl. Boktryckeriet P. A. Norstedt & Söner, 1966, 376–389.

Vasari, Giorgio, *Le vite dei più eccelenti pittori, scultori ed architettori*, Gaetano Milanesi, ed., 9 vol., Florence, Sansoni, 1878–1885.

Venezia e il melodramma nel Seicento, Maria Teresa Muraro, ed., Florence, Olschki, 1976.

Venturi, Lionello, "Le compagnie della Calza (sec. XV-XVII)," *Nuovo Archivio Veneto*, n.s. XVI, II, 1908, 161–221, and XVII, I, 1909, 140–233.

Verdone, Mario, "Lo spettacolo taurino in Italia," *Storia dell'Arte*, 38–40, 1980, 457–469.

Vincenzo Scamozzi 1548–1616, Franco Barbieri and Guido Beltramini, eds., ex. cat., Venice, Marsilio, Centro Internazionale di Studi di Architettura Andrea Palladio, 2004.

Vitruvius Pollio, *De architectura liber primus[-decimus]*, Joannes Sulpitius Verulanus, ed., Rome, Eucharius Silber, n.d., 1488(?).

Vitruvius, 1511. *M. Vitruvius per Iocundum solito castigatior factus cum figuris et tabula ut iam legi et intelligi possit*, Venice, Joannis de Tridino alias Tacuino, M.D.X.I [1511]

Vitruvio, *De Architectura traslato commentato et affigurato da Cesare Caesariano, 1521*, reprint, A. Bruschi, A. Carugo, and F. P. Fiore, eds., Milan, Il Polifilo, 1981.

Vitruvio, *I Dieci Libri dell'Architettura, tradotti e commentati da Daniele Barbaro 1567*, essays by Manfredo Tafuri and Manuela Morresi, Milan, Edizioni Il Polifilo, 1997.

Vitruvius, 2003. *Vitruvius Ten Books on Architecture. The Corsini Incunabulum with the annotations and autograph drawings of Giovanni Battista da Sangallo*, Ingrid D. Rowland, ed., Rome, Edizioni dell'Elefante, 2003.

Vitruvius, *On Architecture*, tr. Richard Schofield, intro. Robert Tavernor, London, Penguin Classics, 2009.

Volpicelli, Maria Letizia, "Il Teatro del cardinale Ottoboni al Palazzo della Cancelleria," *Il Teatro a Roma nel Settecento*, Rome, Istituto della Enciclopedia Italiana, 1989, vol. II, 681–782.

Walker, Thomas, "'Gli Sforzi del Desiderio': Cronaca Ferrarese, 1652," *Studi in onore di Lanfranco Caretti*, Modena, Mucchi, 1987, 45–75.

Walker, Thomas, "Echi estensi negli spettacoli musicali a Ferrara nel primo Seicento," *La corte di Ferrara e il suo mecenatismo 1441–1598: The Court of Ferrra and Its Patronage: atti del convegno internazionale Copenhagen maggio 1987*, Marianne Pade et al., eds., Modena, Pannini, 1990, 337–351.

Warwick, Genevieve, *Bernini: Art as Theatre*, New Haven, CT, and London, Yale University Press, 2012.

Weil, Mark S., "The Devotion of the Forty Hours and Roman Baroque Illusions," *Journal of the Warburg and Courtauld Institutes*, 37, 1974, 218–248.

Weil, Mark S., *Baroque Theatre and Stage Design*, ex. cat., St. Louis, Washington University, 1983.

Weil, Mark S., "The Relationship of the Cornaro Chapel to Mystery Plays and Italian Court Theater," *Papers in Art History from Pennsylvania State University*, Barbara Wisch and Susan Scott, eds., VI, 2, 1990, 459–484.

Westfall, Carroll William, *In This Most Perfect Paradise: Alberti, Nicholas V, and the Invention of Conscious Urban Planning in Rome, 1447–55*, University Park, Pennsylvania State University Press, 1974.

Wiehl, T., "Catalogo delle opere in musica rappresentate nel scolo XVIII in Venezia," *Nuovo Archivio Veneto*, Anno VII, XIV, 1897, 259–345.

Worsthorne, Simon Towneley, *Venetian Opera in the Seventeenth Century*, Oxford, Clarendon Press, 1954.

Ziosi, Roberta, "Il Teatro di San Lorenzo," *I Teatri di Ferrara. Commedia, Opera e Ballo nel Sei e Settecento*, Paolo Fabbri, ed., Lucca, Libreria Musicale Italiana, 2002, 221–280.

Zorzi, Giangiorgio, *Le ville e i teatri di Andrea Palladio*, Vicenza, Neri Pozza, 1969.

Zorzi, Ludovico, *La scena e il Principe. Il luogo teatrale a Firenze*, Milan, Electa, 1975.

Zorzi, Ludovico, *Il teatro e la città*, Torino, Einaudi editore, 1977.

INDEX

Accademia degli Immobili, 238
Accademia degli Intrepidi, 173
Accademia degli Intronati, 244
Accademia dei Riaccesi, 230
Accademia Olimpica, 131–32
    respectability of, 139–40
    statues of, 140–41, 144
    theater commissioned by, 139
Acciaioli, Filippo, 261–62
    proscenium approved by, 264
Achilles, 217
acoustics, 174, 212, 281–82
Adelcrantz, Carl Frederik, 264–65
Adelphi (Terence), 50–51
admission, of audiences, 45
Adria, 75
Alberti, Leon Battista, 21, 80–82, 282
    on ancient theaters, 280
    Sant' Andrea, Mantua, 81
Aldobrandini, Margherita, 200
Aleotti, Giovan Battista, 89–90, 178, 180, 191
    proscenium by, 174, 178, 187–98
    role of, 297
    theater designed by, 173
Alexander VII Chigi (pope), 254, 256, 259
The Amazon of Aragon, 232–33
ambassadors, 44, 212
    from Ferrara, 45
L'Amico Fido (Bardi), 99
Ammanati, Bartolomeo, 109
Amor Costante (Piccolomini), 131
Amore prigioniero in Delo (tourney), 164
    audience at, 165–66
amorini, 37, 93
Amphitryon (Terence), 10
ancient plays
    performances of, 16
    revival of, 23
ancient theaters, 142, 146
    descriptions of, 35
    tourneys in updated version of, 153
    Vitruvius and Alberti on, 280
Andreani, Francesca, 111
Andreini, G. B., 205
Andria (Terence), 10

Antigono (Conte da Monte), 134
Aragonese, victory over Moors, 233
Arcucci, Camillo, 304
Aretino, Pietro, 73
Arianna (Monteverdi), 210, 227–28
Ariosto, Ludovico, 19
Aristotelian unity of time, 76
Aristotle, 139
Arnaldi, Vincenzo, 134
assassination
    of Farnese, Pier Luigi, 177
    Medici, Alessandro de', 70, 122
assault, 207, 210–11
audiences, 111
    accommodations for, 13
    admission of, 45
    at *Amore prigioniero in Delo* (tourney), 165–66
    circulation for, 221
    around dais, 91
    framing elements of, 225
    instrumentalists and singers protected from, 219
    lower-class audience members, 149–50
    perspective of, 147–48
    size of, 283
    sorted by sex and class, 64
auditoriums, 273

Bacchus, 228
Bacchus (Michelangelo), 22, 24–25
Balbi, Giovanni Battista, 232–33
ballet, 228
    theater for, 255
Ballo delle Ingrate, 228
banishment, 211
Barbari, Jacopo de', 49–50
Barbaro, Daniele, 136, 142
Barberini family, 254–55
Bardi, Giovanni, 99
Bargagli, Girolamo, 102
Bartoli, Cosimo, 136
Basilica, 131
Battle of Fornovo, 1495, 17
Battle of Ravenna, 32
Beatrice of Aragon, 12
Bellerofonte, 213–14, 216

323

Bellini, Gentile, 53–56, 222
Benedetti, Zuane di, 207
Benini, Enrica, 91
Bentivoglio, Enzo, 200–1
Bernini, Gianlorenzo, 249, 260, 288, 303–4
Bertani, Giovanni Battista, 138
Bertazzolo, Gabriele, 108
Bezzi, Tommaso, 217–18
Bibbiena, Bernardo Dovizi da, 31, 38, 78
Bibbiena, Francesco Galli, 230–31, 249
Binck, Jakob, 124
blocking, 149
boat race, 51
Bologna, 89, 115, 230–31
  in 1639, 170–72
  in 1628, 164–68
Borgia, Lucrezia, 18
Bramante, Donato, 41–42, 157
Brown, Patricia Fortini, 53–56
Brunati, Antonio, 255
Bruschi, Arnaldo, 41–42
budgetary concerns, 273
Buontalenti, Bernardo, 98–100, 102
Burroughs, Charles, 154–55

La Calandra (Bibbiena), 31, 38, 78
Callot, Jacques, 103–4
canals, 120
Cantelmo, Sigismondo, 13
Capitoline Hill, Rome, 26–27, 39
  theater on, 40–41
Cardinal Bibbiena. See Bibbiena, Bernardo Dovizi da
Cardinals, at comedies, 109
Cassaria (Ariosto), 19
Castel Sant'Angelo, Rome, 160–62
Il Castello di Gorgoferusa (tourney), 176
  impact of, 152
Castiglione, Baldassare, 31–35
  sets described by, 36
Cavalli, Francesco, 232–33
Cefalo (Correggio), 10
celibacy, 291
chandeliers, 83, 102, 226
Charles V (Emperor), 122, 148
Chenda, Alfonso, 169, 172, 209, 212, 230
Cherea, Francesco, 48–50, 59
Chiappini, Paolo, 132–34
Chigi, Agostino, 25
China, 278–79
Christina (Queen of Sweden), 254–56, 258, 262–64
Christine of Lorraine, 102
Christmas, 47
Chrysis (Pius II), 306
Cibo, Innocenzo (Cardinal), 288
cittadini class, Venice, 208, 220
city hall, Modena, theater in, 234

class, 142
  audiences sorted by sex and, 64
  cittadini class, Venice, 208, 220
  lower-class audience members, 149–50
  seating and, 109
  upper class, women in, 8–9
Clement VIII Aldobrandini (pope), 173
Clement X Altieri (pope), 261–62
  death of, 263
Clement XII Corsini (pope), 275
coat of arms
  of Gonzaga family, 17
  of Immobili, 242
  of Medici family, 241
  of Vasa family, 260–61, 264
Codex Coner, 40
Collegio Clementino, 263–64
Colonna, Maria Mancini, 262
Colosseum, Rome, 13, 25–26, 282
Columbus, Christopher, 270
comedies, 10, 115
  Cardinals at, 109
  during carnival season only, 259–60
  earthy humor, 119
  female comics, 111
  of Plautus, 68–69
  return of, 205, 207
  Roman comedy, 277
  Savelli performing, 232
  settings for, 66
  stigma attached to, 232
  success of, 113
  at Teatro San Salvador, Venice, 213
  at Vatican, 38
  in Venice, 118–19
commedia dell'arte, 110–15, 291
  Confidenti troupe of, 117
  disappearance of, 120
  Pedrolino company of, 115
  permanent theaters for, 118–21
  seating for, 209
  spaces invented for, 278
  theater boxes invented for, 221
Il Commodo (Landi), 72
Compagnia degli Accesi, 134
Compagnie della Calza, 50
  last of, 134
Confidenti, 117, 207
  in Tron Theater, Venice, 118
Congregation of the Reform of Ecclesiastical Discipline, 275
Congress of Mantua, 32
Cordaro, Michele, 244
Corinthian columns, 79, 92, 246
Coriolano, Giovan Battista, 164–65
Cornaro, Alvise, 67–68
  theater of, 125–26
Correggio, Niccolò da, 10, 17

INDEX

Cortile Regio, 253
Coryat, Thomas, 112
costumes, 19
   in *Oedipus Rex*, 146
Council of Ten, 48–51, 119–20
   capi of, 211
   lack of supervision by, 207
   records of, 285
court tennis, 170
The Courtier (Castiglione), 31–32
coved ceiling, 273
Cremailles, Jacques de Chassebras de, 222–24
crenellated houses, 36
crowns, 92

dais, 84
   audience around, 91
D'Alibert, Giacomo, 259, 262, 270–71
d'Ambra, Francesco, 87
Danti, Ignazio, 94
de re aedificatoria (Alberti), 280
Decroisette, Françoise, 243
The Defense of Beauty (*La difesa della bellezza*), 189
Deidamia, 216
Delia osia la sera sposa del sole (Strozzi, Giulio), 211
dell'Anguillara, Giovanni Andrea, 109
d'Este, Alfonso I, 105
   fire destroying theater of, 138
   marriage of, 10
   second marriage of, 18
d'Este, Cesare, 173
d'Este, Ercole I, 7–8, 13, 19
d'Este, Francesco, 234
d'Este, Ippolito, 78
d'Este, Isabella, 8, 38
   letters of, 10–13
   marriage of, 10
Dido, or the Burning of Troy, 231
   success of, 232
La difesa della bellezza (*The Defense of Beauty*), 189
digital reconstruction, 219–20
   of Teatro Tordinona, 274
directors, 114
doge, 50, 56
   in Ducal Palace, 47
   Petrarch and, 52
Dolfin, Anzolo, 50
Doric order, 214–16
Doric piers, 89
Dragons, 83
dramma per musica, 263–64
Ducal Palace, Venice, doge residing in, 47
Ducal theater, Modena, 234–38

Eleanora of Aragon, 12, 286
Eleanora of Toledo, 70, 87
Elizabethan theater, 277–78
Epidicus (Plautus), 22

Ermiona (tourney), 168
   production of, 169
   stage for, 169–70
Ersilia (Faustini), 234
Eunuchus (Plautus), 48
Evangelista, Annamaria, 117
executions
   of bulls, 54
   of rebellious nobles, 233

Fano, 246–53
Farnese, Alessandro, 258
Farnese, Odoardo, 177–78, 200–1, 246
Farnese, Pier Luigi, 177
Fat Thursday, 58–59
Feris, Bartolommeo, 236
Ferrara, 12
   ambassador from, 45
   carnival season in, 7
   d'Este family loss of, 173
   Ferrarese diamond patterns, 204
   after 1501, 18–20
   proscenium style from, 198, 240
   Teatro degli Intrepidi, 173–75
   Venice war with, 8
fight in theater, 219
La Finta Pazza, 217, 232
fire, theaters destroyed by, 138, 171
   protection from, 212
   Teatro degli Intronati, 203
   Teatro San Cassiano, 208
fireworks, 153
Fleming, Alison, 96
Flemish tapestries, 33–34
fleur-de-lis, 78
Florence, 32, 87–93
   ambassadors from, 44, 212
   Teatro della Pergola, 238–43
   Teatro di Baldracca, 115–18
Florence Cathedral, 94
Fondamenta Nove, 213
Fontana, Carlo, 217, 264–66, 269, 274
Forster, Kurt, 162–64
Fouquet, Nicolas, 246
Franco, Battista, 109
Franco, Giacomo, 54, 57

Gabrieli, Andrea, 148–49
Gallo, Egidio, 26
Gelosi, 118
Genga, Gerolamo, 60, 287
Giazotto, Remo, 208–9
Giovanna d'Austria, 87
Giustiniani, Lorenzo, 206–7
glasswork, 76
Globe Theater, London, 277–78
gondolas, 120
Gonzaga, Carlo II, 242

Gonzaga, Federico II, 54–56
Gonzaga, Francesco I, 10, 16–17
   coat of arms of, 17
   last years of, 19–20
Gonzaga, Francesco II, 27
Gonzaga, Guglielmo, 108, 112
Gonzaga, Vespasiano, 153
Gonzaga, Vincenzo I, 227
Gonzaga palace, Mantua, 14
Granada, 24
grandstands, 54
   building public, 58
Grimani, Giovanni, 207, 211
   jumping on opera bandwagon, 211–12
Grimani Calergi, Vittorio, 242
Gritti, Andrea, 59
Guarini, Giovanni Battista, 227–28
"La Guerra dei Palchi" (The War of the Boxes) (Giazotto), 208–9
Guitti, Francesco, 199, 201

Habiti d'Huomeni et Donne Venetiane (Franco, Giacomo), 54, 57
Hadid, Zaha, 278–79
Hadrian (Emperor), 160–62
Harrison, Wallace K., 274
Heikamp, Detlef, 99
Henry II (King of France), 77–79, 86–87
Henry III (King of France), 120
Hercules, 56–58, 154–55, 225
Historia Baetica (Verardus), 24
history painting, 71–72
horses, 298
   for jousting, 189
Hôtel de Ferrare, Fontainbleau, 86
hydrology, 189
Hyppolitus (Seneca), 22

Idropica (Guarini), 228
Immortali, 50–51, 56–58
Imperiale, Giovanni Vincenzo, 232
Ingegnieri, Angelo, 148–49
Inghirami, Tomaso, 23
Innocent VIII Cybo (pope), 23
   Belvedere of, 29–30
Innocent X Pamphili (pope), 258
Innocent XI Odescalchi (pope), 263, 269
   death of, 269
Innocent XII Pignatelli (pope), 275
instrumentalists, 199, 203
   protected from audiences, 219
intermedi, 36–37, 93
   sets for, 103
Ionic order, 214–16
Italy
   Italian architecture, 302

Jarrard, Alice, 235
Jesuits, 120

Jewish community, Mantua, 112–13
jousting, 124, 152, 160, 179
   horses for, 189
   knights entrance for, 108
   races and, 52
Julius II della Rovere (pope), 25, 27–28
Juno, 37

knights, 108. *See also* jousting
   knightly combat, 152
   lack of imposing entrance for, 187
   lines of opposing, 164

Lafrery, Antonio, 157
Lanci, Baldassare, 85, 94, 98
Landi, Antonio, 72
leaflets, 293
League of Cambrai, 37
Leaning Tower of Pisa, 72
Lent, 47
Leo X Medici (pope), 38–46
Leonardo da Vinci, 88
Leto, Pomponio, 23
Libreria di San Marco, Venice, 97–98
Lieberman, Ralph, 40–41
lighting, 102, 114, 151. *See also* chandeliers
   of Odeon, Sabbioneta, 157–59
   by torches, 12
Limojon de St. Didier, Alexandre-Toussaint, 220
Lodi, Giacinto, 172
Loggia Cornaro, Padua, 67–69
Lorenzo the Magnificent, 38, 41–42
Louis XIV (King of France), 302
Lyons, in 1548, 77–87

La Maga Fulminata, 209–10
Maganza, Alessandro, 131
Maggior Consiglio, Venice, 47
   banishment from, 50
Malibran, Maria, 222
Manara, Curzio, 231
Manetti, Gianozzo, 21
Mangini, Nicola, 135
Mantegna, Andrea, 13–14
   Triumphs of Caesar, 14–15
   Triumphs of Petrarch, 13
Mantua
   Congress of Mantua, 32
   Court Theater, 105–8
   after 1501, 18–20
   Jewish community relationship with, 112–13
   Mantuan theater of 1501, 13–17, 34
   map of, 108
   Toscano poem on, 106
Marcello, Bernardo, 207
Margherita d'Austria, 122–23
marriages
   Borgia and d'Este, Alfonso I, 18
   d'Este, Isabella, and Gonzaga, Francesco, 10

marriage negotiations, 178
    Medici, Margherita de', and Farnese, Odoardo, 238
    of Medici family, 70–73, 83, 87–93, 102–4
        Rovere, Federigo Ubaldo della, and Medici, Claudia de', 192
        Sforza, Anna, and d'Este, Alfonso I, 10
Mars, 107, 200–1
Maximillian I (Holy Roman Emperor), 16–17
Maximillian II (Holy Roman Emperor), 87
McReynolds, Daniel, 145
Medici, Alessandro de' (Duke of Florence), 70, 122
Medici, Catherine de' (Queen of France), 77–78, 92, 102
Medici, Cosimo de' I (Grand Duke of Tuscany), 70
Medici, Ferdinando de' (Grand Duke of Tuscany), 102
Medici, Francesco I de' (Grand Duke of Tuscany), 99
Medici, Gian Carlo de' (cardinal), 238
Medici, Giovanni de', 38
Medici, Lorenzo de', 38
Medici, Mattias de', 243–44
Medici family, 70
    coat of arms for, 241
    first pope from, 78
    hegemony of, 287
    marriages in, 70–73, 83, 87–93, 102–4
    popes from, 92
Medici-Hapsburg union, 92
Menaechmi (Plautus), 7, 10, 105
Mercury, 200–1
Metropolitan Opera House, New York, 135, 274
Michelangelo, 22, 24–25, 88, 162
Michiel Theater, Venice, 118–21
Milan, 32
    ambassadors from, 44
military glory, 17
Minerva, 252
mock combats, 164
Modena, Ducal theater, 234–38
Monte, Conte da, 134
Monteverdi, Claudio, 200–1, 210, 227–28, 301
Moorish dancers, 64
Moors, Aragonese victory over, 233
Museo del Bargello, Florence, 22
music, 148–49, 202–3
    musical harmonies, 293
musical theater, 36
musicians, 102. *See also* instrumentalists; singers

Naples, 231–34
Neptune, 37
Nicholas V Parentucelli (pope), 21
Nobili, Francesco de', 48
Nolli, Giovanni Battista, 259

Obizzi, Pio Enea II degli, 168, 172, 209
Odeon, Sabbioneta, 153–58
    lighting of, 157–59
    for tourneys as well as plays, 160
Odeon Cornaro, Padua, 67–69

Oedipus Rex (Sophocles), 139
    costumes in, 146
oligarchy, 119
Olympian deities, 93, 103
    masculine, 154–55
    statues of, 157–59
opera
    emergence as art form, 227
    Grimani jumping on opera bandwagon, 211–12
    for political ends, 234
    public, 221, 228
    success of, 213
    Teatro San Cassiano, Venice, and first public performance of, 208–11
Opera House, Guangzhou, China, 278–79
orchestra, 64, 125
    orchestra pits, 251–52
    semicircular orchestra pit, 198
    use of term, 298
    women allowed to enter, Teatro Olimpico, Vicenza, 143
Orfeo (Monteverdi), 227–28, 301
Ortolani, 50–51
Ottoboni, Pietro (Cardinal), 269–70
outdoor performances, 9
oval plan for theaters, 265, 271
    invention of, 275–76
    truncated, 272, 305
Ovid, 30

Padua, in 1636, 168–70
Pagan, Matteo, 53–56
pagan dramas, 23
paintings
    exterior of theater covered in, 135
    history painting, 71–72
    Triumphs of Petrarch, paintings of, 13
    of Venus, 226
Palazzo Caprini, Rome, 154
Palazzo degli Uffizi, Florence, 93–98, 291
    interior of, 104
    Medici theater in, 98–102
    remodeling, 102
Palazzo dei Camerlenghi, Venice, 49
Palazzo dei Conservatori, Rome, 43–44
Palazzo del Podestà, Bologna, 89, 115
    Sala Grande of, 170, 172
Palazzo della Cancelleria, Rome, 23
Palazzo della Pilotta, Parma, 178, 184–90
Palazzo della Ragione, Fano, 247
Palazzo della Ragione, Ferrara, 18
Palazzo della Ragione, Mantua, 14, 113
Palazzo di San Sebastiano, Mantua, 19–20, 27
Palazzo Ducale, Ferrara, 9
    temporary theater in, 11
Palazzo Ducale, Urbino, 33–34
Palazzo Farnese, Piacenza, 122–25
Palazzo Gonella-Venier, Venice, 73–77
Palazzo Pubblico, Siena, 89–90

INDEX

Palazzo Vecchio, Florence, 87
   representation of, 94
Palazzo Venezia, Rome, 28–29
Palladio, Andrea
   Teatro Olimpico, Vicenza, 1580–1585, 136–51
   Venice theater of 1565, 134–36
   Vicenza, theater of 1561–1562, 130–34
   Vitruvius and, 126–30
Palliolo, Paolo, 43–44
papal legates, 114–15, 230
papal prison, Rome, 258
Parigi, Giulo, 103
Paris, Opéra, 179
Parma, 175–92, 200–3
Pasetti, Carlo, 203
Il Pastor Fido (Guarini), 227
patrons of the arts, 10, 228–29
Paul III Farnese (pope), 177
Peace of Bagnolo, 8
pediments, 82, 251
La Pellegrina (Bargagli), 102
Pencaro, Iano, 10–12, 18
pepian, 219
periaktoi, 94, 147, 281–82
permanent theaters
   for commedia dell'arte, 118–21
   early, 105–8
   Teatro Olimpico as, 137
Peruzzi, Baldassare, 24–25, 60
Pesaro, 192–200
Petrarch, 52–53
Philodoxus (Alberti), 282
Piazza San Marco, Venice, 52–53
Piazza Signoria, Florence, 94, 96
Piccola Pianta di Roma, 259
Piccolomini, Alessandro, 131
pigs, killing of, Venice, 59
Pius II Piccolomini (pope), 306
Pius IV Medici (pope), 87, 124
plague, 118
Plautus, 7, 22, 44, 48, 105
   comedies of, 68–69
Poenulus (Plautus), 44
Pola, ancient theater at, 61–63
Povoledo, Elena, 13, 18, 34, 152
Pozzo, Alfonso, 189
preservation
   disuse and, 137–38
   of Teatro Farnese, Parma, 175
Prisciani, Pellegrino, 7–8, 12
The Procession of Corpus Domini in Piazza San Marco (Giovanni Bellini), 53–56
Procession of the Doge on Palm Sunday (Pagan), 53–56
proscenium, 64, 93, 165, 169–70, 212, 239
   Acciaioli approval of, 264
   Aleotti and, 174, 178, 187–98
   for *Bellerofonte*, 214
   Corinthian columns forming, 246
   for *Deidamia*, 216

   depth of, 252
   with Doric piers, 89
   Ferrarese type of, 198, 240
   first, 92
   inscriptions over, 179–82
   opening above, 223
   prominence of boxes in, 273
   proscenium boxes, 220, 222, 231
   for Salone del Cinquecento, Florence, 98
   size of, 260
   stage view through, 164
   of Teatro degli Intrepidi, Ferrara, 89–90
   of Teatro Olimpico, Vicenza, 147
   for *Venere Gelosa*, 215–16
Prosperi, Bernardino, 19
Protestant Reformation, 120
Puppi, Lionello, 132

Ranuccio I Farnese (Duke), 176–79
   death of, 200
Raphael, 44
Rectors of Vicenza, 139–40
remodeling, 102, 243
   Teatro San Moisè, Venice, 210
Riario, Raffaele (Cardinal), 7, 255, 285
   patronage of, 22–25
Il Riccio, 89
Roman Doric pilasters, 153
Roman plays, revival of, 281
Roman theaters, 12, 21
   Colosseum, Rome, 13
   Marcellus, Rome, 197
Rome, 35–36
   Castel Sant'Angelo, Rome, 160–62
   in 1549, 109–10
   of Leo X, 38–46
   Roman comedy, 277
   Sack of Rome, 60–61
   seventeenth-century, 254
   Teatro alle Stufe dei Mellini, oldest theater in, 304
Rosand, Ellen, 217
Rosselli, Pietro, 41–42
Rotondi, Sergio, 272–73
Rovere, Federigo Ubaldo della, 192
Rovere, Francesco Maria I della, Duke of Urbino, 31–32
   ascent of, 286
Rovere, Giuliano della (Pope Julius II), 25
Rucellai, Giovan Battista, 242
Ruffini, Franco, 34, 144–45
Ruzzante, 50–51

Sabbioneta, 153–62
Sack of Rome, 60–61
Sala dalle Comedie, 19
Sala dei Cinquecento, Florence, 90
Sala del Consiglio Generale, 245–46
Sala del Trono, Urbino, 32–33

INDEX

Sala di Pisanello, Mantua, 14
Salle des Machines, Paris, 235
Salle Saint-Jean, Lyon, 79
Salone dei Cinquecento, 87–88, 96, 98
Salone Vasari, 98
San Carlo Borromeo, 176–77
Sangallo, Bastiano da, 73
Sansovino, Francesco, 135
Sant' Andrea, Mantua, (Alberti), 81
Sanudo, Marin, 48, 110–11
    death of, 59
Savelli, Fabrizio (Cardinal), 232
Savonarola, 88
Scamozzi, Bertotti, 143
Scamozzi, Vincenzo, 139, 155
scandalous behavior, 120
scenae frons, 123, 129–32, 144–45
    perspectival urban view fused with, 135–36
    Vitruvius on, 281
scenic effects, 209, 221
Scève, Maurice, 78, 80
Schulz, Jürgen, 74
seating, 83–84
    class and, 109
    for commedia dell'arte, 209
    curved, 107
    innovation in, 235
    steps for, 135
    in Teatro Farnese, Parma, 179, 189–98
    at Teatro Olimpico, Vicenza, 140
    for women, 99, 102, 170
Seneca, 22
Serlio, Sebastiano, 60–67, 82, 85–86
sets, 290
    Castiglione description of, 36
    for intermedi, 103
    painted set in one-point perspective, 19
sex, audiences sorted by class and, 64
Sforza, Anna, 7–8
    marriage of, 10
Sforza, Ludovico, Duke of Milan, 7–8
Shakespeare, William, 277–78
ships, 214
Siena, 89–90, 243–46
Sighizzi, Andrea, 230
singers, 199, 203
    protected from audiences, 219
sipario, 249
Sir John Soane's Museum, London, 217–22, 243–44, 300
Sixtus IV della Rovere (pope), 8
Skippon, Philip, 213
Sofonisba (attrib. Maganza), 131
Sofonisba (Trissino), 131
Sommi, Leone de', 112–13
La Sonnambula (Bellini), 222
Sophocles, 139, 146
Spada, Lionello, 182
Spectacula (Prisciani), 8

stage construction, 9
    perspectival illusion built into, 221
stage machinery, 214, 232–33
staircases, 179
stanze, 47
Stanzione, Massimo, 234
Strozzi, Giovanni Battista, 72
Strozzi, Giulio, 211
Sullivan, Louis, 278–79
I suppositi (Ariosto), 45
Sweden, Queen Christina of, 254–56, 258, 262–64

Tacca, Ferdinando, 238
La Talanta (Aretino), 73
Tavassi La Greca, Bianca, 260
Teatro alle Stufe dei Mellini, Rome, 304
Teatro alli Saloni, Venice, 242
Teatro degli Intrepidi, Ferrara, 173–75, 197
Teatro degli Intronati, Siena, 243–46
    fire destroying, 203
Teatro degli Obizzi, Ferrara, 203–4
Teatro della Fortuna, Fano, 246–53
Teatro della Pergola, Florence, 237–43, 265
Teatro della Sala, Bologna, 242
Teatro di Baldracca, Florence, 115–18
Teatro di Tordinona, Rome, 254
    opening of, 275
    rebuilding of, 275
Teatro Farnese, Parma, 175–93
    plan of, 183–96
    seating in, 179, 189–98
    superiority of, 189
    vastness of, 200
Teatro Formagliari, Bologna, 230–31, 242
Teatro Goldoni, Venice, 207
Teatro Malibran, Venice, 222
Teatro Malvezzi, Bologna, 231, 242
Teatro Novissimo, Venice, 213–17
    first great success of, 232
Teatro Olimpico, Vicenza, 136–51, 183
    proscenium of, 147
Teatro San Bartolomeo, Naples, 234
Teatro San Carlo, Naples, 234
Teatro San Cassiano, Venice, 205–6, 231
    fire in, 208
    first public performance of opera and, 208–11
    flourishing of, 208
Teatro San Giovanni Grisostomo, Venice, 222–26
Teatro San Gregorio, Venice, 242
Teatro San Luca, Venice, murder in, 207–8
Teatro San Moisè, Venice, 205–7
    remodeling, 210
Teatro San Salvador, Venice, 213
Teatro SS. Giovanni e Paolo, Venice, 211–13, 242, 263
    Soane Museum drawing of, 217–22
Teatro Tordinona, Rome, 265–66, 279
    digital reconstructions of, 274
    plans for second, 271

Temanza, Tomaso, 146
temporary theaters, 13
Terence, 50–51
Terminus, 75
Tessin, Nicodemus, 222
theater boxes, 119, 184–85
   destruction of, 140
   extravagant royal box, 266–67
   improved sight lines for, 250
   invented for commedia dell'arte, 221
   marbleized figures holding up, 225
   party walls between, 218–19
   private, 232
   proscenium, prominence of boxes in, 273
   scandalous behavior in, 120
Theater of Marcellus, Rome, 28–32, 61–63, 197, 282
Tito, 263
Tor di Nona, Rome, 258, 260, 304
Torelli, Giacomo, 213, 215–16, 232–33, 246, 248
   stage designing by, 251–52
Toscano, Raffaello, 106
tourneys, 179
   Amore prigioniero in Delo, 164–66
   Il castello di Gorgoferusa, 152
   drama-tourneys, 152, 168, 200
   Ermiona, 168–70
   Odeon (theater) for plays as well as, 160
   tradition of, 152
   in updated version of ancient theaters, 153
   waning popularity of, 203
Trionphanti, *compagnia della calza*, 50–51
Trissino, Gian Giorgio, 68–69, 131
The Triumph of Continence Displayed by Scipio Africanus (Il trionfo della continenza considerato in Scipione Africanus), 252
The Triumph of Partenope Liberated, 233
triumphal arches, 74–75, 78–79, 92
Triumphs of Caesar (Mantegna), 14–15
Triumphs of Petrarch (Mantegna), 13
Trojan War, 33–34, 37
trompe-l'oeil windows, 85
Tron, Ettore, 120, 206
Tron family, 205
Tron theater, Venice, 118–21, 206, 209
tuberculosis, 176–77
Tuileries Palace, Paris, 235
Tuscany, 177–78

the unwashed, 159
uomini famosi, 95–96
upper class, women in, 8–9
Urbino, 31–38

Valmarana, Leonardo, 146, 148
vanishing point, 147–48
Varchi, Benedetto, 92
Vasa family, 260–61, 264
Vasari, Giorgio, 73–74, 90, 94–95, 99, 135

Vatican
   comedies at, 38
   drawing of, 29–32
   drawings preserved in, 244
Vatican Library, 31–32
Vecchio, Cosimo il, 88–89, 94–95
   rule of, 90
Vendramin family, 207
Venere Gelosa, 214–15
   proscenium for, 215–16
Venice, 58
   climate of, 48
   comedies in, 118–19
   Cornaro theater, 125–26
   in 1542, 73–76
   as huge set, 51–52
   Michiel and Tron Theaters, 118–21
   Palladio theater of 1565, 134–36
   Serlio in, 60–67
   theatrical situation in, 47–48
   unusual structure of Venetian society, 119
Venus, 37, 226
Verardus, Carolus, 24
Veremonda, 232–33
Veroli, Sulpizio da, 22
vestigial steps, 93
Via della Pergola, Florence, 238–39
Viani, Antonio Maria, 227
Vicenza, 130–34, 136–51
   Rectors of Vicenza, 139–40
Vigarani, Gaspare, 234–37
Vignola, Giacomo Barozzi da, 122–25
Villa Farnesina, Rome, 25–31
Villa Madama, Rome, 44
Villa Trissino, Cricoli, 68–69
Vitruvius, Barbaro edition, 12, 35, 66, 126–30
   on ancient theaters, 280
   publication of, 136
   reconstruction plan of Vitruvian theater, 134
   on scenae frons, 281

wars, 8
Wittelsbach, Margaret, 17
women, 117–18, 165
   allowed to enter orchestra, 143
   entrances for, 243
   female comics, 111
   mixing of men and, 119
   noble, 65
   in Sabbioneta, 159
   seating for, 99, 102, 170
   set of steps reserved for, 13
   in upper class, 8–9
wool cloth, 303
World War II, 176

Zane, Almorò, 210–11
Zuccaro, Federico, 92, 135